EMERGING INFORMATICS – INNOVATIVE CONCEPTS AND APPLICATIONS

Edited by **Shah Jahan Miah**

Emerging Informatics – Innovative Concepts and Applications
Edited by Shah Jahan Miah

Published by InTech

Janeza Trdine 9, 51000 Rijeka, Croatia

Publishing Process Manager Vedran Greblo

Technical Editor Teodora Smiljanic

Cover Designer InTech Design Team

Additional hard copies can be obtained from orders@intechopen.com

Emerging Informatics – Innovative Concepts and Applications, Edited by Shah Jahan Miah
p. cm.
ISBN 978-953-51-0514-5

For EU product safety concerns:
IN TECH d.o.o., Prolaz Marije Krucifikse Kozulić 3, 51000 Rijeka, Croatia,
info@intechopen.com or visit our website at intechopen.com.

Meet the editor

Dr Shah J. Miah is a Lecturer in Information Systems (IS) of the School of Management and Information Systems at the Victoria University, Melbourne, Australia. Prior to this position, He had academic positions at the University of the Sunshine Coast, Griffith University and James Cook University, Australia. Shah has received his PhD (in the area of Decision Support Systems), jointly from the Institute for Integrated and Intelligent Systems and Griffith Business School, Griffith University, Australia. Shah is an early career researcher who has lead authored over 40 peer reviewed publications include research book chapters, journal and conference papers in different IS areas and taught over 20 different IS/IT subjects for both postgraduate and undergraduate levels. His research interests include Decision Systems Design for businesses; eService solutions design; Information Systems Development Methodologies; and Digital business ecosystems.

Contents

Preface

The title of this book *"Emerging Informatics- Innovative Concepts and Applications"* encompasses emerging concepts and applications of information systems (IS) development. The word *"Emerging Informatics"* expresses focal interest and its meaning which has been reflected on different promising application areas in this book. The word *"emerging"* represents most prominent new concepts or application areas and the word *"informatics"* refers to how the new concepts and applications are created, constructed and purposefully used through particular forms of information models.

Prof. John Gammack and his colleagues (in the Book of Informatics) state that informatics is the *"art and science of information"*. It is about human knowledge and how it is constructed for useful meaning and purpose, for instance enhancing the processes we experience and use in our daily life. Furthermore, *the University of Edinburgh* (URL: http://www.ed.ac.uk/schools-departments/informatics /about/vision/ overview) suggests that *Informatics* incorporates research and learning aspects in a number of existing academic disciplines - Artificial Intelligence, Cognitive Science and Computer Science. It is all about connecting thoughts, concepts and applications to design and guide purposeful knowledge creation. In my book, I am exploring the connecting elements between technologies and different problem spaces in an attempt to design and create artificial systems for human operations and businesses.

Informatics as a discipline has many fields with their own bodies of significant knowledge. Many application areas and concepts are growing through new research explorations nowadays. The new areas and ideas help us outline the problems and produce subsequent solutions for the future. This enhances our understanding of emerging informatics and helps to prepare for the world we will experience tomorrow.

I have edited this book keeping in mind that we should continuously be addressing the demands by providing useful knowledge that contributes to the enhancement of the current body of informatics discipline. The author of each chapter brings their individual research and relevant contributions to their area of interest. I have had no control as editor, over the quality and rigorousness of the research that they have presented in their chapter. I would like to take the opportunity to thank all of the authors for their significant contributions to this book.

The book has been produced for the researchers and industry practitioners who are interested in learning about the emerging fields and applications in informatics. It has been structured into four sections. Section 1 (*Specialised informatics and applications)* provides induced technical concepts to emergent problem solving. Section 2 (*Emerging business informatics and applications)* includes technical concepts for business applications. Section 3 (*Emerging informatics in railways)* includes innovative approaches for effective and efficient railway system design and development. Finally, section 4 (*Emerging web informatics and applications*) includes new technologies for web service design.

I will be pleased if this book could contribute to the human community and its systems on this planet in some small way. I would like to thank all those who have contributed to publishing this work.

Dr Shah Jahan Miah,
Lecturer of Information Systems at Victoria University, Melbourne,
Australia

Section 1

Specialised Informatics and Applications

1

Applications of Geospatial Technologies for Practitioners: An Emerging Perspective of Geospatial Education

Yusuf Adedoyin Aina
Geomatics Technologies Department, Yanbu Industrial College, Yanbu
Saudi Arabia

1. Introduction

Geospatial technology (also known as geomatics) is a multidisciplinary field that includes disciplines such as surveying, photogrammetry, remote sensing, mapping, geographic information systems (GIS), geodesy and global navigation satellite system (GNSS) (Pun-Cheng, 2001). According to the U.S. Department of Labour, geospatial industry can be regarded as "an information technology field of practise that acquires, manages, interprets, integrates, displays, analyzes, or otherwise uses data focusing on the geographic, temporal, and spatial context" (Klinkenberg, 2007). It is a new integrated academic field that has a diverse range of applications (Konecny, 2002). The applications of geomatics are in the fields of precision farming, urban planning, facilities management, business geographics, security and intelligence, automated mapping, real estate management, environmental management, land administration, telecommunication, automated machine control, civil engineering and so on. Even applications of some devices such as cellular phones, RFID (radio frequency identification) tags and video surveillance cameras can be regarded as part of geospatial technologies, since they use location information (Klinkenberg, 2007). So, graduates of geospatial technologies have the opportunity to pursue varying and challenging careers. Apart from offering graduates challenging career paths (both indoor and outdoor); geomatics exposes them to modern, cutting edge and innovative information system and technologies.

The connection between geospatial technologies and information and communication system and technology runs deep. Geomatics fields, especially GIS, have used information and communication technologies such as database management, data sharing, networking, computer graphics and visualization. Thus, some authors (Klinkenberg, 2007; Goodchild, 2011) regard geospatial technologies as part of information technology. Even geospatial technology has had its own free and open source software movement in the open source geospatial foundation (OSGeo) which organizes the free and open source software for geospatial (FOSS4G) conferences. The foundation also support a number of geospatial projects for web mapping, desktop applications, geospatial libraries and metadata catalogue. This relationship has led to further development of geospatial techniques and applications.

There has been a significant growth in geospatial technologies applications in recent years. There is a major increase in the availability of remote sensing imagery with increasing spatial, temporal, radiometric and spectral resolutions. So, users can apply satellite images in wider areas of application. In the field of surveying, advancements in surveying instruments such as electronic distance measurement, total stations, data collectors, 3D laser scanners and automatic level have boosted the applications of surveying in varying areas. In navigation satellite technology, wide area differential GNSS systems are nearly covering the whole world leading to improved accuracy and availability (Fig. 1). In GIS technology, GIS applications have become ubiquitous. They are available on desktops, notebooks, tablets and mobile phones. The trend is towards multidimensional visualization of geospatial data especially with the availability of digital terrain model (DTM) data and light detection and ranging (LIDAR). The drive towards more integration of geospatial technologies within the geospatial domain and with other related domains (such as information technology and telecommunication) (Xue et al., 2002) has further enhanced the growth and development of geomatics applications.

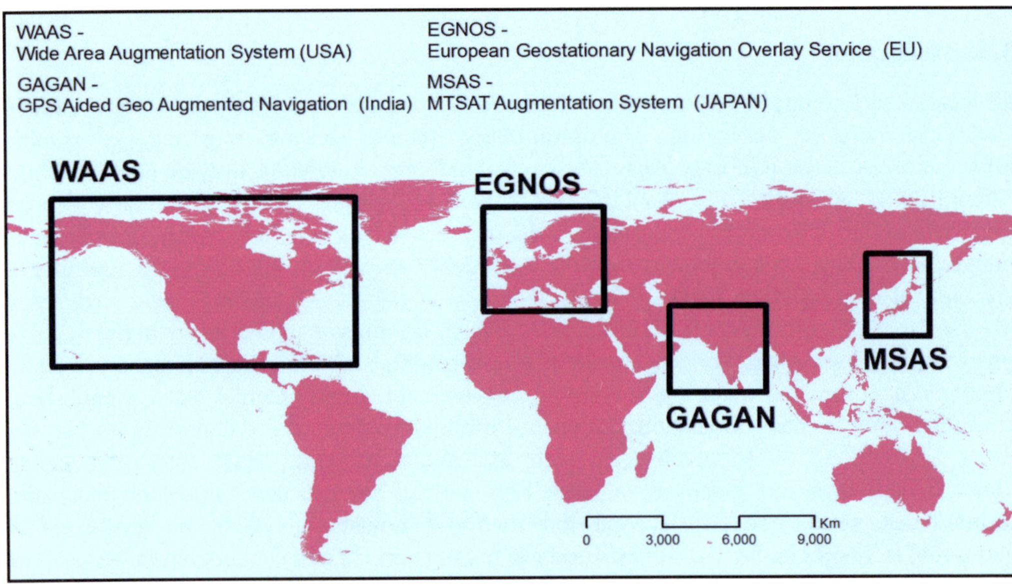

Fig. 1. Global wide-area differential GNSS systems

The current development and expected growth of geospatial technologies have earned it a place as one of the emerging technologies (Gewin, 2004). New job opportunities are being created as geospatial market expands to new areas of applications. The global annual revenues of geospatial market were estimated at $5 billion in 2003 (Gaudet et al., 2003) and the revenues are expected to continue to grow. The American Society for Photogrammetry and Remote Sensing (ASPRS) in its ten-year industry forecast estimated revenues for its geospatial domain at $6.5 billion for this year (Mondello et al., 2004). The expanding geospatial market requires adequate education and training to develop a workforce that will meet current and future market demand.

Despite the increasing utilization of geospatial technologies in different fields, many geomatics departments in colleges and universities are facing the challenge of low student intake and retention. Quite a number of studies (Hunter, 2001; Konecny, 2002; Mills et al., 2004;

McDougall et al., 2006; Hannah et al., 2009; Aina, 2009) have discussed the problem and part of the suggested mitigations is revamping the curriculum and improving the learning experience of the students. Emerging pedagogical methods such as problem-based learning, cooperative learning, student-centred inquiry and active learning could be relevant in achieving effective learning and enhancing learning experience. This article examines the adoption of active learning method as one of the strategies of improving student enrolment and retention in geospatial education. It presents the results of a case study of the active learning approach. It also discusses the emerging trends in geospatial applications, the global challenges of geospatial education and the different strategies to improve geospatial education.

2. Methodology

The sections of the article that discuss the trend in geospatial applications, importance of geospatial technology for higher education and the challenges of geospatial education are based on review of literature. The final section on the adoption of active learning method is based on questionnaire survey, course assessment and teacher's observations. The questionnaire survey was completed by 16 students that enrolled in Geographic Information System and Remote Sensing courses. The questions were aimed at getting feedback from students on the adoption of active learning method. The questionnaire contained seven items with a five-point Likert scale (Highly Agree to Highly Disagree). The questionnaire was composed of the following items:

- There has been a remarkable change in the teaching method of this course
- The current teaching method helps me in learning better
- I am more motivated to learn than before
- The group discussions make me a better learner
- Teaching other members of the class by making presentations helps me in my learning
- I am encouraged to search for more information about the subject
- There is no difference between how I learn now and how I have been learning before

The course assessment is based on students' grades for each of the courses. The course assessment for the semester was compared with the previous semester when active learning method had not been vigorously adopted. Also, teacher's observations on changes in the performance of students were documented.

3. Recent and emerging trends in geospatial applications

It is difficult to exhaustively outline the recent applications of geomatics in an article as the list continues to expand and there are already vast areas of application. "Comprehensive lists of the capabilities of GIS are notoriously difficult to construct" (Goodchild, 2008). However, notable applications can still be highlighted to show what geospatial technologies are capable of and the possible future uses. The development of new applications in geospatial technology is linked with recent development in electronic and information and communication technology (ICT). Geospatial technologies adopt innovative information and communication system concepts and this is evident in the current and emerging geospatial applications highlighted in the following sections. The different domains of geomatics have benefited from these technological developments.

3.1 Geographic information system – Towards multidimensional visualization

GIS is one of the most evolving aspects of geospatial technology. It evolved from desktop application in the 1980s into enterprise GIS in the 1990s and into distributed GIS. Even the technology of distributed GIS is evolving. It has changed from mobile GIS to web GIS and it is currently developing into cloud GIS. The development of cyberinfrastructure has facilitated the distribution of geospatial information as web service and the advancement in visualizing geospatial data. The synergy between cyberinfrastructure and GIS has not only increased the availability and use of geoinformation, but has also enabled members of the public to become publishers of geoinformation (Goodchild, 2011). Map mashups and crowd-sourcing or volunteered geographic information (VGI) (Goodchild, 2007; Batty et al., 2010) and ambient geographic information (AGI) (Stefanidis et al., forthcoming) are being developed by non-expert users to disseminate geoinformation on the web. These emerging sources of geospatial information have become valuable to different societal and governmental applications such as geospatial intelligence (Stefanidis et al., in press), disaster management, real time data collection and tracking and property and services search.

McDougall (2011) highlighted the role of VGI during the Queensland floods in Austalia especially in post-disaster assessment. Crowd sourced geographic information was vital during the floods as people were kept informed of the flood events, "especially as official channels of communication began to fail or were placed under extreme load" (MacDougall, 2011). Crowd sourcing was also applied in managing similar recent events such as Haiti earthquake (Van Aardt et al., 2011) and Japan tsunami (Gao et al., 2011) (Fig. 2). Research

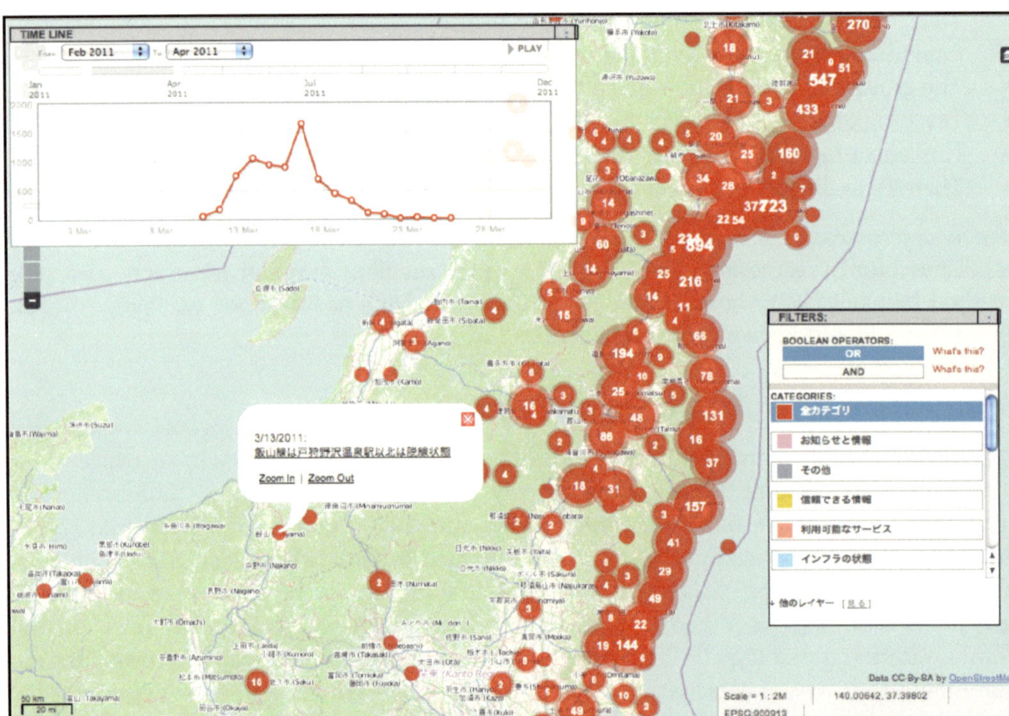

Fig. 2. Number of incidents reported during Japan tsunami (Source: www.ushahidi.com)

studies on varying issues of global concern such as global warming and sea level rise, urbanization, environmental management, global security have also been taking advantage of the emerging opportunities of increased data availability and improvement in visualization techniques. An example of such studies is the work of Li et al. (2009) on global impacts of sea level rise. They used GIS to delineate areas that could be inundated due to the projected sea level rises basing their analysis on readily available DEM data. Alshuwaikhat & Aina (2006) applied GIS in assessing the urban sustainability of Dammam, Saudi Arabia and they concluded that GIS is a veritable tool for promoting urban sustainability.

In the industrial sector, the articles by Ajala (2005; 2006) described how a GIS-based tool was applied by a telecommunication firm to analyze call records and improve network quality. GIS was used to analyze call records on the basis of "the location of subscribers, cells, market share, and handset usage" with a view to improving subscribers' services (Ajala, 2006). In the oil and gas industry, Mahmoud et al. (2005) demonstrated the use of GIS in determining the optimal location for wells in oil and gas reservoirs. The Well Location Planning System consisted different modules for automated mapping, data integration and reporting, overlay and distance analysis, specialized modules and 3D viewer for 3D visualization (Mahmoud et al., 2005). 3D visualization is one of the areas that GIS has become relevant both in the public and private sectors. 3D GIS is applied in generating profiles, visibility analysis and as basis for virtual cities. Figure 3 shows an example of 3D visualization in GIS. The model was developed by using DEM, buildings layer and building heights data. Recent 3D models have improved upon this technique by using high resolution images and incorporating building facade into the model.

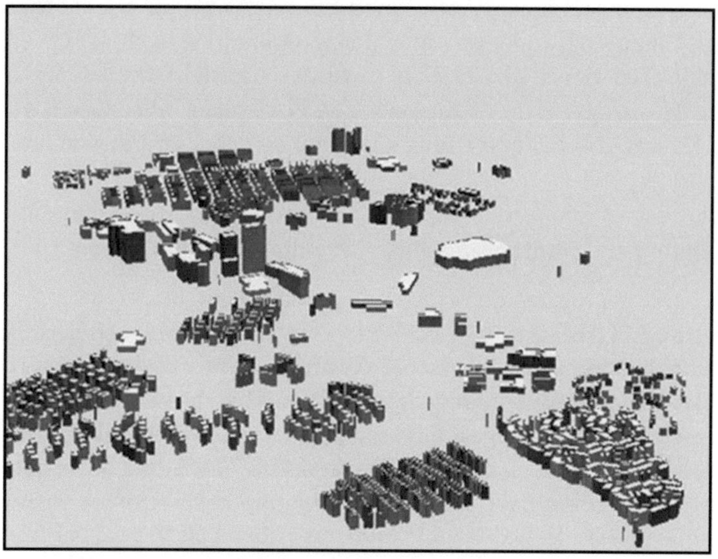

Fig. 3. 3D GIS: Visualization of KFUPM Campus, Dhahran, Saudi Arabia

It is expected that many more GIS applications will be developed in the future and some of the highlighted applications will be improved upon. The future trend is towards 4D visualization by incorporating time component with 3D. Goodchild (2009) opined that future development in GIS will include knowing where everything is at all times, improvement in third spatial dimension, providing real time dynamic information, more access to geographic information and improvement in the role of citizen. These developments indicate that geospatial technologies will be more integrated in the future. For example, the technologies for knowing where everything is at all times will most likely include RFID, GPS, internet, geo-visualization and probably satellite imagery.

3.2 Surveying and GNSS – Towards accurate and timely data collection

The advancements in modern surveying instruments have not only led to improvement in accuracy, but also increasing integration of digital survey data with other technologies. In Olaleye et al. (2011), this development was referred to as "Digital Surveying". Most of the data collected through surveying are now in digital formats that are interchangeable with other geospatial data formats. Even in some instances, survey data can be streamed through bluetooth or wifi to other hardware or software. Another development that has impacted surveying is the proliferation of laser technology. 3D laser scanners are now being used in surveying to collect quick and accurate data, captured as thousands of survey points, known as point cloud. The point cloud can be processed to produce accurate 3D geometry of structures. The use of unmanned aircraft has also made an inroad into surveying (Mohamed, 2010). Using unmanned aircraft in aerial mapping provides opportunity for collecting cheap, fast and high-resolution geospatial data.

GNSS technology has been very crucial to most geospatial technology applications from in-vehicle navigation to civil aviation and automated machine control. GNSS is a component of the unmanned aircraft technology mentioned above. As stated above, the technology is applied in aerial mapping and even in military operations such as US military drones (Chapman, 2003). The trend in GNSS is towards consistent availability and improved accuracy. With the inauguration of Russia's GLONASS and other GNSS systems such as Japan's QZSS, EU's GALILEO and China's Beidou; accuracy and availability will continue to improve.

3.3 Remote sensing and photogrammetry – Prying eyes from above

Remote sensing and photogrammetric technology have been undergoing dramatic changes since the launching of Landsat in the 1970s. Then, it was only United States that was involved in planning and launching remote sensing satellite missions. Now, there are more than 20 countries that own remote sensing satellites. This development has made users to have more access to satellite images. Free image programmes like the Global Land Cover Facility (GLCF) and USGS free landsat archive and OrbView3 data have also improved the availability of images. Users have recently got the opportunity of accessing satellite data through geospatial portals such as Google Earth and Microsoft Virtual Earth. Apart from the improvement in data availability, the quality of satellite imagery has also improved in terms of resolutions. Currently, the image with the highest spatial resolution is GeoEye (0.5m) but there is a plan to launch GeoEye-2 (0.25m) within the next two years. High resolution satellite imagery is valuable to applications in disaster management, feature extraction and analysis, mapping and monitoring changes in urban landscape, infrastructure management, health (Kalluri et al., 2007) and 3D visualization.

Suppasri et al. (2012) showcased the application of remote sensing, especially high resolution imagery, in Tsunami disaster management. Their study includes damage detection and vulnerability analysis. Figure 4 shows tsunami damage detected in their study by using IKONOS imagery. In the same vein, AlSaud (2010) used IKONOS imagery to identify the areas inundated during the Jeddah flood hazard in November 2009. The study was also able to highlight areas that are vulnerable to flooding to help decision makers take preventive actions. Also, in a population estimation study, the population distribution of a rural lake basin in China was successfully mapped using high resolution imagery from Google Earth (Yang et al., 2011). The study applied texture analysis with other procedures to extract building features for population estimation. The extraction of features and information from high resolution imagery is currently an expanding area of remote sensing. Buildings, roads, trees and even DEM data are extracted from images, including LIDAR, to estimate socio-economic information and for visualization.

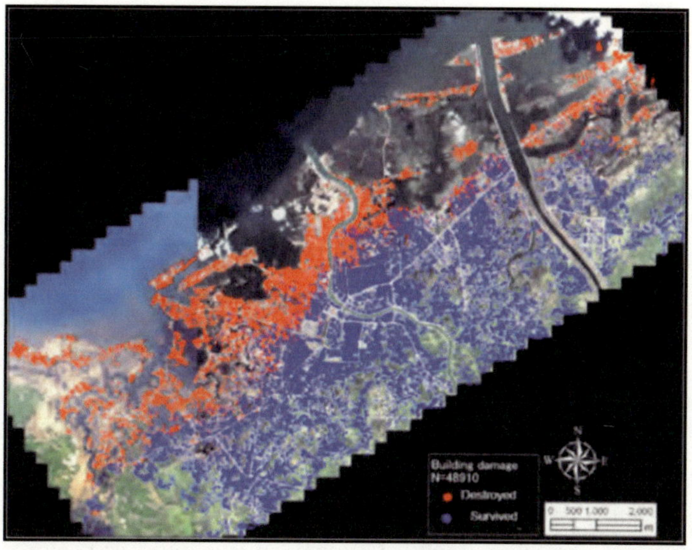

Fig. 4. Detection of tsunami damaged buildings (Red dots indicate damaged buildings and blue dots indicate undamaged buildings) from IKONOS imageries
(Source: Suppasri et al., 2012)

LIDAR images, with high geometric resolutions, have opened new areas of research and applications. LIDAR has been applied in 3D modelling of cities and geometric analysis of structures including utility corridor mapping. One of these applications is the use of LIDAR imagery as a tool for utility companies to monitor electricity transmission lines for vegetation encroachment and line rating assessment (Corbley, 2012). "Airborne LIDAR will become the most widely accepted solution due to its efficiency and cost-effectiveness" (Corbley, 2012). The highlighted applications demonstrate the usage of remote sensing and photogrammetry in a variety of ways. The applications are expanding as we have more satellite sensors "prying eyes" monitoring the earth "from above". Samant (2012) succinctly highlighted this trend by identifying conventional and emerging applications of remote sensing (Table 1).

Application environment	Coventional applications	Emerging applications
Terrestrial	Biodiversity	Health
	Defence	Infrastructure Monitoring
	Disaster management	Cadastral mapping
Hydrological	Energy	Oil and gas
	Climate	Mineral exploration
	Water	Location based service
	Weather	Insurance
Atmospheric	Ecosystem	Property registration
	Forest	Emergency and accident monitoring
	Agriculture	Environmental monitoring

Table 1. Conventional and emerging applications of remote sensing (Source: Samant, 2012)

3.4 Integration of geospatial technologies – Towards a synergy

As mentioned in section 3.1, the current trend is towards the integration of different geospatial technologies. There is hardly any recent geospatial application that does not have components from two or more domains of geospatial technology. The idea of integration started with the use of remote sensing data in GIS and data from GIS serving as ancillary data in satellite image classification. In recent times, the integration has included computer-aided design (CAD), GPS, survey data, internet, RFID, geosensor and telecommunication. Even concepts such as space syntax, cellular automata and agent based modelling (ABM) have been integrated into geospatial technologies (Jiang & Claramunt, 2002; Beneson et al., 2006; Sullivan et al., 2010). Likewise, software vendors have started integrating GIS, GPS and remote sensing functionalities in their packages. The trend towards synergy has been driving emerging applications in geospatial technologies and this might probably continue into the future.

In one of the early study on the integration of geospatial data with wireless communication, Tsou (2004) presented a prototype mobile GIS that "allows multiple resource managers and park rangers to access large-size remotely sensed images and GIS layers from a portable web server mounted in a vehicle". The mobile GIS application was developed for habitat conservation and environmental monitoring. A similar application, geared towards crowd management and pilgrim mobility in the city of Makkah, used location based services and augmented reality technologies to provide Hajj pilgrims with timely information on mobile phone (Alnuaim & Almasre, 2010). In Saud Aramco, (AlGhamdi & Haja, 2011) developed an integrated system, based on mobile GIS technology and high precision surveying process, to monitor land encroachments on land reservations and pipeline corridors. The system generated and propagated encroachment data (to GIS database) based on a change detection process (Fig. 5).

The emerging applications that integrate geospatial technologies with ICT are based on wireless network of spatially-aware sensors "geosensor networks" that "detect, monitor and track environmental phenomena and processes" (Nittel, 2009). Geosensor networks are used in three streams of applications; continuous monitoring (e.g. measuring geophysical processes),

Fig. 5. Monitoring and detection of land encroachment (2007-2009)
(Source: AlGhamdi & Haja, 2011)

real-time event detection (e.g. stream and well water monitoring and warning, Yoo et al., 2011) and mobile sensor nodes (e.g. livestock traceability, Rebufello et al., 2012) (Nittel, 2009).

4. Importance of geospatial technologies in higher education

It can be argued that the importance of geospatial technology in higher education is evident from its varying areas of application. A field of study that its applications cut across different aspects of human endeavour should be valuable to higher education. Sinton (2012) classified the reasons behind geographic information science and technology (GIS&T) education into two; dominant and secondary reasons. The reasons include marketplace, conducting research, competition for students, managing the business of the university and enhancing learning and teaching (Sinton, 2012). Apart from the need for geospatial technology in the marketplace, there is increasing demand for researchers (even in other fields) to have geospatial skills. "Scientists who can combine geographic information systems with satellite data are in demand in variety of disciplines" (Gewin, 2004). Thus, geospatial technology could help enhance the needed "spatial thinking" in higher education.

In addition to supporting varying research studies, geospatial technologies enhance teaching and learning by promoting effective learning environment and critical thinking (Sinton, 2012). Most of the subjects in geospatial technologies are amenable to being taught using emerging and innovative teaching and learning methods such as problem-based learning and inquiry-based learning. For example, GIS courses have components that are taught using real world problem-solving approach. These problem-solving components engender analytical and spatial thinking among learners thereby improving their critical thinking skills.

The myriad of challenging issues facing the world today ranging from urban growth and biodiversity to climate change have spatial dimension. Geospatial technologies are needed in addressing these challenges. "Grappling with local, regional and global issues of the 21st century requires people who think spatially and who can use geotechnologies" (Kerski, 2008). In addition, geospatial technology is interdisciplinary giving its graduates the capability of viewing problems from different perspectives. Tackling these varying global challenges needs multidisciplinary and collaborative approach and training in the needed multidisciplinary perspectives is already embedded in geospatial education.

5. Geospatial education at crossroad: Can active learning help?

5.1 The challenge of low student enrolment

One of the major challenges facing some geomatics and other related departments is low student enrolment. It has been a global issue (Mills et al., 2004; Hannah et al., 2009) and even affects schools in the United Stated (Mohamed et al., 2011) where geospatial market is rapidly expanding (Gewin, 2004). Bennett et al. (2009) in their study on spatial science education in Australia referred to the phenomenon as a "paradox"; there is a steady increase in demand for graduates but no increase in student enrolment. The same trend has been observed in the UK and New Zealand (Hannah et al., 2009), Sub-Saharan Africa (Ruther, 2003) and Saudi Arabia (Aina, 2009). Some of the reasons for low student intake are lack of awareness, weak financial support, misconception that only training is needed not education and being a relatively new field (Mills et al., 2004; AlGarni, 2005; Aina, 2009).

The problem of low student intake is compounded by the fact that geospatial technologies are evolving and schools have to grapple with developing effective method of teaching an ever changing field. In addition, the curriculum has to be designed in a way that will inculcate self-learning in the students to prepare them for self-directed continuous learning after graduation. So, the challenge is not only about student enrolment but also presenting a fulfilling learning experience to the students. Apart from raising public awareness of geomatics, changing the teaching and learning method could help in attracting and retaining students by enhancing their learning experience. There is a "need to identify new paradigms as a basis for developing more resilient and responsive educational programs" (Barnes, 2009).

5.2 Active learning to the rescue?

Active learning is a departure from the traditional teaching method that is teacher-focused, to student-focused approach. It emphasizes active engagement of the students rather than the traditional passive learning. Students should not be like vessels into which the teachers pour ideas and information. The students need to reflect on given information and understand the underlying concepts. Effective learning is not achieved if students are relegated to the "role of passive 'spectactors' in the college classrooms" (Matmti and Delany, 2011). "Effective learners are active, strategic, thoughtful and constructive in linking new information to prior knowledge" (Lipton & Wellman, 1999). A plethora of research about learning indicated that active learning method improves student engagement, learning and retention and enhances learning experience.

Active learning and its variants, such as problem-based learning, are increasingly adopted in teaching geospatial technologies (Shortis et al., 2000; Meitner et al., 2005; Drennon, 2005; Harvey & Kotting, 2011; Schultz, 2012). ESRI, one of the notable GIS vendors, has also adopted active learning methods in its GIS training courses (Wheeler, 2010). Active learning is being embraced to deal with changing geospatial body of knowledge, stimulate critical thinking, improve student engagement and enhance learning experience. Shortis et al. (2000) were able to transform the teaching and learning of plane survey from the traditional passive method to active learning based on web technology. They got positive feedback from students and staff. Likewise, Harvey and Kotting (2011) presented an active learning model for teaching cartography that enabled students to reflect on the "concepts and techniques of modern cartography". Meitner et al. (2005) also reported a successful adoption of active learning in teaching GIS. However, they noted that instructors should be cautious of turning student-focused classroom into "free-for-all" chaos or drifting back to teacher-led classroom. It is not all the activities of the students that will necessarily translate to active learning. Even Prince (2004), had raised a cautionary note on reported result since it is difficult to measure whether active learning works. Shortis et al. (2000) also noted this difficulty when they acknowledged that comparison of examination results might be misleading as the capability of different cohorts are different.

6. From global to local: The case of geomatics at Yanbu Industrial College

The Geomatics Technologies Department at Yanbu Industrial College is facing the problem of low student enrolment. Since the department was created in 2003, student enrolment has not been more than 24 in a year. In addition, the department has not been able to attract high quality students. This poses a challenge of identifying the learning and teaching approach that will increase student motivation, retention and performance. The situation is similar to that of some other geomatics department around the world experiencing low patronage or even closure. The department has taken some measures to reverse this trend. One of the measures is to take the opportunity of the college's drive towards student-centred learning (Matmti and Delany, 2011; Delany, 2011) to reinvigorate the department and transform student learning experience.

The active learning case study that is presented in this article was implemented in teaching two geomatics courses in remote sensing and GIS. There were ten and six students in the remote sensing and GIS classes respectively. Two methods, group discussion and learning by teaching, were adopted in infusing active learning in the courses. In the group discussion, the study material was given to the student to study before the class. In the class, the students were paired into groups and each group was asked to discuss the material and write down two important ideas they understand from the material and two ideas they do not fully understand. Thereafter, a student from each group was asked to explain to the class the ideas they understand and other ideas (difficult to understand) were thrown open for discussion.

The learning by teaching method was based on presentations by the students. The students were divided into groups. Each group was given a topic from the course module to prepare a presentation on. Each group made presentation on the assigned topic in class and other class members had to take note of important points in the presentation. The teacher served as a facilitator in these two approaches by clearing misconceptions about the subject matter, guiding the students on the concepts to focus on and getting feedback from the students. The following sections present the results of the assessment of the methods (as mentioned in the methodology section).

6.1 Comparison of grades

The comparison of grades of the students with the grades from previous semester shows a mixed result as depicted in Table 2. The average class performance for remote sensing and GIS in the previous semester was 2.89 and 2.59 respectively. For the assessed semester, the average grade was 2.65 for remote sensing and 2.67 for GIS. The results show a slight improvement in performance in GIS and a lower performance in remote sensing. The results

Courses	Previous Semester		Assessed Semester	
	Average Performance	No. Of Students	Average Performance	No. Of Students
Remote Sensing	2.89	7	2.65	10
GIS	2.59	8	2.67	6

Table 2. The assessment of student performances for two semesters (Before and after adopting active learning techniques)

also show that the performance in the assessed semester is more consistent than the performance in the previous semester. There was a larger gap between performance in remote sensing and GIS in the previous semester than the assessed semester. As mentioned in section 5.2 above, the result should be interpreted with caution as the cohorts cannot be compared without accounting for differences in students' capability. In the light of this, other means of assessment (questionnaire survey and teacher's observations) were also employed.

6.2 Feedback from students

Table 3 shows the result of students' feedback which indicates that the students were undecided as regards perceiving any remarkable change in the teaching method. The mean and median scores for this item are (3) as shown in Table 3. However, the students acknowledged that the approaches of active learning method had helped them in learning better. With regard to group discussion and presentations, the results show that the students agreed that the methods had helped them in learning better. The students also indicated that they were more motivated to learn than before. The result for information search/library search indicates that though the result is positive, the students were not highly motivated to search for more information about the subject.

Items	Mean	Median	Range	
There has been a remarkable change in the teaching method of this course	2.9	3	4	1 - Highly Disagree 2 - Disagree 3 - Undecided 4 - Agree 5 - Highly Agree
The current teaching method helps me in learning better	4.3	4.5	3	
I am more motivated to learn than before	3.8	4	3	
The group discussions make me a better learner	4	3.5	3	
Teaching other members of the class by making presentations helps me in my learning	3.8	4	2	
I am encouraged to search for more information about the subject	3.6	3.5	2	
There is no difference between how I learn now and how I have been learning before	2.9	3	3	

Table 3. Summary of student survey

6.3 Teacher's observations

There were two changes noted after the introduction of the active learning approaches. Some of the students developed keen interest in searching for additional information that could enrich their presentations and understanding of the subject. And some of them became passionate about the given topic that they felt they were the experts in the topics so others should just accept their findings. So, the presentation exercises also taught the student how to accommodate classmates with different views about the subject. Another noted change was in the answers provided by the students to examination questions. Previously, students responded to exam question by virtually regurgitating the information in the course material. During the assessed semester, responses from students showed that some of them had started explaining issues in their own words different from the expressions in the given material. This indicates that they were able to understand the material better than before. The new approaches did not really affect student attendance. And this is an important issue in the department. The goal of the department is to nurture the students to a level that they can be self-motivated to attend classes and to search for additional information about their subjects. It might be too early for the department to fully assess the impact of the transformation since the method has just been implemented for a semester. The results from the assessment are promising enough to encourage the department to continue on the active learning path.

7. Conclusion

This article has dwelt on three issues that are very important to geospatial technologies. First is the justification for teaching geospatial technologies in higher education by highlighting its growing applications and future trend. Second is the paradoxical issue of low student enrolment at some geomatics departments around the world despite the growing need for geospatial technologies in varying fields of application. Third is the adoption of active learning technique to improve teaching and learning and thereby attract more students. The highlight on the expanding applications of geospatial technologies has shown that different domains of geospatial technologies are continuously evolving and the market demand for geomatics researchers and practitioners is expanding. And this leads us to the justification for having geospatial technologies in any college or university. Apart from the demand for geospatial technologies, other justifications include research, its use by the society and the promotion of emerging learning techniques. The emerging learning techniques could help in solving the problem of enrolment.

A case study of the adoption of emerging teaching techniques at Yanbu Industrial College is presented in this article to show that these techniques could transform geomatics education. Though the implementation is still at an early stage, its effect on student intake is yet to be determined, it has shown promising results. The students were keen to search for additional material on the courses and they answered exam questions from what they understood not what they crammed. If the techniques could not result in an increase in student intake, they might lead to an increase in retention of students once the students realise that geomatics can offer a fulfilling learning environment.

8. Acknowledgments

The author is grateful to the remote sensing and GIS students for participating in this study. The author acknowledges the assistance of Yanbu Industrial College in carrying out this work especially the sponsorship of his participation in an active learning workshop. The author is also grateful to the Editorial Board for its valuable comments. The views expressed in this work are not necessarily that of the college.

9. References

Aina, Y. A. (2009). Geomatics education in Saudi Arabia: Status, challenges and prospects. *International Research in Geographical and Environmental Education*, Vol.18, No.2, pp. 111-119, ISSN 1038-2046

Ajala, I. (2005). GIS and GSM network quality monitoring : A Nigerian case study. *Directions Magazine*, Available from http://www.directionsmag.com/articles/gis-and-gsm-network-quality-monitoring-a-nigerian-case-study/123278

Ajala, I. (2006). Spatial analysis of GSM subscriber call data records. *Directions Magazine*, Available from http://www.directionsmag.com/articles/spatial-analysis-of-gsm-subscriber-call-data-records/123196

AlGarni, A. M. (2005). Future of geo-sciences can be seen everywhere in the Kingdom. *GIS Development*, Vol.1, No.1, pp. 32-34, Available from

AlGhamdi, Y. & Haja, S. (2011). Implementation of a land encroachment survey process in Saudi Aramco based on high precision mobile GIS technology. *Proceedings of the Sixth National GIS Symposium in Saudi Arabia (Online)*, Khobar, Saudi Arabia, 24-26 April, 2011, Available from http://www.saudigis.org/FCKFiles/File/6thSaudiGIS_Papers/T2_3.docx

Alnuaim, H. & Almasre, M. (2010). The use of mobile technology for crowd management in cities: The case of safe pilgrim mobility in the city of Makkah. *Proceedings of The 3rd Knoowledge Cities World Summit*, pp. 1373-1395, ISBN 978-0-646-54655-1, Melbourne, Australia, 16-19 November, 2010

AlSaud, M. (2010). Assessment of flood hazard of Jeddah area 2009, Saudi Arabia. *Journal of Water Resource and Protection*, Vol.2, No.9, pp. 839-847, ISSN 1945-3108

Alshuwaikhat, H. M. & Aina, Y. A. (2006). GIS-based urban sustainability assessment: The case of Dammam city, Saudi Arabia. *Local Environment*, Vol.11, No.2, pp. 141-161, ISSN 1469-6711

Barnes, G. (2009). Geomatics at the crossroads: Time for a new paradigm in geomatics education? *Surveying and Land Information Science*, Vol.69, No.2, pp. 81-88, ISSN 1538-1242

Batty, M.; Hudson-Smith, A.; Milton, R. & Crooks, A. (2010). Map mashups, web 2.0 and the GIS revolution. *Annals of GIS*, Vol.16, No.1, pp. 1-13, ISSN 1947-5691

Beneson, I.; Birfur, S. & Kharbash, V. (2006). Geographic automata systems and the OBEUS software for their implementation. In: *Complex Artificial Environments: Simulation, cognition and VR in the study and planning of cities*, J. Portugali, (Ed.), pp. 137-153, Springer, Netherlands, ISBN 978-3-540-25917-6

Bennett, R.; Ogleby, C. & Bishop, I. (2009). One strategy for repositioning spatial sciences education in Australia. *Journal of Spatial Science*, Vol.54, No.1, pp. 93-104, ISSN 1836-5655

Chapman, G. (2003). An introduction to the revolution in military affairs. *XV Amaldi Conference on Problems in Global Security*, Helsinki, Finland, 25-27 September, 2003, Available from
http://www.accademianazionaledeilincei.it/rapporti/amaldi/papers/XV-Chapman.pdf

Corbley, K. (2012). Why LIDAR has become the "Go To"technology for utility corridor mapping. *Directions Magazine*, Available from
http://www.directionsmag.com/articles/why-lidar-has-become-the-go-to-technology-for-utility-corridor-mapping/228168

Delany, J. (2011). Active learning: How do we know it works? *YIC Campus Times*, No.3, Available from http://www.calameo.com/read/000335779577c886d8dd1

Drennon, C. (2005). Teaching Geographic Information Systems in a problem-based learning environment. *Journal of Geography in Higher Education*, Vol.29, No.3, pp. 385-402, ISSN 1466-1845

Gao, H.; Barbier, G. & Goolsby, R. (2011). Harnessing the crowdsourcing power of social media for disaster relief. *IEEE Intelligent Systems*, Vol.26, No.3, pp. 1541–1672, ISSN 1541-1672

Gaudet, C. H.; Annulis, H. M. & Carr, J. C. (2003). Building the geospatial workforce. *URISA Journal*, Vol.15, No.1, pp. 21-30, ISSN 1045-8077

Gewin, V. (2004). Mapping opportunities. *Nature*, Vol.427, No.6972, pp. 376-377, ISSN 0028-0836

Goodchild, M. F. (2007). Citizens as sensors: The world of volunteered geography. *Geojournal*, Vol.69, No.4, pp. 211-221, ISSN 1572-9893

Goodchild, M. F. (2008). The use cases of digital earth. *International Journal of Digital Earth*, Vol.1, No.1, pp. 31-42, ISSN 1753-8955

Goodchild, M. F. (2009). Goegraphic information systems and science: today and tomorrow. *Annals of GIS*, Vol.15, No.1, pp. 3-9, ISSN 1947-5691

Goodchild, M. F. (2011). Information technology as megaengineering: The impact of GIS, In: *Engineering earth: The impacts of megaengineering projects*, S. D. Brunn, (Ed.), Vol.1, pp. 37-47, Springer, ISBN 978-90-481-9919-8, Dordrecht, Netherlands

Hannah, J.; Kavanagh, J.; Mahoney, R. & Plimmer, F. (2009). Surveying: A profession facing a global crisis ? *Survey Review*, Vol.41, No.313, pp. 268-278, ISSN 1752-2706

Harvey, F. & Kotting, J. (2011). Teaching mapping for digital natives: New pedagogical ideas for undergraduate cartography education. *Cartography and Geographic Information Science*, Vol.38, No.3, pp. 269-277, ISSN 1545-0465

Hunter, G. J. (2001). Ensuring the survival of geomatics engineering at the University of Melbourne. *Surveying and Land Information Science*, Vol.61, No.4, pp. 255-262, ISSN 1538-1242

Jiang, B. & Claramunt, C. (2002). Integration of space syntax into GIS: New perspectives for urban morphology. *Transactions in GIS*, Vol.6, No.3, pp. 295-309, ISSN 1467-9671

Kalluri, S.; Gilruth, P.; Rogers, D. & Szczur, M. (2007). Surveillance of anthropod vector-borne infectious diseases using remote sensing techniques: A review. *PLOS Pathogens*, Vol.3, No.10, pp. 1361-1371, ISSN 1553-7374

Kerski, J. J. (2008). The role of GIS in Digital Earth education. *International Journal of Digital Earth*, Vol.1, No.4, pp. 326-346, ISSN 1753-8955

Klinkenberg, B. (2007). Geospatial technologies and the geographies of hope and fear. *Annals of the Association of American Geographers*, Vol.97, No.2, pp. 350-360, ISSN 0004-5608

Konecny, G. (2002). Recent global changes in geomatics education. *Proceedings of ISPRS Commission VI Symposium (CD-ROM)*, ISSN 1682-1750, Sao Jose' dos Compos, Brazil, 16-18 September, 2002

Li, X.; Rowley, R. J.; Kostelnick, J. C.; Braaten, D.; Meisel, J. & Hulbutta, K. (2009). GIS analysis of global impacts from sea level rise. *Photogrammetric Engineering and Remote Sensing*, Vol.75, No.7, pp. 807-818, ISSN 0099-1112

Lipton, L. & Wellman, B. M. (1999). *Pathways to understanding: Patterns and Practices in the Learning-Focused Classroom*. Hawker Brownlow Education Pty Ltd, Victoria, Australia, ISBN 1864018135

Mahmoud, W. H.; Ahmed, I.; Krinis, D. & Al-Marri, H. M. (2005). Well placement optimization using GIS. *Proceedings of the First National GIS Symposium in Saudi Arabia (Online)*, Khobar, Saudi Arabia, 21-23 November, 2005, Available from http://www.saudigis.org/FCKFiles/File/SaudiGISArchive/1stGIS/Papers/2.pdf

Matmti, R. & Delany, J. (2011). Active learning: Going beyong just telling them information ! *YIC Campus Times*, No.2, Available from http://www.calameo.com/read/000335779577c886d8dd1

McDougall, K.; Williamson, I.; Bellman, C. & Rizos, C. (2006). Challenges facing spatial information and geomatics education in the higher education sector. *Combined 5th Trans Tasman Survey Conference & 2nd Queensland Spatial Industry Conference,* Cairns, Australia, 18–26 September, 2006

MacDougall, K. (2011). Understanding the impact of volunteered geographic information during the Queensland floods. *Proceedings of 7th International Symposium on Digital Earth*, Perth, Australia, 23-25 August, 2011

Meitner, M. J.; Gonzales, J.; Gandy, R. & Maedel, J. (2005). Critical thinking, knowledge retention and strife: Reflections on active-learning techniques. *Proceedings of ESRI Education Users Conference*, San Diego, California, 23-26 July, 2005, Available from http://proceedings.esri.com/library/userconf/educ05/abstracts/a1081.html

Mills, J. P.; Parker, D. & Edwards, S. J. (2004). Geomatics.org.uk: A UK response to a global awareness problem. *Proceedings 20th ISPRS Congress Commission VI*, pp. 1-6, ISSN 1682-1750, Istanbul, Turkey, 12–23 July, 2004

Mohamed, A. H. (2010). Editorial - Unmanned aerial vehicles for surveyors. *Surveying and Land Information Science*, Vol.70, No.3, pp. 107-109, ISSN 1538-1242

Mohamed, A.; Grenville, B.; Sowmya, S.; Benjamin, W. & Adam, B. (2011). A comparative study of geomatics education at select Canadian and American universities. *Surveying and Land Information Science*, Vol.71, No.1, pp. 21-31, ISSN 1538-1242

Mondello, C. M.; Hepner, G. F. & Williamson, R. A. (2004). *10-Year Industry Forecast: Phases I-III – Study Documentation*, ASPRS, USA, Available from www.asprs.org/a/news/forecast/10-year-ind-forecast.pdf

Nittel, S. (2009). A survey of geosensor networks: Advances in dynamic environmental monitoring. *Sensors*, Vol.9, pp. 5664-5678, ISSN 1424-8220

Olaleye, J. B.; Abiodun, O. E.; Olusina, J. O. & Alademomi, A. S. (2011). Surveyors and the challenges of digital surveying and mapping technology. *Surveying and Land Information Science*, Vol.71, No.1, pp. 3-11, ISSN 1538-1242

Prince, M. (2004). Does active learning work? A review of the research. *Journal of Engineering Education*, Vol.93, No.3, pp. 223-231, ISSN 1069-4730

Pun-Cheng, L. S. C. (2001). Knowing our customers: A quantitative analysis of geomatics students. *International Research in Geographical and Environmental Education*, Vol.10, No.3, pp. 322-341, ISSN 1038-2046

Rebufello, P.; Piperno, P. & Drets, G. (2012). Uruguay streamlines livestock traceability. *ArcNews*, Winter 2011/2012, Vol.33, No.4, pp. 32, Available from www.esri.com/news/arcnews/winter1112articles/files/arcnews33_4/arcnews-winter1112.pdf

Ruther, H. (2003). The situation of geomatics education in Africa – An endagered profession. *Keynote Paper at 2nd FIG Regional Conference (Online)*, Marrakech, Morocco, 2-5 December, 2003, Available from www.fig.net/pub/monthly%5Farticles/november_2003/Heinz_Ruther_November_2003.pdf

Samant, H. (2012). Applications : Here, there, every where. *Geospatial World*, January, 2012, pp. 46-53, Available from http://geospatialworld.net/index.php?option=com_content&view=article&id=23930

Schultz, R. B. (2012). Active pedagogy leading to deeper learning: fostering metacognition and infusing active learning into the GIS&T classroom, In: *Teaching geographic information science and technology in higher education*, D. Unwin, N. Tate, K. Foote & D. Dibiase, (Ed.), pp. 17-36, Wiley, Chichester, UK, ISBN 978-0-470-74856-5

Shortis, M.; Ogleby, C. & Kealy, A. (2000). Self-paced learning of plane surveying concepts and field procedures. *International IT Conference on Geospatial Education*, Hong Kong, 6-8 July, 2000, Available from www.geomsoft.com/markss/papers/Shortis_etal_PS_CTMM.pdf

Sinton, D. S. (2012). Making the case for GIS&T in higher education, In: *Teaching geographic information science and technology in higher education*, D. Unwin, N. Tate, K. Foote & D. Dibiase, (Ed.), pp. 17-36, Wiley, Chichester, UK, ISBN 978-0-470-74856-5

Stefanidis, A.; Crooks, A.; Radzikowski, J.; Croitoru, A. & Rice, M. (in press). Social media and the emergence of open-source geospatial intelligence, In: *Social-cultural dynamics and global security: Interdisciplinary perspectives on human geography in era of persistent conflict*, C. Tucker & R. Tomes, (Ed.), US Geospatial Intelligence Foundation (USGIF)

Stefanidis, A.; Crooks, A. & Radzikowski, J. (forthcoming). Harvesting ambient geospatial information from social media feeds. *Geojournal*, DOI: 10.1007/s10708-011-9438-2, ISSN 1572-9893

Sullivan, K.; Coletti, M. & Luke, S. (2010). GeoMason: Geospatial support for MASON. *Technical Report GMU-CS-TR-2010-16*, Department of Computer Science, George Mason University, Virginia, USA, Available from cs.gmu.edu/~tr-admin/papers/GMU-CS-TR-2010-16.pdf

Suppasri, A.; Koshimura, S.; Matsuoka, M.; Gokon, H. & Kamthonkiat, D. (2012). Application of remote sensing for tsunami disaster, In: *Remote sensing of planet earth*, Y. Chemin, (Ed.), pp. 143-168, InTech, ISBN 978-953-307-919-6

Tsou, M. (2004). Integrated mobile GIS and wireless internet map servers for environmental monitoring and management. *Cartography and Geographic Information Science*, Vol.31, No.3, pp. 153-165, ISSN 1545-0465

Van Aardt, J. A. N.; Mckeown, D.; Faulring, J. ; Raqueno, N.; Casterline, M.; Renschler, C.; Eguchi, R.; Messinger, D.; Krzaczek, R.; Cavillia, S.; Antalovich, J.; Philips, N.; Barlett, B.; Salvaggio, C.; Ontiveros, E. & Gill, S. (2011). Geospatial disaster response during the haiti earthquake: A case study spanning airborne deployment, data collection, transfer, processing, and dissemination. *Photogrammetric Engineering and Remote Sensing*, Vol.77, No.9, pp. 943-952, ISSN 0099-1112

Wheeler, C. (2010). ESRI charts a new direction in training. *ArcWatch*, December, 2010, Available from http://www.esri.com/news/arcwatch/1210/feature.html

Xue, Y.; Cracknell, A. P. & Guo, H. D. (2002). Telegeoprocessing: The integration of remote sensing, geographic information system (GIS), global positioning system (GPS) and telecommunication. *International Journal of Remote Sensing*, Vol.23, No.9, pp. 1851-1893, ISSN 0141-1161

Yang, X.; Jiang, G.; Luo, X. & Zheng, Z. (2011). Preliminary mapping of high-resolution rural population distribution based on imagery from Google Earth: A case study in the Lake Tai Basin, Eastern China. *Applied Gogeraphy*, Vol.32, pp. 221-227, ISSN 0143-6228

Yoo, J.; Jazzar, A. B.; Jeong, K. J. & Lee, K. W. (2011). Development of real-time monitoring system integrated with GIS. *Proceedings of the Sixth National GIS Symposium in Saudi Arabia (Online)*, Khobar, Saudi Arabia, 24-26 April, 2011, Available from www.saudigis.org/FCKFiles/File/6thSaudiGIS_Papers/T1_3.doc

2

Ethical Decisions in Emergent Science, Engineering and Technologies

D. A. Vallero
Duke University, USA

1. Introduction

Emerging technologies present unique societal challenges. The public may be reluctant to accept them. The market niches are not always clear. They may have few precedents. They may rely on obscure knowledge and science that is not sufficiently understood outside the laboratory. These and other aspects of emerging technologies can present distinctive challenges to ethics.

Often, research and development of emerging technologies involve a very small group of experts in an esoteric enterprise. This often entails self-enforcement of difficult decisions. It also involves very dedicated and sharply focused researchers and advocates, who may have little incentive or aptitudes to be completely objective about the potential problems associated with their project. This is certainly understandable given that those engaged in advancing technologies have committed substantial intellectual and capital resources to the effort. Indeed, a key reason that many technologists are so successful is their laser-like focus. This is great for advancing the science, but can detract from considering the downsides of a new technology.

Another reason for lack of objectivity is motivation. Researchers at the cutting edge have much to lose if the technologies are delayed or stopped. For example, consider the dilemma of a doctoral student well into dissertation research who discovers a potential misuse of the technology. This could delay the research, or even require retrenchment and significant uncertainty in completing the doctorate. The problem is that doctoral students engaged in cutting edge research likely know more about the details than even the dissertation advisor and other experts on the committee. Indeed, even the ethics experts at the university will not know enough about the details of the research to see the ethical problems.

A third potential reason for missing possible ethical problems with an emerging technology can be traced to the scientific method itself, or at least the manner in which it is applied in cutting-edge research and development. Scientists often rely on weight-of-evidence. Evidence is gathered to support or refute a hypothesis. This often means that in order to keep the research from becoming unwieldy, all but one or a few variables are held constant, i.e. the laboratory condition.

The laboratory mentality can lead to looking at a very tightly confined data set, akin to looking for lost keys only under the light of the lamppost. Add to this the fact that mathematics is the language of science. Any non-mathematical communication is lost or at least valued less than quantitative information. Much of the ethical information is qualitative (e.g. honesty, integrity, justice, transparency, long-term impacts, etc.). When the good and bad aspects of a project are added up, it is not surprising that many of the potentially bad outcomes are underreported.

1.1 Transparency and open communication

Responsible research depends on reliable communication and oversight. That is, there needs to be a set of checks and balances beyond the innovator to ensure that research is not violating scientific and ethical standards. This serves the potential users, the general public and the innovator, since it could well prevent mistakes and misuses, with attendant liabilities for the innovator and sponsors.

Technical communication can be seen as a critical path, where the engineer sends a message and the audience receives it (See Fig. 1). The means of communication can be either perceptual or interpretive (Myers and Kaposi 2004) Perceptual communications are directed toward the senses. Human perceptual communications are similar to that of other animals (Green 1989); that is, we react to sensory information (e.g. reading body language or assigning meaning to gestures, such as a hand held up with palms out, meaning "stop" or smile conveying approval).

Interpretive communications encode messages that require intellectual effort by the receiver to understand the sender's meanings. This type of communication can either be verbal or symbolic. Scientists and engineers draw heavily on symbolic information when communicating amongst themselves. Walking into a seminar covering an unfamiliar technical topic, using unrecognizable symbols and vernacular, is an example of potential symbolic miscommunication. In fact, the experts may be using words and symbols that are used in your area of expertise, but with very different meanings. For example, a biosensor may draw from both electrical engineering and microbiology. Both fields use the term "resistance," but they apply very different meanings. Such dual meanings can be problematic in technical communication. With emerging technologies, such ambiguity is not only frustrating, it can be dangerous.

Technical communication is analogous to the signal-to-noise ratio (S/N) in a transceiver. S/N is a measure of the signal strength compared to background noise. The signal is the electrical or electromagnetic energy traversing from one location to another. Conversely, noise is any energy that degrades the quality of a signal. In other words, for ideal transmission, most of the energy if the signal finds its way to the receiver. Similarly, in perfect communication, the message intended by the sender is exactly what is collected by the receiver (see Fig. 2). In other words, $S/N = \infty$, because $N = 0$. This is the goal of any technical communication, but this is seldom, if ever, the case.

There is always noise. A message is different than what was meant to be sent (i.e. is "noisy,") because of problems anywhere in the transceiver system. For starters, each person has a unique set of perspectives, contexts, and biases. We can liken these as "filters" through which our intended and received message must pass. Since both the sender and the receiver are people, each has a unique set of filters. So, even if the message were perfect, the filters will distort it (i.e. add noise). The actual filters being used depends on the type of message

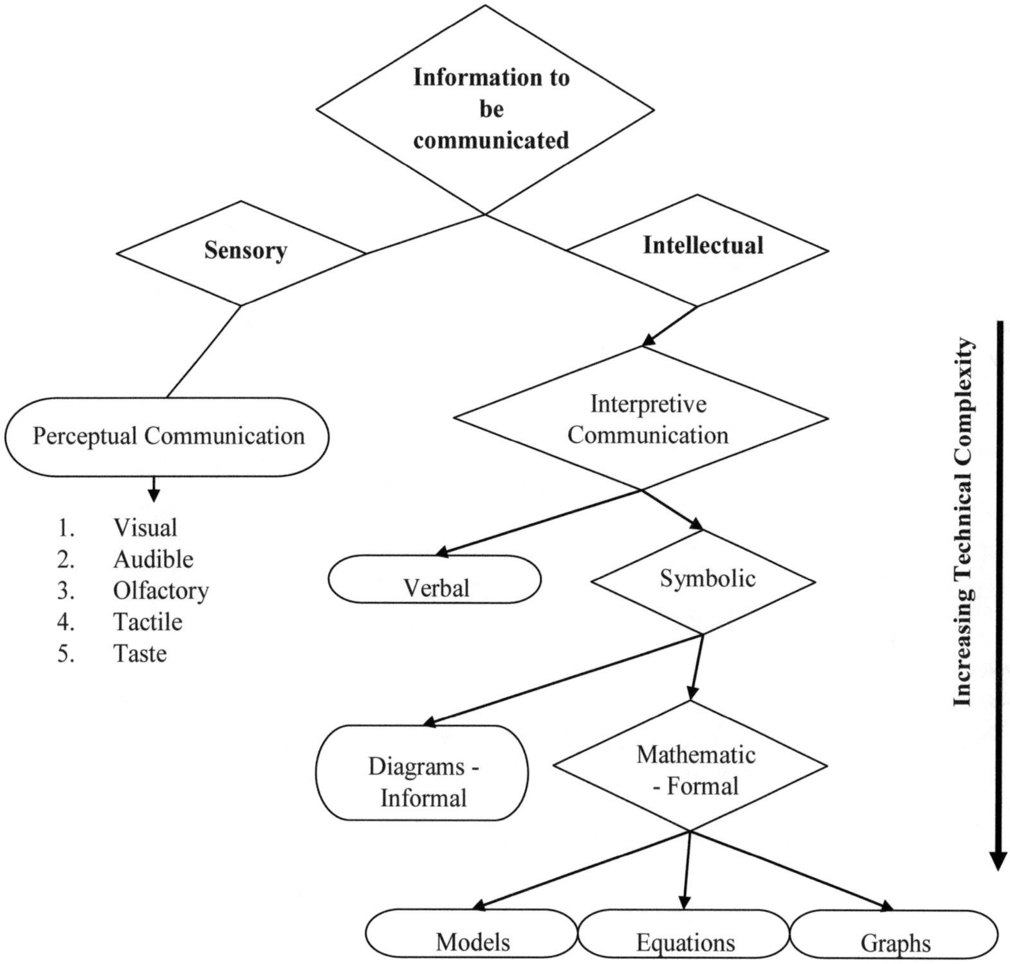

Fig. 1. Human communications. The right side of the figure is the domain of technical communication, but not of most people. Miscommunication can occur when members of the public may be overwhelmed by perceptive cues or may not understand the symbolic, interpretive language being used by an engineer. The potential for misunderstandings of an emerging technology at a public meeting will differ from a more technical setting, depending on the type of communication employed. Source: Myer and Kaposi (2004).

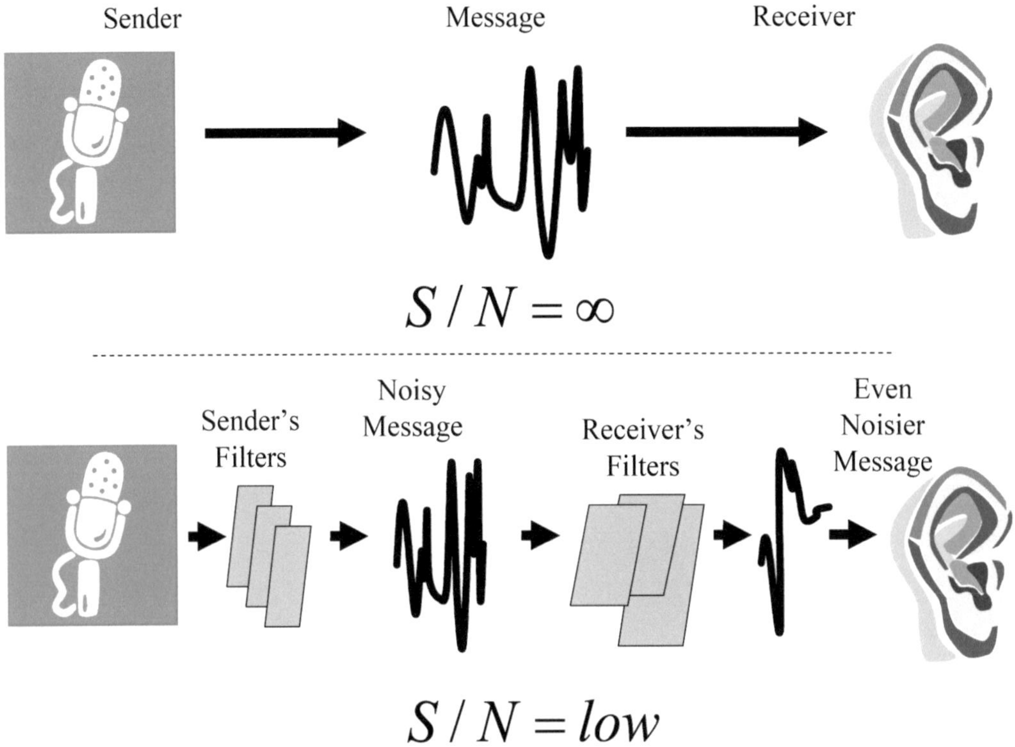

Fig. 2. Transceiver analogy for communications, consisting of three main components: the sender, the message and the receiver. The distortion (noise) that decreases the S/N is caused by filtering at either end of the message. Source: Vallero and Vesilind. (2007).

being conveyed. In purely technical communications, the effect of cultural nuances should be minimal compared to most other forms of communications. Translating highly technical reports written in Spanish or another non-English language might be much easier and straightforward than translating literature and poetry.

One worst case scenario for an emerging technology, or even a novel use of an existing technology, is actually an aspect of justice. For example, uneducated people, those not familiar with a dominant culture's norms, and even well educated people unfamiliar with technical jargon, may be easily ignored.

A tragic example occurred in Bangladesh in the 1990s. An engineering solution to one problem played a major role in exacerbating the arsenic problem. Surface water sources, especially standing ponds, in Bangladesh have historically contained significant microbial pathogens causing acute gastrointestinal disease in infants and children. To address this problem, the United Nations Children's Fund (UNICEF) in the 1970s began working with Bangladesh's Department of Public Health Engineering to fabricate and install tube-wells in an attempt to give an alternative and safer source of water, i.e. groundwater. Tube wells are mechanisms that consist of series of 5 cm diameter tubes inserted into the ground at depths of usually less than 200 m. Metal hand pumps at the top of each tube were used to extract water (Smith et al. 2000). Unbeknownst to the engineers, however, as many as 77 million of the 125 million Bangladeshi people have been exposed to elevated concentrations of arsenic in their drinking water, resulting in thousands of debilitating skin lesions, with chronic diseases expected to increase with time (World Health Organization, 2000).

The engineering solution appeared to be a straightforward application of the physical sciences, but societal warnings were ignored. The tube wells did indeed solve the pathogen problem, but ignored the local people's protesting the use of groundwater in some locations as "the devil's water." The water was not tested for arsenic. Indigenous folklore that suggested problems with the aquifer was ignored. Indeed, this case provides another unfortunate example of misreading an application of an emerging technology. The World Health Organization (WHO) responded by installing thousands of ion exchange resin canisters to absorb the arsenic ion. The system worked well, until the villagers began inquiring what to do with the used canisters, which had reached arsenic concentrations of a hazardous waste. The WHO engineers failed to consider the disposition and disposal parts of the life cycle, and now Bangladesh has tens of thousands of these canisters with the potential to cause acute human health problems (Vallero and Vesilind 2007).

1.2 Transparency and self-enforcement

Designs flaws are often only identified and corrected at the very end of the project: the software crashes, the device fails in real-world test, the project is grossly overbid, or the sensor explodes. This is followed by a search for what went wrong. Eventually the truth emerges, and often the problems can be traced to the initial level of engineering design, the development of data and the interpretation of test results. This is why innovative designers must be extremely careful of their work. It is one thing to make a mistake (everyone does), but misinformation is clearly unethical. Fabricated or spurious test results can lead to catastrophic failures because there is an absence of a failure detection mechanism in engineering until the project is completed. Without trust and truthfulness in engineering, the system will fail. Bronowski (1958) framed this challenge succinctly:

> *All engineering projects are communal; there would be no computers, there would be no airplanes, there would not even be civilization, if engineering were a solitary activity. What follows? It follows that we must be able to rely on other engineers; we must be able to trust their work. That is, it follows that there is a principle which binds engineering together, because without it the individual engineer would be helpless. This principle is truthfulness.*

Thus, responsible conduct related to cutting edge research requires equipping the researcher to be aware of the ethical problems or potential problems, to make the right decisions even at a cost in time and resources and to follow with behavior that carries through one's entire career.

Socrates is said to have defined ethics as "how we ought to live." The "ought" becomes rather complicated in the rapidly advancing and highly competitive world of emerging technologies. Socrates might suggest that the first step toward the proper unfolding of new technologies is a blend of science and ethics: doing what is right and doing it in the right way. Technologists must learn how to survive and thrive, not only as innovators, but as fellow citizens.

2. Ethical awareness and decision making

Instilling ethics at a university or research institution can be quite challenging since most researchers have only briefly engaged in venues outside of those found in their technical discipline. Their experiences with ethics generally have been under the mantle of academic integrity. Thus, it is necessary to build a bridge between academic integrity and research. A common extrapolation in scientific research is to transition from the "data-rich" to the "data-poor"; from the more certain to the uncertain. Ethics falls within the domain of the data-poor and uncertain for most scientists, engineers and technologists. That said, we can start from some basics and transition to the more complex aspects of ethics likely to confront technologists engaged in cutting-edge research and development.

2.1 The drivers education analogy

Research ethics can be likened to driver's education training, where the basics of driving a vehicle from a textbook (i.e. the "Rules of the Road") is augmented by hypothetical cases and scenarios to engage the student in "what ifs" (e.g. what factors led to a bad outcome, like a car wreck?). Society realizes that new drivers are at risk and are placing other members of society at risk. Teenagers are asking to handle an object with a lot of power (e.g. hundreds of horsepower), a large mass (greater than a ton), with a potential to accelerate rapidly and travel at high speeds. The problem is that the new driver cannot be expected to understand the societal implications of using this technology (the automobile). To raise the consciousness (and hopefully their conscientiousness), they are shown films of what happens to drivers who do not take their driving responsibilities seriously. Likewise, ethics training may include films and discuss cases that scare researchers in hopes that this will remind them of how to act when an ethical situation arises. This takes place in a safe environment (the classroom with a mentor who can share experiences), rather than relying on the one's own experiences.

But, memory fades with time. Psychologists refer to this as extinction, which can be graphed much like a decay curve familiar to engineers (See Fig. 3). If an event is not extremely dramatic, its details will soon fade in memory. This may be why ethics training courses employ cases with extremely bad outcomes (e.g. failed medical devices, operations gone horribly wrong, bridge failures, fatal side effects, scientific fraud on a global scale) as opposed to more subtle cases (e.g. the unlikely misuse or off-label use of an otherwise well-designed product).

Extinction could also occur if an unpleasant event happens to someone else, such as the scenarios in the driver's education films. One uncertainty associated with "canned" cases, particularly online "you be the judge" cases, is that the trainee does not directly relate to the situation or scenario. Thus, the individual technologist may not expect the bad outcomes to happen to his or her technology, even if there are strong parallels to one's own real-world situation.

Events are much more memorable when directly translatable to one's own experiences. Anyone who has been in a car wreck will remember it for many years. Hearing about another's case means more if one has experienced a very similar situation. For example, new drivers have little experiential data from which draw, which is analogous to new technologies. By definition, the ethics of emerging technologies must often be extrapolated from rather dissimilar scenarios.

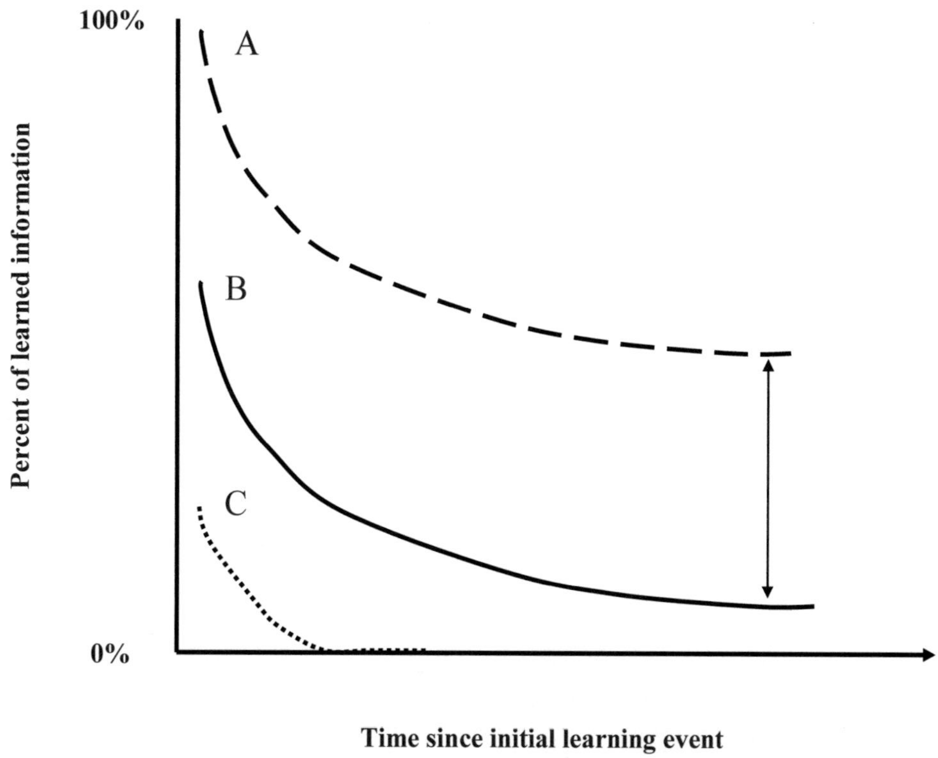

Fig. 3. Hypothetical memory extinction curves. Curve A represents the most memorable case and Curves B and C less memorable. Curve C is extinguished completely with time. While the events in Curves A and B are remembered, less information about the event is remembered in Curve B because the event is less dramatic. The double arrow represents the difference in the amount of information retained in long-term memory. Source: D.A. Vallero (2007). Biomedical Ethics for Engineers: Ethics and Decision Making in Biomedical and Biosystem Engineering. Elsevier Academic Press, Burlington, MA.

Training programs employ some measures to overcome or at least ameliorate extinction. Annual or recurring training programs addressing ethics and responsible conduct are common at many institutions (See Fig. 4).

Governing bodies are increasingly stressing the importance of responsible research. Thus, universities and research institutions have instituted training programs to ensure that research is conducted in a responsible manner. In the United States, for example, the Office of Research Integrity (ORI 2011) requires that all publicly funded entities include Responsible Conduct of Research Training (RCR). This is an important first step in instilling and enforcing ethical behavior, but ethical awareness is merely the first step in decision making related to emerging technologies.

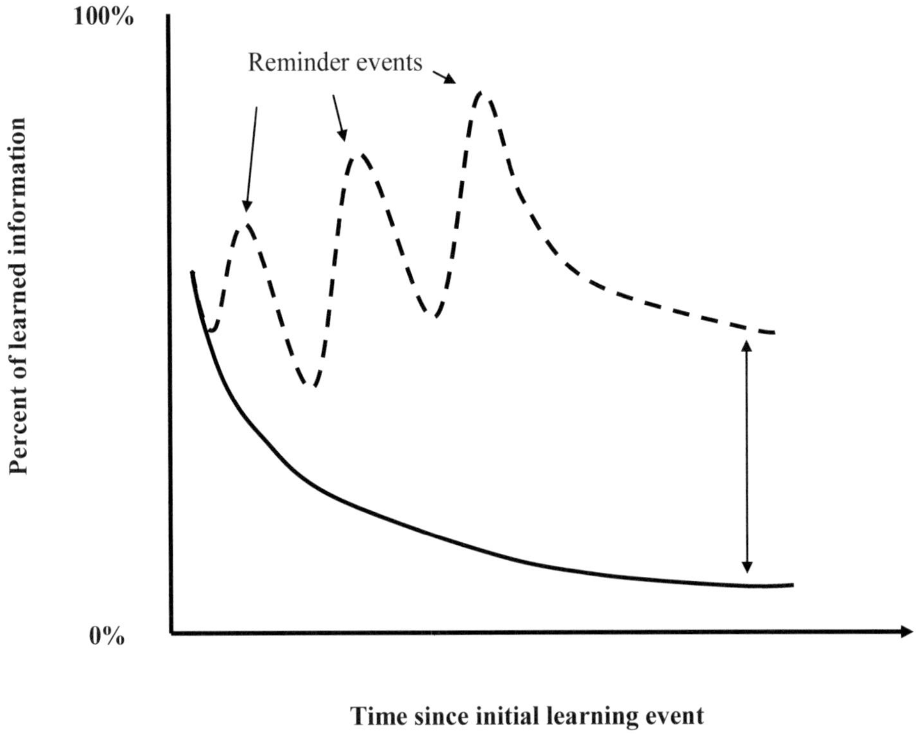

Fig. 4. Hypothetical extinction curves. The solid line represents a single learning event with no reminders (reinforcements). The dashed line shows reminder events in addition to the initial learning event. The double arrow is the difference in retained information retained in long-term memory as result of adding reminders. Source: D.A. Vallero (2007). Biomedical Ethics for Engineers: Ethics and Decision Making in Biomedical and Biosystem Engineering. Elsevier Academic Press, Burlington, MA.

2.2 Ethical decision making

Awareness is followed by sound decision making (Pickus 2008). Learning enough to make the best ethical decision, as is the case in learning to drive a car, results from a combination of formal study, interactive learning, and practice. While considering cases is helpful, it is no substitute for experiential learning. As evidence, technical professions require a period of time during which a newly minted engineer, medical practitioner, and designer can learn from a more seasoned professional. Much of this is to gain the benefits of real-world experience, without the new technologist having to suffer through painful trial and error, making mistake after mistake, before finally learning enough about the profession beyond textbooks to begin practice (society, clients and patients rightfully would not allow this!). But, this stage is also to help the new professional become inculcated into a new scientific and professional community, with its distinct and often unforgiving norms and mores. This can be likened to the new driver spending time behind the wheel with a seasoned driver. Only after a defined accompaniment stage, may the driver be expected to know the subtleties of merging left, parallel parking and other skills gained only after ample practice. Responsibility is gained incrementally. Whereas, the formal professional development stage is a necessary step in ethical growth, it is wholly insufficient for the ethics associated with the complexities of emerging technologies. Returning to our driving analogy, the ethics of emerging technologies is more akin to driving in the LeMans, a grueling, 24-hour race, with varying road conditions and unexpected obstacles. Predicting the benefits and risks associated with an emerging technology (like the LeMans) is much more uncertain than most technical endeavors, with rewards and risk well above that ever experienced by the average technologist (or the average driver).

The path to combined competence and integrity includes a number of steps. First, the researcher learns what is the right thing to do, technically and ethically. Next, the technologist learns how and when to decide what is right under various scenarios. Ultimately, the researcher's behavior reflects moral development. Along the way, at least within the traditional professions, the technologist advances from academic preparation to internships and practica, to membership in professional societies, leading to a morally exemplary career.

Evaluating whether a new technology is "worth it" depends on the metrics employed to compare the benefits to the risks.

Thankfully, most scientists engage in efforts justified by noble ends, even if one's particular research or practice provides but a small contribution to those ends. However, the moral imperative has two parts, the work itself *and* the obligation to do the right thing, i.e. Kant's concept of "duty." If deploying a technology fails to meet either or both of these requirements, it is considered to be morally unacceptable.

Evaluation of the ethics of a technology is not a discrete snapshot of the technology. The entire life cycle must be considered. Any technology that is poorly conceived, designed and operated fails the test of duty, even if the stated purpose is noble. An example would be to miss some key detrimental traits of a strain of genetically modified bacterium that effectively detoxifies a water pollutant. The endpoint, destruction of a pollutant, meets half of the categorical imperative (noble objective), but if the bacteria adversely affect nearby ecosystems by destroying beneficial microbes, the researcher is engaging in unethical behavior. The research fails the test of universalization since, by extension, all such ecosystems would be harmed every time these organisms are used. That is, if all bioengineers behaved this way, the world would be a much riskier place to live. This example also illustrates that emerging technologies are complex, with commensurately complex ethical considerations.

The categorical imperative is actually a professional metric. The distinguishing factor of professionalism is trust. Engineers, physicians and other professionals enter into a social contract that matches professional authority with accountability to the public. The vendor's credo, *caveat emptor,* does not hold for professionals. Rather, their credo is *credat emptor*; "The client can trust us!" As the first canon of National Society of Professional Engineers (NSPE) states, engineers must "hold paramount the safety, health and welfare of the public." Technical professions and research institutes must enhance their members' technical competence to address newly emergent and seemingly intractable problems, such as security, health, and safety. Simultaneously, the profession must instill an ethos that addresses these problems in a just way. The two premises must be integrated into any technological advancement.

The distinguishing characteristic of a professional is what the Ancients referred to as *ethike aretai*. Roughly translated from Greek, it means "skill of character"(Pence 2003). This is a hybrid of both technical competence and ethics; not separate, but integrated throughout the life cycle of an innovation. Thus, the ethical technologist is not only competent and skillful within a technical discipline, but is equally trustworthy and honorable.

3. Predicting benefits and risk

It comes as little surprise that inventors and innovators are better prepared and more willing to predict the benefits of their ideas and nascent projects than the concomitant risks. However, such bias is little comfort when mistakes, miscues and misdeeds are uncovered. As evidence, many of the case studies used in introductory engineering ethics courses have an element of selective bias toward the predicted benefits of an innovation.

The inventor or sponsor of a new medical device is likely to be very optimistic about the benefits, but predicting possible negative outcomes may be more obscure. Better credit card security devices could tread upon privacy. A genetically modified organism may do its job quite well in making medicine or cleaning up wastes, but may have risks, such as adverse effects on biodiversity. What these three seemingly diverse examples have in common is that the benefits are often more obvious and more immediate than the risks, which may be years or decades in the future.

Of course, hindsight is often 20/20 and is always easier than foresight. Predictions of an emerging technology's risks require a balance between being so overly cautious as to lead to loss of innovation and the introduction of large opportunity costs. Likewise, the prediction must not be so optimistic, or the risk prediction so rife with oversimplifications and assumptions, that the risks are mischaracterized or completely missed.

Another common element of the case studies mentioned is that the risks were not completely transparent or even ignored by decision makers (often by people with more power in the decision making process than the engineers or by engineers who had "forgotten" some of the ethical canons of the profession). Sometimes, the only reason the unethical decision making comes to light is a memo or note from a designer that implicates the decision makers at the higher level.

Applying the philosophical tools of *reductio ad absurdum*, do we blame the Wright brothers for the misuse of an aircraft or drone? Do we blame Louis Pasteur for the use of anthrax in bioterrorism? Of course not. Somewhere along the way, however, the misuse of a technology must be properly considered. In the rapidly changing world of genetics, systems biology, nanotechnology, systems medicine and information technology, we do not have the luxury of waiting a few decades to observe the downsides of emerging technologies.

3.1 Risk: The ethical yardstick

Ethical decision making for pending technologies combines technical and ethical factors. It makes use of multiplex optimization or benchmarking, where only certain outcomes are acceptable. A technically acceptable outcome may be ethically unacceptable, and an ethically acceptable outcome may be technically unacceptable. The tools needed to evaluate the benefits and risks of emerging technologies share aspects of most decision support tools.

However, as technologies become more complicated, the potential impacts become more obscure and increasingly difficult to predict. The "sword of Damocles" is comprised of all potential, but unintended consequences. This means that new decision support tools must be employed to consider risks and costs over the life of the technology and beyond.

One metric of the ethics of a technology is whether it poses or could pose *unacceptable risk.* Risk is the likelihood of negative outcomes. Too much risk means the new technology has failed society. Societal expectations of acceptable risk are mandated by technological standards and specifications, such as health codes and regulations, zoning and building codes and regulations, principles of professional engineering and medical practice, criteria in design guidebooks, and standards promulgated by international agencies (e.g. ISO, or the International Standards Organization) and national standard-setting bodies (e.g. ASTM, or the American Society for Testing and Materials).

Specific technologies are additionally sanctioned by organizations. For example, genetic modification of microbes, i.e. medical biotechnologies, are sanctioned by institutes of biomedical sciences, such as the American Medical Association and regulatory agencies, whereas food safety and environmental agencies, such as the U.S. Food and Drug Administration, the U.S. Department of Agriculture and the U.S. Environmental Protection Agency, and their respective state counterpart agencies, are responsible for new biotechnologies in their respective areas. Since emerging biotechnologies carry a reasonable potential for intentional misuse, a number of their research and operational practices are regulated and overseen by homeland security and threat reduction agencies, especially related to microbes that have been or could be used as biological agents in warfare and terrorism.

Of course, two terms used in the previous paragraphs beg for clarity. What is *unacceptable* and what is *reasonable*? And, who decides where to draw the line between unacceptable and acceptable and between unreasonable and reasonable? It is not ethical to expose people to unacceptable risk. The acceptability of a technology has both inherent and use aspects. For example, radiation emitted from a device is inherently hazardous. However, if no one comes near the device it may present little risk, notwithstanding its inherent properties. Thus, the use of the device drives its acceptability. As such, acceptability is value-laden. A device that destroys a tumor may be well worth the exposure to its inherently hazardous properties.

Likewise, deciding whether a risk of a technology is reasonable also depends on its expected uses. One benchmark of technological acceptability is that a risk be "as low as reasonably practical" (ALARP), a concept coined by the United Kingdom Health and Safety Commission (2011). The Commission is responsible for health and safety regulation in Great Britain. The Health and Safety Executive and local government are the enforcing authorities who work in support of the Commission. The range of possibilities fostered by this standard can be envisioned as three domains (see Fig. 5). In the uppermost domain, the risk is clearly unacceptable. The bottom indicates generally acceptable risk. However, the size of these domains varies considerably on perspective. There is seldom consensus and often never unanimity.

Risks in the ALARP region need to be managed scientifically and ethically to produce an acceptable outcome. Thus, the utility of a particular application of a new biotechnology, for example, can be based upon the greatest good that the use of the technology will engender, compared to the potential harm it may cause. For example, consider a genetically engineered bacterium that breaks downs a highly toxic contaminant that has seeped into the groundwater more efficiently than other available techniques (e.g. pumping out the groundwater and treating it aboveground using air stripping). If the only basis for success were cleaning up the site, this would be a fairly straightforward. That is, if goodness were based solely on this utility, the project is acceptable. However, such single-variable assessments are uncommon and can lead to erroneous predictions of outcome. For example, the engineer must evaluate whether the use of the biotechnology can introduce side effects, such as the production of harmful new substances, or whether the genetically engineered organisms could change the diversity and condition of neighboring microbial populations.

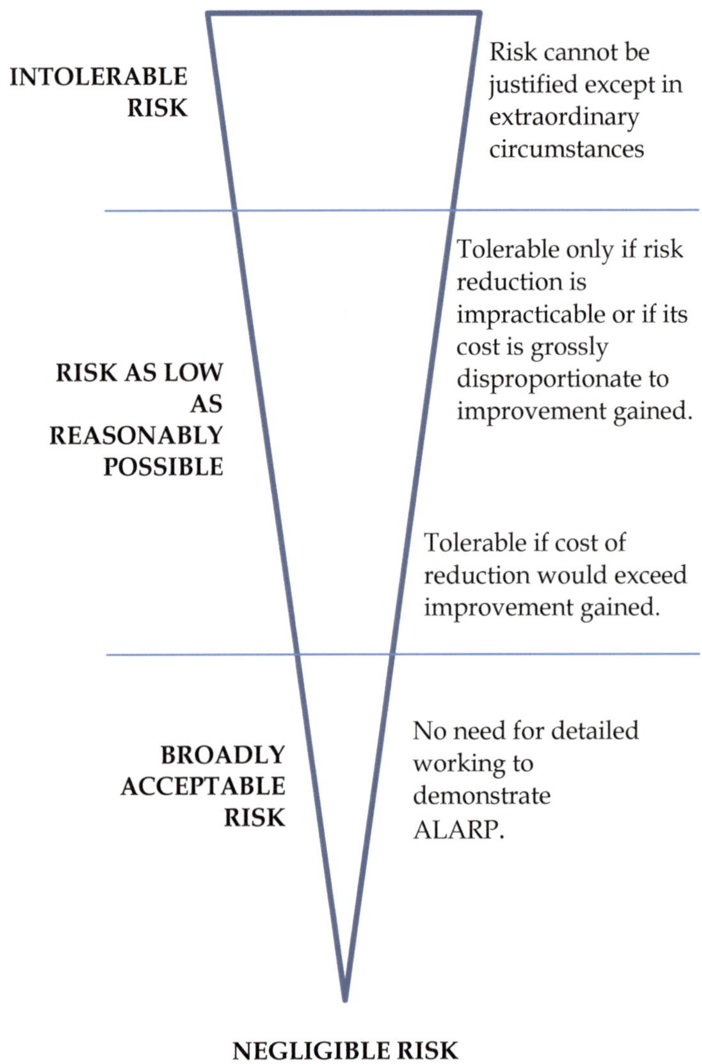

Fig. 5. Three regions of risk tolerance. *Source:* United Kingdom Health and Safety Commission (1998).

Therefore ALARP depends on a defensible margin of safety that is both protective and reasonable Hence, reaching ALARP necessitates qualitative and/or quantitative measures of the amount of risk reduced and costs incurred with the design decisions. The ALARP principle assumes that it is possible to compare marginal improvements in safety (marginal risk decreases) with the marginal costs of the increases in reliability (UK Health and Safety Commission 2011).

To ascertain possible risks from emerging technologies, the first step is to identify the hazard (a potential threat) and then to develop a scenario of events that could take place to unleash the potential threat and lead to an effect. To assess the importance of a given scenario, the severity of the effect and the likelihood that it will occur in that scenario is calculated. This combination of the hazard and exposure particular to that scenario constitutes the risk.

The relationship between the severity and probability of a risk follows a general equation (Doblhoff-Dier 1999):

$$R = f(S, P) \tag{1}$$

Where risk (R) is a function (f) of the severity (S) and the probability (P) of harm. The risk equation can be simplified to be a product of severity and probability:

$$R = S \times P \tag{2}$$

The traditional health risk assessment, for example, begins with the identification of a hazard, which is comprised of a summary of an agent's physicochemical properties and routes and patterns of exposure and a review of toxic effects. (National Academy of Sciences 2002).

The risks associated with emerging technologies are doubly uncertain since the hazards are difficult to predict and the likely exposure can be variable and highly uncertain. Analogies of the risk of the new technology can seldom be directly extrapolated from existing technologies, *and* the emerging technology often takes place at scales much larger or smaller than better documented technologies. For example, if researchers are engineering materials at scales below 100 nanometers (i.e. nanotechnology), even the physical behavior is unknown. Since risk is a function of hazard and the exposure to that hazard, reliable assessment of that risk depends on sound physical characterization of the hazard. However, if even the physics is not well understood due to the scale and complexity of the research, the expected hazards to living things is even less well understood.

Indeed, the ethical uncertainty of emerging technologies is propagated in time and space. For example, many research institutions have numerous *nano-scale* projects (within a range of a few angstroms). Nascent areas of research include ways to links protein engineering with cellular and tissue biomedical engineering applications (e.g. drug delivery and new devices); ultra-dense computer memory; nonlinear dynamics and the mechanisms governing emergent phenomena in complex systems; and state of the art nano-scale sensors (including photonic ones). Complicating the potential societal risks, much of this research frequently employs biological materials and self-assembly devices to design and build some strikingly different kinds of devices. Among the worst case scenarios has to do with the replication of the "nano-machines." Advancing the state-of-the-science to improve the quality of life (e.g. treating cancer, Parkinson's disease, Alzheimer's disease, and improving life expectancies, or cleaning up contaminated hazardous wastes) can introduce different risks (Vallero 2007).

The uncertain, yet looming threat of global climate change can be attributed in part to technological and industrial progress. Emergent technologies can help to assuage these problems by using alternative sources of energy, such as wind and solar, to reduce global demand for fossil fuels. However, these can have side effects, such as the low-probability but highly important outcomes of genetic engineering, e.g. genetically modified organisms (GMOs) used to produce food. GMOs may well help with world food and energy needs, but are not a panacea.

The renowned physicist Martin Rees (2003) has voiced an extreme perspective related to the apprehension about nanotechnology, particularly its current trend toward producing "nanomachines." Biological systems, at the subcellular and molecular levels, could very efficiently produce proteins, as they already do for their own purposes. By tweaking some genetic material at a scale of a few angstroms, parts of the cell (e.g. the ribosome) that synthesize molecules could start producing myriad molecules designed by scientists, such as pharmaceuticals and nanoprocessors for computing. Rees is concerned that such assemblers could start self-replicating (like they always have), but without any "shut-off." Some have called this the "gray goo" scenario, i.e. creating of an "extinction technology" from the cell's unchecked ability to to replicate itself exponentially if part of their design is to be completely "omnivorous," using all matter as food! No other "life" on earth would exist if this "doomsday" scenario were to occur.

Though extreme and (hopefully) unlikely, this scenario calls attention to the problem that ethics usually follows technological advancement. All events that lead to even this extreme outcome are individually possible. Most life systems survive within a fairly narrow range of conditions. Slight modifications can be devastating. So, emerging technologies call for even more vigilance and foresight. Engineers and scientists are expected to push the envelopes of knowledge. We are rewarded for our eagerness and boldness. The Nobel Prize, for example, is not given to the chemist or physicist who has aptly calculated important scientific phenomena, with no new paradigms. It would be rare indeed for engineering societies to bestow awards only to the engineer who for an entire career used only proven technologies to design and build structures. This begins with our general approach to contemporary scientific research. Technologists are often rugged individualists in a quest to add new knowledge. For example, aspirants seeking Ph.D.s must endeavor to add knowledge to their specific scientific discipline. Scientific journals are unlikely to publish articles that do not at least contain some modicum of originality and newly found information.

Innovation is rewarded. Unfortunately, there is not a lot of natural incentive for the innovators to stop what they are doing to "think about" possible ethical dilemmas propagated by their discoveries. However, the engineering profession is beginning to come to grips with to this issue; for example, in emergent "macroethical" areas like nanotechnology, neurotechnology, and even sustainable design approaches (National Academy of Sciences 2004).

Thus, those engaged in emerging technologies are expected to push the envelopes of possible applications and simultaneously to investigate likely scenarios, from the very beneficial to the worst-case ("doomsday") outcomes. This link between fundamental work and outcomes becomes increasingly crucial as such research reaches the marketplace relatively quickly and cannot be confined to the "safety" and rigor of the laboratory and highly controlled scale-ups.

Technological development thrusts the innovator into uncomfortable venues. Rarely is there a simple answer to the questions "How healthy is healthy enough?" And "How protected is protected enough?" Managing risks consists of balancing among alternatives. Usually, no single way to prevent potential problems is available. Whether a risk is acceptable is determined by a process of making decisions and implementing actions that flow from these decisions to reduce the adverse outcomes or, at least to lower the chance that negative consequences will occur (The Royal Society 1992).

Technologists can expect that whatever risk remains after their technologies reach the users, those potentially affected will not necessarily be satisfied with that risk. People want less risk, all other things being equal. Derby and Keeney (1981) have stated that "acceptable risk is the risk associated with the best of the available alternatives, not with the best of the alternatives which we would hope to have available."Calculating the risks associated with these alternatives is inherently constrained by three conditions (Morgan 1981):

1. The actual values of all important variables cannot be known completely and, thus cannot be projected into the future with complete certainty.
2. The physical and biological sciences of the processes leading to the risk can never be fully understood, so the physical, chemical and biological algorithms written into predictive models will propagate errors in the model.
3. Risk prediction using models depend on probabilistic and highly complex processes that make it infeasible to predict many outcomes.

The decision to proceed with most engineering designs or projects is based upon some sort of "risk-reward" paradigm, and should be a balance between benefits and costs (UK Department of Environment 1984). When comparing benefits to costs, values are inaccurate. Given the uncertainty, even a benefit/cost ratio that appears to weigh more heavily toward benefits, i.e. well above 1, may not provide an ample margin of safety given the risks involved.

4. Ethical constructs

For those involved in technologies, there are two general paths to ethical decisions, i.e. duty and outcome. Duty is at the heart of Immanuel Kant's (1785) "categorical imperative":

> *Act only according to that maxim by which you can at the same time will that it should become a universal law.*

The categorical imperative is at the heart of duty ethics (so called "deontology"), invoking the question as to whether one's action (or inaction) will make for a better world if all others in that same situation were to act in the same way. Thus, the technology itself can be ethically neutral, whereas the individual action's virtue or vice is seen in a comprehensive manner. The unknowns surrounding emerging technologies may cause one to add safeguards or even to abandon a technology or a particular use of the technology. The obligation of the technologist is to consider the effects of universalizing one's new technology, from an all inclusive perspective, considering all the potential good and all the potential bad.

Outcome-based ethics (so called "teleology") can be encapsulated in John Stuart Mill's (1863) utilitarianism's axiom of "greatest good for the greatest number of people." Even the most extreme forms of outcome-based ethics are moderated. For example, Mill added a "harm principle" which requires that no one be harmed in the pursuit of a noble outcome. That is, even though an emerging technology is expected to lead to benefits for the majority, it may still be unethical if it causes undue harm to even one person. John Rawls, who can be considered to be a libertarian, introduced another modulation, i.e. the "veil of ignorance." That is, the technologist must project himself or herself behind a veil, not knowing who is harmed the most by the new technology. In fact, the technologist may be the one being most harmed. Thus, the ethics of the technology should be based on its impact on the most vulnerable members of society (pregnant women, the unborn, neonates, children, the infirm, the elderly) , including those in the future. These constructs have in common the need to consider a technology's potential impacts on future and distant people, both the ends and the means during research, development and use of a technology, and the responsibility unique to the developer since he or she is the only one likely to be aware of an ethical breach in its early stages.

Thus, ethics begins with awareness, followed by decisions, and ultimately behavior growing out of these ethical decisions. For engineers, these three steps are codified, at least at the most fundamental level, reflective of duty ethics. The canons of the National Society of Professional Engineers (NSPE 2006) code of ethics captures what engineers "ought" to do. It states that engineers, in the fulfillment of their professional duties, shall:

1. Hold paramount the safety, health and welfare of the public.
2. Perform services only in areas of their competence.
3. Issue public statements only in an objective and truthful manner.
4. Act for each employer or client as faithful agents or trustees.
5. Avoid deceptive acts.
6. Conduct themselves honorably, responsibly, ethically, and lawfully so as to enhance the honor, reputation, and usefulness of the profession.

Such professional canons transcribe "morality," i.e. societal norms of acceptability (virtuous/good decisions and acts) and unacceptability (vicious/bad decisions and acts). These norms are shared by members of society to provide stability as determined by consensus (Beauchamp and Childress 2001). Professional codes of ethics and their respective canons are designed to provide *normative ethics*, i.e. classifying actions as right and wrong without bias. Normative ethics is contrasted with *descriptive ethics*, which is the study of what a group actually believes to be right and wrong, and how it enforces conduct. Normative ethics regards ethics as a set of norms related to actions. Descriptive ethics deals with what "is" and normative ethics addresses "what should be."

Gert (2004) categorizes behaviors into what he calls a "common morality," which is a system that thoughtful people use implicitly to make moral judgments. Humans strive to avoid five basic harms: death; pain; disability; loss of freedom; and loss of pleasure. Arguably, the impetus for many emerging technologies is that they address society's needs and desires. With this in mind, Gert proposes ten moral rules of common morality. The first five directly prohibit the infliction of harm on others. The next five indirectly lead to prevention of harm. Interestingly, these rules track quite closely with the tenets and canons of the engineering profession (See Table 1).

Numerous ethical theories can form the basis for emerging technologies. In large measure, engineering ethics is an amalgam of various elements of many theories. As evidence, the American Society of Mechanical Engineers (ASME 2012) has succinctly bracketed ethical behavior into three models discussed in the next sections.

Engineers shall:	Most Closely Linked to Rules of Morality Identified by Gert
1. Hold paramount the safety, health and welfare of the public.	• Do not kill. • Do not cause pain. • Do not disable. • Do not deprive of pleasure. • Do not deprive of freedom.
2. Perform services only in areas of their competence.	• Do not deceive. • Keep your promises. • Do not cheat. • Obey the law • Do your duty.
3. Issue public statements only in an objective and truthful manner.	• Do not deceive.
4. Act for each employer or client as faithful agents or trustees.	• Do not deprive of pleasure. • Keep your promises. • Do not cheat. • Do your duty.
5. Avoid deceptive acts.	• Do not deceive. • Keep your promises. • Do not cheat.
6. Conduct themselves honorably, responsibly, ethically, and lawfully so as to enhance the honor, reputation, and usefulness of the profession.	• Do your duty. • Obey the law • Keep your promises.

Table 1. Canons of the National Society of Professional Engineers (2006) Compared to Gert's (2001) Rules of Morality.

4.1 Malpractice model

Also known as the "minimalist" model, it may not actually be an ethical model in that the engineer is only acting in ways that are required to keep his or her license or professional membership. It is more accurately defined as a *legalistic* model. The engineer operating within this framework is concerned exclusively with adhering to standards and meeting requirements of the profession and any other applicable rules, laws or codes. Minimalism tends to be retroactive in view; finding fault after failures, problems or accidents happen. Any ethical breach is assigned based upon design, building, operation or other engineering steps that have failed to meet recognized professional standards. This is a common approach in failure engineering and in ethical review board considerations. It is also the basis of numerous engineering case studies.

The minimalist approach to integrity may be particularly problematic if applied to emerging technologies. A failure could be catastrophic, since there are few if any precedents for this technology. That is, meeting performance criteria designed for normal and well-tested technologies may well not prevent problems associated with possible outcomes of untested technologies. The innovator may be the only one with the understanding of the technology to predict problems, and is often certainly in the best position to foresee low probability, negative outcomes. In other words, the innovator may see the flaws of existing performance criteria and rules in assuring the safety, health and welfare. Knowing this places the onus on the innovator, since the regulators may not be aware of the potential risks (sometimes in ethical inquiries, the conclusion is that an engineer "knew or should have known" the risks and declared them before the problems occurred).

4.2 Reasonable-care model

Also known as a due-care model, reasonable care builds on and goes a step further than the minimalist model. The technologist must take reasonable precautions and to provide care in practice (especially in the engineering profession). Interestingly, every major philosophical theory of ethics includes such a provision, such as three mentioned previously, i.e. the categorical imperative in duty ethics, the harm principle in utilitarianism, and the veil of ignorance in social contract ethics.

Determining what is reasonable can be quite subjective, so this model applies a mechanism borrowed from the legal profession, i.e. the *reasonable person standard*. Applying this to emerging technologies, the result of the decision to design or use a new technology is measured against the metric of the degree to which the design and use would be seen as ethical or unethical according to a "standard of reasonableness as seen by a normal, prudent nonprofessional"(ASME 2012).

In a highly technical area, this mechanism should be based on a more knowledgeable *and* reasonable person, i.e. a "reasonable engineer standard" or "reasonable scientist standard." If the innovator is an engineer, for example, this affiliation adds a professional onus. Not only should an action be acceptable to the majority of users it should also be acceptable to one's peers in the profession, as well as to scientists and designers outside of engineering, depending on the technology itself.

An action could very well be legal, and even professionally permissible, but may still fall below the ethical threshold if reasonable people consider it to be wrong.

4.3 Good works model

A truly ethical model goes beyond obeying the law or preventing harm. An ethical innovator excels beyond the standards and codes and does the right thing to improve product safety, public health or social welfare. Doing what is "right" is more than simply avoiding what is "wrong." Much as peace is more than the absence of war, research integrity is more than avoiding immoral acts. It requires a proactive and preventive approach. Ethics must be integrated throughout the design life cycle (Vallero and Vesilind 2007). Certainly, the rules are important, but legality and morality are not completely inclusive (See Fig. 6).

The good works model is rooted in the moral development theories such as those expounded by Kohlberg (1981), Piaget (1965), Rest (1986), and Rest et al. (1999), who noted that moral action is a complex process entailing four components: moral sensitivity, judgment, motivation and character. They and others (e.g., Duska and Whelan, 1975) have noted that the age and education level are the two most important factors in determining a person's likelihood of making moral judgments, prioritizing moral values, and following

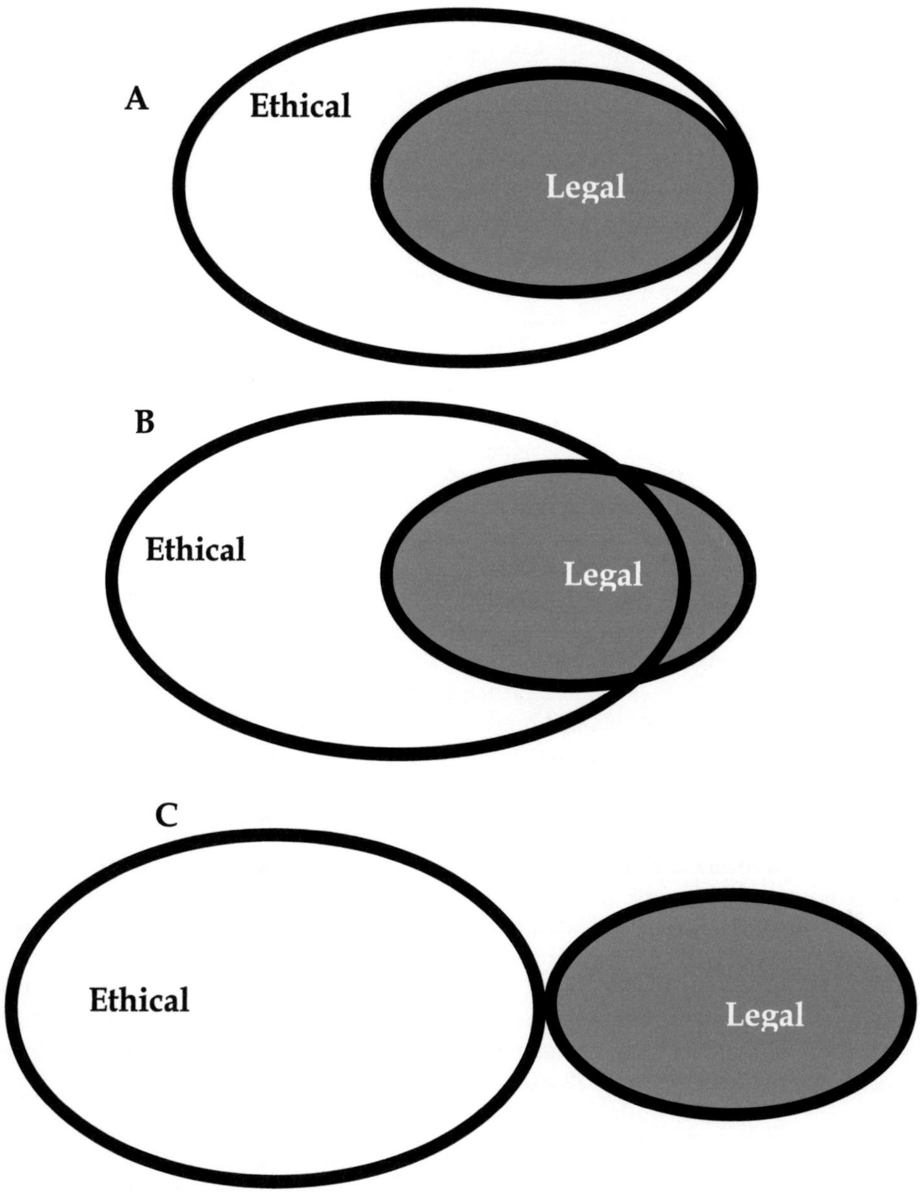

Fig. 6. Ethical decisions differ from legal decisions. Legality can be a subset of ethical decisions (A). An example is a biomedical researcher's responsibility to abide by copyright and intellectual property laws. In addition, ethics also includes extra-legal responsibilities, such as maintaining competence in the scientific discipline. Other situations may arise where a certain amount of legal behavior is, in fact, unethical (B). An example is the paying of bribes or gratuities or conducting research without appropriate informed consent of the subjects, which in certain cultures may be legal or even mandated by regulations. On rare occasions, the laws may be completely unethical (C), such as slavery. Some would argue, for example, that current research like embryonic stem cell and blastocyst research, cloning, and animal experimentation falls into this category.

through on moral decisions. Consistent with Aristotle's argument that the way to achieve excellence is though practice, experience is particularly critical regarding moral judgment: A person's ability to make moral judgments tends to grow with maturity in pursuit of further education, generally reaching its final and highest stage of development in early adulthood. This theory of moral development is illustrated in Table 2.

Pre-Conventional Level	1. punishment-obedience orientation 2. personal reward orientation
Conventional Level	3. "good boy"-"nice girl" orientation 4. law and order orientation
Post-Conventional Level	5. social contract orientation 6. universal ethical principle orientation

Table 2. Kohlberg's (1981) stages of moral development.

During the two earliest stages of moral development, i.e. the "pre-conventional level," a person is primarily motivated by the desire to seek pleasure and avoid pain. This is similar to the malpractice model. The "conventional level" consists of stages three and four: In stage three, the consequences that actions have for peers and their feelings about these actions; in stage four, considering how the wider community will view the actions and be affected by them. The parallel here is with the reasonable-care model. Only a minority reach the "post-conventional" stage, wherein they have an even broader perspective: Their moral decision making is guided by universal moral principles (Kant 1785); that is, by principles which reasonable people would agree should bind the actions of all people who find themselves in similar situations. This stage tracks closely with the good works model.

A normative model can be applied to emerging technologies. The moral need to consider the impact that the use of a technology will have on others forms the basis for the normative model. Pursuing a technological advancement merely with the goal of obeying the law may lead to avoiding punishment for wrongdoing, but it is not usually sufficient for any technological pursuit, let alone one with the uncertainties of emerging technologies. Pursuing a technology with the goal of improving profitability is clearly in line with investors' desires; but presumably customers', suppliers', and employees' desires must also be met at some level. And finally, pursuing an activity with the goal of "doing the right thing," behaving in a way that is morally right and just, can be the highest level of engineering behavior. This normative model of ethical engineering can be illustrated as Fig. 7.

There is a striking similarity between Kohlberg's model of moral development and growth within a technical profession. Avoiding punishment in the moral development model is similar to the need to avoid problems early in one's career. The pre-conventional level and early career experiences have similar driving forces.

The second level focuses on peers and community. The engineer must balance the needs of clients and fellow professionals with those of society at large. Engineering services and products must be of high quality and be profitable, but the focus is shifting away from self-centeredness and personal well-being toward external goals.

Universal moral principles begin to govern actions at the highest level of moral development. The driving force or motivation is trying to do the right thing on a moral (not legal, financial or even advancement of science) basis. These behaviors set an example, now and in the future.

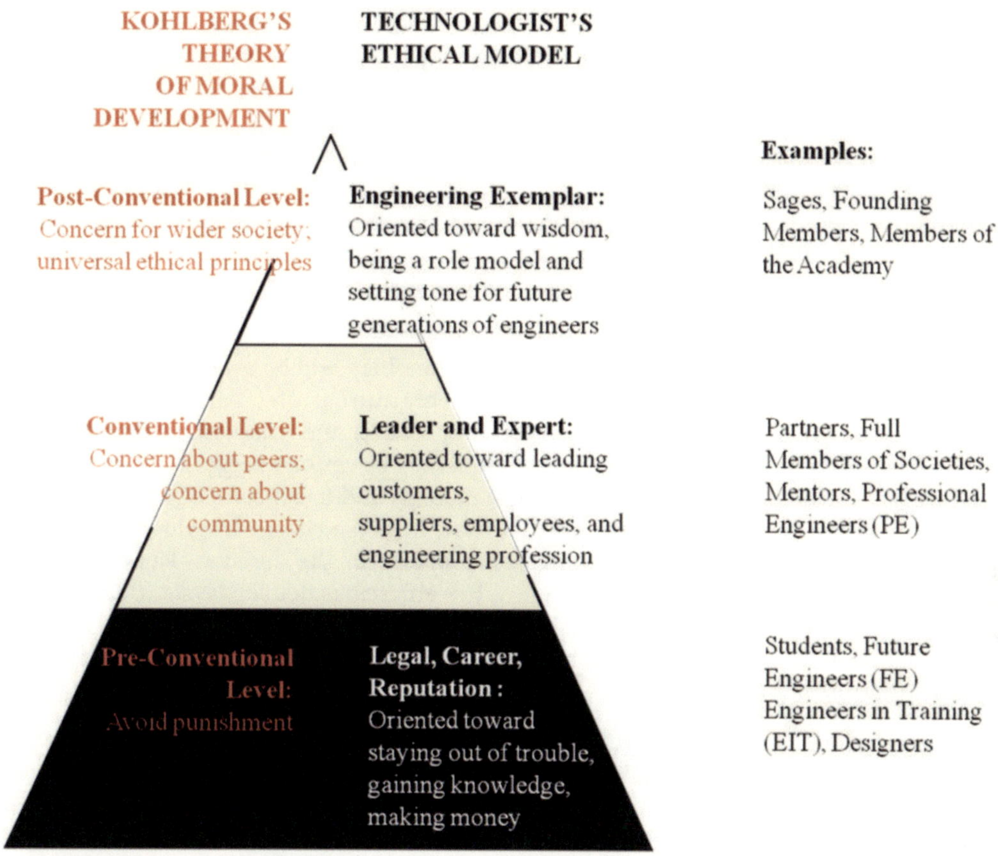

Fig. 7. Comparison of Kohlberg's moral development stages to technological ethics (Vallero 2007).

Ethical content is not an afterthought, but integrated within the decision making process. That is, the engineering exemplars recognize the broad impacts their decisions may have, and they act in such a way that their actions will be in the best interest of not only themselves and the organization they represent, but also the broader society and even future generations.

Much of the ethics training to date has emphasized pre-conventional thinking; that is, adherence to codes, laws and regulations within the milieu of profitability for the organization. This benefits the technologist and the organization, but is only a step toward full professionalism. Those who teach engineering ethics must stay focused on the engineer's principal client, "the public." One interpretation of the "hold paramount" provision mentioned previously is that it has primacy over all the others. So, anything the professional engineer does cannot violate this canon. No matter how competent, objective, honest, and faithful, the engineer must not jeopardize public safety, health or welfare. This is a challenge for such a results-oriented profession.

Technical professionals must navigate through their professional codes. The NSPE code, for instance, reminds its members that "public health and welfare are paramount considerations." Public safety and health considerations affect the design process directly. Almost every design now requires at least some attention to sustainability and environmental impacts. For example, recent changes in drug delivery have been required, such as moving away from the use of greenhouse gas propellants like chlorofluorocarbons (CFCs) and instead using pressure differential systems (such as physical pumps) to deliver medicines. This may seem like a small thing or even a nuisance to those who have to use them, but it reflects an appreciation for the importance of incremental effects. One inhaler does little to affect the ozone layer or threaten the global climate, but millions of inhalers can produce enough halogenated and other compounds that the threat must be considered in designing medical devices.

Technologists must consider how sustainable the technology will be over its useful lifetime. This requires thinking about the life cycle, not only during use, but when the use is complete. Such programs as "design for recycling" (DFR) and "design for disassembly" (DFD) allow the engineer to consider the consequences of various design options in space and time. They also help designers to pilot new systems and to consider scale effects when ramping up to full production of devices. However, if such a change inordinately affects a vulnerable population, this must be weighted properly in the decision. For example, if asthmatics are placed at additional risk due to a less efficacious delivery system, albeit more environmentally acceptable, it is likely not the best alternative. That is, the risk tradeoff between biomedical and environmental values leans more heavily toward the biomedical value (treating asthma effectively).

This illustrates that like virtually everything else in engineering, best serving the public is a matter of optimization. The variables that we choose to give large weights will often drive the design. The technologist must continue to advance the state-of-the science in high priority areas. Any possible adverse effects must also be recognized. These should be incorporated and properly weighted when we optimize benefits. We must weigh these benefits against possible hazards and societal costs.

5. Decision tools

Deciding on whether to introduce a new technology is a choice made under risk and uncertainty. This is why factors of safety are a part of every engineering recommendation. A number of decision support tools are available to aid in predicting the ethical implications of a new technology. Most are at best semi-quantitative. Their major strength lies in their objective descriptions needed for selecting among various alternatives. They even allow for some degree of weighting among physical and social values.

5.1 Net goodness analysis and decision trees

The net goodness analysis aids in the previously mentioned good works model. It estimates the goodness or wrongness of an action by weighing its morality, likelihood, and importance. This is a subjective analysis of whether a decision will be moral or less than moral. It puts the case into perspective, by looking at each factor driving a decision from three perspectives: 1. how good or bad would the consequence be; 2. How important is decision; and 3. how likely is it that the consequence would occur. These factors are then summed to give the overall net goodness of the decision:

$$NG = \Sigma \text{ (goodness of each consequence) x (importance) x (likelihood)} \qquad (3)$$

These analyses sometimes use ordinal scales, such as 0 through 3, where 0 is nonexistence (e.g. zero likelihood or zero importance) and 1, 2 and 3 are low, medium and high, respectively. Thus, there may be many small consequences that are near zero in importance and, since NG is a product, the overall net goodness of the decision is driven almost entirely by one or a few important and likely consequences. There are two cautions in using this approach. First, although it appears to be quantitative, the approach is very subjective. Second, as we have seen many times in cases involving health and safety, even a very unlikely but negative consequence is unacceptable.

The tool can be modified from a purely ethical decision making tool to a risk management tool by incorporating the net goodness into a decision tree. For example, Fig. 8 shows a hypothetical decision on whether to use a GMO (Vallero 2010). The decision is based on the likelihood of various beneficial and adverse outcomes, with ranked importance to three receptors: the environment; public health; and food production. The analysis is qualitative, but can help to identify important factors, as well as potential downstream impacts and artifacts of an immediate decision. The difficulty will be to arrive at probabilities to fill the "likelihood" column. Sometimes these are published, but often will have to be derived from focus groups and expert elicitation. Often, likelihood is presented as an ordinal scale (e.g. high, medium, or low - or 1, 2, or 3).

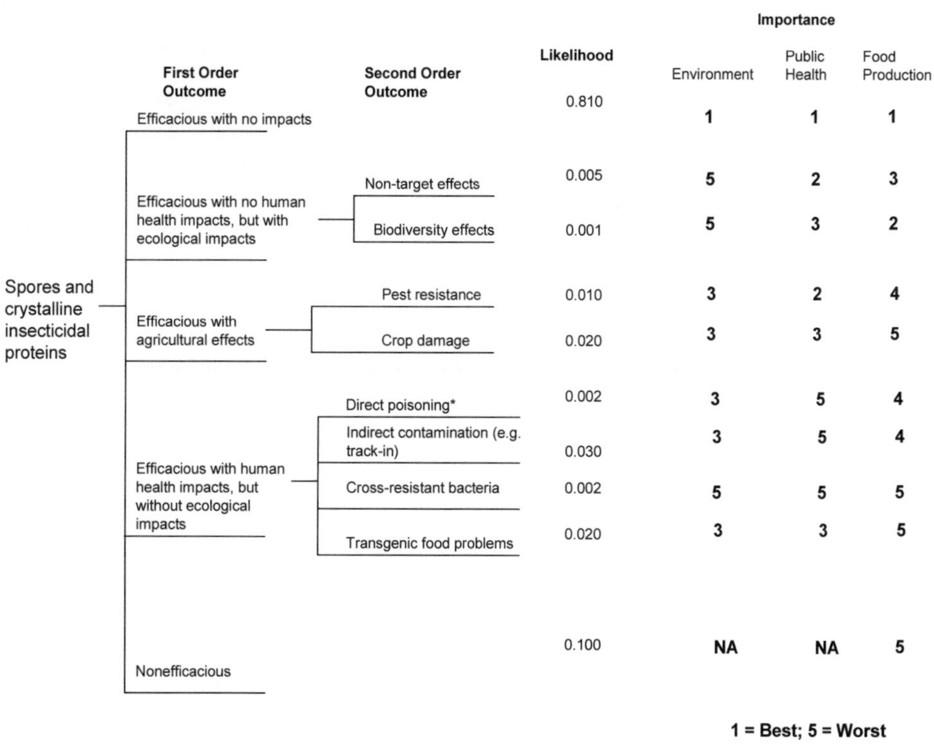

*This has its own decision tree according to vulnerability index, i.e. percentile exposure (high to no exposure) and sensitive subpopulations (children, elderly, asthmatic, etc.)

Fig. 8. Decision tree and net goodness analysis of a decision to insert *Bacillus thuringiensis* genetic material into crops near an ecosystem. Data are hypothetical. Vallero 2010).

5.2 Line drawing

Line drawing (Fledderman 2011) is most useful when there is little disagreement on which moral principles apply, but when there is no consensus about how to apply them. The approach allows the comparison of several real-world precedents for which there is general agreement about right and wrong. The emerging technology (the unknown) is plotted for each important factor (e.g. safety, privacy, etc.) Two of the precedents are extreme cases of right and wrong, respectively. The positive paradigm is very close to being unambiguously moral and the negative paradigm is unambiguously immoral:

NP	Emerging Technology			PP
Negative Feature 1	X			Positive Feature 1
Negative Feature 2		X		Positive Feature 2
Negative Feature 3			X	Positive Feature 4
Negative Feature *n*	X			Positive Feature *n*

Next, the emerging technology (T) is put on a scale showing the positive paradigm (PP) and the negative paradigm (NP), as well as other cases that are generally agreed to be less positive than PP but more positive than NP. This shows the relative position of T:

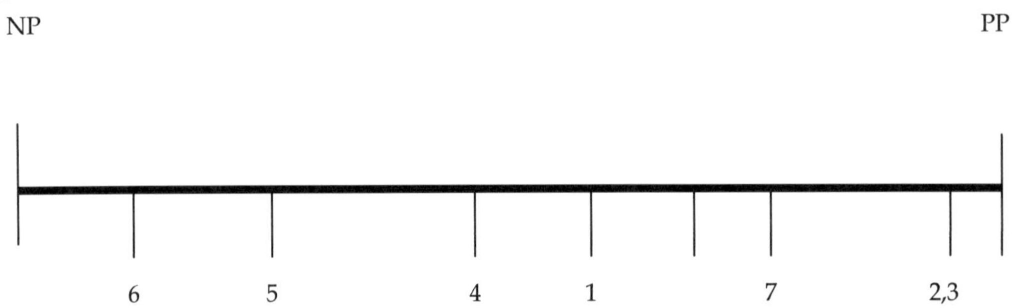

This gives the sense that the new technology is more positive than negative, but still short of being unambiguously positive. In fact, two precedents (2 and 3) are much more morally acceptable. This may indicate the need to consider taking an approach similar to these precedents, at least for the most sensitive factors (those that have influenced the location on the line).

5.3 Charting

Critical paths, PERT charts and other flow charts are useful in ethical analysis if sequences and contingencies are involved in reaching a decision, or if a series of events and ethical and factual decisions lead to the consequence of interest. Thus, each consequence and the decisions that were made along the way can be seen and analyzed individually and collectively. Fleddermann (2011) has used a flow chart for the toxic gas release at Bhopal, India. This flow chart addresses one specific decision, i.e. where to site the plant. Other charts need to be developed for safety training, the need for fail-safe measures, and proper operation and maintenance. Thus, a "master flow chart" can be developed for all of the decisions and sub-consequences that ultimately led to the disaster. A similar chart can used to consider possible contingencies and decision points for an emerging technology, such as the one in Fig. 9 regarding the decision to use a GMO.

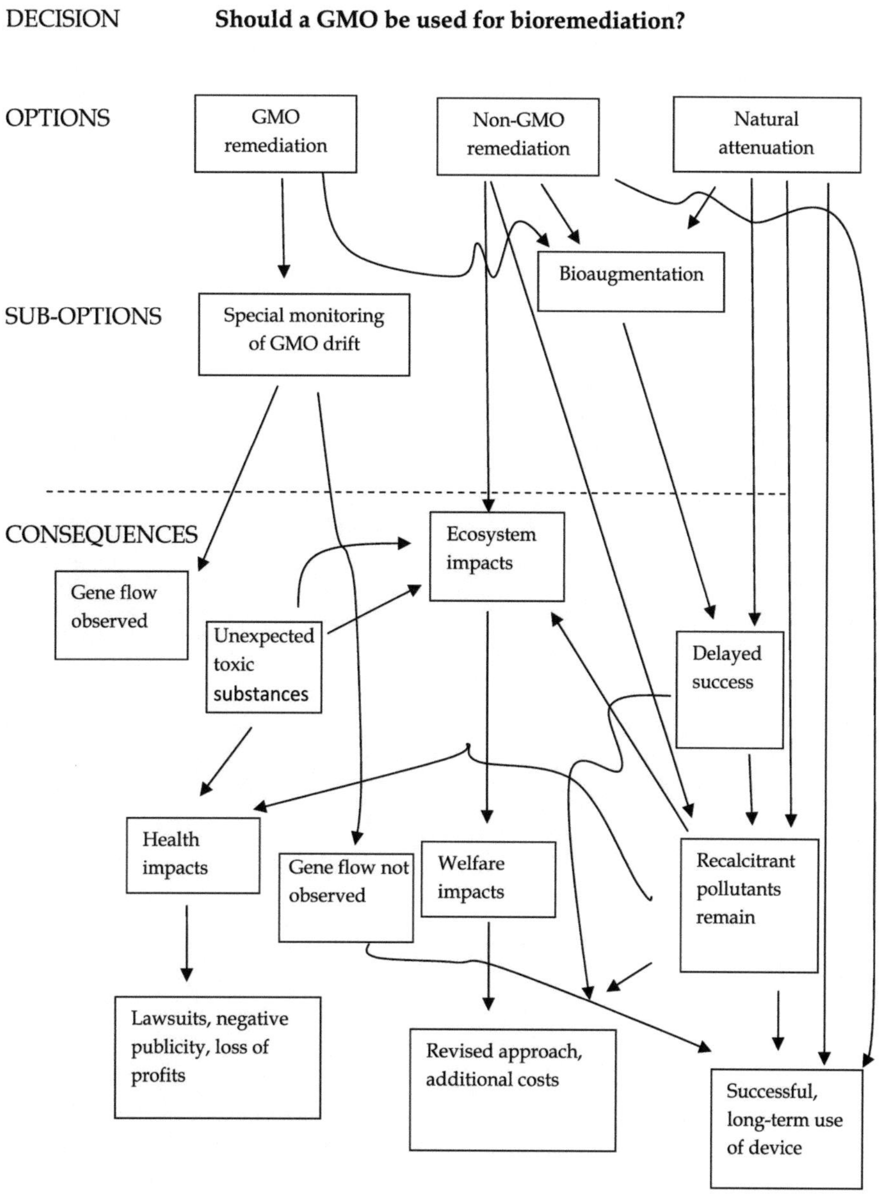

Fig. 9. Flow chart on whether to use a genetically modified organism (GMO) for an environmental cleanup (Vallero 2010).

Event trees or fault trees also support optimization of factors when weighing alternative versions of a technology or ways to mitigate potential adverse effects. This can help to avoid a technology's feature that can cause harm or lead to failures. For example, Fig. 10 shows an event tree that likely will support using a safer material when fabricating a device.

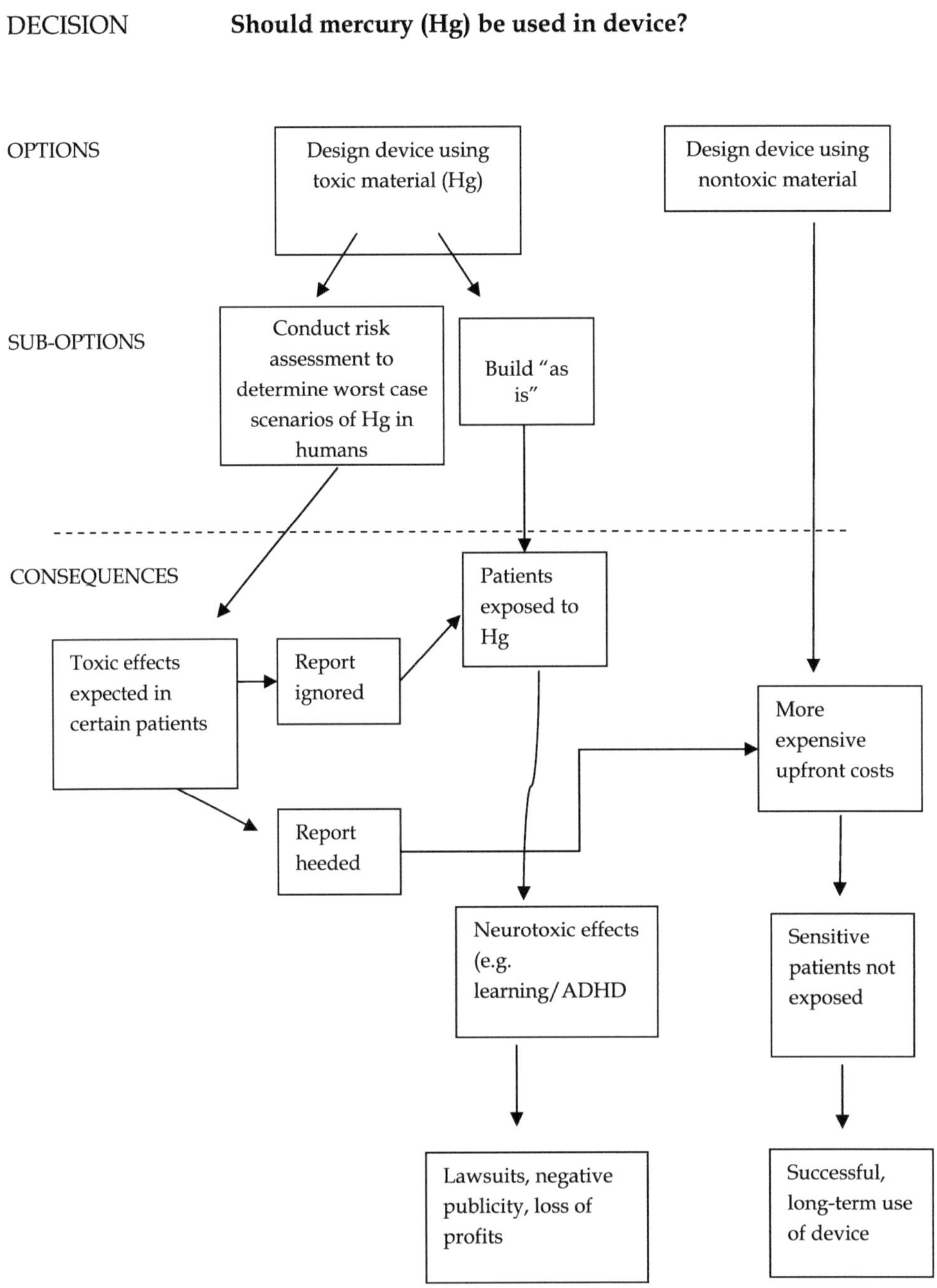

Fig. 10. Event tree on whether to use mercury in a medical device.

6. Responsible conduct of research

Researchers over the past two decades have embarked on ways to ensure that their graduate and faculty research not only advances the state of the science, but do so with integrity. Comparing decision making in emerging areas like these, especially nanomaterials and biotechnologies, to that of more established scientific enterprises combines technical and ethical content of decisions to go forward. As mentioned, Responsible Conduct of Research (RCR) programs at universities include training on ethics topics in specific research areas using proven educational resources, but newer techniques are required when dealing with complex systems (National Academy of Engineering 2003).

Indeed, RCR has been a key part of practical training of research and teaching assistants, provides a bridge between professional and research ethics, helps to ensure transparency and documentation of funding, and is vital to preparing the next generation of scholars by promoting research that both gains the public trust and contributes to the needs of society. As such, RCR provides a means of "preparing stewards of the discipline" as posited by the Carnegie Initiative on the Doctorate. (Duke University 2012). However, research enterprises must to ensure that graduate-level researchers in emerging fields are adequately prepared when confronted with ethical issues associated with emerging technologies (NAS 2004).

RCR training and the professional codes of ethics are starting points for ways to approach emerging technologies.

7. Conclusions

Even a well-conceived, thoughtfully designed and carefully deployed technology can fail to meet ethical standards. For example, a noble outcome does not justify unethical means. Failure to follow appropriate safety protocols (e.g. physical containment in a biotechnology) or or violating research norms (plagiarizing or fabricating data) would be an unethical act. Even if standard protocols are followed, this is not sufficient if they do not properly apply to an emerging technology.

Ethical decisions must embody systems thinking and consideration of worst case scenarios. This goes beyond obvious misuse and abuse. More subtle drawbacks and abuses need to be avoided by researchers and practitioners. Due diligence requires that one considers all possible good and bad outcomes of an emerging technology. Good practice requires that even a good technology needs commensurate safety and security measures to ensure that it is not misused, since emerging technologies have few, if any, completely reliable precedents.

8. References

American Society of Mechanical Engineers - ASME (2011). *Engineering Ethics.* http://files.asme.org/asmeorg/NewsPublicPolicy/Newsletters/METoday/articles/28207.pdf; accessed on January 11, 2012.

Bronowski, J. (1958). *Science and Human Values*, Harper and Row, ISBN: 0060972815, New York, NY.

Department of the Environment, United Kingdom Government (1994). *Sustainable Development, the UK Strategy*, Cmnd 2426, HMSO, London, UK.

Derby, S.L. and Keeney, R.L. (1981). Risk analysis: Understanding 'How safe is safe enough?'" *Risk Analysis*, 1, 3, pp. 217-24. ISSN: 0272-4332.

Doblhoff-Dier, O. (1999). Safe biotechnology 9: values in risk assessment for the environmental application of microorganisms. Trends in Biotechnology. 17, 8, pp. 307-311, ISSN: 0167-7799.

Duke University (2012). Research on Graduate Education. http://gradschool.duke.edu/about/reseduc/index.php; accessed on January 11, 2012.

Fledderman, C.B. (2011). *Engineering Ethics*. Pearson-Hall, ISBN 0132145219, New York, NY.

Green, T.R.G. (1989). Cognitive Dimensions of Notations, In: Sutcliffe, A. and Macaulay, L. *People and Computers V: Proceedings of the Fifth Conference of the British Computer Society*. Cambridge University Press, ISBN: 0521416949, Cambridge, UK.

Kant, I. (1785). *Groundwork for the Metaphysics of Morals*. Translated by Ellington, J.B. (1993). ISBN: 087220166x.

Mill, J.S. (1863). *On Liberty*. Penguin Books, ISBN 0140432078, New York, NY.

Morgan, MG. (1981). Probing the question of technology-induced risk, *IEEE Spectrum*, 18, 11, pp. 58-64, ISSN: 0018-9235.

Myers. M. and Kaposi, A. (2004). *The First Systems Book: Technology and Management* (2nd Edition). Imperial College Press, ISBN: 1860944329, London, UK.

National Academy of Engineering. (2004). *Emerging Technologies and Ethical Issues in Engineering*, The National Academies Press, ISBN: 030909271X ,Washington, DC.

National Academy of Sciences (2002). Biosolids Applied to Land: Advancing Standards and Practices. National Academy Press, ISBN: 0309084865. Washington, DC.

Office of Research Integrity. (2009). U.S. Department of Health and Human Services. Responsible Conduct of Research (RCR). Accessed on October 28, 2011, Available from: http://ori.hhs.gov/education/

Pickus, N. Kenan Institute for Ethics. Duke University. Personal communication. 2008.

Rees, M. 2003, *Our Final Hour: A Scientist's Warning: How Terror, Error, and Environmental Disaster Threaten Humankind's Future In This Century - On Earth and Beyond*, Basic Books, ISBN: 0465068626, New York, NY.

Smith, A.O., Lingas, E.O. and Rahman. M. (2000). Contamination of drinking-water by arsenic in Bangladesh. *Bulletin of the World Health Organization*, 78,9, pp. 1093-1103, ISSN 0042-9686.

The Royal Society. (1992). *Risk: Analysis, Perception and Management*. Royal Society Publishing, ISBN: 9780854034673. London, UK.

United Kingdom Health and Safety Commission (1998). http://www.hse.gov.uk/nuclear/computers.pdf; accessed May 26, 2006.

Vallero, D. (2010). *Environmental Biotechnology: A Biosystems Approach*. Elsevier Academic Press, ISBN: 012375089X, Burlington, MA.

Vallero, D.A. and Vesilind. P.A. (2007). *Socially Responsible Engineering: Justice in Risk Management*. John Wiley & Sons, ISBN: 0471787078, Hoboken, NJ.

World Health Organization. (2000), Researchers warn of impending disaster from mass arsenic poisoning. Press Release WHO/55.

3

Cloud Versus Clouds: Emergency Response Communications at Large Scale Festivals and Special Events – Innovative ICT Applications

David Gration[1] and Shah J. Miah[2]
[1]School of Business, University of the Sunshine Coast, Queensland,
[2]School of Management and Information Systems, Faculty of Business and Law, Footscray Park, Victoria University, Melbourne
Australia

1. Introduction

While considerable effort, if not always success, has been made in terms of the adoption of emergency response and communication technologies on a government level, the ability of private enterprise to adopt such emerging technology has for financial reasons been limited to only certain larger industries, e.g. power industry etc. Here we address the potential use of such systems, through the adoption of emerging technology in situations with short active time-frames, high potential impacts on significant populations, and low management resource contexts. In this chapter we focus on the specific context of special events and festivals as an example of these circumstances.

Studies on risk emergency response to extreme natural events, in the festivals & special events literature, is rare and requires more research (Getz, 2007). There is a lack of research focus on the application of theory to practice covering 'heat of moment' live risk response situations (Sonmez, Backman & Allen, 1993). Special events have been defined as one-off 'specific rituals, presentations, performances or celebrations that are consciously planned and created' (Allen, O'Toole, McDonnell & Harris, 2011, p. 11). They include sporting, cultural, business and celebratory live events. In the typology of specials events, festivals are seen as 'themed, public celebrations' (Getz 2007. p. 31).

Risk management practices, and in particular emergency management planning and response systems, are integral parts of modern special event management practice (Getz, 2007; Allen et al., 2011). The use of technology in special event management is widely adopted but little evidence of its holistic integration into the work practices of event managers has been identified (Knox, 2009). Recent event risk management texts (Tarlow, 2002; Silvers, 2008) accent the project management functions related to risk management but largely fail to address the potential use of ICT (information and communication technology) systems, including emerging technologies, as key components of this knowledge area.

The ability to provide affordable technological infrastructure that can be quickly ramped up in size and is widely accessible to stakeholders is essential when seeking to create a user-friendly and efficient system that enables time critical and multiple-direction decision making communication amongst stakeholders. A potential example of this might include the adoption of smart phone applications as part of such an integrated system. Examples of Mobile Apps being created for specific special events are becoming more commonplace. An example of this is the business event focused Infosalons Group, (Info Salons - Event Technology). This type of targeted communication system is yet to be integrated into a more holistic communication system that covers areas such as emergency management functions.

Extreme Natural Events (ENE), such as cyclones, intensive storms leading to flooding, gale force winds, hailstorms etc., have historically impacted on many areas of the world to one extent or other. Climate change proponents forecast a more rapid increase in both the number and severity of such events. In addressing the risk involved for the tourism industry in managing these types of events Alison Sprecht (2008, p. vii) states that:

'Risk is described simply as resulting from three main factors: (i) the nature of the hazard; (ii) the exposure of the elements to risk; and (iii) the vulnerability of those elements. Vulnerability can be further defined as the product of the susceptibility and resilience of the community and environment to the identified hazards. ENE's are a force of nature and cannot be modified, but risk of loss or damage can be reduced by modifying exposure and vulnerability. For this, a good knowledge of the likely ENE's is fundamental.'

For ENE's and other risk management situations, governments have a long history of utilising a blend of broadcasting media such as television and radio for alerting the public as to the nature and severity of the ENE, and delivering "what to do" information to citizens. Studies suggest the use of different mobile technologies to deliver emergency information in forms of weather warning and location based precautions (Krishnamurthy, 2002; Weiss et al., 2006). Other studies discuss issues of transmitting information through short message service (SMS) via mobile phone broadcasting system (Aloudat et al., 2007). However, these solutions do not provide an independent holistic and systematic framework in which key decision makers such as event managers can ensure appropriate collaboration for transmitting critical information. As such, the designing of an independent ICT based decision support solution, through a new web based sharing provision where decision makers from different agencies can actively communicate and perform decision making is proposed.

Delivering information to and from event attendees would be achieved through systematic and interactive communication linkages with relevant authorities and data sources, hence enabling the prioritising of action-taking in real time. As a specific ICT application, decision support systems (DSS) are gaining popularity to meet the domain-specific demands of clients for informed decision support. New technological provisioning platforms such as cloud computing show significant potential benefits, for the business/supplier as well as for public access requirements, when addressing significant access load demand in a very short time frame. Cloud computing may offer the advantage of a cloud (e.g. Internet or web based provisioning) based DSS service that can meet the emergency communication and decision making needs of key agencies and stakeholders in a wide variety of contexts and populations.

The chapter is organised as follows. Following on from the introduction (section 1) the next section (2) contextualises the major issues being addressed in a case study based on the Woodford Folk Festival in Queensland, Australia. The following section (3) examines the stakeholders and their relationships within the emergency communication system. The next section (4) examines cloud based approaches, while section (5) contextualises this through application to the case study and section (6) considers other advanced technologies for emergency management. The final section (7) provides for discussion and conclusions.

2. Case study Woodford Folk Festival

Our case study, the Woodford Folk Festival, is an Australian regional festival that is held over a six day period each December/January, originally at nearby Maleny it moved to its own property near the town of Woodford in Queensland Australia, in 1994. Here, 400 acres of farmland is being progressively reclaimed as 'environmental parkland'. It's mixed of natural landscape and built physical components can be described as a Blended Festivalscape (Gration, Arcodia, Raciti & Stokes, 2011), with the integration and preservation of natural elements of the environment being critical to consumer satisfaction with their festival experience. Woodford is a regional festival of music, arts and performance managed by the not-for-profit Queensland Folk Federation (QFF) and it currently attracts 100,000 - 120,000 attendees per year from a diverse demographic background. The site was transferred to the local government authority in 2011 with a long term lease being granted back to the QFF.

Fig. 1. Woodfordia Storm Damage - January 2011.

'The Queensland Floods have been a life changing event for many thousands of people and I know that our organisers will rise to the challenge presented to us and build a stronger future'

Bill Hauritz, CEO, Queensland Folk Festival - 14TH March 2011(Woodfordia Mail Media Release)

The sheer size of the site, the numbers attending and the temporary nature of most of the venues on-site make this event vulnerable to significant exposure to risks associated with extreme weather events. The timing of this event, in the Australian Summer 'wet season' increases the likelihood of this type of risk. In many ways the festival site is the equivalent of a temporary small city that has been created to last only a few short days each year. In common with all large scale outdoor special events and festivals, Woodford Folk Festival, is temporary in nature and yet must incorporate risk management plans that reflect the potential magnitude of the risks, the number of people involved (20,000 – 25,000 per day) and the potential for severe negative impacts should the worst occur. Its temporary nature does not lessen the complexity of the risk management task; indeed it can increase the management challenges to be faced.

Risk Management practices at the Woodfordia site are well defined and follow standard industry practices with a comprehensive risk management plan in place and training of all staff, both volunteers and paid, being undertaken. Festival management is required by legislation to manage and control risks associated with the conduct of the festival to ensure the safety of employees, stall-holders, on-site agencies personnel, contractors, volunteers and visitors (WFF Safety, Emergency and Incident Management Plan, 2010, Section 1.3) In addition a 24 hour Emergency Communications Centre (ECC) has been established to liaise with all venues, staff and emergency services. Indeed, both police and ambulance services, alongside a purpose-built medical centre, have a presence on the site during the festival. In the case of an emergency the ECC is converted into the Emergency Incident Control Centre (EICC) by the addition of a room extension to accommodate external; emergency services personnel for coordination purposes.

In terms of web based communications the festival has been increasingly moving to integrate areas as diverse as ticketing, production, administration, volunteer management, customer information and merchandising, alongside the more established promotional functions. In terms of Risk Management, the pro-active workplace health and safety training provided for all volunteers via their website and the reactive monitoring of on-line Bureau of Meteorology (BOM) warnings about weather conditions, as well as accessing of risk management documentation by staff, are the only web based communication activities identified.

During and after the 2010/11 Woodford Folk Festival severe weather conditions resulted, despite extensive drainage works on the site, in excessive disruption on the festival site. There were subsequent significant cost implications in terms of site restoration and future mitigation activities on top of significant box office decreases (approx. 20% downturn). The Courier Mail Newspaper reported that 'while Woodford was dubbed "Mudford" on social networking site Twitter yesterday, visitors continued to arrive into the afternoon' (Courier Mail - *Rain can't dampen Woodford punters' spirits*). The impact on people who attended the event was, while not life threatening, at times significant. Camping areas suffered flooding, car parks became a quagmire, roads and pathways were slippery and increasingly pot-holed leading to risks. The organisers spent a considerable amount of time and resources focused on maintaining safety for the public and allowing the venues to continue to operate. A literal sea of volunteers and paid staff worked to ensure the show could go on – and it did.

The 'wettest ever' festival was followed by an extreme downpour on 11th January 2011 when 180mm was recorded at Woodford. Remedial work on the physical damage to the site was commenced, funded by a combination of fundraising, insurance payouts and government grants. This work will help to restore the site and mitigate some of the potential impacts of similar ENE's in the future. The reality however is that no amount of physical works can fully protect such an exposed site from the ravages of nature without taking away the atmospherics or 'feel' of this blended festivalscape. If the grounds were concreted and all performances were in permanent indoor venues then the desired 'experience' from this festival would be compromised. If we take as a given that mitigating actions have been taken in terms of physical works, within the given boundaries, then it is the non-physical 'human' and 'technology' based systems that deserve closer attention.

The need for cost effective mechanisms for planning, monitoring & controlling risk through improved means of sharing and disbursing knowledge between key stakeholders at events is evident. These stakeholders involve internal and external active participants in the risk management communications process and provide the basis for decision making that will impact on the third stakeholder group, being those travelling to, are on-site, or departing from the festival site (figure 2).

3. Emergency communication network

As can be seen in figure 1 the emergency communication networks utilised by the majority of event managements are vary basic and unidirectional in nature.

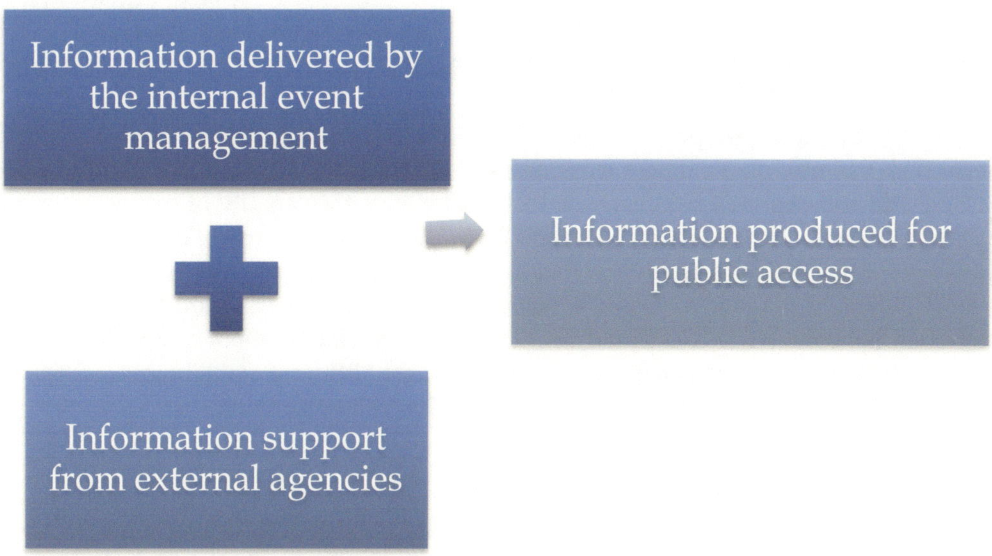

Fig. 2. Information exchange for emergency risk management communication.

In terms of our festival case study, emergency response management relies primarily on a layered communications approach based on private (in venues and offices on site) and public telephone services, mobile telephones supported by two mobile service provider towers and a series of radio communication systems operating during the festival by both festival management and external emergency services. Communications to the Public is via a number of public address systems located in the venues and verbal announcements, with no easy ability for two way communication. A professionally developed risk management plan is accessed through printed and online manuals, notices and other desktop materials and training processes.

The research literature is largely silent on the ways in which effective communications can happen in the 'danger zone', when extreme weather conditions are either happening or threatening to happen. Concentration is primarily on the early stage identification, assessment and mitigation strategies. What is needed is a clear means to bring together up to date information from a variety of sources, combine this data in a manner than integrates with the risk management plan and then enables this information to be communicated, in a timely manner, to relevant stakeholder groups as required. Weather updates from the Bureau of Meteorology (BOM) need to be available to all stakeholder groups to enable them to make personal and corporate decisions. Internal and external management groups need to have access to information from multiple sources (input) and to be able to communicate messages detailing new information to hand, decisions made and actions needing to be taken (output). This information exchange enables the managing, controlling and balancing of risk exposure scenarios directly with each other in real time to avoid confusion and potential duplication. The public need to receive live information updates from BOM, so they can assess this on a personal risk basis, as well as 'massaged' updates from the Emergency Incident Control Centre (EICC) that collates action recommendations from Internal and External management stakeholders. An ideal system would necessitate a feedback loop that provides the Public with the ability to contact the Emergency Incident Control Centre (EICC) in cases of actual or perceived risk to self, others and property being encountered during the event. This feedback loop would enable resources to be better allocated and new or additional information to be placed within the decision-making system.

Given the wide variance in potential input expertise a user-friendly layered approach would be needed. For example volunteer workforces, at events such as Woodford, would require easily learnt and operated risk response tools that ensure the capacity of volunteers is not exceeded (Earl, Parker, Edwards & Capra, 2005). Indeed information flowing back from these volunteers could range from verbal to use of mobile smart phones to, for example, send photographs of a dangerous earth subsidence. How these varied communications are delivered, received, shared, analysed in relation to other information, responded to, and used in deciding on coordinated actions requires a sophisticated communications system which the authors suggest is best handled through cloud based solutions.

4. Cloud based solutions

The term "*cloud computing*"[1] has become popular since October 2007 when Google and IBM jointly announced their collaboration (IBM website announcement, 2010 cited in Vouk, 2008) due to its main benefits such as reduced IT overhead and flexibility in offering cheaper user access. Fitzgerald and Dennis (2010) described cloud based design as a "*circuit-switched service architecture*" that is easier to implement for organisations because "*they move the burden of*

[1] Cloud computing refers to a computing platform in which users have options to use lease connection points into a network for establishing a temporary operation between computers (Fitzgerald & Dennis, 2010). Hayes (2008) described cloud computing as a software application migration from local PCs "to distant Internet servers, users and developers alike go along for the ride" (p.9).

network design and management inside the cloud" (p. 297). As such, Cloud computing provision has been used as a modern architecture of shared computing services. These services are mainly elevated through computing utility rental by service providers on the Internet.

After the introduction of web-based utility services by Amazon.com, many service providers became increasingly interested in utilising the cloud computing platform for launching new services that met their client group demands, including minimising labour and implementation expenses (Santos, Gummadi & Rodrigues, 2009). It is therefore surprising that the use of cloud based services for the effective communication and decision making of multiple parties is still largely overlooked given the potential benefits. As such we provide a conceptual approach of cloud provision to improve communication in event risk management contexts. In theory our concept represents a convergence of communication and decision making through the use of cloud based services.

5. Proposed approach

A SWOT[2] (Strengths, Weaknesses, Opportunities and Threats) analysis of cloud computing within different business perspectives has been described by Marston, Li, Bandyopadhyay, Zhang and Ghalsasi (2011) in which the importance for understanding the business related issues were highlighted. In other words, it is important to thoroughly analyse business problems before implementing the cloud based application. The study (Marston et al., 2011) identified two major trends that create and represent effective cloud computing application. These were 1) "IT efficiency, whereby the power of modern computers is utilized more efficiently through highly scalable hardware and software resources" and 2) "business agility, whereby IT can be used as a competitive tool through rapid deployment, parallel batch processing, use of compute-intensive business analytics and mobile interactive applications that respond in real time to user requirements" (p. 177). According to Marston et al. (2011) the concept of efficiency represents effective use of the computing resources located in geographical areas mainly for offering cheaper access to different services over the Internet. On the other hand, the concept of business agility implies that cloud computing must able to play differing roles for businesses, enabling the use of computational tools on the Internet as free or public access points that can be deployed and scaled as quickly as possible. It also helps reduce the need for the huge upfront investments that characterize enterprise IT setups today (Marston et al., 2011). Following the second principle we propose that the use of cloud based applications for event risk management emergency situations provide a significant improvement to traditional managerial and communication tools.

Cloud based provisioning supports event based emergency management strategies through enabling an appropriate collaboration. This approach, as illustrated in figure 3 below, allows for greatly improved information flows between the multitudes of stakeholders involved in event emergency situations.

Emergency stakeholders at events can be categorised as to their needs, powers and interaction methods (Table 1).

The conceptual model (figure 3) connects different decision makers with public for improved risk and event management practices. It offers a collaborative environment in

[2] SWOT analysis is a tool for evaluating artifacts or organization and its environment

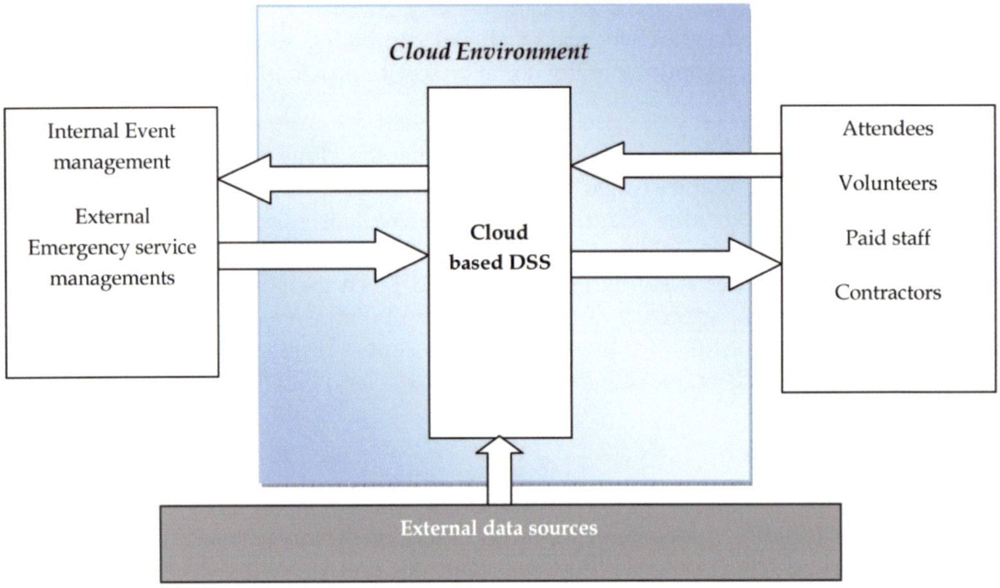

Fig. 3. A conceptual model of cloud based communicational decision support tools (CDST).

which information can propagate freely between multiple stakeholders simultaneously. This approach is far beyond current warning systems of emergency management, as it does support real time information sharing for complex decision making tasks concerning risk situations such as fire control, flooding and, crowd control etc. while at the same time communicating public/attendee announcements and updates through the web based applications on different mobile devices.

Barr et al. (2009) suggested that deploying cloud based applications as an effective management tool makes management significantly easier. However, the system needs to support all of the software management needs for their entire range of activities. For instance, it implies that management needs a systematic way, similar to that of an assembly production line process as opposed to a manual approach. Marston et al. (2011) identified five key advantages of cloud based system including 1) it makes lower the cost of entry for business if there is a lack of resources for widespread deployment of IT services, 2) it can provide an almost immediate access to technological resources, with no upfront capital investments for internal and external users, 3) it can make lower IT barriers to innovation, as can be witnessed from the many promising start-ups, from the popular online applications such as Facebook and YouTube, 4) it can make it easier for enterprises to extend their services - which are increasingly reliant on accurate information to meet the client demand continuously and finally 5) it also makes possible new classes of applications and delivers services that were not possible before.

These benefits (Marston et al., 2011) are applicable in our special event risk management context. 1) The proposed cloud based communications system would lower the entry/conversion costs, 2) it would be easily established without significant infrastructure costs to stakeholders, 3) it would enable the system to be tailored to new trends in communications rather than being tied to existing technology, 4) it can enable event

Stakeholders	Descriptions	Interaction mechanisms
Internal Event Management:	Includes decision-making management positions within the event organisation.	In-person Mobile network Radio network Telephone land lines
External Emergency Service Managements:	Includes Police, Fire, Ambulance, and other decision-making positions with a legal/regulatory responsibility for the event and/or location	In-person Mobile network Radio network Telephone land lines
External Data Sources	External bodies which provide important updates of factual data. Examples could include meteorological monitoring services, traffic monitoring services etc.	Web based Mobile network Public broadcasters (TV, Radio etc.) Telephone land lines (recorded messages) *Note: this is primarily a one-way generalised communication.*
Event Attendees	Includes members of the public travelling to, at, or exiting from the event venue	Public address systems Signage Verbal announcements
Event Volunteers	Voluntary staff working on behalf of event management	On-line training & manuals Verbal communications Public address systems Limited mobile network Limited telephone land lines
Event Paid Staff	Staff working in a paid capacity directly for the event management	On-line training & manuals Verbal communications Public address systems Radio network Mobile network Telephone land lines
Event Contractors	Service providers including artists, technical production companies, caterers etc. who are contracted by the event management to provide event services.	On-line training & manuals Verbal communications Public address systems Mobile network

Table 1. Emergency management stakeholders and their commonly employed communication mechanisms at special events and festivals.

managements to match their communications methods with the changing patterns of their stakeholders (e.g. warnings via Facebook updates to Smart Phones) and 5) the interactivity would enable a whole new range of services to be provided (e.g. traffic congestion updates and suggested alternate exit routes).

The proposed emergency communication framework would provide the foundation upon which future advanced emergency planning, management decision-making and response systems can be grown.

6. Advanced technologies for emergency management

Various applications of advanced technologies for emergency management are being trialed and tested in a number of settings. In their work on the large scale outdoor music festivals, Mogensen and Thomsen (2010) described an integrated approach, the @aGalance System, that provides overview and support collaboration between designated emergency responders. Key components of the communication technological solution proposed by Mogensen and Thomsen (2010) are:

1. GPS and Radio receivers: The media allows communication channel for transmitting information.
2. 3D environment: This enables visual communication through captured live video and digital pictures in the controlled display environment
3. Tracking devices: As an activity indication such as larger movements at the festival area this device tracks down though GPS driven static and remotely controlled cameras.
4. Handheld field devices : This is to connect with centrally located stationary monitors at, for example, the local emergency control centre or with specific response coordinators

However, the system does not provide for a direct communication loop between festival attendees and key management and associated stakeholders.

Bessis, Asimakopoulou and Xhafa (2011) reinforce the argument for a technological roadmap that enables improved application of computational intelligence in disaster management. This study described the merits of cloud computing services for emergency management. In addition, the study also identified next generation emerging technologies for emergency management and decision making. According to Bessis et al. (2011) the next generation technologies are as follows:

Grid computing: Grid computing combines high-end computing nodes, networks and databases in an integrated computing technology. In the emergency management, such infrastructure can support synchronous and asynchronous communication in a collaborative manner.

Web services: Web services use a *service-oriented approach* (SOA) to provide stateless, persistent services. An important merit of this service model is that it is always present for users to meet their information service needs.

Web 2.0: Web 2.0 offers a web based platform where users as individuals or communities are able to communicate online their ideas and feelings on shared topics of interests using available collaborative services. Different Web 2.0 technologies include wikis, blogs, photosharing, bookmarking. All of these technologies can be used as information sharing platforms.

Pervasive computing: Pervasive computing embeds computing and information technologies into our environments by integrating them seamlessly into our everyday lives (Weiser, 2001). Bessis et al. (2011) suggested that pervasive computing has many potential real-world applications ranging from health to environmental monitoring systems through the use of a number of mobile devices such as mobile phones, PDAs, sensors and computers.

Crowd computing: According to the information provided by Bessis et al. (2011), crowd sourcing or crowd computing is a new technology for crowd management. Some studies have proven the potential worth of so-called 'crowd-sourced' mobile phone data (Paulos, 2009; Bessis, 2010). Some of these pilot studies have shown that mobile phones and mobile sensors can be used by ordinary 'citizens' to gather data that could be useful in various settings (Paulos, 2009).

Collective intelligence/complex event processing: According to the information provided by Bessis et al. (2011), the concept of collective intelligence creates a free-flowing system of knowledge with no bureaucratic controller. According to Lévy (1997) the platform can also provide an informational free-for-all where no-one decides what knowledge is worthy of contribution and what should be left out. Gualtieri and Rymer (2009) suggested that complex event processing is best for applications that require near-real-time responses to dynamic, multifaceted, rapidly changing situations (cited in Bessis et al. 2011).

7. Discussion and conclusion

This chapter does not claim to provide answers that will prevent future emergency situations at festivals and events, it does however open up potential ways in which such situations can be managed more effectively and efficiently. Human error and extreme acts of nature will still occur. However, the use and integration of emerging ICT systems into the field of festival and special event management provides great promise in terms of risk mitigation and emergency planning, monitoring, controlling and response management functions.

As mentioned earlier, in many ways the festival site described is the equivalent of a temporary small city with a daily population of between 20,000 and 25,000 residents and visitors. This requires sophisticated risk management plans supported by sophisticated decision making and communications systems. The cost of creating such a system to cover such a short period of time, less than one week, is a challenge that requires innovative approaches. While setting up extensive emergency communications systems to respond to major incidents may be justifiable when addressing the concerns of a major, 1,000,000 or more, city, it becomes increasingly harder to justify major expenditure on infrastructure for smaller towns and indeed, in our research context, festivals and events. Yet, what price can be put on the potential risk to human lives in the event of an extreme emergency incident? Realistic solutions must therefore be sought to mitigate the potential likelihood and consequences of such events through the use of systems that are both affordable and context appropriate.

The future use of pervasive smart phone and pad type technologies are critical to the ability of event and emergency service organisations to create a communications delivery system that can meet the real time challenges of pro-actively responding to emergency situations at events. Many festivals and events are moving towards creating smart phone applications that create an informational relationship between potential and actual consumers of events and the organisers of those events. These applications enable programming, ticketing, site etc. information to be delivered to attendees and purchases to be made. This technology can potentially be used to provide emergency management updates and advice from both event organisers and third parties to attendees. Imagine getting the imagery of approaching storm fronts overlaid onto the festival site map or having the safest road to travel home based on latest road flooding advice from the local roads authority automatically downloaded onto your vehicles GPS system, these propositions are now becoming technologically both feasible and affordable. Communications is a multi-way activity. Such applications could also incorporate means by which attendees could communicate on-site updates of emerging real-time risk issues back to the organisers, providing many more 'sets of eyes' on emerging risk situations.

Examples for potential usage of such systems can be seen with increasing frequency internationally. In 2010 a music festival called 'The Love Parade' was held in Duisburg, Germany. Logistical crowd management issues resulted in more than 500 attendees being injured and 21 deaths with subsequent cancellation of the event and on-going legal cases (Spiegel Online International - *Prosecutors Investigate 16 over Deadly Event*). Critical to the issues involved in this case was the need for better planning, decision-making and communications infrastructure while ensuring information was received and acted on in a timely manner (Spiegel Online International - *Blind Leading the Blind*).

Similarly there was spate of stage collapses in 2011, including the Indiana State Fair disaster in where severe winds of over 60mph had a hand in the deaths of 6 people and many more injured. Media reports stated that 'State Fair management knew and was tracking the weather conditions, yet took no timely action… (in contrast) a local symphony that was to perform nearby cancelled its outdoor performance because of weather and urged spectators to seek shelter' (USA Today - *Safety standards are under a critical eye after stage collapse*). Improved communications, including automated systems, could have vastly improved safety outcomes in these instances.

These more serious examples show the vital need to have the ability to implement an integrated communications strategy that brings together real-time facts and key stakeholders. Such a strategy needs to enable critical decision making in sometimes life threatening circumstances. Given the potential consequences, a system that is robust, affordable, user-friendly and quickly brought on line with sufficient capacity is essential. We believe that cloud based provisioning can provide the framework on which future emergency management systems will be established for special events and festivals. In 'cloud versus clouds' the future is bright.

8. Acknowledgment

The authors wish to acknowledge the assistance of the Queensland Folk Federation and the management and staff of the Woodford Folk Festival for the much valued assistance.

9. References

@aGlance (2011). @aGlance, accessed 26 September 2011, available from: http://www.aglance.dk/

Allen, A., O'Toole, W., McDonnell, I., & Harris, R. (2011). *Festival & Special Event Management* (4th ed.), John Wiley & Sons Australia, Milton, Australia.

Barr, J. von Eicken, T., & Troan, E. (2009). *Application Architecture for Cloud Computing*, White paper, accessed 30 September 2011, available from: http://www.slideshare.net/whitepapers/application-architecture-for-cloud-computing

Bessis, N., Asimakopoulou, E., & Xhafa, F. (2011). A next generation emerging technologies roadmap for enabling collective computational intelligence in disaster management, *International Journal of Space-Based and Situational Computing*, Vol. 1, No. 1, pp. 76-85.

Courier Mail .com.au (28 December 2010). *Rain can't dampen Woodford punters spirits*, accessed 25 September 2011, available from: http://www.couriermail.com.au/entertainment/music/rain-cant-dampen-woodford-punters-spirits/story-e6freqgx-1225977132286

Earl, C., Parker, E., Edwards, M., & Capra, M. (2005). Volunteers in public health and emergency management at outdoor music festivals (Part 2): A European study, The *Australian Journal of Emergency Management*, Vol. 2. No. 1, pp. 31-33.

FitzGerald, J., & Dennis, A. (2010). *Fundamentals of Business Data Communications* (10th ed.), John Wiley & Sons Australia, Milton, Australia.

Getz, D. (2007), *Event Studies: Theory, research and policy for planned events*, Butterworth-Heinemann, Oxford, United Kingdom.

Gration, D., Arcodia, A., Raciti, M., & Stokes, R. (2011). The blended festivalscape and its sustainability at nonurban festivals, *Event Management: An international journal*, Vol. 15, No. 6, pp. 243-359.

Gualtieri, M., & Rymer, R. (2009). *The Forrester Wave: Complex event processing (CEP_ platforms*, accessed 30 September 2011, available from: http://www.waterstechnology.com/digital_assets/1261/progress_apama_forrester_report.pdf

Heyes, B. (2008). *Cloud Computing as software migrates from local PCs to distant Internet servers, users and developers alike go along for the ride*, communications of the ACM, Vol. 51, No. 7, pp. 9 -11.

Info Salons (2011). Info Salons Event Technology, accessed 25 September, available from http://www.infosalonsgroup.com/Content/Event-Technology/3/

Knox, K. (2009). Implications and use of information technology within events, In *Festival and events management: An international arts and culture perspective* (pp. 97-111, I. Yeoman, M. Robertson, J. Ali-Knight, S. Drummond & U. McMahon-Beattie (Eds), Butterworth-Heinemann, Oxford, United Kingdom.

Levy, P. (1997). *Collective Intelligence: Mankind's emerging world on cyberspace*, Plenum Trade, New York.

Marston, S., Li, Z., Bandyopadhyay, S., Zhang, J., and Ghalsasi, A. (2011). Cloud computing – The business perspective, *Decision Support Systems*, Vol. 51, pp. 176–189.

Mogensen, P., & Thomsen, M. (2011). *New Technologies Provide Overview@aGlance at Large Music Festivals*, accessed 30 September 2011, available from http://ercim-news.ercim.eu/en79/rd/new-technologies-provide-overviewaglance-at-large-music-festivals

Paulos, E. (2009). *Designing for doubt: Citizen science and the challenge of change. Proceedings of the 1st International Forum on the Application and Management of Personal Information*, MIT, Cambridge, USA.

Santos, N., Gummadi, K. P. and Rodrigues, R. (2009). Towards Trusted Cloud Computing, accessed 30 September 2011, available from: http://www.mpi-sws.org/~gummadi/papers/trusted_cloud.pdf

Sonmez, S., Backman, S., & Allen, A. (1993), Crisis Management for Event Tourism, *Festival Management and Event Tourism*, Vol. 1, pp. 110-120.

Spiegel Online International (18 January 2011). Prosecutors Investigate 16 over Deadly Event, accessed 1 October 2011, available from: http://www.spiegel.de/international/germany/0,1518,740219,00.html

Spiegel Online International (25 July 2011). Blind Leading the Blind, accessed 8 October 2011, available from: http://www.spiegel.de/international/germany/0,1518,776439-2,00.html

Silvers, J.R. (2008). *Risk Management for Meetings and Events*, Butterworth-Heinemann, Oxford, United Kingdom.

Sprecht, A. (2008). *Extreme Natural Events and Effects on Tourism: Central Eastern Coast of Australia*, Centre for Sustainable Tourism Pty Ltd, Gold Coast, Australia.

Tarlow, P. (2002). *Event Risk Management and Safety*, John Wiley and Sons, New York.

USA Today (17 August 2011). Safety standards under a critical eye after stage collapse, accessed 30 September 2011, available from: http://www.usatoday.com/news/nation/2011-08-16-stage-collapse-safety-regulations_n.htm

Vouk, M.A. (2008). Cloud Computing - Issues, Research and Implementations, *Journal of Computing and Information Technology – CIT*, Vol. 16, No. 4, pp. 235–246.

Weiser, M. (2001). The computer for the twenty-first century, *Scientific American*, Vol. 265, No. 3, pp. 94-104.

Queensland Folk Federation (2010). *Woodford Folk Festival Event Management Plan 2010/11*, Queensland Folk Federation, Woodford, Australia.

Woodfordia Storm Damage (January 2011). *The Woodfordia Mail – Image Gallery*, accessed 15 September 2011, available from: http://www.woodfordia.com/__news/index.php?id=63&galAlbum=1

Woodfordia Mail Media Release (14 March 2011). Media Release - 5pm Monday 14th March 2011, *The Woodfordia Mail*, accessed 15 September 2011, available from http://news.woodfordia.com/index.php?id=58

4

Expert System Design for Sewage Treatment Plant

J. Bouza-Fernandez[1], G. Gonzalez-Filgueira[1],
S. de las Heras Jimenez[2] and D.Vazquez-Gonzalez[1]
[1]University of A Coruña, Ferrol,
[2]Politechnical University of Catalunya, Terrassa,
Spain

1. Introduction

Nowadays the field of centralized control is linked to major production processes or industrial applications, where the flow of information allows optimizing the total production process. In the area of small to medium enterprises (SMEs) (Wang & Kai-Yi, 2009), however it is still underdeveloped (Liao, 2009). Perhaps the reason is not the lack of capacity for the design or the cost of the technology, but the lack of vision and lack of skills, in addition to the benefits obtained with this type of automation. Added to this that the current diversity and technological capability allows to choose a wide range of both technical and economic possibilities. As a result, it is possible to select the technology in order to balance the binomial needs-costs.

In this line shows an application of centralized control, that is linked to a sewage treatment plant (Jiayu & Linan, 2009; Zhu & Liu, 2008) for the timber industry (Fig. 1), as a solution that not only reduces costs in human resources, but also increases the reliability and safety of the process compared to plants that operate semi-automatically and even, with respect to distributed control systems. Thus, from a control element single it is possible to manage, monitor and supervise, in real time, the whole system.

Fig. 1. Sewage Treatment Plant

Despite that there are not known major applications of expert systems in sewage treatment, there are many attempts to apply knowledge-based systems in this area (Mikosz, 2001). However, these experts systems are not be able to maintain a continuous control of the plant, with data gathered through the on-line sensors.

The following flow chart (Fig. 2) shows the design procedure used in this project.

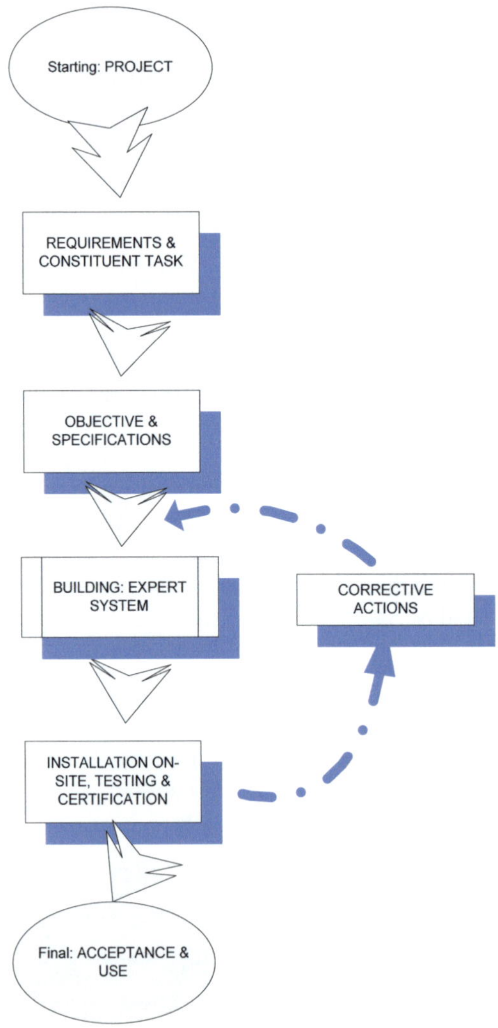

Fig. 2. Flow chart of design procedure

As far as the first phase, and starting point for this project, is concerned to a sewage plant for the Wood Products Industry which operates semiautomatic mode and with permanent presence of several operators to carry out the monitoring and supervision of the installation has been chosen. The system proposes that it should be possible to reduce the human presence to a single operator from a single point of control and that may be simultaneous with other plant processes. In addition to synchronize the various processes of the plant in order to improve the efficiency of the system, which affect the costs of production and levels of quality obtained in the purification process. Moreover, it is vital to minimize "human error" providing the operator with accurate and timely information accompanied by a set of records and alarms. This will increase the security of the system, and therefore, also, it will avoid any possible risk of environmental contamination.

This chapter discusses the relevant aspects for building an expert system that reaches the above requirements (Bouza-Fernandez, 2012). With regard to solve this problem of control such as application of the fuzzy logic (Kang, Yan-min & Guo-chuan, 2009), it is thought that was not appropriate for two reasons:

1. First, this manufacturing process is correctly defined with level 2 GRAFCET and its non-linear structure is properly resolved with the monitoring and supervision of Ph and temperature magnitudes by means of the interface human machine (HMI) design, without the need to develop complex mathematical models.
2. And second, selecting the technology solution in order to balance the binomial needs-costs, is an overriding aspect to comply with requirements demanded by customers. Day-to-day routine that designers must face, is "to develop the best solution in the shortest time and at the lowest cost".

Day-to-day routine that designers must face, is to develop the best solution in the shortest time and at the lowest cost. Although that aspects of installation and starting on site are not discussed in this document, if it is necessary to highlight its importance to carry out the project successfully. It must be said that these functions must be realized by qualified personnel in compliance with the guidelines of designer and respecting all safety rules. A complete verification of the operation and its safety will be done in this phase of the project, too. And the results will be contrasted with the specifications and tests carried out on the phase of building. If necessary, the pertinent corrections are made. In addition to this verification made by the Builder or Designer, usually another inspection is carried out by certification bodies or insurance companies.

A common factor of all the stages defined in this structure is that they suppose an evolution "from start to finish", that is to say, the concept of reference is described previously with approximation and later, it's perfected little by little and established of precise form. This structure allows a breakdown of the project in economic costs in their different stages, something fundamental for his acceptance and development. In this way, it is possible to minimize the risks inherent in his building, use, time and costs.

2. Objective and specifications

Following the flow chart design process described in Fig. 2, the objective and the specification of the system are defined in this section.

The objective of the control system is to improve efficiency and quality of the whole process of purification in two aspects:

a. On the one hand it involves a study of the process restructuring it or modifying those steps or elements deemed inefficient.

b. In the other hand it provides continuous monitoring of sewage treatment. Also displays historical process data and manage the process notices provided by the system. This not only allows real time monitoring of the plant but also to make predictions or future prospects.

There is a relationship between the different elements of the control system SCADA and the work they do within the system. With these automated systems achieve optimize sewage treatment with comparison of actual and theoretical graphics. Modification of the existing situation assumptions are made and are valued, quantifying their effects to the objectives set. Therefore, the objective of operation of the plant is granted.

From a technological perspective, the following requirements for the development of the system control have been established:

a. Take advantage of, where possible, equipment and processes of the plant that is the object of this study.
b. The control system must govern all elements of the wastewater treatment plant performance, and monitor its proper functioning.
c. A program must be available for their daily operations and for emergencies and maintenance.
d. Provide clear and detailed system status, based on records and alarms, to facilitate human decisions making, if were necessary.

On the basis of these requirements, and prioritizing the relation cost-versatility, for the implementation of the system the following were chosen:

a. A series PLC Siemens S7-200 control system [SIMATIC, 1999; Siemens, 1998, 2000].
b. "WinCC Flexible SCADA" Siemens Software to design and monitor the Human-Machine Interface [Siemens, 2005](Penin, 2006). Fig. 3 shows a scheme of blocks of this system.
c. Re-using of existing equipment when it not minimizes the requirements for the control system. Elements strictly necessary are added for increasing the efficiency of the system.

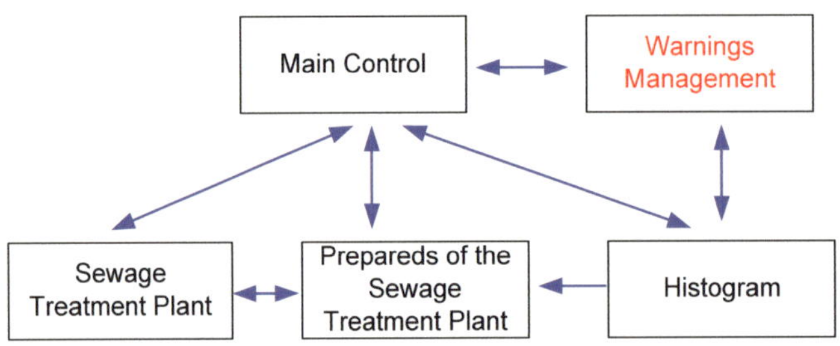

Fig. 3. Human-machine interface

3. Building an expert system

To design an automated system and its control for process, main part of this project, the procedure used is defined in Fig. 4.

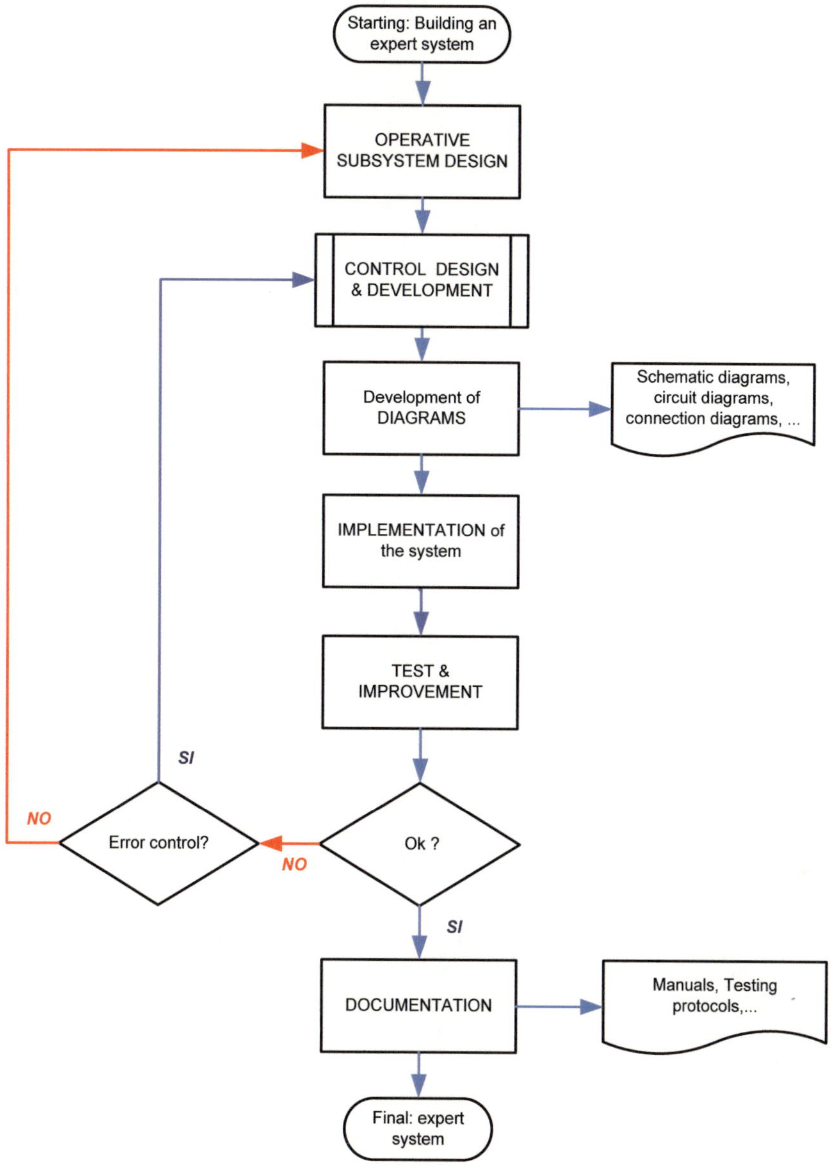

Fig. 4. Procedure for building an expert system

With reference to the development of the operative part of the system, it is necessary to do two basic aspects:

1. Description plant and process control.
2. Selection and sizing of components

As to the first point, the process of purification consists of the following processes: Filtering, elimination of the colloids through the process physical-chemical clotting and flocculation, treatment to regulate the Ph of the water, biological treatment and finally, decanting and sludge extraction. In Fig. 5 is shown a sewage treatment plant scheme where have place these processes.

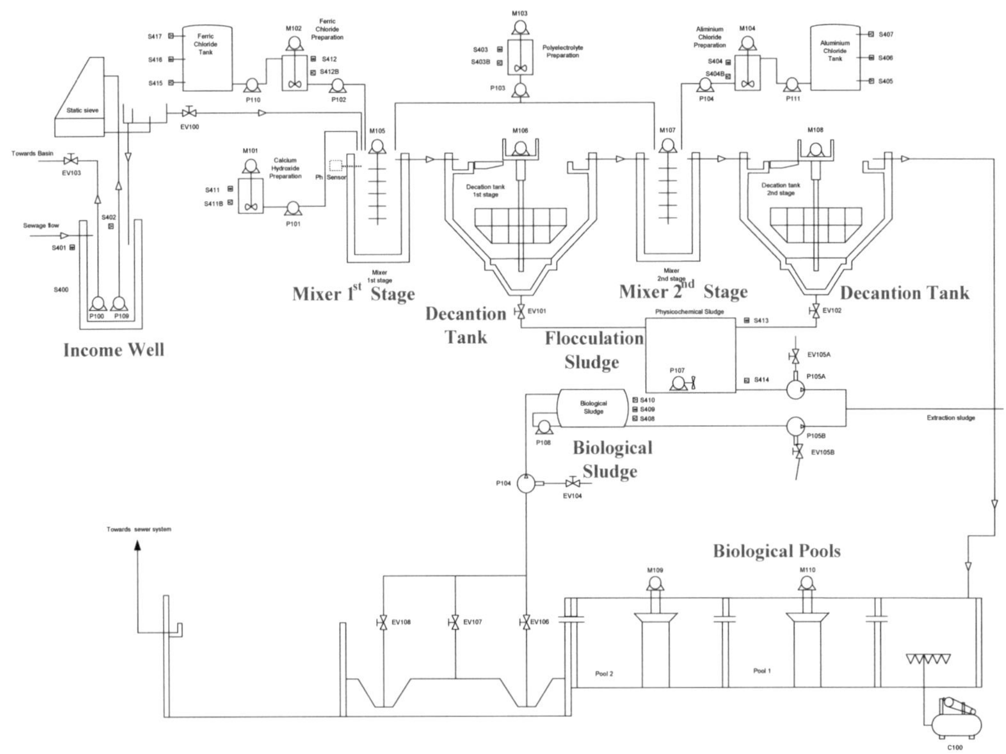

Fig. 5. Sewage Treatment Plant Scheme

The control system must govern all elements of performance of the sewage treatment Plant, and monitor its proper functioning. Moreover, it has to have a program for its daily operations and emergencies. All this accompanied by an information system supported by records and alarms to facilitate human decisions making, if were necessary. The control system may operate automatically according to operating programs daily and/or manually in case of emergency or tuning on.

Normally, in each of the control processes in a plant a programmable automation model is chosen. The process used here is continuous. Due to need for an algorithm as open as possible, in order to be able to work in different PLC's, depending on the needs of clients, and the capacities of the system, it has opted for a program in language of contacts that allow to be implemented in any PLC of the market. There is a cycle of working with seven processes that operate simultaneously or selectively. The activation of each of the processes will depend on the necessity to activate the process in question (Lira et al., 2003). The processes of the system are following:

- Process 1: "Water filling process".
- Process 2: "Process of polyelectrolyte preparation":
- Process 3 "Process of calcium hydroxide preparation"..
- Process 4: "Process of Ferric Chloride Preparation"..

- Process 5: "Process of Aluminium chloride preparation".
- Process 6. "Process of physical-chemical sludge removal".
- Process 7: "Biological sludge Extraction Process".
- Process 8: "The emergency stop".

The water to be treated is stored in a basin. The purification process starts when the water enters the storage basin at the entrance well, in the well there is a pump that constantly circulates the water towards a static sieve which takes care of the solid waste. Once the water from the entrance well reaches the work level, it is directed to the mixer of the first stage.

In the mixers of the 1st and 2nd stage a variety of preparations will be added to water: ferric chloride, poly-electrolyte and aluminium chloride, to decant the water pollutants by coagulation and flocculation (process where colloids come out of suspension in the form of floc or flakes), in a solid waste called flocs. In order that this process takes place under optimum conditions of pH, calcium hydroxide will be added at the 1st stage. A motor will be continuously working throughout the process for mixing the different chemicals preparations to water. The waste water treated with these agents will be moved to some decanters in where the solid remains of the process, or flocs, will collect and will be stored in a deposit for that purpose. And the cycle of waste water treatment by biological treatment in pools will continue.

In the pools, the "biological treatment", it is made by the growth of a bacterial flora that eats dirt. The Ph level in the pools should not be very high because but bacteria responsible for the purification will not carry out its work correctly as it will protect itself due to the high Ph level. There is also in these pools a flow of sludge, which is removed in proportion to the water flow in it. In this way the excess of bacterial population is removed and recycled at the same time, which in turn maintains its capacity for purification. To maintain a level of oxygenation appropriate in the pools, air is injected, producing a bubbling of air from the bottom together with the action of some ventilators.

Both the sludge from the decanters and sludge extracted (Lindberg, 1997) from the pools of biological treatment will be removed to some tanks. In these tanks will be working some motors to prevent it from solidifying. To remove the sludge from the tanks will be used some pumps operated by some air motors, taking advantage of the air installation that exists to inject air into the pools.

In the second point for the selection and sizing of components, a deep knowledge of technology is needed. Diminishing the importance of this fact may bring irreparable losses in addition to endanger human lives. In their technical catalogues and software some manufacturers print the phrase "Failure or improper selection or improper use of the products and/or systems described herein or related items can cause death, personal injury and property damage". Depending on the engineer's previous experience the information and assistance required from manufacturers may vary considerably.

With the description of these two aspects, what has been tried to highlight is the need to consider many other factors, besides cost and technical performance when attempting to choose a make or type of system components.

As for the second phase, "Control Design and development", develops the functional and operational aspects of the expert system and will be dealt with in depth in the next section. The estimate of the same ones, in programmable controller, option chosen in this project, is achieved frequently using a complex mathematical model or control algorithm. Obviously, the 'programmable' attribute increases the potential and the flexibility that has the designer but in contrast increases the complexity, the number of possible solutions and the time spent. Because of this there is a need to define procedures that save time and complexity, and that allow to obtain the optimum solution.

In phase 3, schematic diagrams and circuit diagrams will be made, which are particularly important to build the system and subsequently for realizing the installation and maintenance on site. These diagrams reflect the composition of the built system and will include all units of measurement, technical data of elements and their reference numbers.

For the phase 4, implementation of the control system, it will be necessary know specifications and principles of functioning of control elements used, that will be fundamental for their implementation.

In phase 5, 'Test & Improvement', is to compare the expert system built with the initial requirements and the specification. This complete control of their functioning and operating mode must be made prior to its installation on site.

And last, but not least important, the documentation is an essential prerequisite to facilitate installation, final preparation and maintenance of the designed system. The documentation of the individual phases, including control programs should be available so on paper as on digital media. It goes without saying that the real state of the built expert system must coincide with the documentation.

4. Control development and design

The control system must govern all elements of performance of the sewage treatment Plant, and monitor its proper functioning. Moreover, it has to have a program for its daily operations and emergencies. All this accompanied by an information system supported by records and alarms to facilitate human decisions making, if were necessary. The control system may operate automatically according to operating programs daily and/or manually in case of emergency or tuning on. To design and develop the control for process, the following procedure has been established in Fig. 6. In this procedure, first all input variables that are to do with the control will be identified. And its constitution and behaviour will be scrutinised, as well as the margins of tolerance defined by the specification of the system. This allows to not only set the input parameters that will have to work with to solve the control algorithm but also to choose the appropriate control type: command or feedback control.

Normally, in each of the control processes in a plant we choose a programmable automation model. The process used here is continuous. The process involved in water waste removal can be separated into in different stages that must happen sequentially and correctly. Once the plant specifications have been laid down we continue to programme the plant design, a descending design “top-down” is used. Due to need for an algorithm as open as possible, in order to be able to work in different PLC’s, depending on the needs of clients and the capacities of the system. The algorithm is implemented according to the Grafcet of the second level, Fig. 7, and the system requirements listed above.

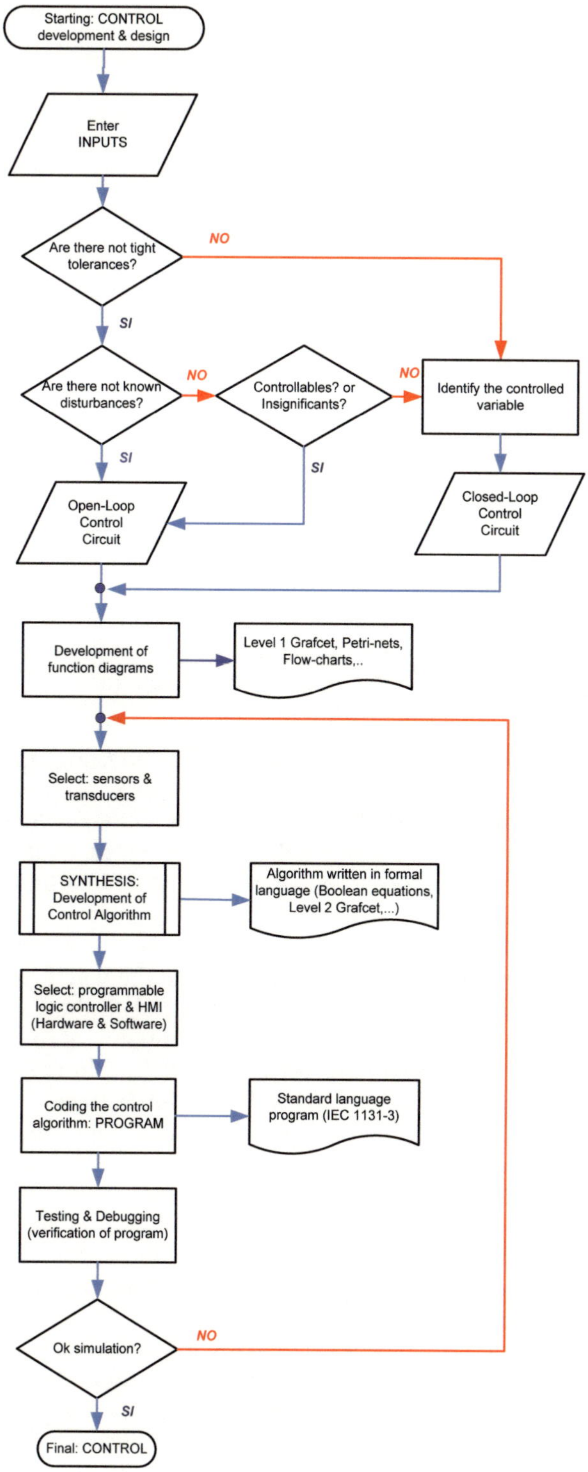

Fig. 6. Procedure for design and development of process control

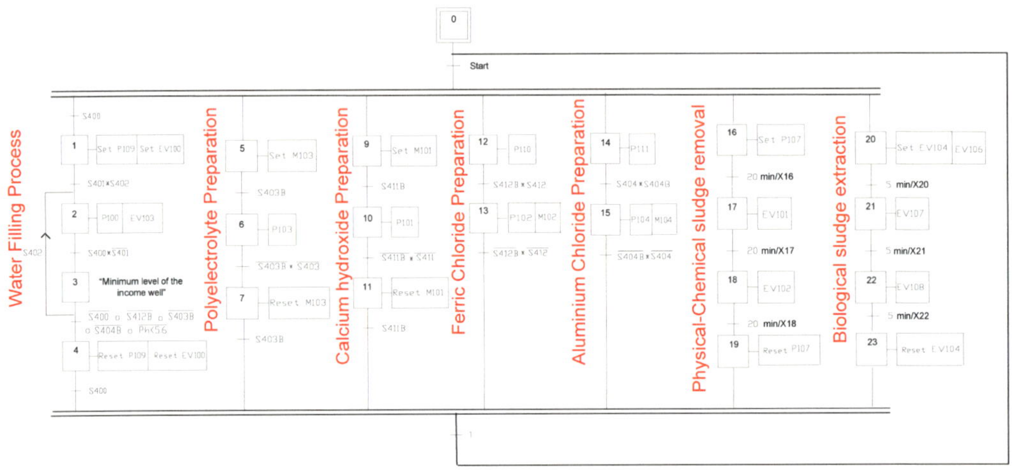

Fig. 7. Level 2 GRAFCET

The Table I and the Table II contain the description of input and output variables respectively used in the program. The analysis of GRAFCET of the second level, that represents the flow diagram of the states of the process, concluded that there is a cycle of working with seven processes that operate simultaneously or selectively. The activation of each of the processes will depend on the necessity to activate the process in question (Lira et al., 2003). The processes of the system are following:

a. Branch 1: "Water filling process". It starts with the "starting up" of the system and when the sensor S400, minimum level of water in the entrance well, is activated. Under these circumstances the pump P109 will start which will circulate water from entrance well through the static sieve. Then it will open the valve EV100 that will allow the passage of water to 1st stage mixer. When sensors S401, due to work level, and S402, due to maximum level of water, are activated in the well, it will launch the P100 pump and will open the EV103 valve to discharge excess water from the entrance well towards the pool. This latter process will stop when the water in the well reaches the minimum level. The activation of the P109 pump and of the EV100 valve that cause water to flow into the other stages, will be cancelled if any of the sensors of minimum level of the tanks of preparation are activated (ferric chloride or polyelectrolyte or aluminium chloride) or if the Ph level in the "Mixer for 1st stage" is less than 5.6.
b. Branch 2: "Process of polyelectrolyte preparation": When activating the "Start-up", this starts the M103 motor that turns the contents of the tank that contains the polyelectrolyte preparation and the water to mix. If the S403B sensor is activated, which is the minimum level of the deposit, the P103 pump, will be activated and this is responsible for providing the preparation to the mixer 1st and 2nd stage. If minimum level sensor is disabled or the emergency stop is activated, the motor of remover in the tank of prepared of polyelectrolyte will stop.
c. Branch 3 "Process of calcium hydroxide preparation". When activating the "Startup", it starts the motor M101 responsible for mixing the calcium hydroxide prepared solution in the preparation tank. If the S411B sensor minimum level of preparation is activated, the P101 pump which provides the mixture of the 1st stage will be activated. Disabling the minimum level sensor of preparation (S411B) or activating the emergency stop will stop the M101 motor.

Inputs	**Function: Level Sensors**
I0.0	Minimum level. Income Well (S400)
I0.1	Reference level. Income Well (S401)
I0.2	Maximum level. Income Well (S402)
I0.3	Maximum level. Ferric Chloride Preparation (S412)
I0.4	Minimum level. Ferric Chloride Tank (S415)
I0.5	Reference level. Ferric Chloride Tank (S416)
I0.6	Maximum level. Ferric Chloride Tank (S417).
I0.7	Maximum level. Calcium Hydroxide Preparation (S411).
I1.0	Maximum level. Polyelectrolyte Preparation (S403).
I1.1	Maximum level. Aluminium Chloride Preparation (S404)
I1.2	Minimum level. Aluminium Chloride Tank (S405).
I1.3	Reference level. Aluminium Chloride Tank (S406).
I1.4	Maximum level. Aluminium Chloride Tank (S407).
I1.5	Minimum level. Biological Sludge Tank (S408)
I1.6	Reference level. Biological Sludge Tank (S409).
I1.7	Maximum level. Biological Sludge Tank (S410).
I2.0	Maximum level. Physicochemical Sludge Tank(S413).
I2.1	Minimum level. Physicochemical Sludge Tank (S414).
I2.2	Minimum level. Ferric Chloride Preparation (S412B).
I2.3	Minimum level. Aluminium Chloride Preparation (S404B)
I2.4	Minimum level. Calcium Hydroxide Preparation (S411B).
I2.5	Minimum level. Polyelectrolyte Preparation (S403B).
Inputs	Function: Analog Sensors
AIW0	Ph value. Mixer 1st Stage
AIW2	Temperature. Mixer 1st Stage
Inputs	Function: Memory
M0.0	Start
M0.1	Emergency Shutdown
M0.2	Reset of the System
M0.3	Empty income Well
M1.0	Emergency Shutdown Light
M1.1	Set/Reset of EV101 &EV102. Drain valves of Decantion Tanks (1st & 2st stage)
M1.2	Set/Reset EV105A.
M1.3	Set/Reset EV105B.

Table 1. Program inputs

Outputs	Function
Q0.0	Recirculating Pump towards Basin(P100)
Q0.1	Recirculating Electro-valve towards Basin (EV103)
Q0.2	Pump. Income Well (P109).
Q0.3	Electro-valve. 1st Stage Mixing (EV100).
Q0.4	Pump. Calcium Hydroxide Preparation (P101)
Q0.5	Mixing Motor .Calcium Hydroxide Preparation (M101).
Q0.6	Pump. Ferric Chloride Preparation (P102).
Q0.7	Pump. Ferric Chloride Tank (P110).
Q1.0	Mixing Motor. Ferric Chloride Preparation (M102)
Q1.1	Mixing Motor. 1st Stage (M105)
Q1.2	Mixing Motor. 1st Stage Decantion Tank (M106)
Q1.3	Sludge Extraction Electro-valve. 1st Stage Decantion Tank (EV101)
Q1.4	Mixing Motor. 2nd Stage (M107)
Q1.5	Mixing Motor. 2nd Stage Decantion Tank (M108)
Q1.6	Sludge Extraction Electro-valve. 2nd Stage Decantion Tank (EV102)
Q1.7	Mixing Motor. Polyelectrolyte Preparation (M103)
Q2.0	Pump. Polyelectrolyte Preparation (P103)
Q2.1	Pump. Aluminium Chloride Tank (P111)
Q2.2	Pump. Aluminium Chloride Preparation (P104).
Q2.3	Mixing Motor. Aluminium Chloride (M104).
Q2.4	Submergible Pump. Physicochemical Sludge Tank (P107).
Q2.5	Recirculating Pump. Biological Sludge Tank (P108).
Q2.6	Electro-valve for control of Extraction Pump. Physicochemical Sludge (EV105A)
Q2.7	Electro-valve for control of Extraction Pump. Biological Sludge (EV105B).
Q3.0	Electro-valve for control of Extraction Pump. Pools Sludge (EV104).
Q3.1	Extraction Electro-valve. Pools Sludge (EV106).
Q3.2	Extraction Electro-valve. Pools Sludge (EV107).
Q3.3	Extraction Electro-valve. Pools Sludge (EV108)
Q3.4	Air Injection Motor. Pool 2 (M109).
Q3.5	Air Injection Motor. Pool 1 (M110).
Q3.6	Air Compressor (C100).

Table 2. Program outputs

d. Branch 4: "Process of Ferric Chloride Preparation". With the system in motion the P110 pump that supplies ferric chloride to preparation tank to reach the maximum level detected by S412 sensor. Then in turns starts the M102 motor, responsible for removing the preparation, and the P102 pump that supplies the preparation in 1st stage mixer. Disabling the prepared minimum level S412B sensor or activating emergency stop, the M102 motor and P102 pump will stop.

e. Branch 5: "Process of Aluminium chloride preparation". It is similar to the branch 4, by changing the designation of sensors and actuators. Its output is the mixer stage 2, instead of stage 1. With the system in motion, the P111 pump starts which supplies aluminium chloride preparation in the deposit up to the maximum level detected by S404. Then it will launch the M104 engine, responsible for mixing the preparation, and the P104 pump that supplies the preparation in 2nd stage mixer. Disabling the preparation minimum level S404B sensor or activating emergency stop, will stop the M104 motor and P104 pump.
f. Branch 6. "Process of physical-chemical sludge removal": When activated the "Startup" in the SCADA panel, the submersible P107 mixer is put into operation that ensures the physical-chemical sludge does not solidify. Twenty minutes after the process starts, the EV101 opens to extract the sludge from decanter of 1st stage for another 20 minutes. Immediately the EV101 closes and the EV102 opens to remove, in this case, the sludge from the decanter of 2nd stage for another 20 minutes. This cycle is repeated continuously unless the process is stopped.
g. Branch 7: "Biological sludge Extraction Process". When "Startup" on SCADA panel is activated, it starts the EV104 valve that operates the P104 pump, responsible for the extraction of biological sludge, and opens EV106 valve that connects the aspiration of the pump. After 5 minutes, the EV106 closes and the EV107 and EV108 valves opens for another 5 minutes each alternately connecting to the pump suction.

With regards to "the emergency stop": If emergency stop in the SCADA is activated the entire installation will stop and remain locked until reset is activated. The activating the emergency stop paralyzes all motors and pumps and puts the valves in a stand by position, leaving different system processes to be automatically locked until the system is rearmed.

This description Grafcet is translated and converted into Boolean equations for development the control program for this process. In order to codify the program, the Boolean equations are converted ladder diagrams (Fig. 8) to create logic networks but using certain techniques to express and identify the sequence logic equations that control the system outputs. Besides, ladder diagrams allow to be implemented in any PLC of the market.

Finally, the expert system specifications chosen for this design are:

a. SCADA System:
   Display and management of real time processing.
   Displays alarms and warnings.
   Display alarm history, and notices.
   Information about the protocol for each alarm or warning activated.
   Two way communication with S7 PLC.
b. The PLC Program:
   Include functions and sequences of the plant standards.
   Must establish procedures for cases of failure or emergency. With warning signs and alarms well marked.
   Structured programming to facilitate any changes or upgrades.

Allow two-way communication with the SCADA system (Cao, 2009; Tian et al., 2008).
Reading and interpreting all types of signals: analogue or digital
Control and supervision of the actuators and field elements.

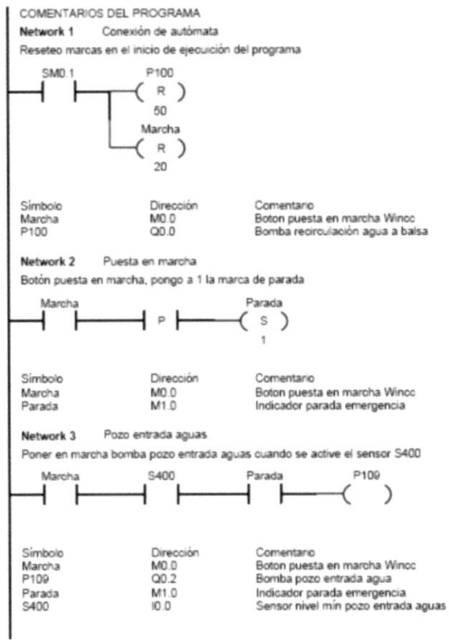

Fig. 8. Ladder diagrams

5. Synthesis: Problem solution

The design and development of the control program is of vital importance due to it constitutes the means for controlling the process. For the controller to carry out its intended task, a control program is necessary. The planning and design work for this process is complex. The following procedure, shown in Fig. 9, has been established in order that the program can be easily developed, verified and documented. An important part of this procedure is the division of programming tasks into two fundamental blocks: on the one hand to solve the sequential problem, on the other hand to implement safety (emergency stop, alerts,...) and operating modes (start conditions, reset, empty income well,...). The following Table 3 provides a good practice guide.

1. Plan your program on paper first "80% of your time should be spent working out the program, and only 20% keying it in"
2. Keep documentation of all elements used in the program and add so comments as necessary.
3. Assume the program will find every error sequence possible, "design safety into it !"
4. Keep programs simple and readable. Comments would be helpful
5. Try sectional development and verifying if possible.
6. Analysis of operation program in situations where it is safe to do so and simulate failures.

Table 3. Good programming practice

The sequential problem has been structured with definite sections dealing about specific areas of process. By adopting this approach, the programs developed are reliable and can be easily understood.

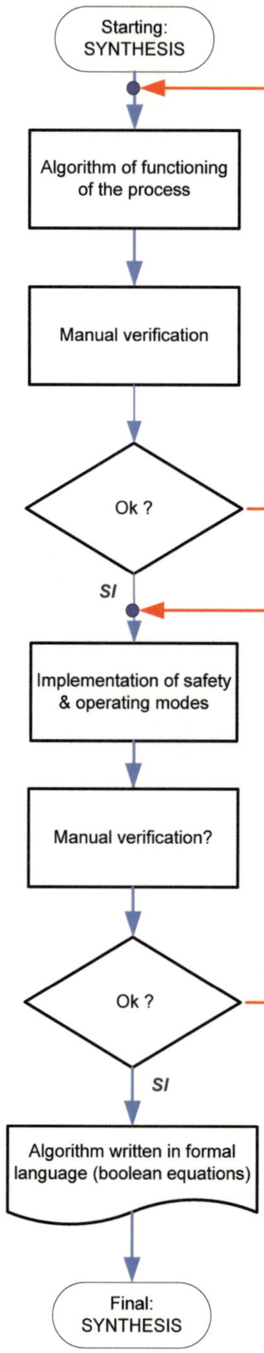

Fig. 9. Procedure for design and development of process control

For example, one of the complicated aspects of the process is the need to control and maintain constant the pH and temperature of water coming from the entrance well. To take the measurement, two transducers are used that convert physical quantities, temperature and pH, into two signals of intensity. This signal intensity, shown in Fig. 10, is received by the PLC via an analog module (EM235) that makes the conversion for its interpretation and comparison with the desired values and thus the corrective actions in the system are made. Thus, one of the calculations is the conditioning of the analog sensors. So the Ph transducer provides as output a variable current signal from 4 to 20mA that reads analog module of the PLC and it becomes a 12-bit digital value. This value is stored in the analog input word,

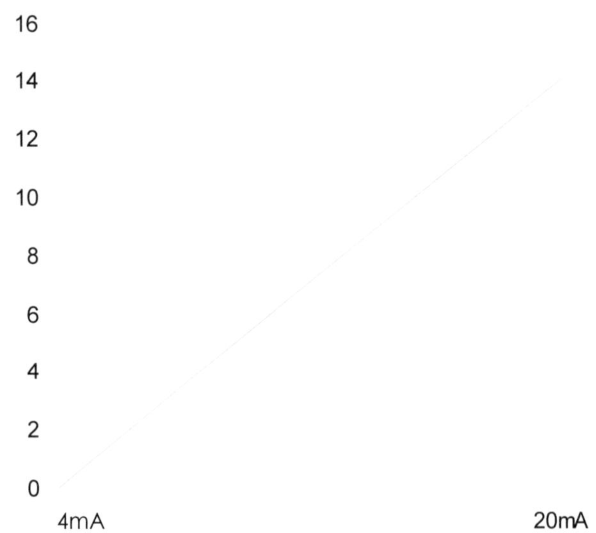

Fig. 10. Current's variation in function Ph

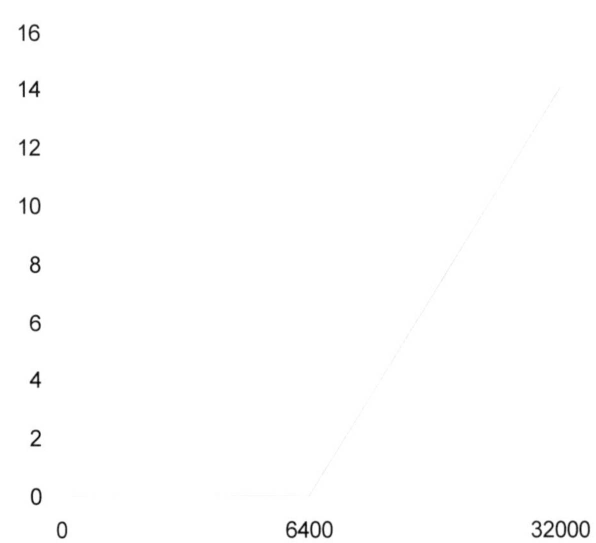

Fig. 11. Variation of AIW0 analog input in function Ph

AIW0, and because of the signal has a unipolar format, your range will be between 6400 and 32000 as is shown in Fig. 11. Therefore it will be necessary to scale and standardize this variable to the actual range of pH, from 0 to 14.

Using the equation:

$$y-y_0 = m.(x-x_0) \quad (1)$$

and solving for the values of the extremes, is obtained the slope of the line depending on the analog input value.

$$m = (14/25600)=0.0546.10^{-3} \quad (2)$$

So the equation to implement in the PLC program to know the real value of Ph is:

$$14\text{-Ph} = m.\ (3200\text{-AIW0}) \quad (3)$$

So for:

a. Ph=5; y0=9.71mA=15543 that is the value to compare in the PLC program as a minimum value of Ph.
b. Ph=7; y0=12mA=19200, that is the value to compare in the PLC program the maximum value of Ph.
c. Ph=5.8; y0=10.63mA=17000, that is the value to compare in the PLC program as a minimum value of Ph.

6. Implementation and results

It has been initiated to implement an expert system in the total control of the process and has been complemented with a set of records and alarms. This has revealed in real time the operation state of the process, which it allows to carry out analysis functions, correct them and act appropriately. It has been developed a Supervisory Control Acquisition Data Analysis (SCADA) system that is structured in a main screen from that is obtained access to the other four: Sewage Treatment Plant, Prepared of the Sewage Treatment Plant, Warnings, and Histogram.

6.1 Main screen

The main screen, that is shown in Fig. 12, gives access to all screens. It allows handling the whole process: start, emergency stop, reset and empty the entrance well. It also displays the different states of the system in the box "System Status".

6.2 Sewage treatment plant screen

From the screen shown in Fig. 13 and Fig. 14 the overall process of purification of the sewage plant is monitored and controlled. One of the important aspects of the process is the need to control and maintain constant the pH and temperature of water coming from the entrance well. To take the measurement, two transducers are used that convert physical quantities, temperature and pH, into two signals of intensity. The state of the system and the different processes are displayed, in addition of showing the levels of pH and temperature of the water in the entrance well.

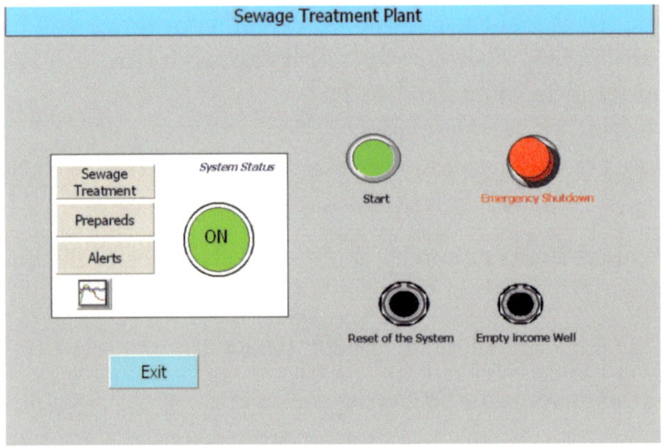

Fig. 12. Menu of Main Screen Sewage Treatment Plant

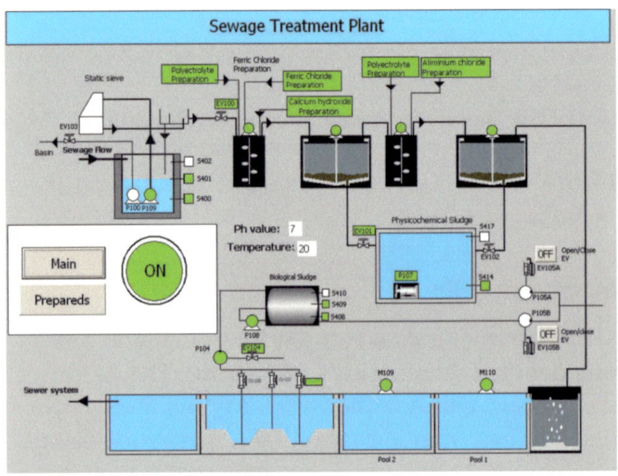

Fig. 13. Main Screen Sewage Treatment Plant in status operation normal

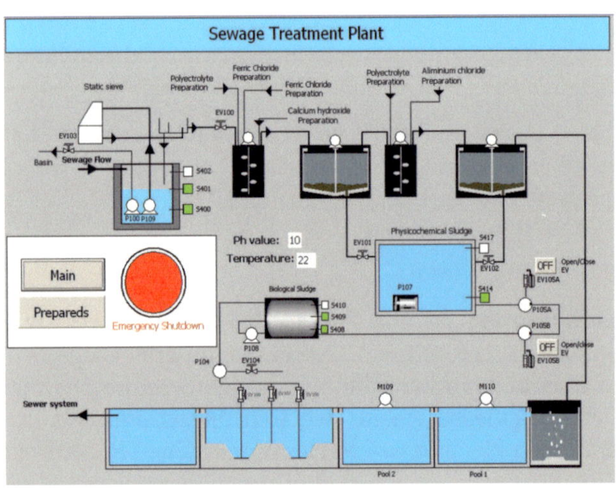

Fig. 14. Main Screen Sewage Treatment Plant. Powered emergency shutdown

6.3 Prepared of the sewage treatment plant screen

This screen displays the different preparations which are going to add to water for physical-chemical treatment of flocculation and coagulation. Fig. 15 shows this treatment

Thus, from this screen is possible to control the levels of the different machines needed to perform the different functions in the purification process, such as the pumps and motors.

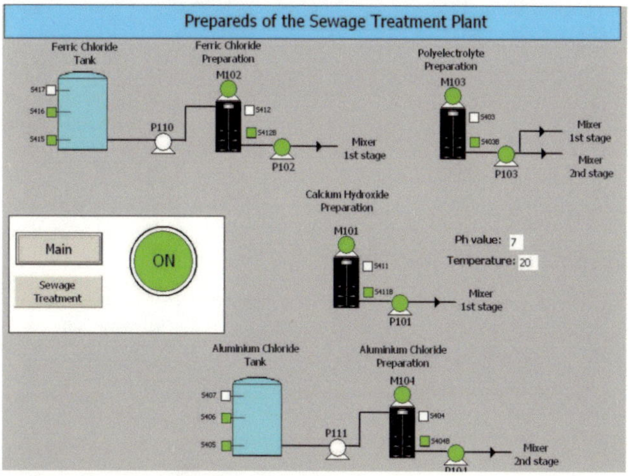

Fig. 15. Prepared of Sewage Treatment Plant Screen

6.4 Warnings

This screen displays warnings and system alarms set up. In both cases, shown in Fig. 16, apart from the source, reflects the date and time.

In the proposed control system, in addition to the specific warnings of the system HMI that reports the state of service, are defined the following:

a. Warnings Service. It reports irregularities in the service or in the process of the Sewage Treatment Plant, and the effects on the efficiency of the process. These warnings are automatically generated and are a necessary information for the operator in making decisions. For example, inadequate levels of temperature or pH will be referred to in messages to report this fact (see alert in Fig. 16).
b. Alarms. These show states of malfunction or danger in the process. These alarms require mandatory action by an operator after its recognition, and are usually accompanied by the shutdown of the system to remedy the problem (for example in Fig. 14). It is distinguished, in this project, among two types of alarms, according to the typology of signal: binary notices for level sensors in the different tanks, and announcements concerning the analogue temperature sensor and pH sensor, for which it has set an upper limit and lower one involving a failure or risk at the plant.

6.5 Histogram screen

Fig. 17 shows the two analogue variables, Ph level and temperature, depending on the time, when the system is on, and Fig. 18 shows when the system there is an emergency shutdown.

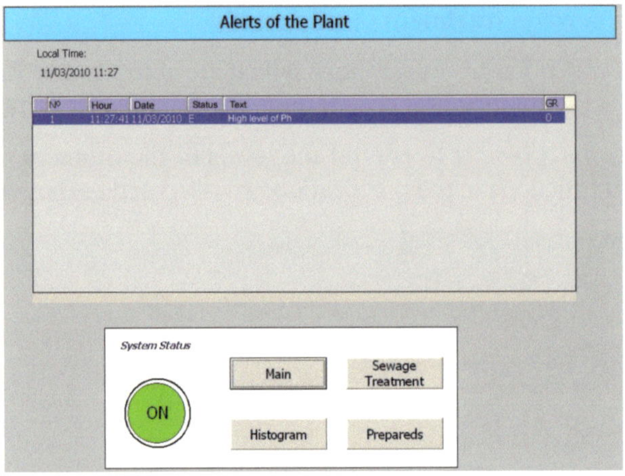

Fig. 16. Warnings Screen Sewage Treatment Plant

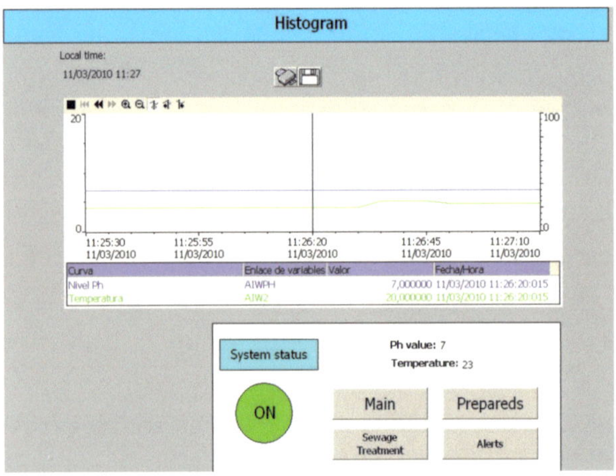

Fig. 17. Histogram Screen when the system is on

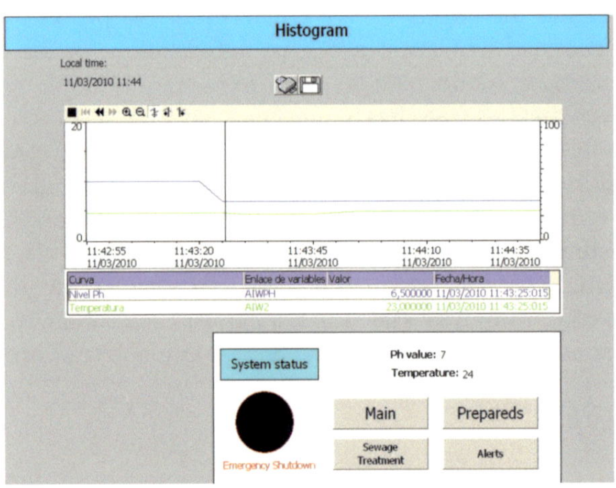

Fig. 18. Histogram Screen when the system is down

7. Conclusion

This work has been carried out using a process of control, supervision and monitoring of a purification plant intended for the wood Industry. It has been initiated to implement an expert system in the total control of the process and has been complemented with a set of records and alarms. This has revealed in real time the operation state of the process, which allows us to carry out analysis functions, correct them and act appropriately.

The choice of a PLC as a control device, not only has guaranteed the interconnectivity and compatibility of the various equipments through interfaces and protocols, but also has also facilitated the interoperability with the used SCADA implementation. At the same time, there are advantages of allowing using industrial PLC, and especially in this project, it gives flexibility for future upgrades or modifications of the process. The WinCC SCADA with which has been developed the Human-Machine Interface ("HMI") of the system, in addition to its compatibility with the PLC, has helped reduce the processing times of the project due to its versatility and ease of programming.

The reduction of the presence in human staff to a single operator, is not detrimental to the operation of the installation, because the expert system proposed improves the quality of work of the operator and minimizes "human error". All this has an impact on increasing the security of the installation, and in short, prioritises environmental protection, the main objective of this process.

8. References

Bouza-Fernandez, J. (2012). "Development and optimization methodologies for the design and efficient implementation of electro-hidraulic and electro-pneumatic systems" Ph.D. dissertation, Dept. Naval and Oceanic Engineering, University of A Coruña, A Coruña, Spain, 2011.

Cao, L. (2009). Wireless mesh monitoring system for sewage treatment plant, *Computing, Communication, Control, and Management, 2009. CCCM 2009. ISECS International Colloquium on* , vol.4, no., pp.350-353, Sanya 8-9 Aug

Jiayu, K. , Linan, M. (2009). An expert system for anaerobic wastewater treatment process, *Information and Automation, 2009. ICIA '09. International Conference on,* pp.422-425, Zhuhai, Macau, 22-24 June

Kang S., Yan-min S., Guo-chuan F (2009). The Application of the Fuzzy Controller Based on PLC in Sewage Disposal System. *2009 International Conference on Artificial Intelligence and Computational Intelligence,* pp.154-158. ISBN: 978-0-7695-3816-7/09. DOI 10.1109/AICI.2009.403.

Liao, J.Q. (2009). Economic analysis on urban domestic sewage treatment, *Computing, Communication, Control, and Management, 2009. CCCM 2009. ISECS International Colloquium on,* vol.2, no., pp.334-339, Sanya, 8-9 Aug

Lindberg, C. F. (1997) *Control and estimation strategies applied to the activated sludge process,* Ph.D. dissertation, Uppsala University, Uppsala, Sweden

Lira, V.V. , da Rocha Neto, J.S., Barros, P.R. & van Haandel, A.C. (2003). Automation of an anaerobic-aerobic wastewater treatment process, *Instrumentation and Measurement, IEEE Transactions on,* vol.52, no.3, pp. 909- 915, June

Mikosz, J. (2001) Application of expert systems in wastewater treatment: Wastewater sludge and solid waste management, *Report No 9. M. Hopkowicz, B. Hultman, J. Kurbiel, E. Plaza (Editors), TRITA-AMI REPORT 3088*, p. 137

Penin A.R., (2006) Sistemas SCADA. Marcombo S.A, Spain

Siemens, (1998). Autómata Programable S7-200, Configuración, instalación y Datos de la CPU, Ref.: 6ES7-398-8AA03-8DA0

Siemens, (2000). Manual de Programación. Software de Sistema para S7-200. Diseño de programas, Ref.: 6ES7-810-4CA04-8DA0

Siemens, (2005). Wincc. Manual de Configuración. Vol. 1, Ref.: 6AV6392-1CA05-0AB0

SIMATIC (1999) S7-200 Programmable Controller System Manual

Tian, J., Wu, H., Gao, M. (2008). Measurement and control system of sewage treatment based on wireless sensor networks", *Industrial Technology, 2008. ICIT 2008. IEEE International Conference on*, vol., no., pp.1-4. Chengdu 21-24 April

Wang, E.M.-Y.; Kai-Yi L.(2009); A human factors improvement on supervisory alarms in wastewater treatment system, *Industrial Engineering and Engineering Management, 2009. IE&EM '09. 16th International Conference on*, vol., no., pp.618-621, Beijing, China, 21-23 Oct

Zhu Z., Liu, J. (2008). Remote monitoring system of urban sewage treatment based on Internet, *Automation and Logistics, 2008. ICAL 2008. IEEE International Conference on* , pp.1151-1155, Qingdao, 1-3 Sept

5

Visualization the Natural Disasters Simulations Results Based on Grid and Cloud Computing

E. Pajorova and Ladislav Hluchý
Institute of Informatics, Slovak Academy of Sciences, Slovak Republik

1. Introduction

Every year, forest fires, floods and landslides cause enormous damage of vegetation and fauna, environment and property and bind significant human resources. Particularly in national parks and natural reservations, unique areas of high degree of protection can be devastated by fire. For instance, during the destructive forest fire in the Slovak Paradise National Park (Slovakia) in 1976, very unique vegetation was destroyed in the Kyseľ Gorge, where the recovery into the former state will last 200 years .

Till now (thirty three years after the fire), this locality is closed for tourists because of the vast damages. Topic of a lot of projects is how to prevent such disasters. Our research in institute is oriented on GRID and Cloud computing. A lot of international projects oriented on natural disasters utilize the HPC (High Performance Computing), grid or cloud computing and within such solution raises requirement of visualization service for presentation of the intermediate or final research results. Our basic aim of our research resolved in projects is the creation Visual service for the Modelling and 3D Rendering of Natural Disasters, before Fire, floods and landslides. Changing input data of Fires spread using to generate new outputs very quickly. Grid and actually Cloud computing on a lot of Clusters and On-line 3Dvisualisation service can allow new scenes of Natural disasters spread. Outputs are using for far adjustment to liquidation the Natural Disasters. 3D_visualization service for animation Natural Disasters should integrate visualization requests of any kind of application solved in our institute and before solved in international projects oriented on environmental problems. The natural disasters like fires and floods or landslides become subject of science in research institutions more and more frequently Many applications from this area are using different kinds of simulation tools, which are producing output data for displaying the results of the computation. The purpose of the visualization service is to model and display results of various simulations of natural disasters like are fire spread in time, fire intensity, flood velocity, landslide activity etc Such service requires unified standards like integration of input data formats and especially creation of unified visualization tool. The purpose of 3D viz. service is to model and display intermediate or final results of various simulations of natural disasters like fire spread in time, its intensity and erosion or floods in time or landslides as well. The output of the service is various scenes of terrain by different simulation outputs. Output of the service can also be the files representing the virtual reality of natural disaster and also files, which are generated as input for VR-Systems. 3D service was tested with outputs from applications, which were solved in our institute and also by data from applications of the international natural disasasters projects (Astaloš, 2010) .

Natural disasters simulation is a very complicated, challenging problem sensitive to the input data required. Therefore, intense research and development of sophisticated software systems and tools is extremely important for Natural disasters fighting management purposes (Gruz, 2003). For example for Slovak forests, original methodology for forest vegetation classification and new fuel models have been developed and proper forest fire simulations related to the locality Krompla (National Park Slovak Paradise), where the large destructive fire appeared in 2000 and its reconstruction have been analyzed. These efforts induced the need of better auxiliary tools for 3D visualization of obtained simulation results and for animation of the forest fire spread. In this paper, new 3D visualization technique for real forest fire simulation and fire behavior and for flood and landslide modeling is described (Orland, 1994). The importance is increasingly expanded for environmental problems (Glasa, 2011).

2. On-line visualization as a sequence application in grid environment

Grid-based applications that generate visualization outputs on-the-fly require a unified application framework. With regards to the Grid computational environment, it is advantageous to divide the performation of Grid applications into three separate phases.

1. Fetching the data from a simulation application
2. Transforming the data into a displayable form and the creation of virtual scenes
3. Displaying the scenes

2.1 Fetching the data from simulations

The first, computational phase is submmision the application to the HP, Grid or Cloud environment. The whole application consists of a large number of consecutive series of jobs. The output from a given series becomes the input for the next series.

The user must prepare the data on the Storage Element and provide the configuration file before launching the job controller. Data can be added even while the application is running (providing the relevant rules are kept). During its run the user can observe the contents of directories with input and output data on the Storage Element. The simulation outputs are treated as input data by the visualization process. The job controller starts their processing by launching the visualization tool. This is the subject of visualization phase.

2.2 Transformation the data into a displayable form

The aim of this phase is the transformation of the data into a displayable form and the creation of virtual scenes according to the requirements of the client. This phase is carried out by a visualization tool, which is together with its controlling agents, is the crux of this article. Apparently, the best approach is to create a separate visualization tool for each type of simulation. Only closely related applications, for instance different simulations of environmental phenomena, enable an usage of a shared control script. The user is free to decide in which phase of the computation the visualization tool is activated. Alternatively, the tool can be run after the whole computation is completed. While the computations are performed, the user can observe the contents of directories with input and output data on the Storage Element. A simulation output is in a certain phase considered to be the input for the visualization process. In the next cycle, the user prepares a new configuration file and runs the visualization tool as a new application.

2.3 Displaying the scenes

The purpose of this final phase is the display and analysis of output files from the second phase.This phase takes place on the client graphical device or in Grid to instal plugin. In new design for on-line visualisation tool is included also online approach for rendering . Examples from visualization scenas are shown on pictures.On Figure 1. and on Figure 2. - we can see pictures from big Fire in Krompla region - Slovak republik. Figure 3. and Figure 4. - pictures show visualization results from flood on river Vah.

Fig. 1. Large Fire in Krompla region - Slovak National Park "Slovensky raj", firespread in time 6 days

Fig. 2. 3D - firespread visualization result of Krompla region

Fig. 3. Picture of Flood visualization result - river Vah - Slovak region

Fig. 4. Picture of Flood visualization result - river Vah - Slovak region

3. Scientific gateway

Thanks to e-infrastructures, researchers can collaborate, communicate, share resources, access remote equipment or computers and produce results as effectively as if they and the resources they require were physically co-located. However, to properly achieve those results, community-oriented e-science environments are required. E-sciences ask for developing user-friendly interfaces, which sophisticated implementations are also known as science gateway. The science gateway is important component of many large-scale Earth, astronomical, environmental and natural disasters science projects. Developing the sciences portals and the science gateways is coverage of requirements of large scale sciences such as Natural Disasters, Earth science, Astronomy and all sciences which are using grid, cloud or cluster computing and high-performance computing infrastructure.

3.1 Visualization tool and its integration in a scientific gateway

Through user-friendly web interfaces such as e-Science gateway integrated into the same environment, researchers and scientists can securely and transparently access computational and data sources, services, tools, sensors, etc. Science gateway is a computational web portal that includes a community-developed set of tools, applications, and data customized to meet the needs of a targeted community. It can hide the complexity of accessing heterogeneous Grid computing resources from scientists and enable them to run scientific simulations, data analysis and visualization through their web browsers (Paulech, 2008). Scientific gateways are able to provide a community-centric view, workflow/dataflow services and a strong support in accessing to the cyber infrastructure including grid and cloud based resources. In each of science contexts, scientific gateways play a key role since they allow scientists to transparently access to distributed data repositories (across several domains and institutions) and metadata sources to carry out search & discovery activities, as well as visualization and analysis ones, etc. Finally, scientific gateways can play an important role in training students (at the academic level) in the different scientific disciplinas, attract new users and representing a relevant centralized knowledge repository in the sciences context. Our paper deals with the position of visualization as one of the main components of scientific gateway. The scientific web portal - gateway cumulate all types of visualization. Since 2004 numerous scientific gateways have been developed. Lot of scientific gateways were funded by the TeraGrid Science Gateways program (Wilkins, 2008). The gateway paradigm requires gateway developers to compile and install scientific applications on a variety of HPC clusters available from the resource providers in TeraGrid, to build service middleware for the management of the applications, and to develop web interfaces for delivering the applications to a user's web browser. Consequently many web-service frameworks (Kandaswamy, 2006), (Krishnan, 2006) have been designed and applied in building domain-specific science gateways. Some of them enable workflow based on the web services [4], but they commonly don't provide solutions to support web interface generation. Developers was usualy hindered. Usualy they need to spend a lot of time learning web programming, especially JavaScript and AJAX Technologies to implement a user-friendly and interactive web interface to these services. Developed visualization tools by us take acces on properties to include them to the Scientific gateway. For example our design propose a new web based application framework for astronomy and asttrophysics environment. We start from rich experimences in lot of grid and cloud based project in e-Sciences environment. We start with proposing new framework enables astronomy and astrophysic science gateway dewelopers based on last one web resources. Visualization tool is part of gateway and proposes a new based application framework for astronomy and astrophysics environment. The framework including the can import the astronomy specific workflow scripts easily can generate web appliance for running astronomical applicationworkflows and visualization the outputs results directly from workflow execution, online visualization through their web browsers.

4. Visual representation of datasets

Simulation and execution with a huge data usually spend long execution time. Good solution for execution is represented by grid and actually on cloud computing. In both infrastructures visualization has the main position as a way to control the execution process. Visual control has in all infrastructure very useful position. The modal parametric studies applications include, for example, astronomical simulations. The simulation was realized as a sequence of parameter studies, where each sub-simulation was submitted to the grid as a separate parameter study. The job management was rather time consuming due to the analysis of failed jobs and to their re-submission. Visualization is included as a visual control process. Client asks for visualization is a "visualization client". Output data on the storage element are the inputs data for visualization jobs. Visualization workers are to modify data to the formats, which can be visualized, but also to prepare the typical visualization scenes. Client can render such scenes on the browser, can make the visual control and modify executions. For example, to immediately understand the evolution of the investigated proto-planetary disc we have developed a Visualization Tool (VT). The VT is composed of several modules, which are responsible for creating scenes and converting data to, the "visualize": format. The VT is designed as a plug-in module. The components generating rendering scenes are easy to exchange, according to the requirements of the given application. In case of our gridified application the output data of the simulation located on the SE can be used directly as the input for the VT. The final product of the VT includes a set of files containing data in the VRML (Virtual Reality Modeling Language) format. These output files can be rendered by many available VRML web-browsers. The whole visualization process is maintained through a visualization script, whose basic function is invoking the individual VT components in successive steps, transferring data, and handling error events. The script is written using the Bourne shell scripts and all VT modules are implemented in the C++ language. The VT can be embedded into the framework described above, or can be used separately as a stand-alone program. By using the on-line VT the client can stop the execution process, change the input parameters and restart the execution process again. In grid environment, such architecture can be used for all applications from different science spheres which have the character of a parametric study. Actually, the research community needs not only "traditional" batch computations of huge bunches of data but also the ability to perform complex data processing; this requires capabilities like on-line access to databases, interactivity, fine real-time job control, sophisticated visualization and data management tools (also in real time), remote control and monitoring. The user can completely control the job during execution and change the input parameters, while the execution is still running. Both tools, the tool for submission designed before and continued sequential visualization tool, provide complete solution of the specific main problem in Grid environment. The position of the visualization tool as a visual control process is shown in figure 1. Astrophysics scientists are able to run scientific simulations, data analysis, and visualization through web browsers. Through Earth and astronomical science gateway scientists are able to import they sophisticated scripts by which the VT can be activated as well, as the output from workflow executions without writing any web related code (Paulech, 2008).

4.1 VT as a new discovery for presenting academic research results

Advance in sciences and engineering results in high demand of tools for high-performance large-scale visual data exploration and analysis. For example, astronomical scientists can now study evolution of all Solar systems on numerous astronomical simulations. These simulations can generate large amount of data, possibly with high resolution (in three-dimensional space), and long time series. Single-system visualization software running on commodity machines cannot scale up to the large amount of data generated by these simulations. To address this problem, a lot of different grid-based visualization frameworks have been developed for time-critical, interactively controlled file-set transfer for visual browsing of spatially and temporally large datasets in a grid environment. To address the problem, many frameworks for grid and cloud based visualization are used. We can go through evolution of sophisticated grid-based visualization frameworks with actualized functionality, for example, Reality Grid, UniGrid and TerraGrid. All of the frameworks have been included in the visualization. Frameworks were created during grid-based projects and create new features for presentations of the academic research results in visualization. Visualization resources enabled by the astronomical science gateway the top of research experiences. Multiple visualizations generated from a common model will improve the process of creation, reviewing and understanding of requirements. Visual representations, when effective, provide cognitive support by highlighting the most relevant interactions and aspects of a specification for a particular use. The goal of scientific visualization is to help scientists view and better understand their data. This data can come from experiments or from numerical simulations. Often the size and complexity of the data makes them difficult to understand by direct inspection. Also, the data may be generated at several times during an experiment or simulation and understanding how the data varies with time may be difficult. Scientific visualization can help with these difficulties by representing the data so that it may be viewed in its entirety. In the case of time data varying in time, animations can be created that show this variation in a natural way. Using virtual reality techniques, the data can be viewed and handled naturally in a true three-dimensional environment (e.g. depth is explicitly perceived and not just implied). All these techniques can allow scientists to better understand their data. Viewing the data in this way can quickly draw the scientist's attention to interesting and/or anomalous portions of the data. Because of this, we encourage scientists to use scientific visualization from the beginning of their experiments and simulations and not just when they think they have everything operating correctly. This also allows scientists to develop a set of visualization tools and techniques that will help them understand their data as their research matures. For example, depending on of our astronomical example, in order to understand immediately the evolution of the investigated proto-planetary disc we have developed a Visualization Tool (VT) for astronomers. Educational visualization uses a simulation normally created on a computer to develop an image of something so it can be taught about. This is very useful when teaching a topic which is difficult to see otherwise, for example, proto-planetary disk, its evolution or evolution in Solar system. It can also be used to view past events, such as looking at the Solar system during its evolution stage, or look at things that are difficult. For astronomers, the VT has in education roles well.

5. Architecture of Visualization Tool (VT)

3D visualization service for animation of natural disasters applications, astrophysical applications and all complicated applications based on HPC (High Performance Computing), grid and Cloud computing should integrate visualization requests. Many applications from this area are using different kinds of simulation tools, which produce output data for displaying the computation results. The purpose of the visualization service is to model and display the results of various simulations. Such service requires unified standards such as integration of input data formats and especially creation of unified visualization tools.

When running parametric simulation with a large number of jobs (such astrophysical simulations), the main problem was in the grid infrastructure reliability. The job management was rather time consuming due to the analysis of failed jobs and to their re-submission. Moreover, the jobs, waiting in a queue for a long time, were blocking the simulation. To overcome these problems, we developed an easy-to-use framework based on pilot jobs concept that uses only services and technologies available in EGEE (Enabling grids for E-science) infrastructure, grid middleware gLite and Bourne Shell scripting language. The framework consists of pilot jobs - workers, and of automatic job management script. Workers are running the application code in cycle with input datasets downloaded from a storage element using remote file access. The storage element contains the input, working and output areas (as subdirectories of the directory created by the user for each parameter study). The user prepares input datasets on user interface and transfers them into the input area before starting the simulation. The working area is used by workers to store static information about computing nodes (name of the computing element and computing node, CPU type and available memory), and to monitor information updated in regular intervals, datasets, that are currently processed, and statistics about processed datasets. Output data is stored into the output area, where the user can see the progress of simulation. To check the progress, the user only needs to list the contents of the output folder. The storage element is accessible also for grid FTP clients, therefore grid portals can also be used to watch the progress. To identify hanging jobs or jobs that perform too slowly, workers are periodically sending monitoring information to the storage element. To avoid termination of workers by the queuing system, workers are running only for a limited time. The main function of the job management script is to maintain the defined number of active workers with detection of failed submissions, finished and waiting workers. The script uses job collections to speed up the start up and automatic blacklisting of full and erroneous sites. In case of our application the output data of the simulation located on the storage element can be directly used as the input for the visualization tool. The whole process is shown on Figure 5. The architecture of the submission process is shown in Figure 6.. The architecture of the visualization process is shown in Figure 7..

As an example we present a visualization tool which has been used on parametric astrophysical simulations and natural disaster simulations. The first simulation project is a collaboration among Astronomical Institute (Slovakia), Catania Observatory (Italy) and Adam Mickiewicz University in Poznan (Poland). The second project performed natural disasters simulations computed at our institute. The applications were ported to EGEE grid infrastructure by the Institute of Informatics Slovak Academy of Sciences (Slovakia), (Astaloš, 2010).

Natural disasters simulation is a very complicated, challenging problem sensitive to the input data required. Therefore, intense research and development o sophisticated software systems and tools is extremely important for natural disasters fighting management purposes. For example for Slovak forests, original methodology for forest vegetation classification and new fuel models have been developed and proper forest fire simulations related to the locality Krompla (National Park Slovak Paradise), where the large destructive and its reconstruction have been analyzed. These efforts induced the need of better auxiliary

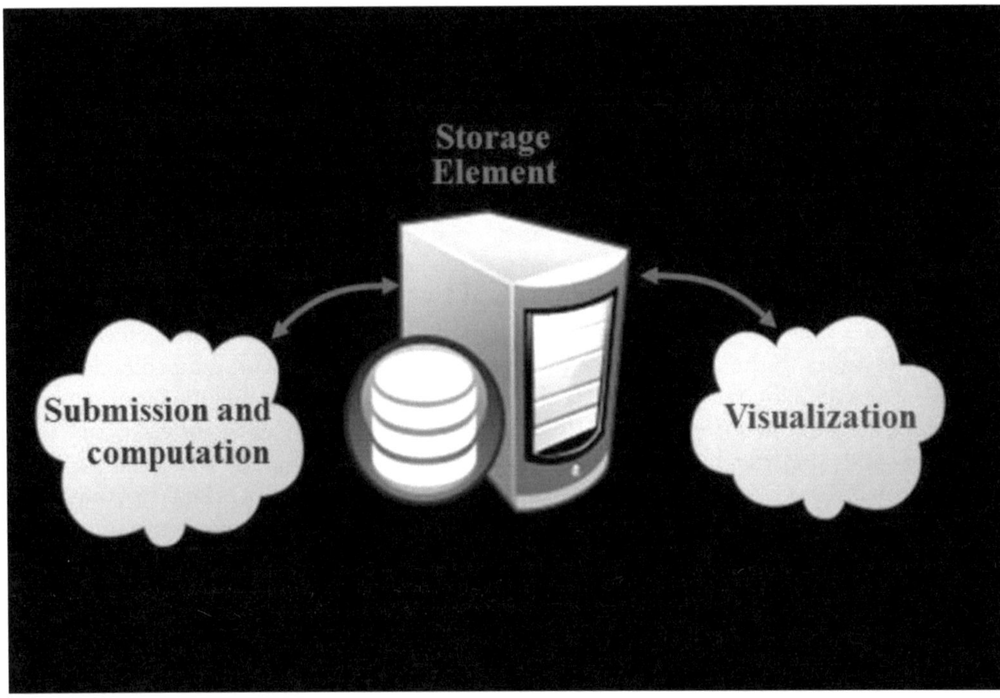

Fig. 5. Schema of all process - process of submission and on-line visualization

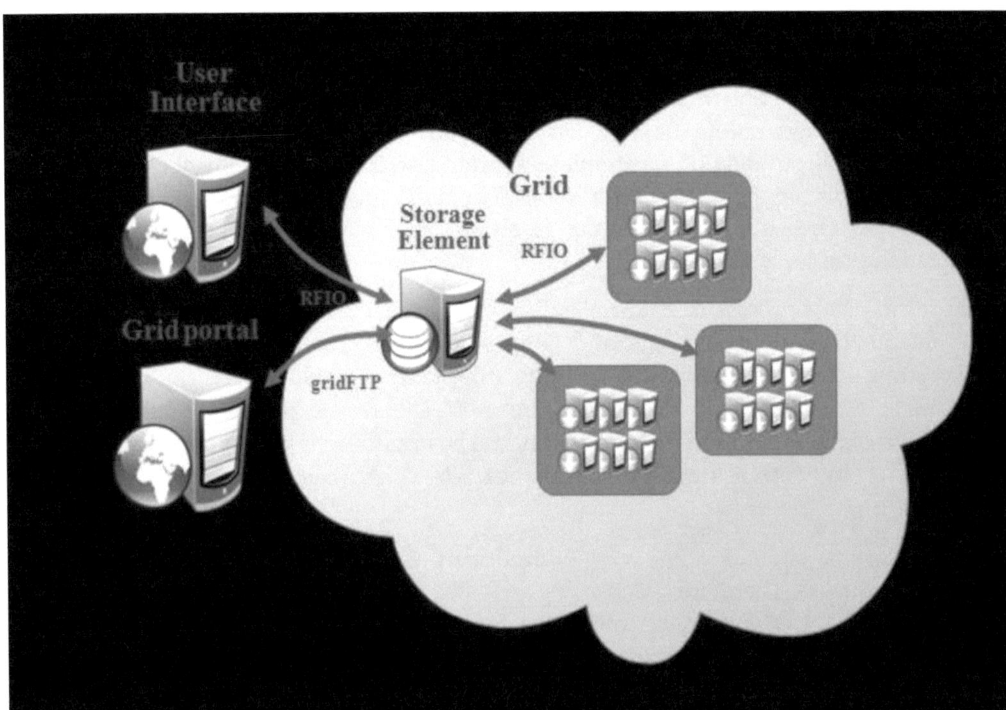

Fig. 6. Schema of process of submission application to the grid.

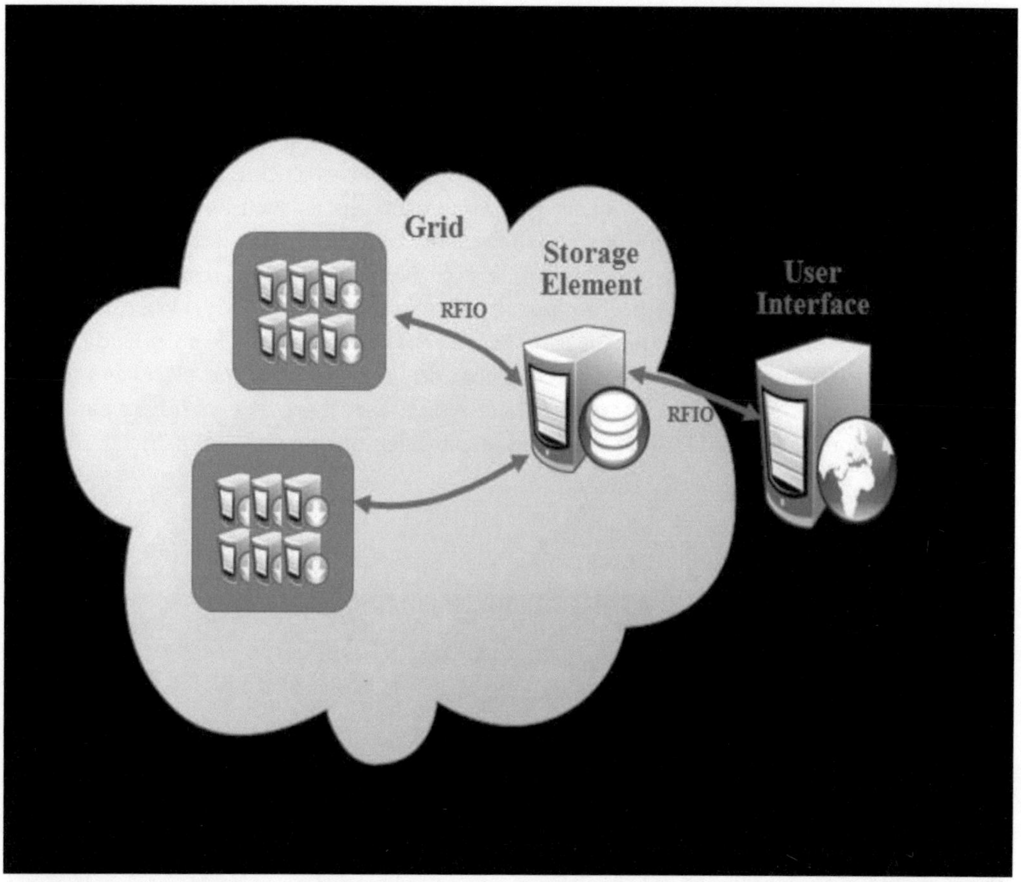

Fig. 7. Schema of on-line visualization process.

tools for 3D visualization o obtained simulation results and for animation of the forest fire spread. The importance is increasingly expanded for environmental problems. VT tool for Earth Science provides pictures from simulations big Fire in Crompla region and from flood in river Vah. VT tool for astronomical applications provides pictures from simulation of the evolution of proto-planetary disc from 1Myr to 1000 Myr. An unsolved question of the Solar System cosmogony is the origin of comets and minor bodies with respect to the Solar System evolution. In the past, authors predicted the existence of reservoirs of the objects and tried an effort to explain the origin and subsequent evolution of these reservoirs. Several partial theories have been developed to clarify the problem. Recently, the researchers try to present a unified theory of the formation of small-body reservoirs in the Solar System (the Kuiper Belt, the Scattered Disc), situated beyond the orbit of Neptune. In our application we developed a new improved model for explaining the formation of the Oort Cloud. One has to assume dynamical evolution of a high number of particles under gravitational influence of the giant planets: Jupiter, Saturn, Uranus, Neptune, the Galactic Tide and nearby passing alien stars. Before our work, only two similar simulations have been performed by Duncan et al. in 1987 and by Dones et al. in 2005[8]. In our application we assumed 10038 test particles. It is several times more than in the previous simulations. Our extensive simulations required very large computing capacity. To complete our model on a single 2.8GHz CPU would last about 21 years. Using the grid infrastructure, the whole computation lasted 5 months; thus, it was more than 40 times faster. The result of our simulation is dynamical evolution of orbits of test particles during the first giga year of the Solar System lifetime. Detailed study of this first giga year evolution results in a general agreement with the results of previously mentioned models as well as in new facts and questions. Having used the mentioned visualization tool we obtain lot of visualization results, pisctures and video files, which absolute represent our research results. Specifically, Figure 8. shows the evolution of proto-planetary disc in the time of 1 Myr. We can see that during the 1000 Myr time that the particles were replaced from inside to outside of the spheres. Figures 9. and 10. show the result of dynamical evolution of Oort-cloud as a part of proto-planetary disk after its evolutionary stage which was the first Gyr (giga year) from different positions. Picture 11. shows expanded particles during the fly of imagine space ship.

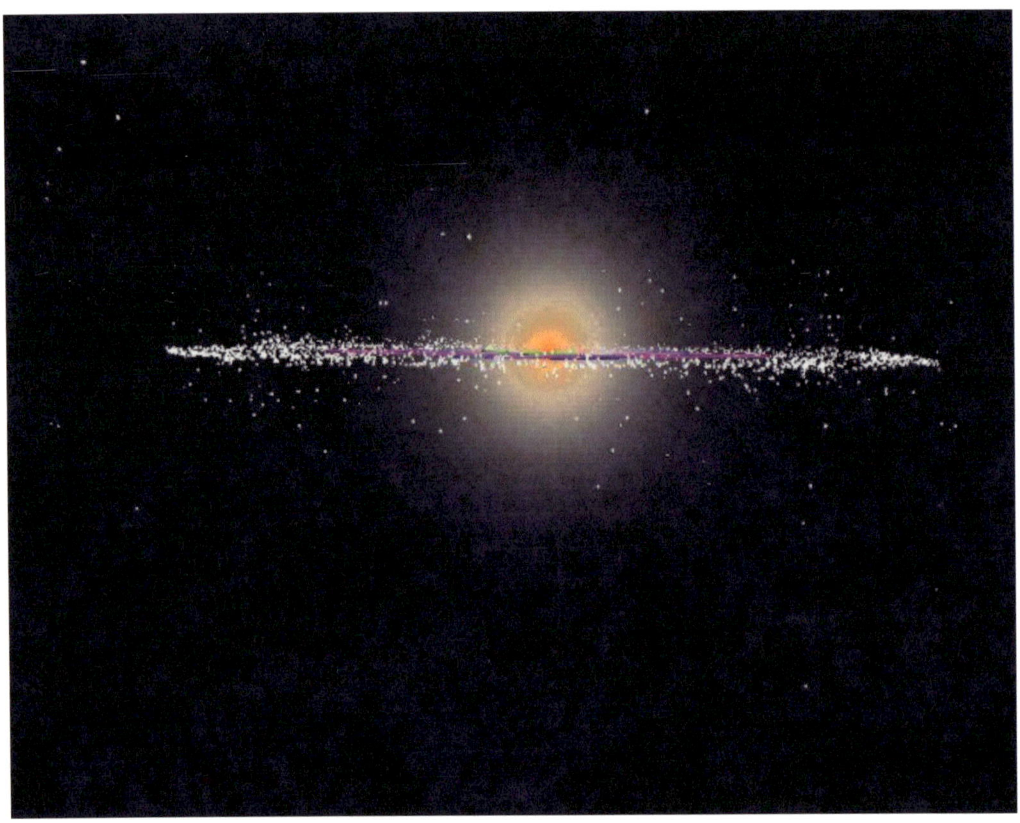

Fig. 8. Visualization output from research results in Astrophysics science simulations.

Fig. 9. Visualization output from research results in Astrophysics science simulations - second position.

Fig. 10. Visualization outputs from research results in Astrophysics science simulations. Dynamical evolution of O-orth cloud - thirth position.

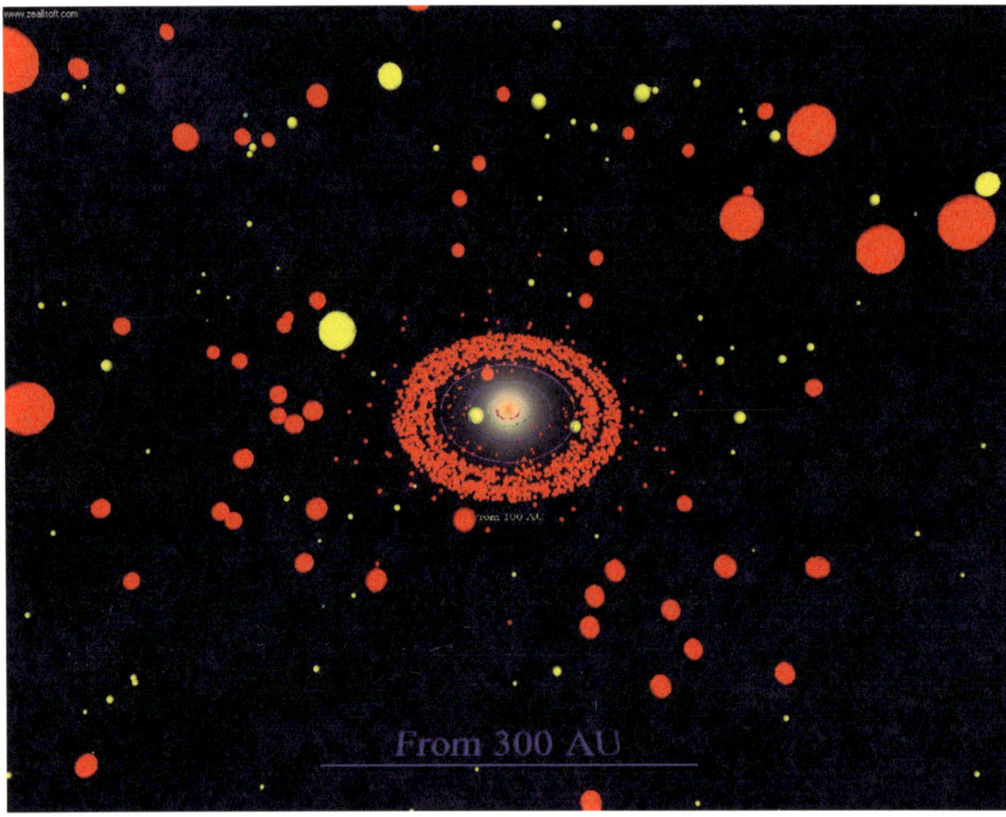

Fig. 11. Visualization outputs - red poinds are expanded particles which we can see during the from fly of imagine space ship.

6. Cloud computing – Such a web portal for disasters management

For approaching of Natural disasters as is for example out of control wild fire, flood, landslides near your environs, people certainly need to have some disaster planning in place. However, with cloud computing, this disaster management and planning is not something you have to worry about when it comes to your computer. *Disaster Management or Recovery Plan* - this is a plan for the unexpected (such as natural disasters, fires, planes falling out of the sky, etc.) To comes information technology and especially disaster management, cloud computing is the way to go. In fact, it basically serves AS your disaster management plan. When all of your valuable information is stored outside of your computer, then you no longer have to be concerned with the destruction of your files and valuable information, in the unfortunate instance that your computer network is destroyed. *Disaster recovery* traditionally involves the backup of all a company's data on backup servers, which can be easily accessed. These backup servers can be on site or contracted out, but the ownership of the hardware or subcontracting of these services can be quite expensive and form a substantial part of an IT budget for an organization. A cloud disaster recovery service brings peace of mind to businesses that can't necessarily afford the hardware and capital costs involved with in-house disaster recovery provision. It completely eliminates the need for expensive hardware, as data stored in the cloud is on the servers of service providers. Then those service providers, in turn, have their own system of remote backup servers at different locations which constantly back up any customer data that they receive. This way, you are able to access it at any time. If your data is saved in the cloud, it will have a number of backups which can assist in data recovery for any material stored in it. This creates a type of organizational back-up that any individual business may find very expensive to duplicate.

7. Conclusion

The goal of the article is to describe the VT architecture and to support the visualization as essential component in new portals - gateways technologies and to show some examples. For the future we want to extend the use of the VT for other scientific disciplines in addition to astronomy, but also for Earth Sciences with all visualization aspects. For the future we plan to participate in a project in which the main activity will be to create and operating a pan-European e-Science Support Centre as a global astronomical environment in which portals such as gateways with visualization included will be as part of essential requirements. In the future we want instead of grid infrastructure to use the cloud resources. Actually, the research community needs not only "traditional" batch computations of huge bunches of data but also the ability to perform complex data processing; this requires capabilities like on-line access to databases, interactivity, fine real-time job control, sophisticated visualization and data management tools (also in real time), remote control and monitoring. The user can completely control the job during execution and change the input parameters, while the execution is still running. The science gateway is important component of many large-scale Earth, environmental and natural disasters science projects. Developing the sciences portals and the science gateways is coverage of requirements of large scale sciences such as Earth or natural disasters and all sciences which are using grid, cloud or cluster computing and high-performance computing infrastructure. Visualization of research results have a main position in Science Gateway. Actually and for a future we are continued by this way, it means to integrate visualization of Natural disasters to different sciences gateway.

8. Acknowledgement

This work was supported by Slovak Research and Development Agency under the RPEU-0024-06 project, and by VEGA project No. 2/0211/09, as well as by EGEE III EU FP7 RI project: Enabling Grids for E-science III (2008-2010) FP7-222667 and also projects RECLER ITMS: 26240220029 and SMART II ITMS: 26240120029.

9. References

Wilkins-Diehr, N.,Gannon, D., Klimeck, G., Oster, S. Pamidighantam, S., 2008. TeraGrid Science Gateways and Their Impact on Science, *IEEE Computer* 41(11):32-41, Nov 2008.

Cruz, M.G., M.E. Alexander, and R.H. Wakimoto. 2003. 3D Nature, LLC. 2002. Using VNS (Manual). Arvada, CO: 3D Nature, LLC. Assessing canopy fuel stratum characteristics in crown fire from fuel types of North America. International Journal of Wildland Fire. 12: 39-50.

Orland, B. 1994. SmartForest: a 3-D interactive forest visualization and analysis system. In Proceedings, Decision Support 2001 - Resource Technology 94, 181-190. Bethesda, MD: American Society for Photogrammetry and Remote Sensing.

Glasa, Ján and all. Analysis of forest fire behaviour by advanced computer fire simulators. In Communications : Scientific Letters of the University of Žilina, 2011, vol. 2, p. 26-31. ISSN 1335-4205.

Astaloš, Ján and all. Slovak Participation In The World LHC Computing Grid. In 6th International Workshop On Grid Computing For Complex Problems, November 8 - 10, 2010, Bratislava: GCCP 2010 Proceedings. Eds. L. Hluchý, P. Kurdel, J. Sebestyénová. - Bratislava : Institute Of Informatics SAS, 2010, P. 21-27. ISBN 978-80-970145-3-7.

Wilkins, Diehr and all. TeraGrid Science Gateways and Their Impact on Science, *IEEE Computer* 41(11):32-41, Nov 2008.

Paulech, Tibor and all. Extended modeling of the Oort cloud formation from the initial protoplanetary disc. On 4th International Workshopon Grid Computing for Complex Problems. Oct. 27-29 2008 page 142-150.

Kandaswamy and all. 2006 Building Web Services for Scientific Grid Applications. *IBM Journal of Research and Development* 50(2-3), 2006.

Krishnan, L. and Stearn, B., et al. 2006 Opal: Simple Web Services Wrappers for Scientific Applications. *IEEE International Conference on Web Services (ICWS 2006),* Sep 18-22, Chicago.

6

An Emerging Decision Support Systems Technology for Disastrous Actions Management

Shah Jahan Miah
School of Management and Information Systems,
Faculty of Business and Law, Footscray Park, Victoria University, Melbourne, Australia

1. Introduction

Climate disaster and catastrophic incidents create emergency problems that need urgent responses by authorities. To protect human communities and human systems from the impact of disasters, rescue teams and decision makers both from government and non-government agencies need to work closely in a systematic manner. Information collected from different sensors and sources must be shared at different decision making levels. However, Government policy and decision makers at various levels lack appropriate technology needed to assist for decision support that could help them work within their context effectively. Research addressing such a context specific decision support issue for managing and fostering the possible impacts on affecting human communities and taking required actions has to date been limited. An IT based solution integrating new technological provisions can have potential benefit for such problem situations in providing good coordination in decision making for authorities.

The purpose of the chapter is to introduce a conceptual approach of emerging decision support systems (DSS) development in enhancing contextual support in decision making. We analyse the requirements of outlining a technological solution model for addressing disaster management problem situations in which decision makers at different levels can have the information support to respond effectively.

The chapter will be organised in the following way. The next section will provide an overview of the issues in such a DSS solution design for disaster emergency decision making. The following section will describe different DSS technologies and their purposes. The fourth section will include different disaster management aspects considered by previous studies. The section following will describe the proposed DSS model that may have application for decision makers. Section six will present a discussion on the delimitations of the proposed approach in the chapter and finally the outline further research directions will be discussed.

2. Problem background

Traditional DSS models have had limited success supporting decision makers in their problem specific situations for disaster management. Specially, for enabling decision makers' context specific reflection, a decision support framework is required for different stakeholders. Technological provisions for on-site or remote access solution concepts are not new in the use of DSS applications. Although some existing DSS solutions integrate GIS provisions, they lack appropriate process that are required to address concurrent data capturing for decision making and relevant decision sharing in users' context. Buzolic, Mladineo, and Knezic (2002) developed a DSS solution for disaster communications through decision processes in the phases of preparation, prevention and planning of a protection system from natural and other catastrophes, as well as in phases throughout interventions during an emergency situation in the telecommunications part. The DSS model is based on a GIS that only capture location specific necessary data. Using a combination of GIS and multi-criteria DSS approach, according to natural catastrophes such as floods, earthquakes, storms, and bushfires, data regarding the vulnerability of the telecommunications system are generated (Buzolic et al. 2002) in the system model. Similarly, Mirfenderesk (2009) described a DSS designed for mainly to assist in a post-disaster situation. However, this DSS model is used traditional technique for pre-disaster flood emergency planning. As a post-disaster measure it can identify vulnerable populations and assist in the evacuation of those at risk (Mirfenderesk, 2009). Rodríguez, Vitoriano and Montero (2009) developed a DSS for aiding the Humanitarian NGOs concerning the response to natural disasters. This DSS has been developed avoiding sophisticated methodologies that may exceed the infrastructural requirements and constraints of emergency management by NGOs. The used method is not technically novel enough to capture decision makers' context. A relatively simple two-level knowledge methodology is utilised in this approach that allows damage assessment of multiple disaster scenarios (Rodríguez et al. 2009). Apart from these DSS approaches, there some disaster management solution have been developed such as MIKE 11 (Designed by Danish Hydraulic Institute) (Kjelds and Müller, 2008) and SoKNOS (Service-Oriented ArchiteCtures Supporting Networks of Public Security--a service oriented architecture based solution design by the German federal government) (SoKNOS, 2011), but they are still in the embryonic or conception stage of design. None addresses the technical requirements of using business intelligence techniques. Therefore issues remain in designing a relevant decision process with support for policy making and operational levels for disaster impact assessments to meet emergency requirements for the safety of humans and other living beings in emergencies.

Drawing upon the above, in the proposed DSS solution, the architecture comprises several technological layers. The first layer collects disaster information from a range of different sensors or sources. This collected information is then processed through a business analytics method (Davenport and Harris, 2007) before storage in knowledge repositories. In the second layer, analysed results with context details are stored in knowledge repositories with their enhanced semantics. The *Protégé* based knowledge framework (Gennari et al. 2003) is employed for knowledge codifications through a controlled vocabulary principle. Finally, the third layer (called data fostering unit) handles the codified knowledge through different decision making policies or rules (for example, rules based decision making- Miah, Kerr and Gammack, 2009) in various decision making levels. Figure 1 illustrates more detail descriptions.

The digital eco-systems research paradigm provides a powerful and broad methodological foundation for such a DSS solution design for addressing the information needs of different stakeholders. A digital ecosystem enables a platform that facilitates self organizing digital system solutions aimed at creating a digital environment for stakeholders in organizations

(Louarn, 2007). This paradigm supports development of emerging technologies for knowledge interactions between software solutions and users (Miah, 2009). Under this framework, an appropriate perspective of socio-materiality is identified for solution design; in which decision maker's social and material characteristics (e.g. organisational policy, rules and management principles) within the changing context can be captured analytically. The fundamental nature of the socio-material practice perspective is important to capture, including themutually constituted view of the stakeholders/decision makers in their own work context (Wagner, Newell and Piccoli, 2010). In this sense, the DSS structures and internal processes for examples the analytics rules and routines associated with a best practice configuration can be outlined as different decision makers draw upon in their situated practices (Wagner et al. 2010; Orlikowski and Scott, 2008). Given the focus of this study upon understanding how the material aspects of technology are entangled with the social for obtaining appropriate decision making practices, this perspective is grounded in the notion that what people do is always locally defined and emergent (Orlikowski, 2000). This view offers potential benefits for such a BI technique oriented DSS solution design that will adapt to various policy and decision making context.

3. Emerging technologies of disaster DSS

DSS based applications are well- known and extensively applied in disaster management. Various technologies are used for instances, in natural disaster management, such as flood control and forescasting, hazard management and pre and post activities management. Table 1 illustrates various DSS design applications in previous studies.

There are many technologies that have been used in DSS application development for the purpose of disaster situation management. Bessis, Asimakopoulou and Xhafa (2011) highlighted potential use of next generation emerging technologies in managing disaster situations. The technologies are namely: *grid computing* (an information sharing solution that allows integrated, collaborative use of distributed computing resources including servers (nodes), networks, databases, and scientific tools managed by multiple organisations); *web services* (an information sharing infrastructure to provide stateless, persistent services and resolves distributed computing issues); *cloud computing* (a service solution that is defined as incorporating virtualisation and utility computing notions as a type of parallel and distributed system); *pervasive computing* (also known as ubiquitous computing, a means to enable resource computation and utilisation in a mobile or environmentally-embedded manner); and *crowd computing* (a service platform and sometimes called 'crowd-sourced' mobile phone data from citizens) (Bessis et al. 2011).Our findings suggest that there are three main approaches that are used for decision support design in different purpose specific disaster managements, namely: integrated dynamic model based, GIS based and cloud computing based approaches.

Asghar et al. (2006) described a dynamic integrated model for disaster management from their previous study on a single DSS design. The model handles specific decision-making needs through the use of combining more than one model. Literature in Asghar et al. (2006) suggested that different DSS systems are designed for various categories of disasters and most of the time DSSs are based on specific models and decision support needs. However, there are different needs of decision support in disaster management in that one single model may not be sufficient to cope with the problem situations (Asghar et al. 2006). Asghar's et al integrated model is decomposed into modular subroutines that are functionally independent in the problem space.

Purpose of decision support solutions	*Descriptions*
Assilzadeha and Mansora (2011) Hazard Decision Support System (HDSS)	HDSS states the scheme, which has to be developed to cater to the requirements of pre, during and post disaster activities. During the events of the disaster, the approach enables user to send and retrieve information as required through the use of handheld devices such as mobile and PDAs. In addition, users can obtain urgent messages or alerts transmitted on their mobile phones in the form of SMS.
TELEFLEUR (Cioca and Cioca, 2010) TELEmatics-assisted handling of FLood Emergencies	The solution is developed for the prevention and management of floods, which combines telematic technologies with advanced meteorological and hydrological forecasting encapsulated in a decision support system.
GIS Based DSS (Buzolic, Mladineo & Knezic, 2009)	The DSS is developed for disaster communications through decision processes in the phases of preparation, prevention, and planning of a protection system from natural and other catastrophes, as well as interventions during an emergency situation. The model captures the necessary location-specific data.
Post and pre disaster DSS (Mirfenderesk, 2009)	The decision system is designed to assist mainly in the post-and pre disaster situation. As a post-disaster measure it can identify a vulnerable population and assist in the evacuation of the population at risk.
Integrated DSS (Asghar, Alahakoon and Churilov, 2006)	The DSS approach is described as dynamic integrated model for disaster management decision support. The model is created on the basis of a given disaster scenario and described the main components of the framework and usefulness of the proposed integrated model. The intelligent technique is used to select the group of subroutines to create the integrated model.

Table 1. Different purpose and technologies used for disaster management DSS development

Gupta (2011) described various stages involved in the preparation of GIS based DSS for disaster management in India. The solution includes the development of an integrated geo-database that consists of various thematic maps, demographic data, socio-economic data and infrastructural facilities at remote level (Gupta, 2011). Gupta's approach uses a menu driven system that is used by administrators who may not have in-depth knowledge of working in GIS. Adityam and Sarkar (1998) also describe a GIS-based DSS for Indian cities affected by cyclones. However, the approach is focused on disaster preparedness and planning through the use of GIS technologies.

The term "cloud computing" has become popular due to its contribution to shared computing applications. Fitzgerald and Dennis (2010) described cloud based design as a "*circuit-switched service architecture*" that is easier to implement for organisations because "*they move the burden of network design and management inside the cloud*" (p. 297). As such, cloud computing provision has been used as a modern architecture of shared computing services. When Amazon.com provided web-based utility services, many service providers became interested in utilising the cloud computing platform for launching new services that met their client group demands through its stable infrastructure (Santos, Gummadi & Rodrigues, 2009). Many studies found cloud computing useful in public safety and disaster management applications. In theory, the approach supports a convergence of interactions and decision making in a broader community perspective.

4. Disaster management aspects

In disaster situations involves a number of entities such as disaster management authorities, teams and individuals from more than one location that are geographically distributed. The entities can be for example medical teams, rescue services, police, civil protection, fire, health and safety professionals, and ambulance services that will be required to communicate, cooperate and collaborate - in real time - in order to take appropriate decisions and actions (Bessin et al. 2011, Graves, 2004; Often et al., 2004). This implies that decision making for such combined action taking is rather multifarious due to diverse information processing from different sources. Carle et al. (2004) suggest that *"there are frequent quotes regarding the lack and inconsistent views of information shared in emergency operations"* (Bessin et al. 2011 p. 77). Carle et al. (2004) also reported that information exchange during an emergency situation is very important and can be very diverse and complex and at analysing information is very important, yet none of the current technologies support such needs.

Disaster managers play important roles in disaster situations. Asimakopoulou and Bessis (2010) and Bessis et al. (2010) note that disaster managers are required to identify the site of people and evaluate their present and projected impacts, because there is no real benefit in sending rescue team to a place if there is no one actually present. This implies that disaster managers need analysed information to make such a quick decision in an appropriate way. Because, it is important to urgently send the rescue team to a place where there is a great risk of someone or many injured. It is straightforward to construct many plausible scenarios where knowledge can be collected from various emerging technologies to the benefit of the disaster managers and the society. In other words, access to shared information regarding the number, whereabouts and health of people in an area struck by a disaster will significantly enhance the ability of disaster managers to respond timely to the reality of the situation. The aforementioned challenges are so vast and multifaceted that it is clearly insufficient to address all of them here.

A framework for analysing disaster management activities is outlined by Wallace & De Balogh, (1985). The proposed framework uses pre and post event based activities for identifying scope of DSS development. The approach can be useful to guide the implementation of DSS technologies for specific purpose.

As mentioned previously, a service oriented architecture based solution in the public security sector called SoKNOS (SoKNOS, 2011) has been developed, in which different technological and user oriented objectives will be investigated such as machine-readable semantics, user-friendly workplace, highly-reliable system behavior and integral data processing. Another objective is machine readable semantics to provide relevant services to user contexts using appropriate machine readable coding in developed technology. Further objective is the user-friendly workplace, which concerns fulfilling decision makers' desires through technological features. This aspect relates to how the technology will accommodate current user's problem scenario and information flow appropriate to particular situation. To

Type	*Operation control Timeframe = 6 months*	*Management control Timeframe = 6months to 1 years*	*Strategic planning Timeframe = more than a year*
Structured tasks	Pre-event such as Inspection Inventory of resources	Pre-event such as Development of resources Development of reporting formats	Pre-event such as securing budgetary and legislative support for programs
Structured tasks	Post-event such as Damage assessment Epidemiological surveillance	Post-event such as Treatment of injured Deployment of relief forces	Post-event such as allocation of scarce resources Development of zoning and regulatory standards
Semi structured tasks	Pre-event such as warning and alerting Meteorological data assessment	Pre-event such as Development of procedures for conducting post event damage and loss assessment	Pre-event as such enforcement of zoning and similar standards Tests and exercises
Semi structured tasks	Post event such as Notification of responsible officials Evacuation plan implementation	Post event such as Declaration of state of emergency Set up triage/reception centers	Post event such as administration of disaster relief Determination of priorities of needs
Unstructured tasks	Pre-event such as Unanticipated personnel problems Exacerbating events	Pre-event such as Replacement for loss of key Personnel and equipment	Pre-event Actions to be considered in legal of unexpected findings (e.g. geological fault under a nuclear facility)
Unstructured tasks	Post-event such as equipment malfunction Impacts not foreseen	Post-event such as Coping with secondary effects such as epidemics Search and rescue	Post-event such as Decision to relocate populace Major recovery expenditures

Table 2. Activities under disaster management scenario
(adapted from Wallace & De Balogh, 1985)

achieve the objective of developing reliable system behaviour, the technology should demonstrate robust behaviour that helps achieve reliability through its innovative mechanisms. The integral data processing requires the technical development that combines internal and external data readable to decision makers. These objectives are useful in motivating further technology development for disaster management; however, this project is still in its conceptual stage. From this perspective this study adopts the principle "*technology should demonstrate robust behaviour that helps achieve reliability*" to outline a business intelligence technique based DSS model in this chapter that guides a conceptual solution design.

5. Proposed DSS framework

Recent research in business intelligence (BI) suggest that the approach can be supportive for any decision support solutions including its underlying architectures, tools, databases, applications, and methodologies (Raisinghani 2004). Negash (2004) provides a definition of BI as follows:

"combine data gathering, data storage, and knowledge management with analytical tools to present complex internal and competitive information to planners and decision makers"

Turban et al. (2008) describes BI's main purposes as enabling interactive and easy access to data, its manipulation and transformation to provide business managers the required decision support. This implies that the approach can add value to decision makers in a disaster management situation where they need to process and transform diverse data. As such, the BI approach is now widely adopted in the world of application design for decision making aid (Watson and Wixom 2007). Drawing from this, this study outlines a BI based conceptual solution in which diverse data are retrieved and manipulated through an analytics filter at the initial stage. Figure 1 illustrates the proposed solution model. The first layer ranges from data sources to knowledge repository; the second from knowledge repository to data fostering; and the third extends from data fostering unit to user group access. At the first layer, the aim is to create meaningful data for storing in the knowledge repository.

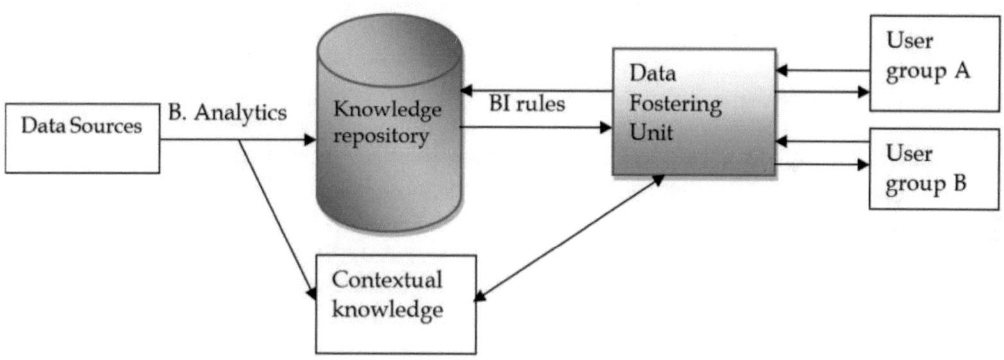

Fig. 1. Conceptual solution model of the proposed decision support systems

After storing the data in the knowledge repository, using an ontology model defined in protégé II (Gennari et al. 2003), the data fostering unit (second layer) use BI rules which will be generated from contextual knowledge to transform the meaningful information to different decision makers at the third layer. It is suggested that BI heavily relies on advanced data collection, extraction, and analysis technologies (Watson and Wixom 2007). In the proposed process, business analytics ensures advanced data collections from a range of data sources with context specific detail knowledge. To extract the data, BI rules ensure appropriate contextual information generation of the stored data to improve decision making. In the data fostering unit, (third layer) the user group can select options relevant to their context, for example by defining parameters for the BI rules. During the events of the disaster, the user is able to send and retrieve information through the use of handheld devices such as mobile and PDA. The data fostering unit can even transmit urgent message and alerts to mobile phones in the form of SMS.

6. Discussion and conclusion

The chapter discussed the potential of a new BI based decision system design to manage disastrous situations. In the context of a decision-support application, the chapter described technologies used in previous applications. The proposed BI based decision system solution used a rule-based approach for ensuring appropriate decision-making through the application of BI both in data storing and retrieving. This initiative reinforces a shift from the traditional DSS application design to a business focused user context specific DSS provision, which allows flexibility and situation specific reflection of real world emergency situations. At the same time, decision makers can actively perform effective decision making, liaise with relevant authorities for sharing data (e.g. relevant climate forecasting, weather conditions) and action-taking on real problems while in the emergency location.

The chapter presented a conceptual solution approach for the target problem area in which decision making needs contextual reflection. The goal was to establish a theoretical foundation for designing and evaluating decision system solution within a real management environment. Outlining the requirement of decision system design the chapter explored a range of DSS techniques and their usage in application areas. It was argued that traditional initiatives are far from a solution that can address situation specific issues and sensitivity of decision makers at different levels.

7. Further research directions

The chapter introduced various DSS applications for disaster management to outline an emergent requirement of context sensitive DSS design. While the findings presented in this chapter are based on a review of previous relevant research, they represent only an early stage analysis of developing a DSS solution in the target application area. Further research will be required for designing a specific knowledge repository using ontology design principle within a real problem scenario that will be capable of working with BI provisions. The interactive users' provisions in such DSS application design can also be a challenge. In this purpose, user specific provisions are required for each user groups to enable improved decision making or action taking through data transition into actionable information. An in-depth study is also required for system integration considering a wide range of BI rules development form 'rules of thumb' (scientific knowledge and practice based understanding) of the emergency situations and to ensure compatibility of the different components within the mobile and wireless operating environment. For acquiring the domain knowledge, further research is required for empirical investigations and which will help outline all of the required 'rules of thumb' in the target area of decision making.

Further to evaluate the outlined DSS technique, a test environment for such solution design will be required for ensuring appropriate information generation according to the different user groups' requirements. This test will also help identify technical difficulties of the proposed solution and various process-oriented challenges associated with user's acceptance and satisfaction.

8. References

[1] Adityam, K.V. & Sarkar, D. (1998), URL: Development of a GIS-Based Decision Support Systems for Indian Cities Affected By Cyclones, Bangladesh Ganges Delia, pp. 239-249, URL: http://cidbimena.desastres.hn/pdf/eng/doc12307/doc12307-contenido.pdf

[2] Asghar, S. Alahakoon, D. & Churilov, L. (2006). A Dynamic Integrated Model for Disaster management Decision Support Systems, *International Journal of Simulation*, vol. 6 (10–11) , pp. 95–114, URL: http://ducati.doc.ntu.ac.uk/uksim/journal/Vol-6/No.10-11/Paper8.pdf

[3] Assilzadeh, H & Mansor, S.B. (2011). Natural Disaster Data and Information Management Systems, Commission Report, University Putra Malaysia, URL: http://unpan1.un.org/intradoc/groups/public/documents/apcity/unpan025913.pdf

[4] Bessis, N., Asimakopoulou, E., & Xhafa, F. (2011). A next generation emerging technologies roadmap for enabling collective computational intelligence in disaster management, *International Journal of Space-Based and Situational Computing*, Vol. 1, No. 1, pp. 76-85.

[5] Buzolic, J., Mladineo, N., & Knezic, S. (2009). Decision support system for disaster communications in Dalmatia, *International Journal of Emergency Management*, vol. 1 (2), pp. 191-201

[6] Carle, B., Vermeersch, F. & Palma, C.R. (2004) Systems improving communication in case of a nuclear emergency, International Community on Information Systems for Crisis Response Management (ISCRAM2004) Conference, 3–4 May 2004, Brussels, Belgium.

[7] Cioca, M. & Cioca, L.I. (2010). Decision Support Systems used in Disaster Management, Decision Support Systems, *InTech Publisher*, URL: http://www.intechopen.com/articles/show/title/decision-support-systems-used-in-disaster-management

[8] Davenport, T.H. & Harris, J.G. (2007). Competing on analytics: the new science of winning, Harvard Business School Publishing Corporation, USA.

[9] FitzGerald, J., & Dennis, A. (2010). *Fundamentals of Business Data Communications* (10th ed.), John Wiley & Sons Australia, Milton, Australia

[10] Gennari, J. H, Musen, M.M, Fergerson, R.W.,Grosso, W.E., Crubezy, M, Eriksson, H., Noy, N.F. & Tu S.W. (2003). The evaluation of Protégé: An Environment for Knowledge Based systems development, *International Journal of Human-Computer Studies*, vol. 58 (1), pp. 89 - 123.

[11] Graves, R.J. (2004) Key technologies for emergency response', International Community on Information Systems for Crisis Response (ICSCRAM2004) Conference, 3–4 May 2004, Brussels, Belgium.

[12] Gupta, R.D. (2011). GIS Based DSS for Natural Disaster Management: A Case Study of Allahabad District, Geospatial Media and Communications Pvt Ltd, URL: http://geospatialworld.net/index.php?option=com_content&view=article&id=15869%3Agis-based-dss-for-natural-disaster-management-a-case-study-of-allahabad-district&catid=145%3Anatural-hazard-management-overview&Itemid=41

[13] Kjelds, J.T. & Müller, H.G., (2008). Integrated Flood Plain & Disaster Management using the MIKE 11 Decision Support System, URL: http://www.icimod.org/?opg=949&document=1248, Retrieved on May 21, 2011

[14] Louarn, M. L. (2007). The technologies for digital ecosystems: cluster of FP6 projects, Digital Business ecosystems, European Commission, Information Society and Media, 2007

[15] Miah, S. J. (2009). A new semantic knowledge sharing approach for e-government systems, *4th IEEE International Conference on Digital Ecosystems*, Dubai, UAE, pp. 457-462

[16] Miah, S.J., Kerr, D. & Gammack, J. (2009). A methodology to allow rural extension professionals to build target-specific expert systems for Australian rural business operators, *Journal of Expert Systems with Applications*, vol. 36, pp. 735-744

[17] Mirfenderesk, H. (2009). Flood emergency management decision support system on the Gold Coast, Australia, *The Australian Journal of Emergency Management*, vol. 24 No. 2.pp.

[18] Negash, S. (2004). Business Intelligence, *Communications of the Association for Information Systems*, Vol. 13, pp. 177-195

[19] Orlikowski, W.J. (2000). Using Technology and Constituting Structures: A Practice Lens for Studying Technology in Organizations, *Organization Science*, vol. 11, pp. 404-428.

[20] Orlikowski, W.J. & Scott, S.V. (2008). Challenging the Separation of Technology, Work and Organization, *Academy Of Management Annals*, vol. (2:1), pp. 433-474.

[21] Otten, J., Heijningen, B & Lafortune, J.F. (2004) The virtual crisis management centre. An ICT implementation to canalise information, *International Community on Information Systems for Crisis Response (ISCRAM2004) Conference*, 3–4 May 2004, Brussels, Belgium.

[22] Raisinghani, M. (2004). *Business Intelligence in the Digital Economy: Opportunities, Limitations and Risks*, Hershey, PA: The Idea Group.

[23] Rodríguez, J. T., Vitoriano, B., & Montero, J. (2009). A natural-disaster management DSS for Humanitarian Non-Governmental Organisations, *Knowledge-Based Systems*, vol. 23, pp. 17–22

[24] Santos, N., Gummadi, K. P. & Rodrigues, R. (2009). Towards Trusted Cloud Computing, accessed 30 September 2011, URL: http://www.mpi-sws.org/~gummadi/papers/trusted_cloud.pdf

[25] SoKNOS (2011), Service-Oriented Architectures Supporting Networks of Public Security Sector, URL: http://www.soknos.de/index.php?id=197&L=0 retrieved on May 20, 2011

[26] Turban, E., Sharda, S., Aronson, J. E., & King, D. (2008). *Business Intelligence: A Managerial Approach*, Upper Saddle River, NJ: Pearson Prentice Hall.

[27] Wagner, E.L., Newell, S. & Piccoli, G. (2010). Understanding Project Survival in an ES Environment: A Socio-material Practice Perspective, *Journal of the Association for Information Systems*, vol. 11 (5), pp. 276-297

[28] Wallace, A.W. & De Balogh, F. (1985). Decision Support Systems for Disaster Management, Public Administration Review, vol. 45, pp. 134-146. URL: http://www.jstor.org/stable/10.2307/3135008

[29] Watson, H. J. & Wixom, B. H. 2007. The Current State of Business Intelligence, *IEEE Computer*, vol. 40:9, pp. 96-99.

Section 2

Emerging Business Informatics and Applications

7

Information Security Management Accounting

Diego Abbo
Candidate School of Systems Enginireering SSE- University of Reading (UK), Italy

1. Introduction

Increased computer interconnectivity and the popularity of Internet are offering organizations of all types unprecedented opportunities to improve operations by reducing paper processing, cutting costs, and sharing information. However, the success of many of these efforts depends, in part, of an organization' ability to protect the integrity, confidentiality of the data and systems it relies on.

Many people seem to be looking for a silver bullet when it comes to information security. They often hope that buying the latest tool or piece of technology will solve their problems. Few organisations stop to evaluate what they are actually trying to protect (and why) from an organizational perspective before selecting solutions. In the field of information security the security issues tend to be complex and are rarely solved simply by applying a piece of technology.

Furthermore the growing of interdependency of the complex integrated information systems will continue and accelerate and more technologies are integrated to deliver rich services. Today there is no way to model, understand, monitor and manage the risks presented by the growth of these systems. That also means that the investments in information security can't have the appropriate accuracy and follow the common principle of redundancy increasing the non-productive costs of the businesses and/or services that are supporting by the above mentioned systems.

On the other hand the failure of information security during the past decade are nothing short of spectacular. The inability of organisations to prevent increasingly dramatic compromises has led to huge financial losses, produced a great deal of embarrassment, and put every sector of the global economy at risk. Despite increasingly draconian legal, commercial, and regulatory activity, the losses continue to mount, national interests are still at risk, and "information crimes" proliferate unabated.

Security is a delicate matter. It is one of the important elements in modern communications today and has many implications on modern life. In order to manage the complexity of this subject it is essential to define the scope of the global research that should focus the protection of the information which definition is the collection of facts and can take many forms (text, numbers, images, audio and video clips).

The core tenets of information protection are confidentiality, integrity and availability, (also defined the CIA triangle) and the perspective of information security is to reduce both the number of events that are causing information security breaches and the range of damages that are related to the aforementioned breach events. The research field must focus the frame that get under control the information that should be protected. In general terms we can assume that the information is moving, in a delivering system, from a point of production to a point of utilization, and a delivering system can be considered a multiple progressive segments of points of departure and points of arrivals for the information in accordance with the logical atomism.

Logical atomism is a philosophical belief that originated in the early 20th century with the development of analytic philosophy. The theory holds that the world consists of ultimate logical "facts" (or "atoms") that cannot be broken down any further.

The information is produced (processed) in one physical site, stored in the same or in another site and communicate through a physical meaning to the site of utilization. All the three entities (production, communication and utilization) exploit instrumental items as facilities that are hosting pertinent devices, hardware, software, operation systems, applicative programs, files, physical meaning of communication (internal and external network) and are linked to the human factors as operational management policy, training, working activities and the end purpose of the delivered information. The delivering systems have information end users that exploit it for a specific aim. Information and all the instrumental items that are components of a delivering system need specific dedicated interdepartmental protections in order to reduce the possibility of information breaches.

Therefore the field of application for this research is individuated in:

- The physical outer edge that contain all the instrumental items for producing, communicating and utilizing the information, the running of the associate information delivering system and its security architecture;
- The state of art of security engineering and management;
- The risk of breaches in the CIA triangle and in which way those breaches are influencing/damaging the purpose of the information end user;
- The set of methodology to individuate pertinent and useful metrics and its validation.

In accordance with the definition of security: "the protection of resources from damage and the protection of data against accidental or intentional disclosure to unauthorized persons or unauthorized modifications or destruction", the research field should be inclusive of the security analysis of all the physical and digital information dimension, the purpose that is sparking off the production, the delivering and the end user information exploitation; furthermore the negotiating power with the threat and the consequences for the end user information purpose of the different kind of breaches.

The actual state of art should deal with four problems that are the addressee of information security research.

The first research problem consists in establishing the appropriate information security metrics to be exploit by those who have the control of the information. Metrics is a term used to denote a measure based on a reference and involves at least two points, the measure and the reference. Security in its most basic meaning is the protection from or absence of danger. Literally, security metrics should tell us about the state or degree of safety relative to a reference point and what to do to avoid danger. Contemporary security metrics by and large fail to do so. They tell us little about the actual degree of "safety" of our system processes, much less about the organization as a whole. They say little about the appropriate course of action, and they are typically not specific for the needs of the recipient.

Security metrics are not well developed outside of a narrow range of IT- centric measures. While these measures may be useful for managing specific technologies such as patch management or server hardening, they are little use in "managing" overall security. There is little to guide the direction of a security program or provide the basis for making decisions.

Indeed, Andrew Jaquith of the Yankee Group expressed it well at the Metricon 1 metrics conference in 2006 during a keynote speech :

"Security is one of the few areas of management that does not possess a well understood canon of techniques for measurement. In logistics, for example, metrics like "freight cost per mile" and "inventory warehouse turns" help operators understand how efficiently trucking fleets and warehouse run. In finance, "value at risk" techniques calculate the amount of money a firm could lose on a given day based on historical pricing volatilities. By contrast, in security there is exactly nothing. No consensus on key indicators exists."

Considering any system that is delivering information from point A (where physically the information is produced or stored) to point B (final information end user) trough a range of A* intermediate points (where A* can range from 0 to ∞) the resolution of the first problem wants to introduce and validate as a baseline tool for security analysis, the following metrics:

- The measure of the functional cost of the implemented security safeguards all along the course of information ;
- The forejudged calculus of probability of breaches (complementary to the estimate percentage rate of security performances) linked to a given functional cost;
- The individuation of the pertinent domains. The domain is a logical entity through which is analyzed the tri-mission situation (e.g. Legal domain, Architectural framework domain, Governance domain and so on). The domains represent both a point of view of a functional perspective and an organizational filter of a dedicated analysis.
- The rate of information system burdening, in terms of loss of effectiveness for the end user purposes, due to security implemented safeguards.

The second research problem looks for the identification of appropriate security indicators that can be used to link the metrics of a security engineered system (first problem metrics) to mathematical indicators; those are representatives of the security of system independently of the technology employed and can also be a baseline of comparison with other systems or interconnected systems. The indicators can be seen as the negotiation power that is in force between the protection of the purpose of an information system and the possible threats. To create an array of security indicators it is both a mean of measuring the operational efficiency of information security and a tool to create regulatory standards for security.

The third research problem is related to the risk analysis. At the moment there is a consolidated literature that shows the way to identify, evaluate, estimate and treat the risk based on empirical methods. However that literature seems to be inappropriate for the information systems overall when they are interconnected with different security standards and the information is becoming under the control of different entities. The solution can be individuated by considering the risk analysis with the existing methods and correlating it directly to the purpose of the information end user.

The fourth research problem consists in the evaluation of return of investment (ROI) for information security implementation.

2. Information security

The analysis of the actual state of art engages the general definition of security: (Abbo, Sun, Feb 2009 pp 195 - 200) "Security is a function of the interaction of its components: Asset (A), Protector (P) and Threat (T) in a given Situation. These can be represented in the equation:

$$S = f(A;P,T) Si.$$

This logical formula is the inspiring baseline for the whole research from Manunta (2000, p. 20) who states that security is the contrived condition of an Asset. It is created and maintained by a Protector in antagonism with a reacting counterpart (Threat), in a given Situation It aims to protect Asset from unacceptable damage.

For the three actors we can give the following definitions:

Asset: Any person, facility, material, information or activity that has a positive value to an owner - (Tipton F. H. – Henry K. 2007 - p. 789 -)
Protector: A person, an organization or a thing that makes sure that something or somebody is not harmed, injured, damaged etc; (OXFORD Dictionary)
Threat Any circumstance or event with potential to cause harm to a system in the form of destruction, disclosure, modification of data, and/or denial of service. Threat is the broadest category in a classification, becoming more specific as it moves through vulnerability, exploit, and attack - (Slade R. 2006 -)

The mere presence of interaction among all three actors (A, P, T) only means that a security context is present as some ongoing processes amongst actors. Further analysis shows that Figure 1 represents a security problem, which has still to be solved.

This definition is the preamble for further related research defined "**theory of sets for security situations** with the application of Venn diagrams.

Venn diagrams or set diagrams are diagrams that show all possible logical relations between a finite collection of sets (aggregation of things) They are used to teach elementary set theory, as well as illustrate simple set relationships in probability, logic, statistics, linguistics and computer science.

The importance of an asset to an organization does not simply depend on the monetary cost of the asset, but rather is based on the value of the asset to the organization (Rogers B.B., p. 75) . Before a consequence of loss of an asset can be reasonably evaluated, the organization itself must be thoroughly understood, which is the purpose of an infrastructure characterization. The infrastructure characterization seeks to gain an appreciation of this organizational environmental and to establish designs constraints under which the security system must operate. An infrastructure characterization consists of defining the critical missions and goals of the organisation, the infrastructure that is necessary to accomplish the mission, the legal, regulatory, safety and corporate framework, and the vulnerabilities that the organisation faces.

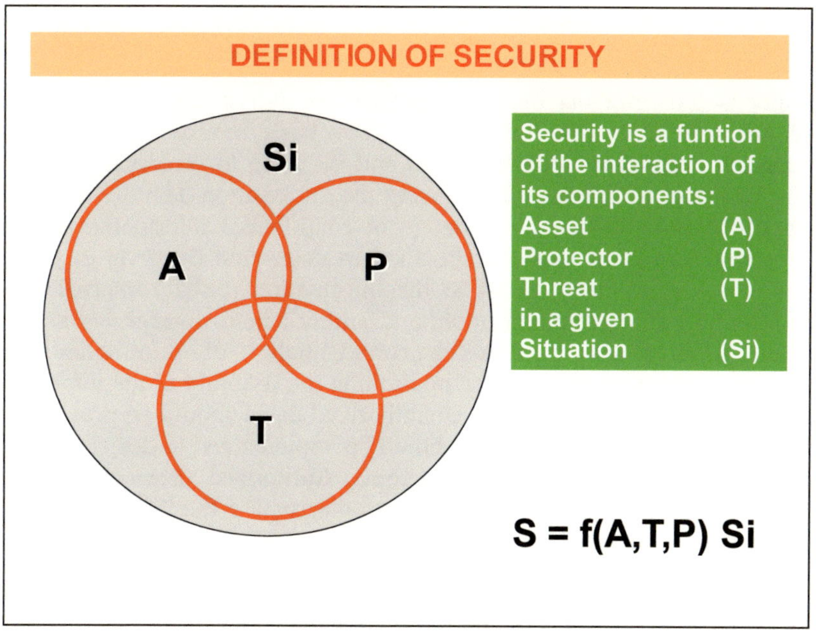

Fig. 1. Definition of Security with the application of set diagrams.

The Assets of information security issues usually include three to five elements. Examples of major security categories include confidentiality, privacy, integrity, authentication, authorization, and non repudiation. The E-Government Act of 2002, section 3542 (B), defines integrity, confidentiality, and availability attributes or security (Barker C. W. p.308):

Availability: The property of ensuring timely and reliable access to and use of information . Availability is the principle that information is accessible when needed. The two primary area affecting the availability of system are denial of service due to the lack of adequate security controls and loss of service due to disaster, such an earthquake, tornado, blackout, hurricane, fire, flood and so forth. In either case, the end user does not have access to information needed to perform his or her job duties. The criticality of the system to the user and its importance to the survival of the organization will determine how significant the impact of the extended downtime becomes.

Integrity: Guarding against improper information modification or destruction, which includes ensuring information non repudiation and authenticity.

Integrity is the principle that information should be protected from intentional, unauthorized, or accidental changes. Information stored within the files, databases, systems, and networks must be able to be relied upon to accurately process transactions and provide accurate information for business decision making. Controls are put in place to ensure that information is modified through accepted practices. Management controls such as the segregation of duties, specification of the systems development life cycle with approval checkpoints, and implementation of testing practises assist in providing information integrity. Well-formed transactions and security of updated programs provide consistent methods of applying changes to systems. Limiting update access to those individuals with a need to access limits the exposure to intentional and unintentional modification.

Confidentiality: Preservation of authorized restrictions on access and disclosure, including means for protecting personal privacy and proprietary information.

Confidentiality is the principle that only authorized individuals, processes, or systems should have access to information on a need-to-know basis. In recent years, much press has been dedicated to the privacy of information and the need to protect it from individuals, who may be able to commit crimes by viewing the information. Identity theft is the act of assuming one's identity through knowledge of confidential information obtained from various sources. Information must be classified to determine the level of confidentiality required, or who should have access to the information (public, internal use only, or confidential). Identification, authentication, and authorization through access controls are practises that support maintaining the confidentiality of information. Encryption information also supports confidentiality by limiting the usability of the information in the event it is viewed while still encrypted. Unauthorized users should be prevented access to the information, and monitoring controls should be implemented to detect and respond per organizational policies to unauthorized attempts. Authorized users of information also represent a risk, as they may have ill intentions by accessing the information for personal knowledge, personal monetary gain, or to support improper disclosures.

The three attributes or the three pillars are also known as C.I.A triangle and are considered as classes of dimensions considering the Committee on National Security System (CNSS) model (Whitman p.5).

This security model, also known as the Mc Cumber Cube after its developer, John Mc Cumber, is rapidly becoming the standard for many aspects of the security information Systems (see Figure 2).

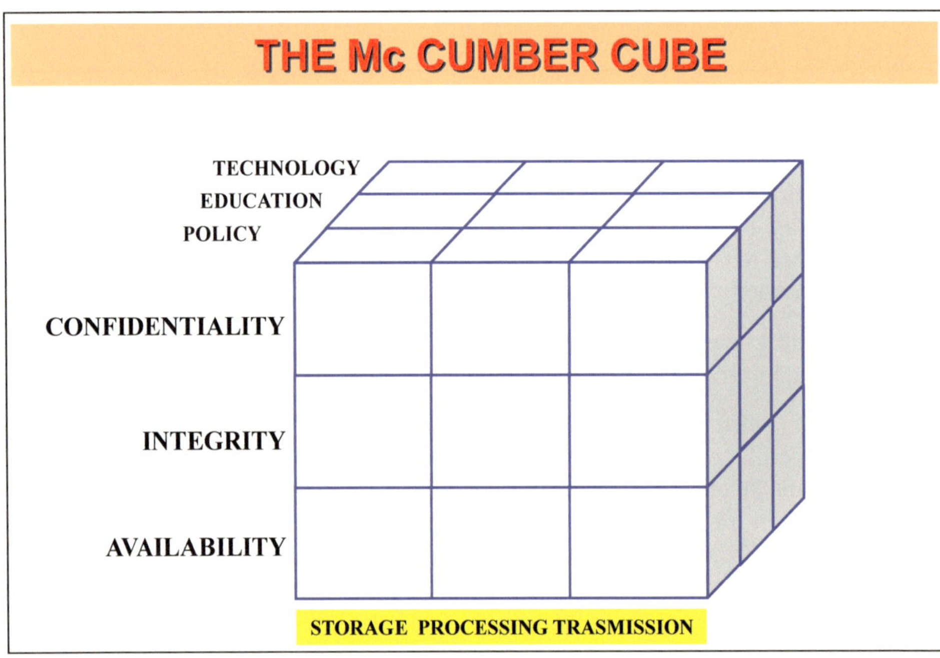

Fig. 2. The Mc Cumber cube is a model recognized by the Committee on National Security System (CNSS).

If we extend the relationship among the three dimensions represented by each axes shown in figure, we end up with a 3x3x3 cube with 27 cells. Each cell represents an area of intersection among these three dimensions that must be addressed to secure information system.

When using this model to design or review any information security program, we must make sure that each of the 27 cells is properly addressed by each of the three communities of interest. For example, the cell representing the intersection between the technology, integrity, and storage areas is expected to include controls or safeguards addressing the use of technology, to protect the integrity, of information while in storage.

While this model covers the three dimensions of information security, it omits any discussion of detailed guidelines and policies that direct the implementation of controls. However this system is very good if reused for the calculation of percentage of the single resource employed in the information security in order to define the amount of the investment.

However, in a given Situation, the ICT security is regarded as layered systems. A layered security needs to be incorporated for any assessment and evaluation process by ensuring the multiple facets of a customer's information security profile are addressed. There have been hundreds of interpretations of layered security but everyone agrees on some core areas to be addressed: network perimeter protection, internal network protection, intrusion monitoring and prevention, host and server configuration, malicious code protection, incident response capabilities, security policies and procedures, employee awareness and training, physical security and monitoring. *These areas are key points of failure within the information security architecture at many organizations"* (Rogers R., pp 5-6).

The issue is something born with the humankind's security perception, since the primordial communities, fully shown by physical layers of defensive concentricity in most archaeological evidences.

Any pertinent situation is seen by the information professional as a set of 10 organizational domains as follows (Tipton F. H. - Henry K pp. xvi-xvii):

a. **Information Security and Risk Management**: Addresses the framework and policies, concepts, principles, structures, and standard used to establish criteria for the protection of information assets, to inculcate holistically the criteria and to assess the effectiveness of that protection. It includes issues of governance, organizational behaviour, ethics, and awareness. This domain also addresses risk assessment and risk management.
b. **Access control**. The collection of mechanisms and procedures that permits managers of a system to exercise a directing or restraining influence over the behaviour, use and content of a systems.
c. **Cryptography.** Addresses the principles, means, and methods of disguising information to ensure integrity, confidentiality, and authenticity in transit and in storage.
d. **Physical (environmental) Security**. Addresses the common physical and procedural risks that may exists in the environment in which an information system is managed.
e. **Security architecture and design**. Addresses the high level and detailed processes, concepts, principles, structures, and standards to define, design, implement, monitor, and secure/assure operating systems, applications, equipment, and networks. It

addresses the technical security policies of the organisation, as well as the implementation and enforcement of those policies.

f. **Business continuity and disaster recovery planning.** Addresses the preparation, processes, and practice required to ensure the preservation of the business in the face of major disruptions to normal business operations.

g. **Telecommunications and network security.** Encompasses the structures, transmission methods, transport formats, and security measures used to provide integrity, availability, and confidentiality for transmissions over private and public communications network and media.

h. **Application security**. Refers to the controls that are included within and applied to system and application software. Application software includes agents, applets, operating systems, databases, data warehouses, knowledge-based systems etc. These may be used in distributed or centralized environment.

i. **Operations security**. Addresses the protection and control of data processing resources in both centralized (data centre) and distributed (client/server) environment.

j. **Legal, regulations, compliance, and investigations**. Addresses general computer crime legislation and regulations, the investigative measures and techniques that can be used to determine if an incident has occurred, and the gathering analysis, and management of evidence if it exists.

For the actual state has defined 13 domains as exhaustive of cloud computing pertinent situation (CSA Guidance 2009):

Domain 1: Cloud Computing Architectural Framework
Domain 2: Governance and Enterprise Risk Management
Domain 3: Legal and Electronic Discovery
Domain 4: Compliance and Audit
Domain 5: Information Lifecycle Management
Domain 6: Portability and Interoperability
Domain 7: Traditional Security, Business Continuity and Disaster Recovery
Domain 8: Data Centre Operations
Domain 9: Incident Response, Notification, and Remediation
Domain 10: Application Security
Domain 11: Encryption and Key Management
Domain 12: Identity and Access Management
Domain 13: Virtualization

The key issues are that the Situation of previous Manunta's formula [S = f(A;P,T) Si] can be viewed, in the information security environment, as a set of well defined interdependent domains each one with its organizational and operational autonomy and protection.

In addition each domain concurs with its own security share to the general protection and any security breach to a single domain reflects consequences to the breached domain and/or to other domains and/or to the general business. Furthermore a more appropriate keyword is in " security of information infrastructure" than "information security" with the following definition:

Information infrastructure. It is the satellite, terrestrial, and wireless communication system that deliver contents to homes, businesses and other public and private institutions.

It is the information content that flows over the infrastructure whether in the form of databases, the written word, a film, a piece of music, a sound recording, a picture or computer software.(Hyperdictionary).

One of the sensitive issue regarding the information infrastructure security is its measurability that means "security metrics". Security metrics are not well developed outside of a narrow range of IT -centric measures. (Brotby W. C - 2009 – pp. 13,14)

While these measures may be useful for managing specific technologies such as patch management or server hardening, they are of little use in managing overall security.

3. The risk perception

The risk is a word that admirably serves the forensic needs of new global culture and its calculation is deeply entrenched in science and manufacturing and as a theoretical base for decision making (Douglas pp 22-23).

Generally speaking Risks are generally classified as "speculative" (the difference between loss or gain, for example, the risk in gambling) and "pure risk", a loss or no loss situation, to which insurance generally applies (Broder p.630).

According to common understanding relating to the information infrastructure the risk focused assets are usually identified as the availability, confidentiality and/or privacy, integrity, authentication and no-repudiation. The risk analysis is tailored on the traditional definition of risk, according to the ISO/IEC (2002, p 2), that states "*combination of the probability of an event and its consequences, but the term risk is generally used only when there is at least the possibility of negative consequences.*"

This is defined Probabilistic Risk Assessment -PRA- (Brotby W. C p.205-). The PRA has emerged as increasingly popular analysis tool especially during last decade. PRA is a systematic and comprehensive methodology to evaluate risks associated with every life-cycle aspect of a complex engineered technological entity from concept definition, through design, construction, and operation, and up to removal from service.

Risk is defined as a feasible detrimental outcome of an activity or action subject to hazards. In PRA risk is characterized: the magnitude (or severity) of the adverse consequence(s) that can potentially result from the given activity or action, and the likelihood of occurrence of the given adverse consequence(s). If the measure of consequence severity is the number of people that can be potentially injured or killed, risk assessment becomes a powerful analytical too assess safety performances.

If the severity of the consequence(s) and their likelihood of occurrence are both expresses qualitatively (e.g. through words like high, medium, or low) the risk assessment is called qualitative risk assessment. In a quantitative risk assessment or a probabilistic risk assessment, consequences are expressed numerically (e.g. the number of people potentially hurt or killed) and their likelihoods of occurrence are expressed as probabilities or frequencies (i.e. the number of occurrences or the probability of occurrence per unit time).

In security applications, the probability of occurrence (P_O) is given by:

$$P_O = P_A (1 - P_E)$$

Where P_A is the probability of an attack and P_E is the probability of effectiveness of the security system (Rogers B.B., p. 76).

Organizations have the option of performing a risk assessment in one or two ways: qualitatively or quantitatively (Abbo, Sun - May 2009 pp 342 -346).

Qualitative risk assessment produce valid results that are descriptive versus measurable (Tipton F. H. - Henry K p. 56).

A qualitative risk assessment is typically conducted when:

- The risk assessors available for the organization have limited expertise in quantitative risk assessment;
- The timeframe to complete the risk assessment is short;
- The organization does not a significant amount of data readily available that can assist with the risk assessment.

The quantitative risk assessment is used by an organization when it becomes more sophisticated in data collection and retention and staff become more experienced in conducting risk assessment.

The hallmark of a quantitative risk assessment is the numeric nature of analysis. Frequency, probability, impact, countermeasures effectiveness, and other aspects of the risk assessment have a discrete mathematical value in pure quantitative analysis.

The risk is associated to a negative event and to the fact that for any negative event, normally, we have pure damages (the costs of the pure loss) resilience damages (the costs of reset) and consequential damages (can be the loss of image, business activity or a step of the threat to pursue other more harmful aims) (Innamorati, pp.61-62 -- my translation).

However if we consider the speculative risk it should be considered also the "positive consequences" in accordance with the concept widely accepted in the business world of no risk no return (LAM pp. 4-5).

The division of risk are limited to three common categories:

Personal (having to do with people assets);
Property (having to do with material assets)
Liability (having to do with legalities that could affect both of the previous categories, such as errors and omissions liability).

Finally it should be taken into consideration the environment in which risk management is situated (Jones, Ashenden p 244):

" Figure 3 depicts the environment in which risk management is situated. At the bottom of the diagram is the concept of trustworthiness (the trust is the predisposition to expose oneself to a security risk). In turn, this has a direct relationship to governance processes in an organization, and this influences an organization's ability to demonstrate compliance.

However should be point out that risk identification and risk estimation is both human and social activity (Tsohou A., Karyda M., Kokolakis S., Kiountouzis p.202). Different people (end -users, stakeholders, etc) or from they have been told by friends. Many factors may influence the way risk is perceived; some of them include the familiarity with the source or danger, the ability to control the situation and dreadfulness of the results.

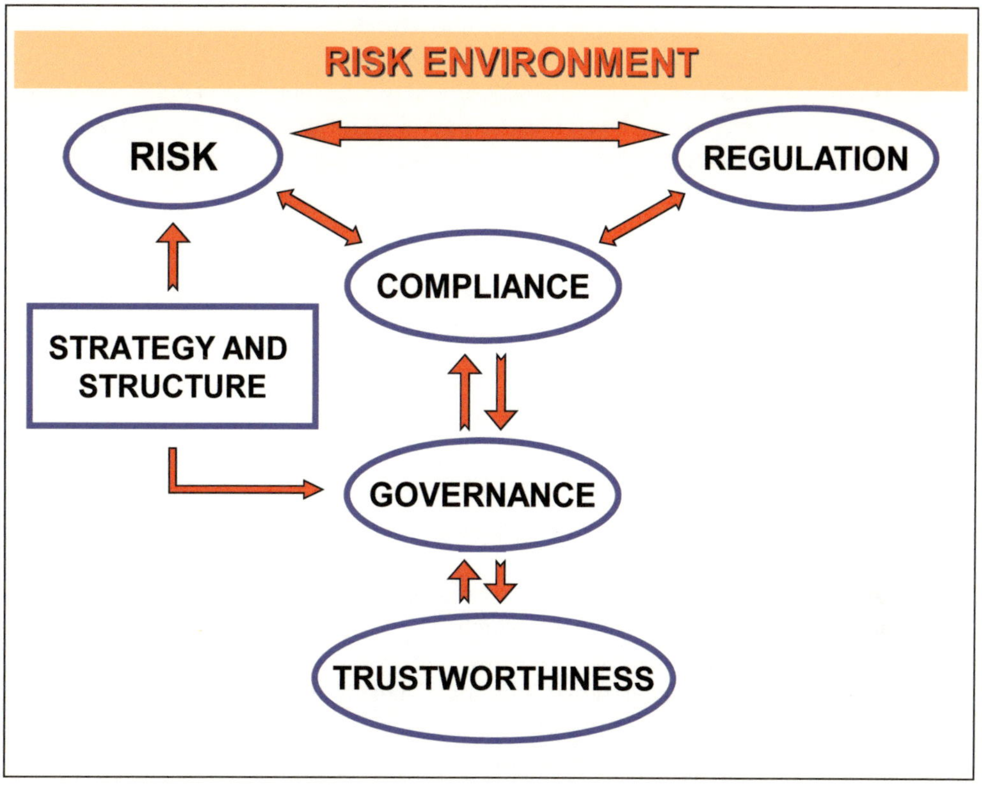

Fig. 3. The risk environment actors.

Therefore, people's ranking of threats may not coincide with that IS security professionals. In essence, much of the people's knowledge of the world comes from perceived stimulus-signs, signal and images.

4. The actual risk management approach

The top edge of security management is represented by the International Standard that adopts the "Plan-Do- Check-Act" (PDCA) model which is applied to structure all Information Security Management Systems (ISMS) process (ISO/IEC 27001 p. v–vi).

The adoption of PDCA model will also reflect the principle the principles governing the security of information systems and networks. This is a robust model for implementing the principle of those guidelines governing risk assessment, security design and implementation, security management and reassessment.

Risk management as define by "random house dictionary" as "the technique or profession of assessing, minimizing, and preventing accidental loss to a business, as "through the use of insurance, safety measures etc" (Tipton F. H. - Henry K p. 56):

A systematic approach to information security risk management is necessary to identify organizational needs regarding information security requirements and to create an effective information security management system - ISMS - (ISO/IEC, 27005 p.3-6).

This approach should be suitable for the organization's environment, and in particular should be aligned with overall enterprise risk management. Security efforts should address risks in an effective and timely manner where and when they are needed. Information security risk management should be an integral part of all information security management activities and should be applied both to implementation and the ongoing operation of an ISMS.

Information security risk management should be a continual process.

The process should establish the context, assess the risks and treat the risks using a risk treatment plan to implement the recommendations and decisions.

Risk management analyses what can happen and what possible consequence can be, before deciding what should be done and when, to reduce the risk to an acceptable level. Information security risk management should contribute to the following:

- Risks being identified
- Risks being assessed in terms of their consequences to the business and the likelihood of their occurrence
- The likelihood and consequences of these risks being communicate and understood
- Priority order for risk treatment being established
- Priority for actions to reduce risks occurring
- Stakeholders being involved when risk management decisions are made and kept informed of the risk management status
- Effectiveness of risk treatment monitoring
- Risks and the risk management process being monitored and reviewed regularly
- Information being captured to improve the risk management approach
- Managers and staff being educated about the risks and the actions to mitigate them

The information security risk management process can be applied to the organization as a whole, any discrete part of the organization (e.g. a department, a physical location, a service) any information system, existing or planned or particular aspects of control (e.g. business continuity planning).

The information security risk management process consists of context establishment, risk assessment, risk treatment, risk acceptance, risk communication and risk monitoring and review.

The level of risk is estimated on the basis of likelihood of an incident scenario, mapped against the estimated negative impact. The likelihood of an incident scenario is given by a threat exploiting vulnerability with a given likelihood.

The following shows the risk level as a function of the business impact and likelihood of the incident scenario. The resulting risk is measured on a scale 0 to 8 that can be evaluated against risk acceptance criteria. This risk scale could also be mapped to a simple overall risk rating according to the matrix in table 1 (CSA 2009, p. 21):

- Low risk: 0-2;
- Medium risk 3-5;
- High risk 6-8

Likelihood of incident scenario / Business impact	Very Low Very Unlikely	Low Unlikely	Medium Possible	High Likely	Very High Frequent
Very Low	**0**	**1**	**2**	**3**	**4**
Low	**1**	**2**	**3**	**4**	**5**
Medium	**2**	**3**	**5**	**5**	**6**
High	**3**	**4**	**5**	**6**	**7**
Very High	**4**	**5**	**6**	**7**	**8**

Table 1. Estimation of risk levels based on ISO/IEC 27005: 2008.

The subsequent management of risk is facing three basic options (Broder p. 641).

- The risk can be avoided, eliminated, or reduced to manageable proportions;
- The risk can be assumed or retained;
- The risk can be transferred to a third party. The transfer to a third party generally implies transfer of liability to an insurance carrier.

The consequent step of risk management is its reduction within levels of acceptance introducing safeguards that reduce the rate of the product probability by consequences, where both the terms are included under an ordered category as it is shown in figure 4.

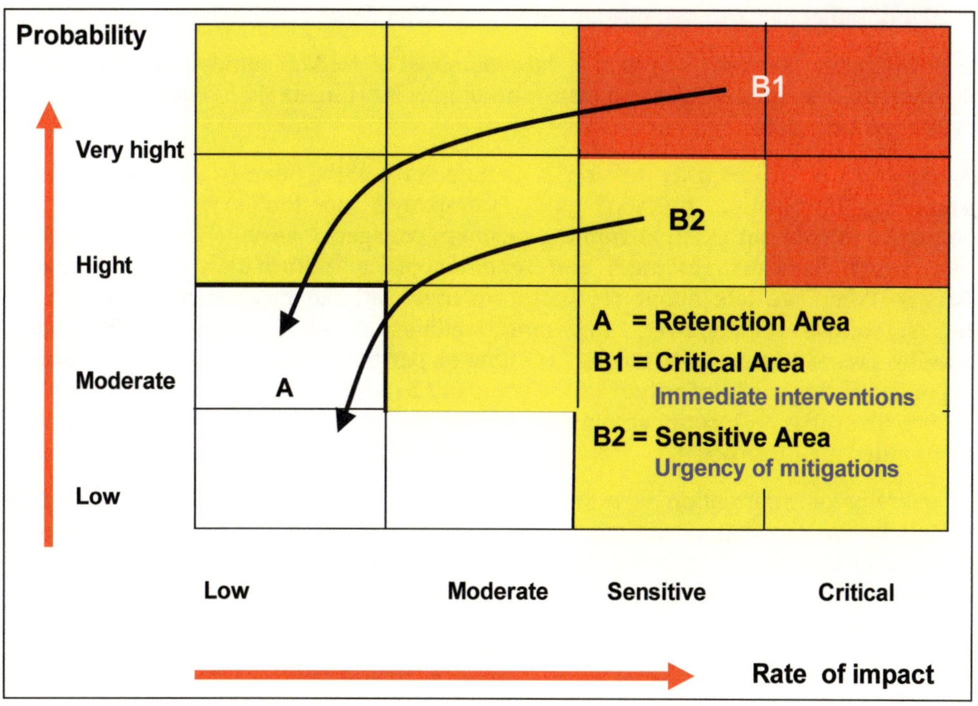

Fig. 4. Levels of risk acceptance.

Risk are always understood in relation to overall business opportunity and appetite for risk. Sometimes risk is compensated by opportunity (ENISA 2009 p.22). The European Network and Information Security Agency (ENISA) in its report regarding Cloud Computing Risk Assessment.

The risks identified in the assessment are classified into three categories:

a. Policy and organizational risks;
b. Technical risks;
c. Legal risks;

5. The ABBO's Information Models for Security – A.I.M.S.

A system is a collection of interacting components, policies and procedures that are integrated and organized to react to an input and produce a predictable output and have a feedback. Everything is not a part of the system is called the surroundings (Rogers B.B., 2006 pp. 67-71). The components themselves and the relationships among them determine how the system works.

A complex system is defined as a diverse system of sub- systems working together toward a common goal.

Complex systems may be deterministic or probabilistic. The goal of deterministic system is to produce the same output every time given a specific input. The performance of a deterministic system can be modelled and predicted by mathematical tools such as algebra and calculus. On the other hand, probabilistic systems do not always produce the same output, but rather a distributed output with a central tendency.

The ICT Security Company's System is the core model of A.I.M.S. family. It is made of three sub - systems like three entities in a close market how it is illustrated in Figure 5 (Abbo, Sun, Feb 2009 pp 195 - 200).

The first entity is "ICT security mission" a manufacturer of the other two entities considered customers: "Information mission" and "Company's mission" We should consider Company's mission an external running business engaged internally in an innovation e-policy which dedicates resources and requirements to information and ICT security missions. When we talk about resources we mean all the instrumental items: money budgets, software, manpower, hardware, facilities, training, know-how capabilities, operating procedures etc. that can be full- time or par-time dedicated. All those assets are component of the "chain of value" of the company to fulfill its mission and it's possible to measure them like an income account in a fiscal period. The three entities are obviously well-founded on information.

The quantity of information is normally encapsulated in **business information flows (B.I.F.s)** the we can defined as a summation of Acts, Facts, Requested Information and Delivered Information in a given timing:

$$\frac{\Sigma\ \{\text{Acts, Facts, RI, DI}\}}{\Delta T}$$

The facts consist on the potential productivity of the infrastructural architecture and the acts all the human and automatic actions connected with the architecture.

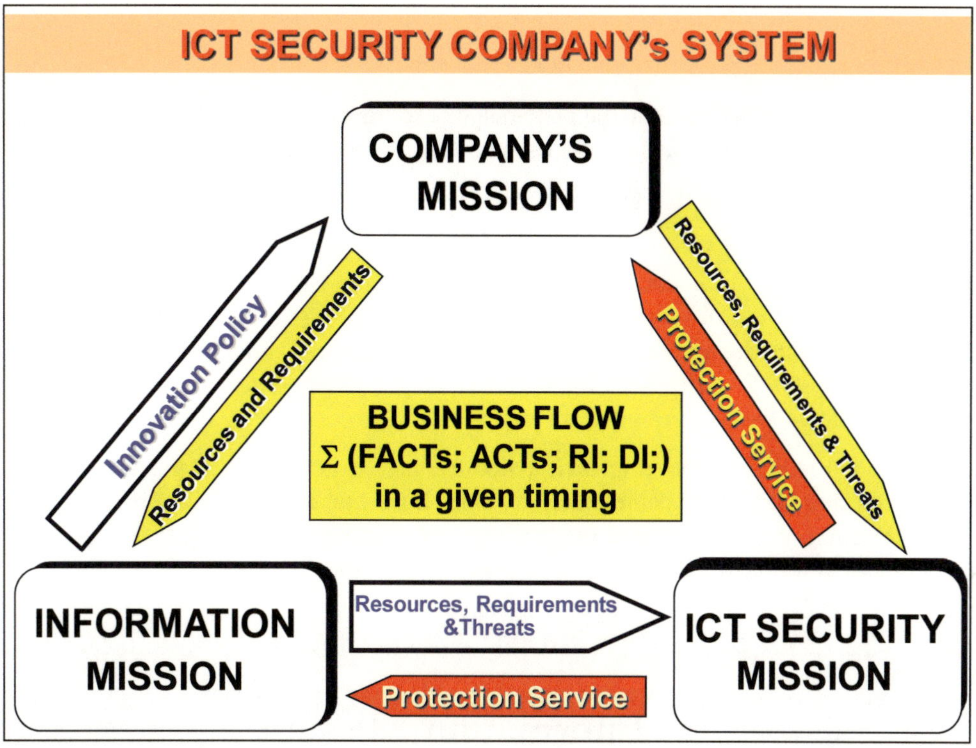

Fig. 5. The three missions are the entities of a close market where Company and Information are the two customers of Security Services.

"Information mission" is a pure deterministic system. It is designed to deliver business flows either on demand or automatically. Its competitive advantage is done by the effective business information flows per unit of time:

$$\frac{\text{Numbers of B.I.F.s}}{\text{Unit of time}}$$

"Company Mission" is both a probabilistic and deterministic system

It is designed to exploit the on - demand Business Information flows for a commercial objective either a service or a good. It is the only Mission in which there is the coexistence of pure risk (loss no-loss situation) and speculative risk (loss or gain situation). Its competitive advantage is done by the summation of profit per any Business Information Flow in the fiscal period:

$$\frac{\Sigma(\text{single BIF x its own profit})}{\text{Fiscal } \Delta T}$$

"Security Mission" is a pure probabilistic system. It's designed to protect the effectiveness of the business information flows according to the C.I.A. triangle. Its competitive advantage is done by One minus the probability of occurrence of a negative event divided by the functional cost of the Security Mission:

$$\frac{1 - P_O}{\text{Functional cost}}$$

The functional cost is defined like the percentage of resources of the business system budget that is invested for the defensive measures to protect the information (Author definition).

One of the key point is the that any instrumental item can have a multiple use one for each entity.

For instance an employer is dedicating his working time to Company Mission" but he/she is spending a percent of this working time to "Information mission" for duty purposes (e.g. production of digital documents, connection with the network) and smaller percent of time is dedicated at ICT Security Mission (e.g. unlock the door, enter the system with the password, updated the security software etc).

The focal point is that considering each single resource in terms of 100 percent functional units we can share it in three complementary slots. If we put on graphics the percent of each relevant resource that is dedicated respectively to the Information mission and to the ICT security mission we have the ISO-line of balanced budget (see Figure 6).

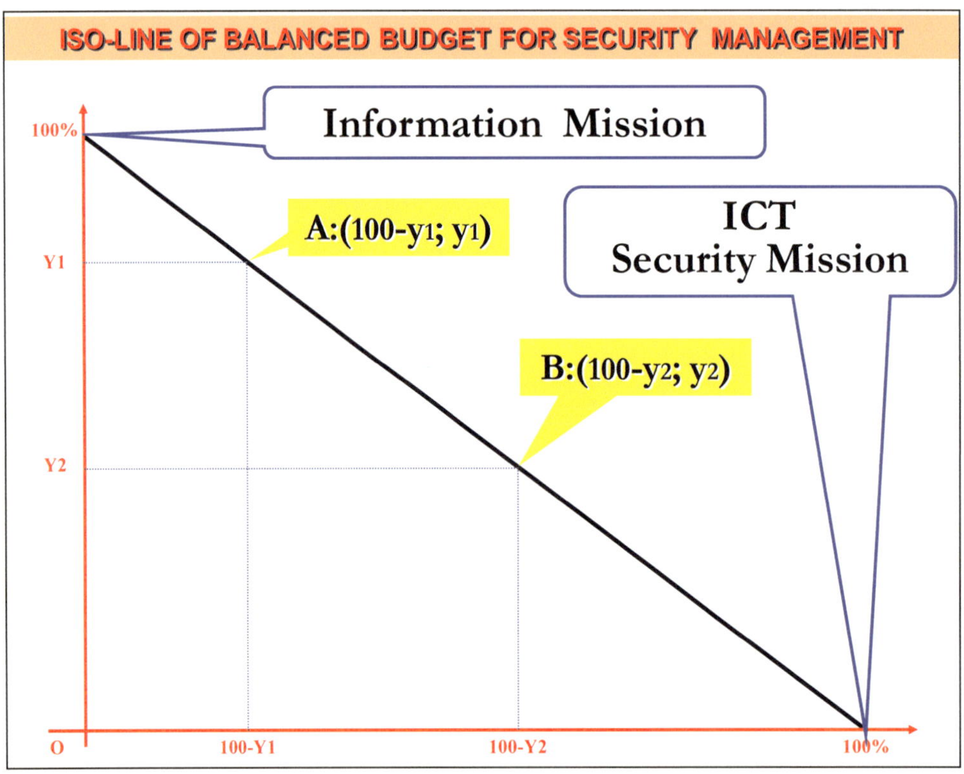

Fig. 6. The entire resources dedicated to IS systems are divided in two shares: the first rate is specific for information mission and the complementary one, dedicated to security, represents the functional cost. This graph representation belongs to the "two reciprocal exhaustive variables model". (Abbo, Sun, Nov 2009 pp 289 - 293).

Having several classes of resources, we should produce a graphic for each class of resource and compare in analytical context, or to use a mathematical system of nth equations. It should be outlined that the values in the graphic ranges from 0 to 100 and they are expressing percentage and the amount of resources that is given to ICT security mission is subtract from information mission budget. We should introduce the definitions of real cost and functional cost of the resources.

The real cost is the prize of a resource in the external market and is clearly represented in the balance sheet of the Company's mission. The functional cost is the percentage of each single resource that we should invest for the defensive measures of the resource for its operational survival.

By definition we can assume that ICT security mission represents the percentage of "Information mission" it should be employed for its survival and in an extensive sense to the "Company mission" survival. The real cost is measured in actual currency and ranges from zero to infinity, the functional cost it is a percentage ratio and ranges from zero to one hundred and by dimensions it is a pure number. Now we can associated, in the same graphic the ISO-line of balanced budget the curve of security performance: y = SP(x) that associates to every combination of functional cost of Information mission a point of security performance (see Figure 7). The combination of the functional costs is efficient only in the area represented by the integral of the realistic curve. The value of security performance is

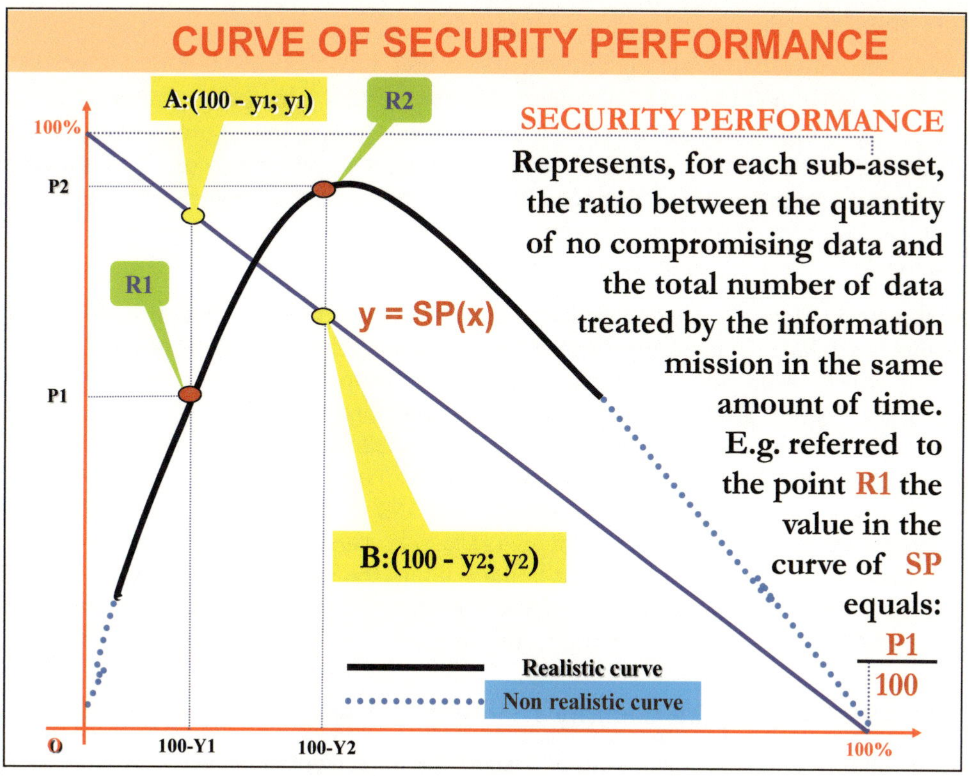

Fig. 7. The curve represents the level of security performance dependable from the functional cost. (Abbo, Sun, Nov 2009 pp 289 - 293).

represented by the ordinate of each point in the realistic curve that is a percentage value. The difference between one hundred and the value of security performance represents both the value of "threat performance" and the "quantitative risk analysis" for any model that has same premises and surrounding conditions.

The calculation of functional cost should be something of relatively easily to individuate in a strictly accounting way and its acceptance as an analytical tool addresses any possible scenario represented by all the families of security performances in every Information System (IS) context. In addition any change in the security architecture of an existing or projected Information System should take always into consideration both the functional cost and the rate of security performance..

By an analytical point of view that means to draw the curve **y = SP(x)**: the functional cost is fixed but the correspondence with the value of Security Performance Curve is variable that should be conquered on the field. While functional cost and security performance rates are variables that should be considered in the strategic planning, the dynamic confrontation is related to the operational planning. The tactical context should be tailored, in the middle period, for monitoring intrusions in order to:

- create a continuative operational feed back for a better security proficiency;
- match together the quantitative and qualitative risk analysis;
- create a kind of "field continuative intelligence" versus the Threat attempts and breakages.

The current use of data mining investigations and link analysis techniques it can be proficiently integrated with the "broader intelligence of the "Company's Mission" or with any allied IS security systems. Actually all the domain is largely unexplored in the sense that the "IS intelligence abilities" are mainly used in the relations either between the Information and Company missions or between the Company mission and its delivering customers. In the other hand the reporting capacity for IS security purposes ranges mainly in the operational planning for "daily purpose statistics".

The implementation of the same existing process between the Information and Company missions like CRM, Business intelligence and the appropriate definition of indicators and warning will be a proper way to close the security loop for any implementing stage of security governance. The capacity of reporting like any "measurable issue" is limited by two main considerations. The first is the capacity of measurement both by a technical and by a managerial point of views. In the specific case the reporting capacity of the security disruption (or attempt of intrusion) should consider if the technological tools can be proficient enough and if its employment on a large scale can create managerial bias on the of IS architecture governance. The second is the willing, the needs or the convenience of the Company mission management to implement a reporting process function in the tactical domain, the threshold of implementation and the level of accuracy.

6. The ASThMA (ABBO's Security Theoretical Measurement Algorithm)

Actually, in a given Information Security System, the implementation view should go deeper in the organizational aspects, creating operational patterns that are always dependable from "functional cost" and "security performance" (Abbo, Sun - May 2009 pp 342 -346).

A way to build-up operational patterns is to consider the Information domain that needs to be secured like horizontal interlocking sets, each one with its technical, organizational and formal security issues. The sets can be considered the domains of the pertinent situation Each domain has its functional cost and a class of security mitigation measures that can be considered mathematical variables. The mitigation measures belong to two main categories:

- Preventive measures that reduce the probability of a negative event on the Y- axis of the previous figure 4
- Protective measures that reduce the rate of impact in case of occurrence of a negative event on the X- axis of the previous figure 4

Any domain can be seen as a mathematical function that links the implementation of the measures with a probability of occurrence or a reduction percentage of the rate of impact .

In the Y-axis we should have n-integrated domains and for each one a function that states: the probability of effectiveness of the security system versus a negative event and/or a category of homogenous negative events is function of the interaction of the implemented preventive measures:

$$P_E = f(Pm1; Pm2; \ldots Pmn)$$

The mathematical union of all the domains is given the global probability of the effectiveness of the security system. This mathematical union equals an algorithm called ASThMA and the results can be put on the pertinent matrix (table 2)

Pertinent parameters / Domains	**Functional cost**	**$1 - P_E$**	**P_A**	**P_O**
1st Domain	%	%		%
2nd Domain	%	%	%	%
(Nth-1) Domain	%	%	%	%
Nth Domain	%	%	%	%
Mathematical Union of all Domains	%	%	%	%

Table 2. The ASThMA matrix for preventive measures. All the numbers are percentage value. PE represents the probability of effectiveness of security system, PA the probability of an attack and PO the probability of a negative event and/or a category of homogenous negative events.

A similar assumption can be done also for the domain of X-axis where the generic probability is substituted by the percentage rate of impact of a negative event and/or a category of homogenous negative events is function of the interaction of the implemented protective measures(table 3).

It should be remarked that in each domain there are quantitative variable that can be expressed with a numerical entity and qualitative variables that can be expressed with an on/off implementation and a coefficient of quality. It is important to establish the appropriate indicators that reflect aspects of situation and which calculation is done by mathematical formulas. The set of indicators is called A.S.I.A. (ABBOs' Security Indicators Array). The validation of those indicators consists in their usefulness for a dual reason:

Domains \ Pertinent Parameters	Functional cost	Percentage of pure damage reduction	Cost of resilience	Time of resilience	Consequential damages
1st Domain	%	%	Currency	Δt	%
2nd Domain	%	%	Currency	Δt	%
(Nth-1) Domain	%	%	Currency	Δt	%
Nth Domain	%	%	Currency	Δt	%
Mathematical Union of all Domains	%	%	Currency	Δt	%

Table 3. The ASThMA matrix for protective measures. It takes into consideration for every domain the functional cost, the percentage of immediate damage reduction, the cost and the time of reset (resilience parameters) and consequential damage of a negative event and/or a category of homogenous negative events. The consequential damages consider a future percentage reductions of Company Mission (loss of image, business activity etc.).

- the creation of a metrics, independent from the technology, that immediately give evidence links among security architectural safeguards, risks for the architecture and the business purpose of the architecture, surrounding environment and negotiation power with the treat;
- the frame (upper and lower level) for international security recognized standard- A.S.I.A. is including , but are not limited to, the following set of indicators

TPP - Threat Penetration Power indicator

$$(\Sigma Ei\ At)\ Ka\ /\ Tp \quad \text{where}$$

Ei Numbers of events that should take place for the threat reaching its aim
At Skilfulness coefficient that ranges from 0 to 1
Ka Time of alert for any event that should take place for the threat reaching its aim
Tp Penetration time of the threat

TM - Threat Motivation indicator =

$$Tib\ /\ \Sigma Ei\ Twc \quad \text{where}$$

Tib Incoming benefits that the threat has after reaching its aim
Ei Numbers of events that should take place for the threat reaching its aim
TwcWorking costs that the threat should afford for any single event;

TR - Threat Deterrence indicator =

$$Pt\ \Sigma Ei\ Twc \quad \text{where}$$

Pt Penetration time of Threat;
TwcWorking costs that the threat should afford for any single event

RE - Resilience Elasticity indicator

Rc /Ti where

Rc Cost of reset. After a negative vent
Ti Total income of the business supported by the information system

Fc **Functional cost** It is the percentage of resources of the business system budget that is invested for the defensive measures to protect the information. It is a number that ranges from 0 to 100

WoS - Weigh of System indicator

= Cs / Ti where

Cs Cost of safeguards
Ti Total income of the business supported by the information system

$\mathbf{P_o}$ Probability of occurrence

$\mathbf{Cp_o}$ Conditional probability of occurrence. It is the probability of a further negative event, given the occurrence of an initial negative event.

All the previous indicators should be abstractedly applied to any information architecture independently of the employed technology.

7. Conclusion

The aforementioned paragraphs set out some fundamental aspect linked to security and risk analysis.

Firstly security is framed as a engineered system where the input is a malevolent human attack upon a business architecture and the desired output is a defeated adversary and an intact asset. In the design of the engineering security system the desired output is the risk evaluation and expressed by numbers that are the result of the formula likelihood or probability of occurrence and severity of the consequence(s) both normally express qualitatively.

Secondly the three pillars (C.I.A. triangle) are seen as a whole **and not specifically considered as a multiple value entity** and consequently the investments and the implementation of safeguards are indiscriminate. It would be more appropriate to link the value of availability, confidentiality, and integrity with the asset and liability statement for any class or set of information, at the end of the suitable working timeframe.

Thirdly the security system **is not considered as an economical system** in the sense that there is no leverage between performances and investments. The implementation of safeguards in an information system match the risk reductions in the supported business system but it is not compared with the Return of Investment (ROI) of the information safeguards. That is a consequence of the shortcoming of the above mentioned system feedback.

Fourthly The implementation of safeguards in an engineered system increase the weight of the system itself and bias the efficiency of the mission.

Fifthly the increasing inter-connections between IS systems **makes more and more difficult the estimation (and by consequent he management) of a given risk** by the traditional statistical and /or among different information infrastructures.

The purpose of seeing the IS security models (like the ICT Security Company's System, the formula of Security and all the others mentioned in the publication) is to create a scientific approach to understand the nature of Is security issues, and to manage the connected problems in the most possible consistent way. The main advantage of an analytical approach is not only the possibility of always estimating costs, but also proficiency, adaptations and re-usability of an IS security architecture. Actually the IS security is perceived as a common sense knowing where the dominant perception is linked to experience; but the build-up of security performing rules requires a point of view beyond the pure empirical reports. The main perspective of IS security analysis is to create a "reference lay-out, in order to make global, measurable and repeatable lay-outs.

The creation of models should be done by accurately considering and analyzing also the growing of interdependency of the complex integrated information systems that will continue and accelerate as more technologies are integrated to deliver rich services. Today we have no way to globally model, understand, monitor and manage the risks presented by the growth of these systems in other words to have the risk assessment in the forensics domain.

The build-up of an interactive set of controlled models is the most suitable way for maintaining a "risk estimation forensics capacity" that should be able to evaluate, make real-time understandable, monitor and manage the measured rate of the security defensive profile of interconnected systems, align information architectures with organizational goals, and help these process to cooperate.

The applications are inclusive of all the IS architecture and a scientific analytical approach should became a the necessary doctrinal baseline when entering in an unplanned "systems of systems" where functionality override resilience.

The impact of implementing the above mentioned solutions in terms of social, political, economical costs compared with the improvements of market benefits and if it is taken seriously by the Government can positively influence the GDPs

8. References

Abbo D. – Sun L. (Feb - 2009) "*Security analysis of information systems*" IADIS International Conference - e-Society Proceedings Vol II – Edited by Piet Kommers and Pedro Isaìas Barcellona – SPAIN.

Abbo D. – Sun L. (May - 2009) "*The patterns for information system security*" ICEIS 11th International Conference on Enterprise Information Systems- Proceedings of Information System Analysis and Specification – Edited by Josè Cordeiro and Joaquim Filipe Milan – ITALY.

Abbo D. - Sun L. (Nov - 2009) *"The information infrastructure protection anlysis"* IADIS International conference - Proceedings of Applied Computing 2009 vol.II- Edited by Hans Weghorn, Jörg Roth and Pedro Isaìas Rome - ITALY

Barker C. W.(2006) *E-Government Security Issues and Measures* - HANDBOOK OF INFORMATION SECURITY vol. 1, Editor- in-Chief Hossein Bidgoli published by John Wiley & Sons NJ USA

Broder, J.F. (1993) *Encyclopaedia of Security Management* - Techniques and Technology, Butterworth-Heinemann, Burlington MA USA.

Brotby W. C (2009) *Information Security Management Metrics – A definitive guide to effective security monitoring and measurement* Auerbach Publications Boca Raton FL US

CSA - Cloud Security Alliance - (2009), *Security guidance for critical areas of focus in cloud computing V2.1* – URL http://cloudsecurityalliance.org/csaguide.pdf

CSA Guidance – Cloud Security Alliance – (2009), *Security Guidance for Critical Areas of Focus in Cloud Computing*- URL http://cloudsecurityalliance.org/guidance.html

Douglas M. (2005) *Risk and blame* - Routledge NY, USA.

ENISA -European Network and Information Security Agency- (2009) *Cloud Computing Risk Assessment* -- URL: http://www.enisa.europa.eu/act/rm/files/deliverables/cloud-computing-risk-assessment

Hyperdictionary *Meaning of National Information Infrastructure* -- URL: http://www.hyperdictionary.com/computing/national+information+infrastrucure.

Innamorati, F. (2002) *La security d'impresa*, Insigna Edizioni Simone, Milan ITALY

ISO/IEC, Guide 73 (2002) *Risk management - vocabulary – guidelines for use in standards*, Geneva CH.

ISO/IEC, 27001 (2008) *"Information technology – Security techniques – Information security management system – Requirements"* Geneva CH

ISO/IEC, 27005 (2008) *"Information technology – Security techniques – Information security risk management – Annex E: information security risks assessment approaches"* Geneva CH.

Jones A. - Ashenden D. (2005) *Risk management for computer security*, Elsevier Butterworth-Heineman, Oxford UK

Lam J. (2003) *Enterprise risk management – from incentives to controls*, John Wiley and Sons, NJ USA

Manunta, G. (2000) *Defining Security* Diogenes paper n.1 Cranfield Security Centre- The Royal Military College of Science, Hampshire UK

Rogers B.B. (2006) *Engineering Principles for Security Managers* – THE HANBOOK OF SECURITY Edited by Martin Gill - Palgrave Macmillan, London, UK .

Rogers, R. (2005) *Network Security Evaluation using the NSA-IEM*, Syngress Publishing Inc. Rockland, MA - USA,

Slade R. (2006) *"Dictionary of information security"* Syngress Publishing Inc. Rockland, MA - USA

Tipton F. H. - Henry K. (2007) *Official (ISC)2 Guide to the CISSP CBK*, Auerbach Publications New York - USA

Tsohou A., Karyda M., Kokolakis S., Kiountouzis E. (2006) "*Formulating information systems risk management strategies through cultural theory Information*" - Management & Computer Security Vol. 14 N° 3

Whitman, E.M., Mattord, J.H., 2008. *Management of Information Security*, Thomson Course Technology, CANADA, 2nd edition.

8

RFID, an Emerging Wireless Technology for Sustainable Customer Centric Operations

Stuart So
The University of Queensland, Australia

1. Introduction

The main applications in the first wave of RFID have been in the supply chain mainly for improving the distribution of physical assets in the systems (Hardgrave and Miller, 2008; Sarma, 2008). The burgeoning use of RFID technology extends its applications to both upstream (supplier management) and downstream (retail and service) of manufacturing supply chains. RFID tags, also called "smart labels", together with other pervasive computing technologies realizes lean thinking in real-life and creates a smarter operating environment through adding *value* not only to customers with user-friendly shopping experience but also to merchants with agile and responsive store operations. Harrison and Hoek (2008), define *value* as relative advantage in general which is specified as *perceived benefit* obtained from the products or services in terms of the final customer, while as *economic profitability* in terms of the management, and the concept can be extended to other supply chain stakeholders as *value stream* which represents the *value-adding processes* beginning as raw materials from suppliers that are progressively converted into finished product bought by end-customers, such as aluminum is converted into one of the constituents of a can of coke. Being one of the management best practices, lean thinking preaches simplification and elimination of wasteful tasks, which is applicable to overly complex and nonintegrated processes that are inefficient and provide little added value. The firms following these practices have seen such dramatic improvement in performance that lean has spread across entire supply chains leading users to map their business processes to drive out *wastes* in operations, and becoming a lean enterprise has the potential to improve operations, reduce costs and deliver services with shorter lead times (King, 2009).

Ohno (1988) identified seven kinds of manufacturing *waste* that need to be eliminated: *overproduction; transportation; inventory; motion; defects; over-processing;* and *waiting*. These seven wastes represent the most commonly wasted resources and associated wasteful manufacturing activities which do not add value or are unproductive, in which the concept can be applied in non-manufacturing. Womack and Jones (2003) defined the eighth waste, i.e. delivering goods or services *not meeting customer need*, which represents a key attribute of a customer-centric lean enterprise. Lean thinking is proved to be an effective management system for manufacturing to improve overall efficiency and to enhance the work environment, in which the "getting more with less" concept can be applied in any type of business upon value creation (Aikens, 2011; Russell and Taylor, 2009). By offering the benefits of reducing complexity, improving efficiency, speeding delivery, and understanding customer needs, lean thinking has gained the wide acceptance in non-manufacturing (Heizer and Render, 2007; Russell and Taylor, 2009). Successful cases of adopting lean thinking in services have been applied in some instances to insurance (Swank, 2003), healthcare (Miller, 2005), government (Gupta, 2004), library (So and Liu, 2007), and retailing (Heizer and Render, 2007; Russell and Taylor, 2009; So and Sun, 2010).

To adopt lean services effectively in operations, firms need to made changes on three aspects: (i) *standardization of tasks and procedures* which can be achieved by, for example, documenting the process flow, training, automating tasks, etc., such that people can be freed to spend more time being creative on value-added work, (ii) *consolidating common processes* to eliminate non-value-added cost and duplicative efforts that customers are not willing to pay for, and (iii) *eliminating loop-backs or delay* which will result in improving productivity levels (Swank, 2003; George and Wilson, 2004; Hanna, 2007). The fast-paced characteristics and changing customer expectations of the markets lead apparel retail to the characteristics of short lifecycle and high impulse purchase which are sensitive to inventory shrinkage and product flow delay in the supply chains. Also, the perception of customers on retail services would affect their purchase decision. Realizing lean thinking in apparel retail operations with RFID technology creates a leaner operating environment which offers not only user-friendly shopping experience to customers but also more agile and responsive store operations to retailers with less wasteful sales and operations process. Adopting lean services in apparel retailing may equally beneficial to this industry with potential of creating both user- and eco-friendly retail environment.

The purpose of this research is to provide management and practitioners with insights on implementing and adopting lean services in contemporary retail environment enabled with RFID, a communication technology that add value to the customer chain in apparel retailing through providing smart and agile service operation. This paper presents supportive literature on the principles and the process of value creating activities based on lean thinking (Womack and Jones, 2003) and CCOR model (SCC, 2010a) aimed at improving profitability. A case study is presented to demonstrate how the convergence of these two management approaches can be applied to an apparel retailer based on a novel RFID-enabled smart apparel system aimed at improving its service operations that lead to increased customer conversion. Lastly, the implications of adopting this new initiative in creating leaner and smarter retail operations are discussed with the purpose to ensure the delivery of maximum value as a strategic tool for apparel retailers.

2. RFID technology and sustainability

2.1 Fundamental of RFID technology

RFID is an automatic identification (Auto-ID) technology developed by Auto-ID Center at Massachusetts Institute of Technology, relying on storing and remotely retrieving data using devices called RFID tags and readers (Auto-ID Center, 2002; Doyle, 2004; EPC, 2004; Finkenzeller, 2000; Shepard, 2005). With RFID technology, physical asset will have embedded intelligence that allows them to communicate with each other and with the tracking points (Auto-ID Center, 2002; IBM, 2003; VeriSign, 2004). Leading companies and business networks adopt management best practice enabled with new technologies and strategies such as lean thinking, eco-design, life-cycle assessment and close-loop production, which offer merchants improved resources management and greener value chains (UN, 2003). Information and communication technologies (ICT), e.g. RFID technology, add great values to retail sales and operations processes through enabling consumers to find information and alternative products and services more easily online leading to a greener and less wasteful consumption practice by helping them to make sustainable choices (UN, 2011).

A RFID system essentially consists of three main components: RFID tag, RFID reader, and backend information system with middleware sitting between reader and backend system for carrying out data capturing, screening and routing (Glover and Bhatt, 2006). An RFID tag is a small object that can be attached to or incorporated into physical asset such as book, clothing, or person. When an RFID tag passes through the electromagnetic zone, it detects the reader's activation signal. The reader decodes the data encoded in the tag's integrated circuit (silicon chip) and the data is passed to the host computer for further processing (Finkenzeller, 2000; Hawrylak *et al.*, 2008; Shepard, 2005). RFID tags generally fall into two categories: passive, and active. Passive tags receive the most publicity and are currently being used by large retailers such as Wal-Mart and Metro to track inventory, and by the U.S. Department of Defense to track supplies (Hawrylak *et al.*, 2008). Unlike active tags, passive tags do not contain onboard power source and derive the power for operation from RFID interrogation signal in the course of communication (Finkenzeller, 2000; Hawrylak *et al.*, 2008; Shepard, 2005).

Passive RFID tags communicate using one of two methods: near-field and far-field (Hawrylak *et al.*, 2008). Far-field RFID tags support longer communication range than near-field tags, but they are comparatively more sensitive to tag orientation. The type of tags required for a RFID system would depend on their business applications, site conditions and system design requirements. In case of supply chain and retail applications, far-field RFID systems are used extensively. According to Hawrylak *et al.* (2008), the sensitivity of the system to RFID tag orientation is critical in many applications. The communication method used by far-field RFID system easily causes false detection and hence the design of middleware and upper layer application software becomes critical in order to effectively screen unwanted RFID signals emitted by nearby irrelevant product items.

2.2 RFID in enabling sustainable retail operations

Tracking the movements of product items in operations can be determined by three variables in a three-dimensional space, in which the first two are related to the "time" and "space" of item movement, while the third dimension concerns item identification by using RFID tags that carry Electronic Product Codes (EPCs) (Sarma, 2008). On this ground, RFID reader works with middleware to provide backend information systems with an "inventory snapshot" in its field of view which may cover a small corner of warehouse, distribution centre (DC) or backroom of retail store that essentially provides a series of item management function for improving the efficiency of supply chains including: (1) finding, (2) tracking, (3) tracing, (4) item count, and (5) time-intersections. Through querying of this corpus of data gathering from operations, two key metrics, i.e. *shrinkage* (caused by theft, damage, loss, and etc.) and *lead times* that concern operations visibility are evaluated (Hardgrave and Miller, 2008). In particular for apparel retailing, the "lost sales" causing by (1) misplacement, (2) damage, (3) theft, (4) shipping error, and (5) counterfeit of items can be reduced with the use of RFID which ultimately lead to increased product availability and total cost saving (Ustundag and Tanyas, 2009).

Back in June 2003, Wal-Mart, a US retailer, strictly required its top 100 suppliers to implement RFID technology by tagging the pallets and cases in the supplies for operation improvement through sending real-time inventory data from individual store to suppliers (Hardgrave and Miller, 2008; Roberti, 2004). Wal-Mart and its suppliers use the real-time data to improve replenishment with out-of-stocks reduced by 16% by tracking cases of goods with RFID tags carrying EPCs, where this data enables suppliers to measure the execution of promotions and boost sales which benefit to both parties (Roberti, 2005; 2007). The Wal-Mart case demonstrates an RFID implementation that only predominately affects only a small portion of the supply chain (from retailer distribution centre to store backroom) and makes use only limited RFID system capability (e.g. finding and counting items at pallet level and case level only). Given this limited scope of exposure and application, determining the payback and ultimately creating business value are challenging.

In supporting the lean thinking initiative, three mini-cases are presented to illustrate how the application of RFID technology combined with the EPCs benefits apparel retail management:

1. **Marks & Spencer**, one of Europe's largest retailers, has expanded its RFID deployment to include six clothing departments across 53 stores (Hess, 2008). The company uses RFID to track goods as they move throughout the supply chain into its stores. Apparel is individually tagged and eventually ends up on the sales floor. Store employees can quickly read racks of the RFID-tagged items by passing an RFID reader past the apparel. Tagging the items at the manufacturing point allows Marks & Spencer to monitor its shipments more accurately as they arrive in stores.
2. **Levi Strauss & Co.**, a U.S. apparel retailer, demonstrated the value of RFID technology in inventory management through item-level tracking (Wasserman, 2006). The company has reported that sales clerks can complete a storewide inventory in about an hour, a process that used to take two days. That inventory data is used on the sales floor to replenish sizes, colors and styles of clothing. Levi says the in-store use of item-level RFID on clothing in Mexico City, which started in 2005, has increased sales.
3. **American Apparel**, a U.S. apparel company, which operates more than 180 stores in 13 countries, is jumping into item-level RFID tagging and product tracking (O'Connor, 2008). The company saw quick benefits from the technology. The weekly process of taking inventory of all items in the store, which previously took four workers eight hours to complete, could now be accomplished with just two people in two hours. This gives employees more time to assist customers directly, and carry out other tasks.

As seen from these examples, many RFID-based apparel retail systems is mainly used to improve accuracy or efficiency of business logistics in relation to inventory management or checking out of product items but however do not address all the concerns on sales-floor management, e.g. improving shopping experience or item availability. RFID technology is traditionally offered to the retail segment for improving business logistics. Some apparel retailers use RFID technology in product authentication or article surveillance. Apparel retail is a season-driven and time-sensitive industry. In today's fast-paced society, customers with more sophisticated buying needs and increased choices but have less time to devote to shopping. Apparel retailers have to face the challenge of adapting quickly and efficiently to keep up with fashion and buying trends to meet customer demand, in view of the shelf-life of most product items are just around 20-40 days before their first markdown (Wasserman, 2006).

An innovative system design and new configuration are needed for coping with changes. By re-designing services with RFID and CCOR model, clothing items carried by customers can be automatically detected with mix-and-match recommendations provided in real-time.

3. Re-designing services with CCOR model

Service design is considered as part of operations management that concerns the production of goods and services. Shostack (1982, 1984) is one of the earliest contributors in designing services that are process driven and customer focus with the methodology named service blueprinting. Shostack (1982) identified three important concepts in service design: (i) *process charts* for illustrating the operations processes flow, (ii) *PERT charts* for visualizing the project yields, and (iii) *systems/software programs* for supporting the service operations. Shostack (1984) further introduced the process of designing a blueprint which includes the steps of: (i) *identifying processes,* through mapping the processes that constitute the service, (ii) *isolating fail point,* by identifying the vulnerabilities of the service delivery system on the process chart, (iii) *establishing time frame,* as standard execution time which is below the maximum delay time tolerable by the customers, and (iv) *analyzing profitability,* based on the service execution time which is considered as cost component of service that should be minimized. However, the leakage of sales prospects, i.e. customer conversion is not included as a measurement of service profitability and the metric should be used in designing customer focused retail services.

Developed by Supply-Chain Council's (SCC), CCOR model expands the application range of the supply chain operations reference (SCOR) model, which is also a methodology, diagnostic and benchmarking tool developed by SCC for standardizing the process of supply chain management, from improving supply chain processes to enhancing service operations of a firm at its customer touch points (Saegusa, 2010). CCOR model provides a standard framework of high-level customer chain definitions that enables firms to benchmark their processes with other firms that use the same approach, and then identify and implement the changes needed to improve their customer chain which aims at cutting cost and time for subsequent improvement programmes (SCC, 2010a). The process reference framework adopts a standardized approach to speeding up the improvement programmes (Magnusson, 2010; SCC, 2010a) which includes three major steps: (i) *reengineering business processes* by capturing the 'As-is' business activity structure and deriving the future 'To-be' state, (ii) *benchmarking* by quantify the operational performance of similar companies and establish internal targets based on the 'best in class' results which involve defining metrics for making comparison, and (iii) *best practice analysis* by adopting suitable management practices and software or technological solutions that result in superior performance.

CCOR model defines the value-creating processes in the sales operations of a firm as the collection of business activities along the customer chain in which both the pre-sales and post-sales activities in the sales execution processes are designed to convert customer needs into sales orders (Magnusson, 2010). According to SCC (2010a, 2010b), the sales execution processes are triggered by planned or actual events including customer visits, responding to customer inquiries, creation of customer solutions, processing of claims and support calls, which are organized into four major process groups:

- *Relate* - The process of establishing and maintaining relationships with customers,
- *Sell* - The process of establishing an understanding of the customer's needs and presenting and/or developing a solution to meet those needs,
- *Contract* - The process of pricing a solution and gaining customer agreement, and
- *Assist* - The process of providing after-sales support for products/services.

The sales operations and related service support tasks happened on the shop floor of a retail store that concern customer conversion involve mainly pre-sales activities, which are organized into three process groups, i.e. '*relate*', '*sell*' and '*contract*' (SCC, 2010b), and can be adapted as the basis for mapping the value creating activities to shopping process in retail operations.

Figure 1 depicts the concept of customer conversion in the customer chain processes. By visualizing the conversion of potential customers of the target markets to contract customers at each stage of the shopping processes, CCOR model measures the value of the services developed in the chain through enhancing the speed and flexibility of the operations in each process group leading the retailer to overall profitability improvement in response to the evolving markets and changing customer demands (SCC, 2010a, 2010b). The conversion metrics can be adopted for measuring the profitability of new service in two folds, i.e. overall profitability, and profitability by process group so that retailers can lay different emphasis on the process groups in performance tuning according to their business priority and resource availability.

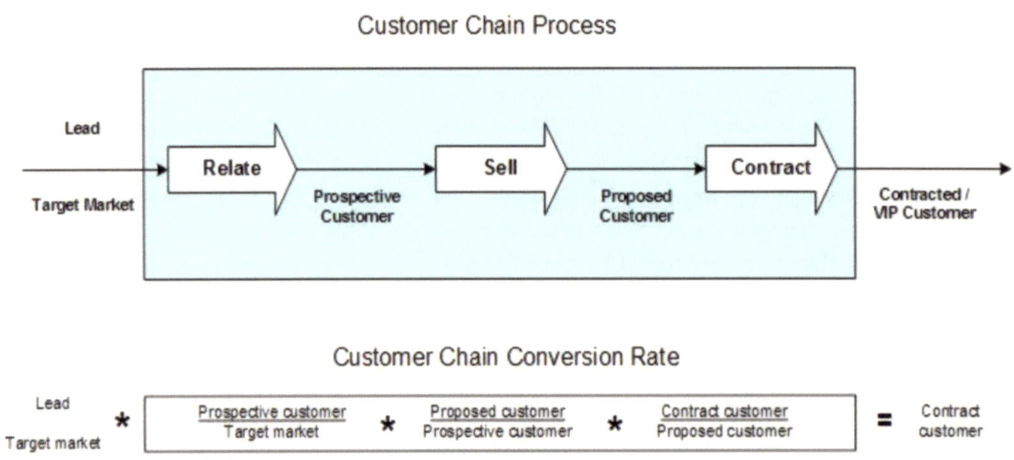

Fig. 1. Customer Chain Process and Conversion Rate

4. Realizing lean services with RFID technology

Lean thinking began in manufacturing and is originated in Toyota with names 'Toyota production system (TPS)' or 'Just-in-time (JIT) manufacturing' beginning back in 1960s, aiming for a total management system that works for any type of business and stresses value creation (Ohno, 1988; Womack and Jones, 2003; Womack *et al.*, 1991). It is a strategic move to adopt lean thinking as a total management system and the success is determined by how well a company coordinates all of its internal process, including activities with its suppliers and customers that create *value* to products and services (Russell and Taylor, 2009). Lean thinking enriches customer value based on the principle that the final customer should not pay for such as the cost, time and quality penalties of wasteful processes and this is achieved by adopting five lean principles as a cyclical route to seek perfection (Harrison and Hoek , 2008; King, 2009; Womack and Jones, 2003):

- *Specify value* - value is specified in two fronts, (i) representing the customer value, which may include: increasing *delivery speed* and enhancing *service flexibility*, and (ii) representing the shareholder/management value in the business aspect which may include *reducing cost* and *inventory* or *acquiring new knowledge/skill.*
- *Identify and map value stream* - the whole sequence of process steps in the supply chain with all the activities required for a company's product and services, no matter value added and non-value added, should be identified for the next step.
- *Make value flow in the supply chain* - Wasteful tasks/processes are removed by lean principles in which JIT or pull systems enable flow.
- *Enable customer pull* - By working collaboratively with suppliers to make only on response to a signal from the customer in downstream supply chains. Pull enables the value stream to produce and deliver the right materials at the right time in the right amounts with minimal inventory.
- *Pursue perfection* - continuous improvement of all processes through empowering employees actually doing the work to remove waste and to design and implement more effective process, which is generally known as 'kaizen' in Japanese.

Lean service is the adoption of lean thinking in services, which are suitable nearly for any working environments no matter they are operational or support in nature (Aikens, 2011; Russell and Taylor, 2009; Voehl and Elshennawy, 2010). An important value created by the adoption of lean thinking is the reduction of customer order fulfillment time by eliminating non-value-added wastes from the processes (Ohno, 1988), and other value creating objectives such as reducing lead-time or inventory can also be applied to services by streamlining the processes so that businesses can be more responsive to changes (George and Wilson, 2004; Russell and Taylor, 2009). In the past decades, information technology (IT) has continued to expand into key manufacturing and service delivery systems, and more importantly, into their process workflows and supporting procedures where this expansion has been seen lately in the retail sector that implement lean thinking in the service operations (Husby and Swartwood, 2009; Martin, 2010). IT applications facilitate simplification, automation, integration, and monitoring of business processes, as well as the management and control of material and information flows that fully realized the lean thinking initiative in services (Martin, 2010). With the emergence of wireless computing, the "*Internet of Things*" is now happening where the things such as people and physical assets in organizations can be enabled with a wireless capability to provide visibility throughout the business and real-time tracking of inventories, movements, security and safety forms the basis of business process improvement (Hawrylak *et al.*, 2008).

Through streamlining and automating operations processes with real-time asset and personnel visibility, RFID-based lean services in the "last 50 feet" of the supply chains resulting in improved item management in store management as well as enhanced customer experience which enables retailers to cope with customers of more sophisticated buying needs in the fast-paced society who have less time devoted to shopping (Doyle, 2004;

Hardgrave and Miller, 2008; Sarma, 2008). Hence, adopting lean services with RFID technology in retail operations supporting Martin (2010)'s IT capabilities becomes feasible and brings improvements to the operation as a whole. A case study of RFID applications in realizing lean services in apparel retailing is presented below aiming to provide insights on formulating relevant adoption tactics based on real-life experience.

5. Case study and discussions

5.1 Research design

Case study research is used in this study considering the strength of its likelihood of generating novel theory and replicating or extending the emergent theory (Eisenhardt, 1989). A comprehensive case study on an apparel retailer, Firm A and its technology partner, Firm S has been conducted by exploring various aspects of the design and implementation of RFID-based lean services in Firm A's retail stores aimed at improving customer conversion based on CCOR process model. In this research, an embedded single case study using qualitative approach (Remenyi *et al.*, 1998; Sanders *et al.*, 2000; Yin, 2009) was adopted to explore the details about the acceptance of a novel system-driven lean service in the context of apparel retailing from design, implementation to result assessment. Special emphasis is placed on RFID application in realizing lean services for retail sales support operations by improving customer experience, operation efficiency and item availability. Semi-structured interviews are conducted in Firm A, including staffs and customers at the retail stores who involve in using the new services and staffs at the back-office who make related decisions and provide figures about customer conversion. In addition, informal observations are carried out on site where the researcher participated as staff member or customer. Triangulation is used in the study to improve validity (Yin, 2009). Therefore, the members of Firm A and technical support staffs in Firm S are also interviewed. The findings that concern the experience and expectation from end-users are compared and contrasted with the implementation experience of the developer so that conclusions and strategic implications can be realistically drawn from the case study.

5.2 Background

Prior implementing the new initiative, mix-and-match suggestions on clothing were provided to customers in an old fashion way through staff members on the sales floor based on their experience and/or designers' suggestions by either showing photos in the product catalogues or locating the matched products on racks. Moreover, management of items on the sales floor and inventory in the back-store were relied on bar-codes. Due to the constraint of bar-code technology, store operation was highly manual-based where the availability of staff was crucial as their full participation in the operation processes was required. In order to streamline the operation processes and improve customer experience, Firm S has come-up a RFID-enabled smart retail apparel system in collaboration with Firm A to support the lean service initiative. With the new system, customers are now provided with computerized recommendations on mix-and-match of clothing items with on-screened product information details, which offer a unique shopping experience ensemble to meet their buying needs instantaneously. In addition to the customer relationship enhancement functions, the system enhances shop management by improving the security and inventory management and minimizing shrinkage at the store.

5.3 Approach of developing innovative retail services

The approach of orchestrating the service innovation project by Firm S includes two dimensions: (a) *project deliverables,* regard creating innovative lean services, and (b) *project management,* regards managing the process of creating project deliverables in a controllable manner. Unlike project management, obtaining project deliverables requires understanding of the product markets and has no established rules to follow. Products of apparel retail typically have **short shelf-life**, in which the markets are characterized by: (1) *short lifecycle,* as the product is designed to capture the mood of moment and hence the saleable period is very short, (2) *high impulse purchase,* as the buying decisions for these products are mainly made at the point of purchase, and (3) *high volatility,* which is sensitive to *shrinkage* and *dwell time* of the inventory and ultimately influence the efficiency, operations visibility and total cost of the store operations (Christopher *et al.,* 2004). Besides, customers' perception on the sales dynamics such as service levels and operation efficiency, could also affect their purchase decision.

The approach depicted in **Figure 2** aims at improving the 'As-is' processes with most suitable management practice (e.g. lean thinking, six-sigma, or CCOR model). Based on lean thinking, various value creating activities can be identified as the basis of new services for addressing corresponding market characteristics, and the 'To-be' processes of new services are created by automating/streamlining with suitable enabling technology. In practice, the metric for measuring proposed customer refers to all transacting customers, while it refers to repeated customers (VIP) when measuring contract customer. The approach can be applied to not only tangible services, but also online services considering value creation as the goal.

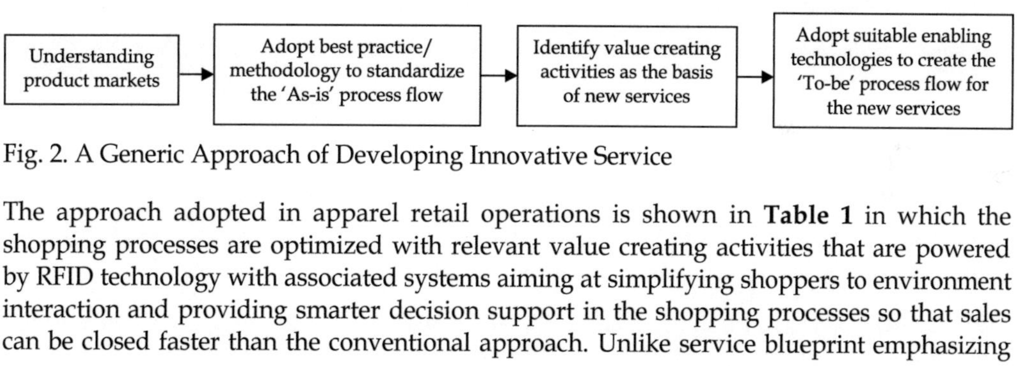

Fig. 2. A Generic Approach of Developing Innovative Service

The approach adopted in apparel retail operations is shown in **Table 1** in which the shopping processes are optimized with relevant value creating activities that are powered by RFID technology with associated systems aiming at simplifying shoppers to environment interaction and providing smarter decision support in the shopping processes so that sales can be closed faster than the conventional approach. Unlike service blueprint emphasizing

Shopping process	Value creating activities in new services	Market chars.	Enabling technologies for new services
Search and locate	Product catalog and inventory records	(3)	Clothing with RFID tags and clothing items with mix-and-match photos database for: (a) enhancing customer experience, and (b) improving operation efficiency and visibility
Dressing mirror	Mix-and-match suggestion on clothing	(1), (2)	
Fitting room	Mix-and-match suggestion on clothing	(1), (2)	
Checkout at POS	Automatic/contactless checkout process	(3)	Clothing with RFID tags and RFID-enabled ePOS application systems

Table 1. Identifying Value Creating Activities for Apparel Services

service delivery time reduction (Shostack, 1982;1984), lean apparel services are customer oriented which emphasize creating customer value through suggesting mix-and-match of clothing items in a smart (e.g. photo displayed in response to the detected RFID-tagged items) and agile (e.g. contactless and personalized services) way.

5.4 Adoption of lean services in apparel retail

Apparel retailers face the challenge of adapting quickly and frequently to keep up with product change and buying trend to meet customer needs. Lean services are introduced to better manage store operations in a more efficient manner as well as to bring customers with fresh new shopping experience so that the retailer will stay competitive in the markets through automating the customer touch points which are beneficial to both the customers and retailer. Based on the approach in **Figure 2**, a value stream map of the 'As-Is' processes is created where purchase orders are initiated to upstream suppliers based on customer purchase representing the ultimate business value and the retailer should maintain the value flow in the supply chain through improving customer conversion continuously. The approach is depicted in **Figure 3**.

Based on the CCOR model, value stream mapping of the in-store pre-sales activities was defined systematically through organizing the CCOR processes, i.e. '*relate*', '*sell*' and '*contract*' in the retail services operations so that value is created from the use of RFID-driven lean systems which improves customer conversion. Under these three CCOR process groups, lean services are developed based on the value creating activities shown in **Table 1**. **Table 2** illustrates the mapping of lean services and the operation processes from the perspective of CCOR, customer and retailer aimed at delivering target business value.

CCOR Process	Retailer Process	Customer Process	Lean Services and Systems	Values Contributed
Relate and sell	Remove product from shelf	Search and locate	Product catalogue and inventory management database	Locate product more quickly and accurately
			RFID-based article surveillance systems	Security control
	Mix-and-match suggestion	Dressing mirror	RFID-based dressing mirror systems	Enhance customer experience
		Fitting and changing	RFID-based smart fitting room systems	Enhance customer experience
Contract	Checkout and transaction automation	Payment	RFID-based point-of-sales systems	Automate the checkout process
			RFID-based article surveillance systems	Security control and alert

Table 2. Mapping of Processes and Lean Services with Intended Values

With far-field RFID technology, lean services are realized in the apparel stores through offering a variety of intelligent services that essentially extend the RFID application to the "last 50 feet" of apparel supply chains for improving the efficiency of store execution and in particular, sales-floor operations such as customer conversion and item management (Hardgrave and Miller, 2008; Heizer and Render, 2007; Magnusson, 2010; Russell and Taylor, 2009; Sarma, 2008). Providing suggestions on clothing mix-and-match is one of the new initiatives of lean services in apparel retail. Together with the following store management functions, interactions at the customer touch points in the retail operation can be improved with the expected values as detailed in **Table 2**.

- *Mix-and-match suggestions*: enhance customer experience, through providing suggestions personalized for VIP or registered customers based on their transaction history by discovering purchase patterns, i.e. estimating preferred choices through using data-mining technique or machine-learning algorithm. However, only standardized recommendations are offered to casual customers;

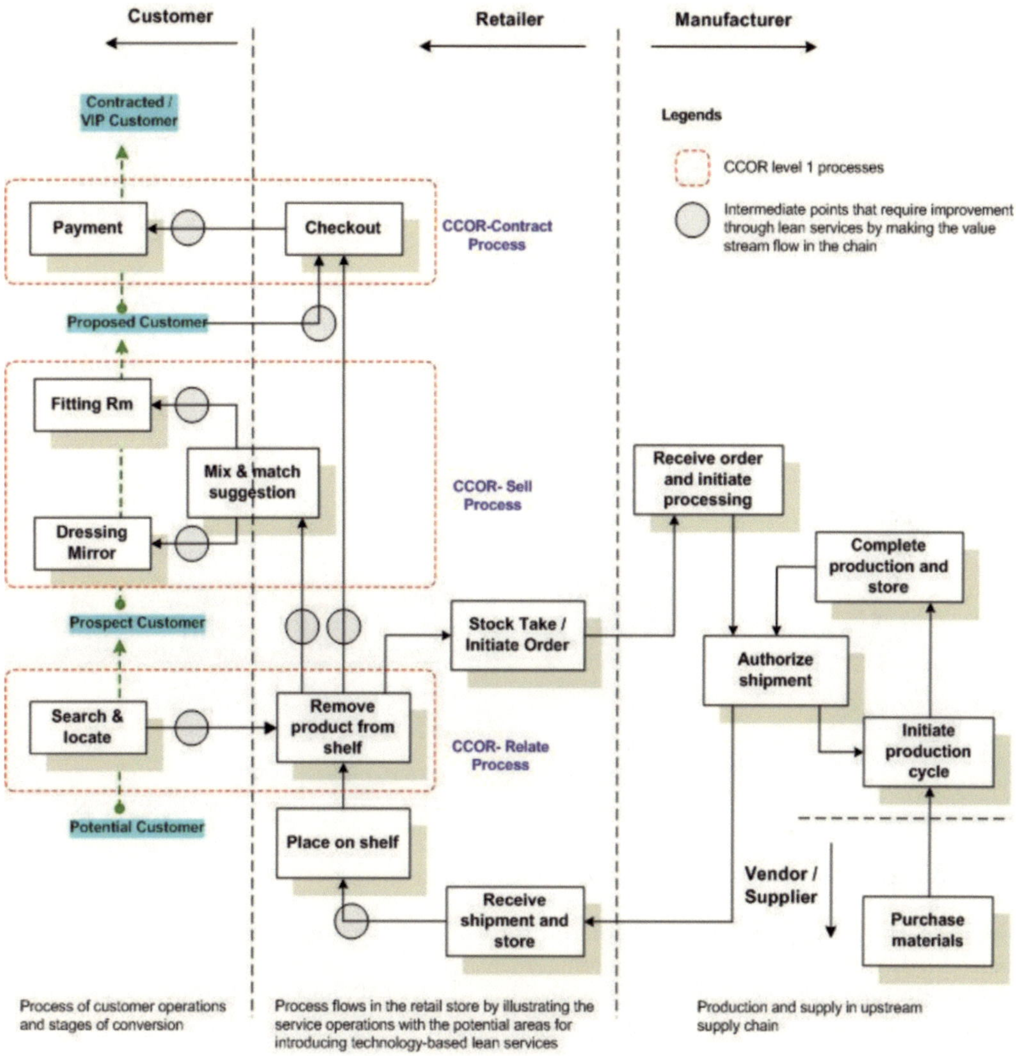

Fig. 3. 'As-is' Processes of Apparel Retail Service Operations

- *Product catalogue and inventory management*: enhance product visibility and improve search efficiency through tracking and tracing items automatically in the back-store and on the sales-floor;
- *Article surveillance*: brings *security control* capability by identifying and detecting items that are not check-out at the Point-of-sales (POS) locations, and
- *Transaction process automation*: includes the features like contactless check-out of items with bulk processing capability for improving POS process workflow and ultimately enhancing customer experience in which the contactless feature is not available in the conventional bar-code technology.

5.5 Lean service improvement with RFID-based apparel applications

The smart apparel retail system has a number of modules including *smart fitting room* and *smart dressing mirror* enabled with RFID technology with the promise to enhance shopping experience by offering responsive mix-and-match capability based on real-time analysis of customers' behavioral data stored in its database together with the implementation of essential shop management functions under a lean service environment in Firm A's retail stores. **Figure 4** shows the basic operations and flow of shopping process associated with the RFID-enabled smart fitting room and smart dressing mirror that were designed based on the process flow mapping in **Figure 3** and **Table 2**.

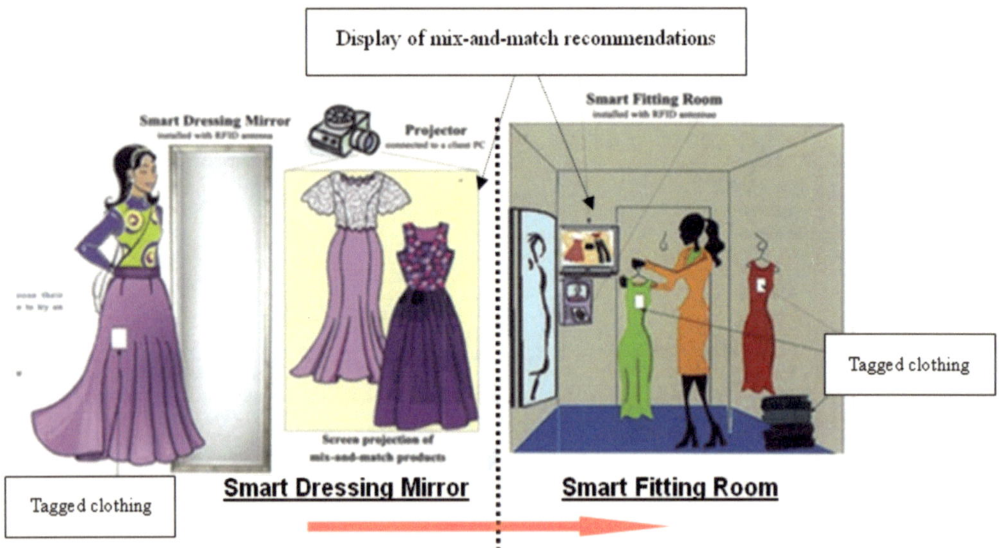

Fig. 4. Smart Fitting Room and Smart Dressing Mirror

Both smart dressing mirror and smart fitting room are equipped with RFID readers embedded with middleware and intelligent apparel application which respond to any tagged clothing item associated with registered product ID and can be further associated with relevant product data and photo image stored in the backend databases on the in-house networks. It is the design objective that *mix-and-match suggestions* are provided to customers in a faster and easier way than conventional human method. For arousing customer interest, smart dressing mirror is the first access point in fashion shop providing simple mix-and-match recommendations through image projection or high resolution TV display. When customer presents the tagged clothing items in front of the dressing mirror, the product images and mix-and-match image slide show of the products are displayed on the adjacent screen. Based on the suggestions, customer may proceed to smart fitting room equipped with a touch-screen display which has the capability of showing detail product information including product ID, price, color, size, and inventory status in an organized mean, while specific information such as VIP discount and preferred choices are customized for registered customers. **Figure 5** shows the screen displays of smart fitting room module. The product search flow is similar to smart dressing mirror previously accessed by the customer.

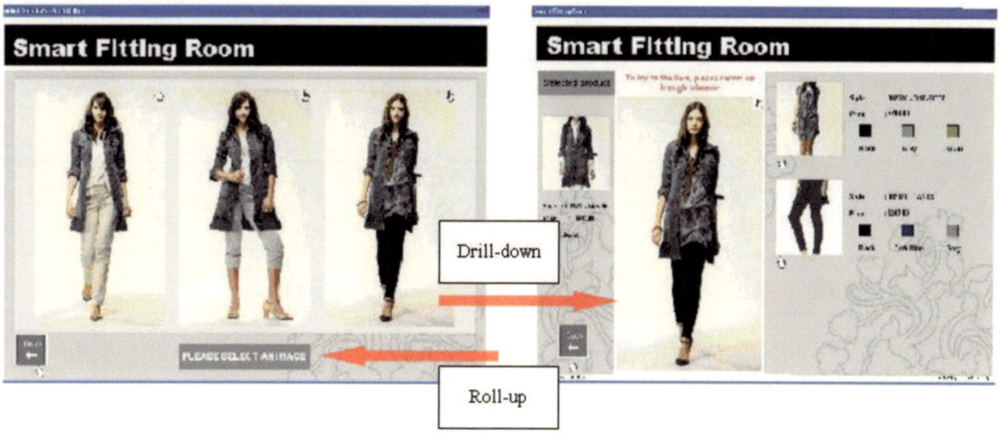

Fig. 5. Roll-up and Drill-down of Mix-and-match Suggestions

As shown in **Figure 5**, clothing items that are picked by customers are tracked and recorded by the smart apparel system with valuable "on-the-spot" business intelligent data associated with customer identity. With the new system, customers are able to resemble the style that they want to portray in a more autonomous manner and less relies on the staff on the sales-floor, not to mention unpacking clothing items for trial in virtually unlimited number of times, which is very inefficient and wasteful. Besides, retailers may gain instant access to the customer preferences and buying behavior captured in the shopping process, which enable them with the capability of offering personalized mix-and-match suggestions and formulating marketing strategies and business plans based on actual customer needs.

Lastly, the *electronic point-of-sales (ePOS)* module which is the last access point in the shopping process provides contactless check-out functions in the *inventory management* and *transaction processing* routines with the transaction records automatically updated in the database. Besides, the *article surveillance* module plays the role of gatekeeper by generating alert message to shop assistants via the ePOS if it detects any tagged item that is not properly check-out and the results are shown in **Figure 6**. The 'To-be' processes of lean services essentially collapse the manual tasks in the three process groups into different smart apparel system features delivered sequentially by the software for smart dressing mirror, smart fitting room, ePOS and article surveillance modules that are responsive to the

Fig. 6. Active Monitoring at ePOS and Display of Alert Message

detection of RFID-tagged clothing and human touches on the screen. The performance improvements in terms of customer conversion are summarized in **Table 3**, which indicates that the overall profitability has been significantly increased by more than twice after adopting the new approach.

Shopping process	CCOR process	Customer Conversion Rates (Based on the formula in Fig.1)	Before Implementation	After implementation
Search and locate	Relate	Prospective / Target market	48%	50%
Dressing mirror & Fitting Room	Sell	Proposed / Prospective	24%	38%
Checkout at ePOS	Contract	Contract / Proposed	57%	77%
		Overall profitability	**6.57%**	**14.63%**

Table 3. Customer Conversion Rates of Process Groups

5.6 Discussions and implications

The case study demonstrates the use of CCOR model that systematically creates the value stream of lean services for an apparel retailer based on a hierarchical process mapping method by walking through all the pre-sales activities happening on the retail shop floor (See **Figure 3**). The convergence of these two management systems was not explored in previous studies. Based on the interview results, the pre-defined values shown in **Table 2** based on the lean services objectives, help streamline the operation processes and enhance the customer experience on the service operations such that the bottom line and customer satisfaction of the retail sales are improved in two years' time which exceeds the management's expectation. As shown in **Table 3**, the number of contract customers is increased significantly by about 20% and contribute over 45% to the sales revenue in each year despite of the stringent competition. More importantly, the customer conversion rate is improved from about 6% to exceeding the market average, which is about 12% in apparel retailing (Conroy and Bearse, 2006). According to the retailer, casual customers, VIP customers and first-line staffs are all beneficial from the new initiatives with improved operational execution and decision-making assistance that lead to increased customer conversion rate by delivering a better customer experience.

The case study provides not only insights but also strategic implications to apparel retailers on realizing lean services with RFID technology. Both the merchant (Firm A) and its RFID supplier (Firm S) have to consider various practical issues in addition to merely look for obtaining business values when implementing the services that heavily rely on emerging technology. Hence, interview results obtained from the users in Firm A and staffs in Firm S are consolidated in association with the system functions and they are presented below:

- The strategic intent of offering *mix-and-match suggestions* based on visual effects and rich information is to close the sales faster than conventional approach. Addressing the complexity and security concerns of RFID technology is the key to success as the moment of truth can never be captured if customers do not actually use it. Based on the user feedbacks, there exist problems concerning *ease of use* and *data privacy* which should be resolved before launching the new technology.

- Improving the accuracy and efficiency of operations is the purpose of applying RFID technology to *product catalogue* and *inventory management*. Based on the user feedbacks, the new RFID application software need to be integrated with existing system and hence, product developer has to design and develop their RFID products compatible with major business applications in retail, for example, ePOS systems and ERP systems. Without proper compatibility with other retail business applications, the use of RFID technology could be limited. Besides, many ePOS systems have bundled with low cost bar-code reader as input device. RFID product suppliers may consider product integration through forming strategic alliance with ePOS vendors. Hence, *cost advantage* and *compatibility* are the critical success factors.
- Existing *electronic article surveillance* (EAS) devices based on magnetic technology are mature and competitive in prices. Although the apparel retailer expects the new RFID system to help save cost in the long term, the price of RFID-based EAS needs to be competitive in order to compete with existing technologies. Otherwise, the new product would be hard to survive alone. Alternatively, it can be sold in bundled with other products as a total solution before it comes to the end of product life cycle. Hence, *time to the market* and *cost advantage* are very important.

6. Conclusion

The study introduces an innovative RFID application that realizes lean thinking in the pre-sales service operations of an apparel retailer aimed at customer service excellence with improved customer conversion rate and greener operations. The study has made a contribution to practices by establishing a systematic approach in the creation of value stream for lean services with the use of CCOR model which has not been studied in previous research. Practitioners and researchers in the field of organizational improvement will systematically define the value stream of a retail firm and improve the services at customer touch points based on this approach. According to the retailer, various kinds of customer including prospective customers and contract/VIP customers are beneficial from this new initiative leading to an increasing customer conversion. However, in reality, getting new idea adopted, even if it has obvious advantages, is often very difficult which may take quite a lengthy period and may fail in the process of adoption (Rogers, 1995). Therefore, strategic implications of applying RFID technology to lean services are discussed with the purpose to alleviate the practical problems and user concerns so that lean services can deliver maximum value to apparel retailers. Four practical issues are identified based on the interview results: (i) *ease of use*, (ii) *data privacy*, (iii) *cost advantage*, (iv) *compatibility*, and (v) *time to the market*. Developers of lean services, RFID suppliers and apparel retailers need to take note on these issues when developing or acquiring the new services.

7. References

Aikens, C.H., 2011. *Quality inspired management: the key to sustainability*. NJ: Prentice Hall.

Auto-ID Center 2002. *Technology Guide*. US: Auto-ID Center, Massachusetts Institute of Technology.

Christopher, M., Lowson, B. and Peck, H., 2004. Fashion logistics and quick response. *In:* Fernie, J. and Sparks, L., eds. *Logistics and Retail Management – Insights into Current Practice and Trends from Leading Experts*. US: Kogan Page, 82-100.

Conroy, P. and Bearse, S., 2006. *The changing nature of retail: planting the seeds for sustainable growth - customer conversion*. US: Deliotte & Touche.

Doyle, S., 2004. Auto-ID technology in retail and its potential application in marketing. *Journal of Database Marketing & Customer Strategy Management*, 11 (3), 274-279.

Eisenhardt, K.M., 1989. Building theories from case study research. *Academy of Management Review*, 14 (4), 532-550.

EPC, 2004. *The EPCglobal Network™: Overview of Design, Benefits, & Security*. New Jersey: EPC Global Inc.

Finkenzeller, K., 2000. *RFID Handbook: Radio-Frequency Identification Fundamentals and Applications*. US: John Wiley & Sons.

George, M.L. and Wilson, S.A., 2004. *Conquering and complexity in your business: how Wal-Mart, Toyota, and other top companies are breaking through the ceiling on profits and growth*. NY: McGraw Hill.

Gupta, V., 2004. Why every government agency should embrace the lean process. US: *American Public Works Association Reporter*.

Hanna, J., 2007. *Bringing 'lean' principles to service industries*. US: Harvard Business School Working Knowledge.

Hardgrave, B.C. and Miller, R., 2008. RFID in the retail supply chain: issues and opportunities. *In*: Miles, S.B., Sarma, S.E. and Williams, J.R., eds. *RFID Technology and Applications*. NY: Cambridge University Press, 113-120.

Harrison, A. and Hoek, R.V., 2008. *Logistics management and strategy: competing through the supply chain*. UK: Pearson Education Limited.

Hawrylak, P.J., Mickle, M.H. and Cain, J.T., 2008. RFID Tags. *In*: Yan, L., Zhang, Y., Yang, L.T. and Ning, H., eds. *The Internet of Things*, (pp.1-32). USA: Taylor & Francis Group, Auerbach Publications.

Heizer, J. and Render, B., 2007. *Principles of operations management*. 7th ed. NJ: Pearson Education, Inc., Prentice Hall.

Hess, E., 2008. RFID Apps bring unique set of requirements [online]. Integrated Solutions. Available from: http://www.integratedsolutionsmag.com/ [Accessed 13 February 2009].

Husby, P.C. and Swartwood, D., 2009. *Fix your supply chain: how to create a sustainable lean improvement roadmap*. NY: Taylor & Francis.

IBM, 2003. *Applying Auto-ID to Reduce Losses Associated with Shrink*. US: Auto-ID Center, Massachusetts Institute of Technology.

King, P.L., 2009. *Lean for the process industries: dealing with complexity*. NY: Taylor & Francis.

Magnusson, L., 2010. DCOR & CCOR overview [online]. Supply Chain Council. Available from: http://archive.supply-chain.org/galleries/default-file/SCC%20EC06%20MAGNUSSON%20DCOR_CCOR.pdf [Accessed 31 May 2010].

Martin, J.W., 2010. *Measuring and Improving Performance: Information Technology Applications in Lean Systems*, Boca Raton, FL: Taylor & Francis.

Miller, D., 2005. Going lean in Healthcare. *In*: Innovation Series 2005. Cambridge, MA: Institute for Healthcare Improvement.

O'Connor, M.C., 2008. American apparel makes a bold fashion statement with RFID [online]. *In*: Roberti, M., Prince, P. and Linne, A., eds. *RFID journal*. Available from: http://www.rfidjournal.com/article/print/4018 [Accessed 13 February 2009].

Ohno, T., 1988. *Toyota production system*, Portland: Productivity Press.

Remenyi, D., Williams, B., Money, A., and Swartz, E., 1998. *Doing research in business and management*. London: SAGE Publications.

Roberti, M., 2004. *Wal-Mart begins RFID rollout* [online]. RFID Journal. Available from: http://www.rfidjournal.com/article/articleview/926/1/1/ [Accessed 22 March 2009].

Roberti, M., 2005. *EPC reduces out-of-stocks at Wal-Mart* [online]. RFID Journal. Available from: http://www.rfidjournal.com/article/articleview/1927/1/1/ [Accessed 20 July 2009].

Roberti, M., 2007. *Wal-Mart, suppliers affirm RFID benefits* [online]. RFID Journal. Available from: http://www.rfidjournal.com/article/articleview/3059/1/1/ [Accessed 20 July 2009].

Rogers, E.M., 1995. *Diffusion of Innovation*, NY: Free Press.

Russell, R.S. and Taylor, B.W., 2009. *Operations management: creating value along the supply chain*. 6th ed. NJ: John Wiley & Sons, Inc.

Saegusa, T., 2010. SCOR and beyond: case studies in implementation and new practices for transformation [online]. Japan Business Create Co., Ltd. Available from: http://www.jbc-con.co.jp/seminar/pdf/E080317.pdf [Accessed 04 June 2010].

Sarma, S., 2008. RFID technology and its applications. *In*: Miles, S.B., Sarma, S.E. and Williams, J.R., eds. *RFID technology and applications*. NY: Cambridge University Press, 16-32.

SCC, 2010a. Customer chain [online]. Supply Chain Council. Available from: http://supply-chain.org/ccor [Accessed 04 June 2010].

SCC, 2010b. CCOR WG action report [online]. Supply Chain Council. Available from: http://www.supply-chain.gr.jp/download/scor_wg/2008/4_CCOR/action_report.pdf [Accessed 04 June 2010].

Shostack, L.G., 1982. How to design a service. *European Journal of Marketing*, 16(1), 49-63.

Shostack, L.G., 1984. Design services that deliver. *Harvard Business Review*, 62(1), 133-139.

So, S. and Liu, J., 2007. Learning from failure: a case study of adopting radio frequency identification technology in library services. *International Journal of Technology Intelligence and Planning*, 3 (1), 75-95.

So, S. and Sun, H., 2010. Creating ambient intelligent space in downstream apparel supply chain with radio frequency identification technology from lean services perspective. *International Journal of Services Sciences*, 3 (2/3), 133-157.

Swank, C.K., 2003. The lean service machine. *Harvard Business Review*, 81(10), 123–129.

UN, 2003. *United Nations guidelines for consumer protection*, NY: United Nations.

UN, 2011. Marrakech Process - SCP Issues for Business and Industry [online]. United Nations. Available from: http://esa.un.org/marrakechprocess/ [Accessed 11 October 2011]

Ustundag, A. and Tanyas, M., 2009. The impacts of radio frequency identification (RFID) technology on supply chain costs. *Transportation Research Part E*, 45 (1), 29-38.

VeriSign, 2004. *The EPC Network: Enhancing the Supply Chain*. US: VeriSign Inc.

Voehl, F. and Elshennawy, A., 2010. Lean service. *In*: Salvendy, G. and Karwowski, W., eds. *Introduction to service engineering*. NJ: John Wiley & Sons, Inc.

Wasserman, E., 2006. *RFID is in fashion* [online]. *RFID Journal*. Available from: http://www.rfidjournal.com/article/print/2408, [Assessed 13 February 2009].

Womack, J.P. and Jones, D.T., 2003. *Lean thinking: banish waste and create wealth in your corporation*, NY: Free Press.

Womack, J.P., Jones, D.T., and Roos, D., 1991. *The Machine That Changed the World*. NY: Harper Collins.

Yin, R.K., 2009. *Case study research: design and methods*. 4the ed. London: SAGE Publications.

9

Reorganization of Existing Business-Information Model in Purpose to Improvement Production Process

Zoran Nježić and Vladimir Šimović
The Faculty of Teacher Education,
Croatia

1. Introduction

Production processes supported by IT systems, improve the organizational structure of production with better insight into all aspects of production; and provide planning, monitoring and managing with all phases of production flows. The goal of this work is to investigate the current state of the production environment (working people, manufacturing resources, the material used ...) and suggest the information models which will improve the existing state.

The results of simulation experiments locate the congestion and bottlenecks of production, suggest and provide guidance for further development of complex information flows of production. Furthermore, that structure refers to the creation the production of feedback information generated in the actual environment, and thus become the correction factor to the production-entry zone.

It is assumed that within the information systems except than finished products that require a small number of business operations and phases, can be processed and inquiries about the complex finished products (where have lot of different production operations and materials needed to obtain the finished product). To make such a production cycle to be effective, it's requires a minimum level of knowledge about the creation and manufacture products by the external client that defines the query, because it is based on the confirmed offer runs a complex manufacturing process of projecting and managing of production flow to produce the ordered product. In this report wants to give the proposal a few information models that will automate and simplify making of business documents in order to reduce the time required for their production.

2. Conditions of construction of information-production structure

In current situation is also included set up information organization which is fundament for the further upgrading and updating with new information flows. By this, it's includes the definition of flow for automated creation of production business documents; for both internal and external business correspondence. Furthermore, with advanced production - business information systems with a high degree of automation it's allows the generation of complete documents or records (eg, queries, quotes, job orders, production reports ...) according to external inquiries by clients through the web interface.

With that is necessary and a minimum level of knowledge about the project layout and manufacture products by the external client that defines the query, because on the confirmed offer runs a complex manufacturing process of projecting and managing the production flow of the final product. It is also proposed to implement the subsystem for feedback production information which can have affect on the input values for the appointing calculations of the finished product. Through this subsystem it made a correction of the set current value to getting a new planning and calculation production parts. Implementation mechanism of the efficiency of production it can expect a significant influence on getting quick and accurate financial and statistical status of resources to additionally contribute to the management and establishing the development direction of organizational structure.

3. Basic Information model

In the first phase of building a information system there is only one database, which includes limited minimal elements for projecting and planning of production processes. Figure 1 shows the initial phase of information system under which they achieved the minimum requirements of the functioning of the productive structure (cost of materials and production resources). Under financial and material-financial system is provided capturing all input materials, articles, finished half products with the corresponding cost and the manufacturing specifications for the finished product. It's also included the creation offer to customer basic on the elements and inquiries through the making production calculations.

Through such a basic system the time required to produce a final offer request conditional on the complexity of the finished product. Increasing the number of necessary operations and different materials to produce the finished product is conditioned by the increase in working time required to produce final offer. From this existing base model is created order, work order for production, and complete final activities at the finished work order (post calculation estimates, billing and complete material and financial reports).

On daily bases production comes to the greatest congestion in the preparation of project offer and daily reporting about actual production activities; financial and results about the production efficiency. Increased number of inquiries on a daily basis requires significant expenditure of time working people for their preparation, and with that it's open space for the introduction of additional information subsystem for the automated preparation of production calculations. Except the final offer, from this subsystem is also expected to give automated the time listing of all production stages and production operation, and complete listing of all materials which is a implement in final product.

From this record will be created an orders for the necessary materials and any additional external manufacturing operations that cannot be realized in own production structure. From the manufacturing subsystems is created a work order which becomes the final document; which included all information about projecting and making final products with all operations and materials at each production stage.

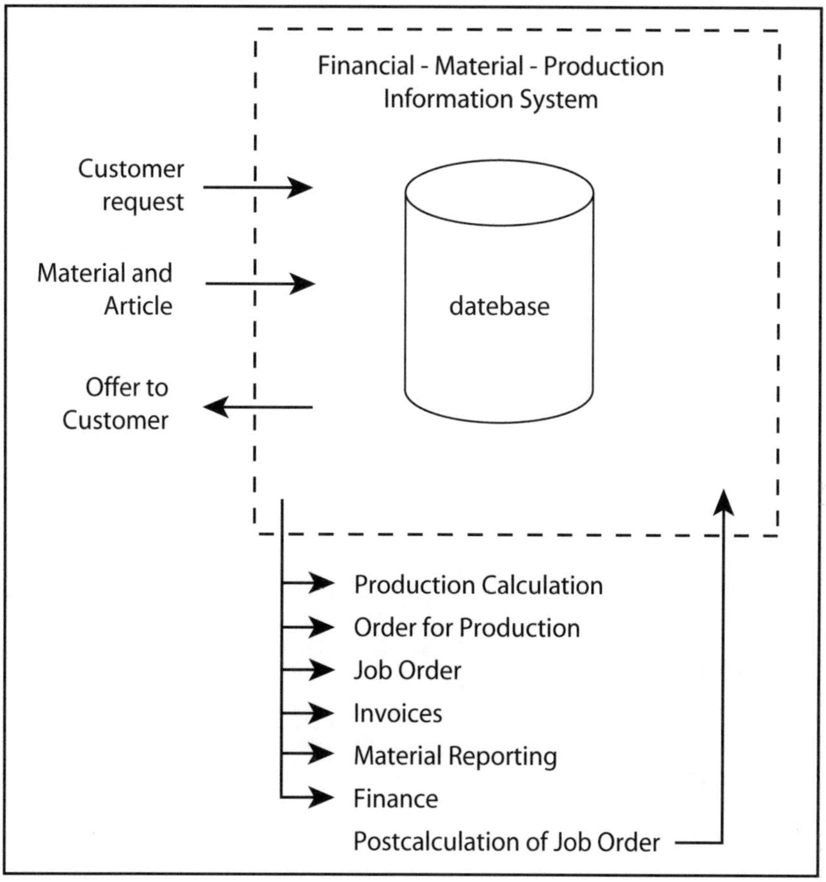

Fig. 1. Basic information - production model

4. Model of integrating between various information systems

In introducing the information subsystem for developing an automatic calculation part, more time becomes available for persons working in the production sector which can then be used for improving the quality and additional production control. Figure 2 presents an organizational scheme with an automation and calculation part which was expanded from the subsystem base.

A new, expanded organizational production scheme was obtained based on two different information systems - financial-material (serves for a complete financial part which includes prices of material, production activities and resources, creation of all business documents and reports) and production (development of working versions of tenders, complete production planning, time and status reports of individual activities - work orders).

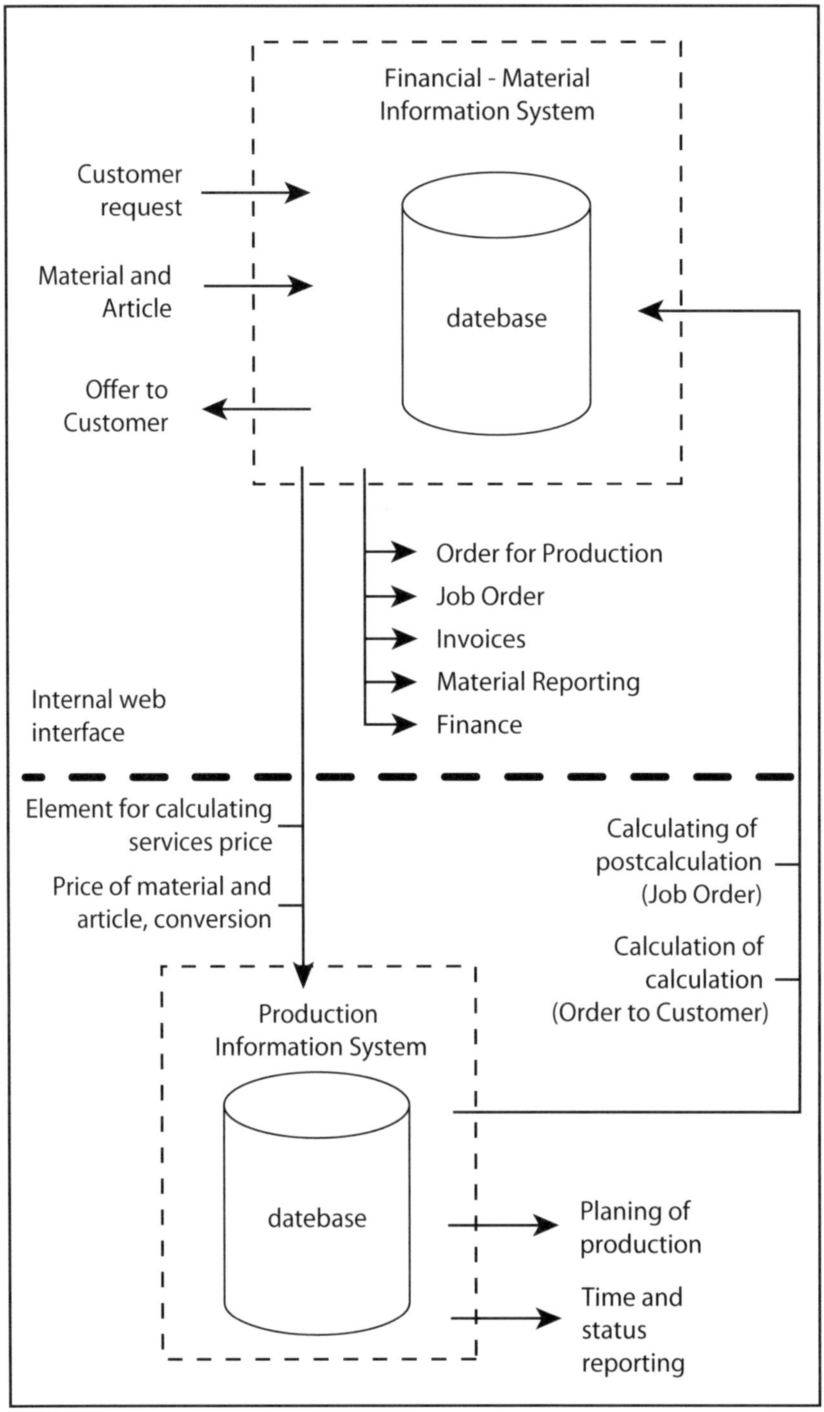

Fig. 2. Integration between different information systems

The integration part which links the two information systems communicates by transferring information for production, i.e. current prices of materials, articles, resources as well as the appropriate conversion of necessary elements for the production cycle. The integrated interface enables the transfer of necessary information for the production calculation considering that in such a scheme those elements are entered through the financial-material sector integrated in an appropriate information system.

From the production part, the final project yields a final calculation of the work order and the results are sent for finalization into the financial-material system. In the construction of a model presented in Figure 2 requests by the production organization itself had to be taken into consideration. They refer to the transition period of training workers in other sectors. Training refers to acquisition of knowledge which defines the final product in the maximal capacities of the organization itself, and expanded with other elements that can be upgraded to the existing product.

Considering that such knowledge is broad and concrete it is inevitable that a significant amount of time for their acquisition is necessary as well as for their actual application. The period of training can last for several years because of the work activities which are present on a daily basis, and the existing information structure which has to be in place.

In comparison with the basic model, production planning, time and status reports were introduced. This includes a variable digital display of the load of all production resources through a varied period of time; from daily to weekly planning using an automatic system of confirming an offer as an order. The internal web interface transfers the automatic calculations according to clients' requests through the financial-material information system. In that way the existing communication between the client and production organization is maintained. Completed post calculations are also transferred according to the financial system for the final processing of the work order.

Further enhancement in the restructuring of the existing links and appropriate activities which can accelerate communication with the external client and communication within the organization itself is shown in the model in Figure 2. Figure 3 represents a significant reorganization primarily through communicative activities with external clients which take place directly through the production system. In order for the presented model to become active in the organization it is necessary to carry out a reorganization of work activities and knowledge of people participating in the production process. This is evident in positions in the production structure from which the final offer emerges.

In the previous model (Figure 2) the final document is generated in the financial-material system to which the entire calculation part for the ordered product is transferred. This leaves the possibility for correcting the suggested price (adding workers or changing the amount of particular material for the production itself) of the production system.

However, such a possibility has to exist in the production system itself. The suggested model in Figure 3 clearly shows the reorganization of links in positions of creating orders and work orders for the purpose of reducing the time necessary for their development and in reducing possible mistakes in transferring between two information systems.

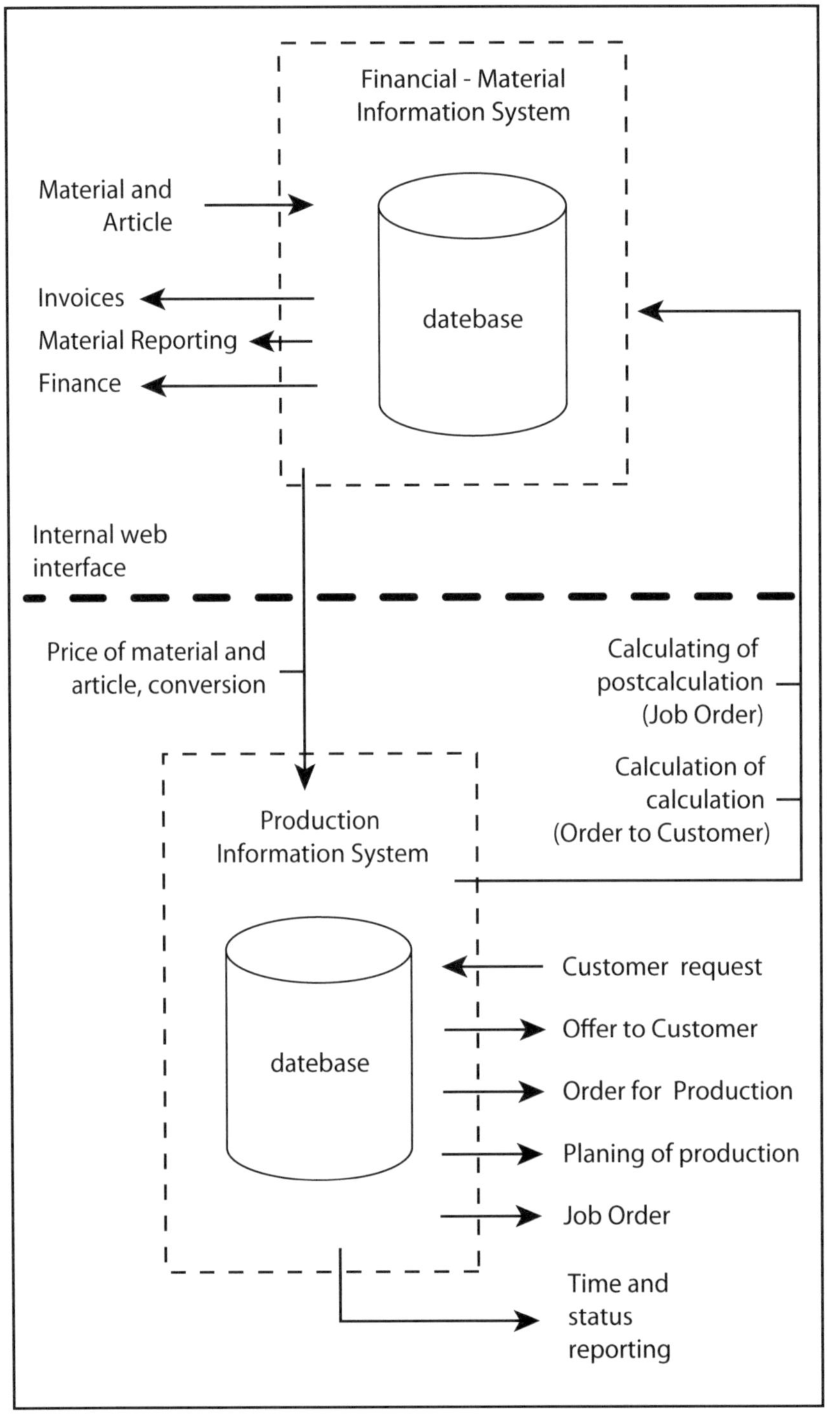

Fig. 3. Extended integration between different information systems

4.1 Analysis of the complex financial-production information model

The advanced way offers possibilities of direct - automatic communication in the client-production communication through which the calculations are generated as valid business documents. At that level, the client must take responsibility of correctly defining elements for the finished product (e.g. through a web interface), since based on those specification an automatic project for the finished product is created. An offer is generated based on the confirmed order and work order as well as complete production planning of resources.

Having such a system enables the client to see and monitor all the production processes defined. Information systems without such options of "openness" towards clients (independent work specification and product monitoring) are extremely complex and demanding, and their implementation is possible only in rare systems which already have and existing automatic structure of the Figure 3 type.

Only organizations like that can expect an increased number of orders and work orders which opens an area for further quality investment into production resources and training of people who can manage such complex production structures. Figure 4 presents a highly computerized production model in which the interaction of the system with the external client is minimal. This enables rapid information searches which will manage further business activities on the client's side. Such a model enables independent creation and change of desired input parameters by the client with immediate results for the desired inquiry.

Such an advanced business organizational model yields extra work time which can be further directed to planning, development and control of the final product for the purpose of obtaining a more quality and more competitive product. This also leads to room for creating new products whose construction is based on the existing base by extending it to new production resources. By expanding the production capacity and resources there is a possibility for selecting different production directions in order to obtain a cheaper yet high quality product as well as obtaining a sequence of cost-effectiveness of various technological production flows.

With the existence of a module for planning and monitoring production it is possible to visually control the suggested processes and resource occupancy, and thuds influence their change and reorganization (automatic re-calculation for the resources of necessary time and people). In such a way production management becomes simpler, controlled and transparent making the time for locating production congestion and delay almost minimal.

5. Information models support by feedback production information

To make the information system was more comprehensive and effective; it is further proposed the implementation of subsystems for feedback generating information that can further affect the input values for the appointing calculation of the finished product. Through this subsystem performs the correction of the set current value, which affects the gain of the new planning and calculation production parts. Permanent changes in factors

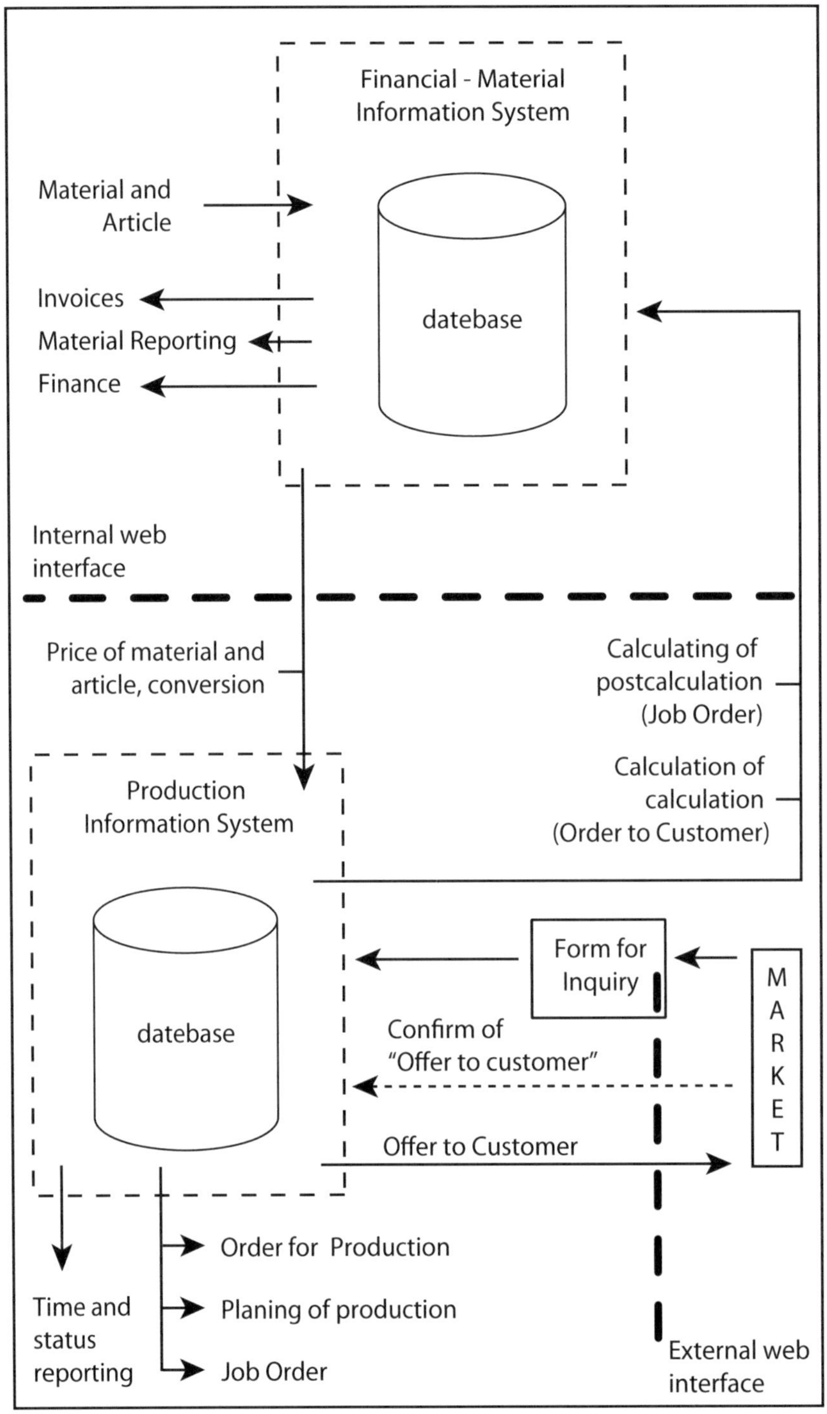

Fig. 4. Complex integration between different systems with web interface to market

that influence on overall calculation of the final product determines introduction of mechanisms which will be based upon on actual changes in the elements for calculating production costs. Except a fixed set of elements (cost articles, semi products, materials, resources, amortization costs) are important factor is set working hours for all manufacturing operations in the development of the final product. How is the final product complex, in its production is related to several dozens of different operations. This is precisely the space within which occurs a continuous change, and it is necessary to introduce mechanisms that will be registered this time changes, and based on these corrected set of input values. Implementing additional mechanisms affect the efficiency of production to obtain more accurate production time for each working phase, and thus financial - statistical state of resources for stable production lines and establishing new directions of development of the organizational structure.

5.1 Improving production capacity with production information feedback

Susceptibility to constant change of elements which influence the calculation of the final product calls for the introduction of a mechanism on which real changes of factors for the calculation of production costs will be based. In addition to set elements (article price, work in process, materials, resources, cost depreciation) the set working times for all production operations in the finalization process have an important role. Since the final product is complex, its production is related with dozens of different operations. This is the area within which constant changes occur and where it is necessary to introduce mechanisms which will record such time changes based on which it will correct set input values. The result of that is the new corrected calculation which represents the actual state of the production resources in a particular structure. Figure 5 shows the model of production flow organization which can collect actual production information for correcting the set values.

In an ideal structure, automatic tools for selecting, analysis and transfer if information into the basis can be implemented, however the lack of such tools is evident in the resources for developing such complex operations (several different mechanical activities), which is why the production line is sometimes interrupted. It is on such resources that the embedding of tools based on manual duration production activities by workers involved in the production process is anticipated. In combining automatic and manual tools at the level of the entire production, all necessary production information can be obtained (real time, delays, problems) which significantly increase the existing structure. Furthermore, such tools can be used in status reports of each work order through the model of monitoring the production flow for each product. In such a way the production flow becomes transparent and monitoring becomes visible through planning models and the organization of production processes.

The model in Figure 5 encompasses the production environment within which the system for gathering production information is implemented. Setting up such a system demands considerable investment and taking responsibility of all participants in production operations by being independently engaged and in controlling for improving the quality of the final product.

Depending on the content of the work order is defined workflow and sequence of individual operations on the resource for making the product. Depending upon the operating times of individual phases is calculated the time occupancy of resources, and its planned occupancy of on a daily (short term) and over daily (long term) basis. This means

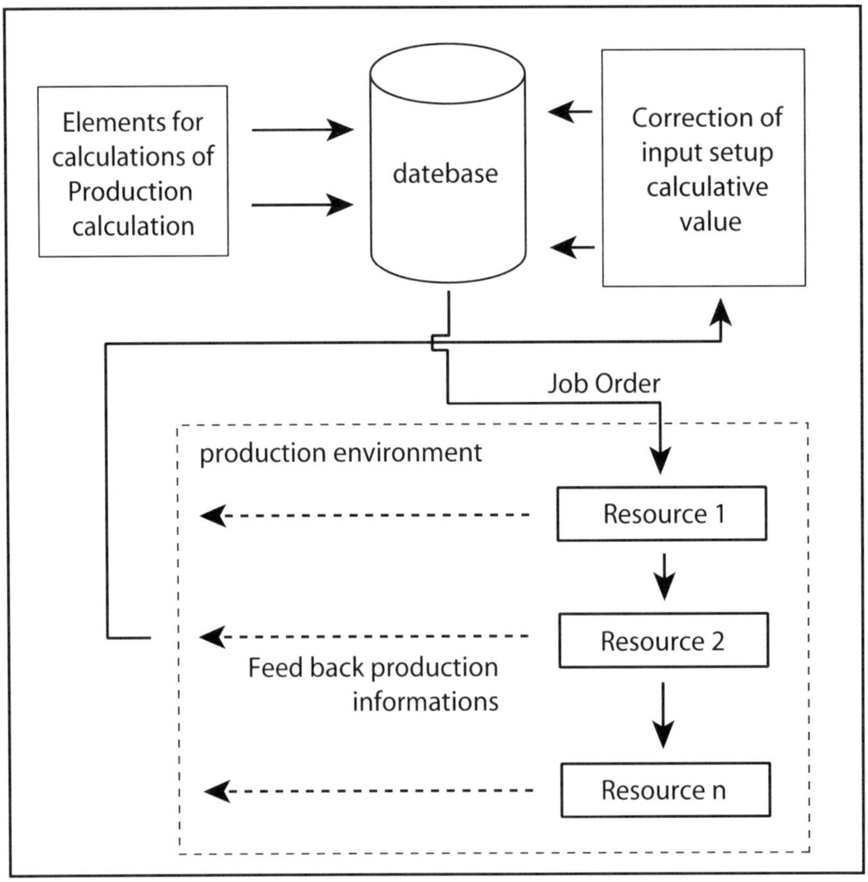

Fig. 5. Model of feedback production information

that the same work order to occupy a different time-workload of particular resources after entering corrective factors received with backward connections. It wills also feedback production information will impact on change workflows in manufacturing the product in terms of seeking alternative and profitable work processes. With that comes to correcting the total cost of production, and thus to more competitive on the market.

In such a model, the input for calculating the production of the final product can be done by the external client (Figure 4) or internally by the person in charge within the organization (Figure 1, 2, or 3). Further creation of business documents is automatically generated based of the entered production elements.

6. Simulation experiment of production processes

Simulating the manufacturing processes and business activities with corresponding resources, the goal is locating the congestion and bottlenecks with the proposal and reference to the solutions that to optimize production flows. Furthermore, the simulation of production is expected to set up connections that define the production cycle with effective results in terms of competitive price and quality ratio of finished product. Also, simulation of production flows suggests to new proposals and solutions for improving, standardizing, managing and planning process through support of information systems. Results of the simulation research is expected to obtain the order of cost effectiveness individual resources, and make the necessary investment to renew (extend or reduce) the productive capacity of the organization.

According to the presented organizational models an IT system was constructed which experimentally correlated production resources, materials, work time, supporting production activities and appropriate financial values. Production processes encompass necessary materials and logs which define particular production orders, and new production resources which expand the existing organizational structure. At the end of the production process there is always a new product, show on Figure 6.

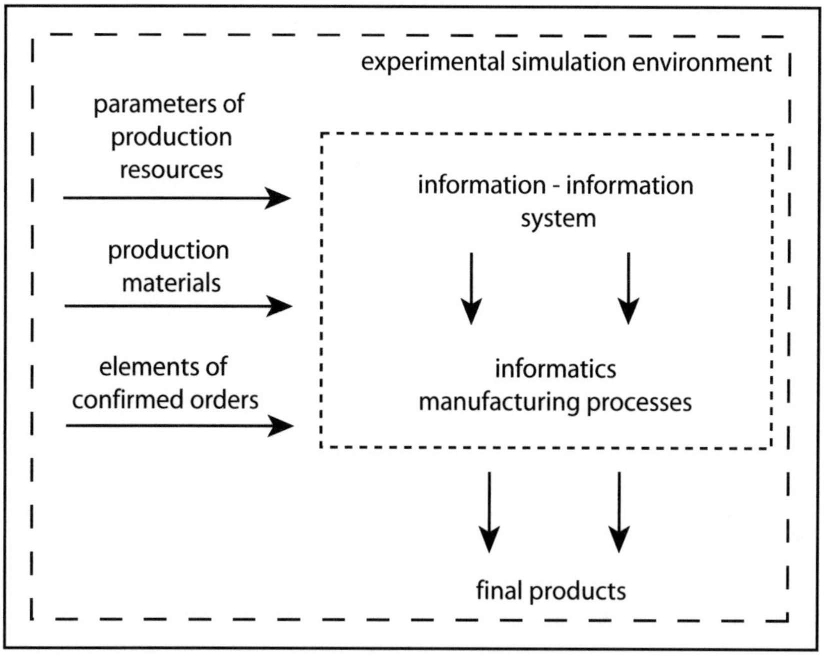

Fig. 6. Model of experimental simulation process

In information defined resources are installed a real properties of production, and is set informatics description of the working environment within which the simulation was tested. Research has focused on projecting of virtual manufacturing of components with all parameters and defined the production norms. The results of simulations of production contribute to the establishment of new ways to manage the existing work processes, and upgrading on overall planning of the production cycle. This tends to find a stable production plan, which is characterized by flow without delay from one side, and on the other side the financial profitability and competitiveness in the total price of the product. With simulation is also possible a planning and designing the working environment which is actual realization is predicted in future for a particular time period. With this approach it influence on opening and planning of new workplaces, on new organizational structures, and to increase the level of knowledge for managing production. Applying such approach allows the predictions of new work structures without causing damage and material costs.

The goal is to automated generating production flows for a new product with a focus in finding the most profitable working operations and corresponding resources. Studying the bottlenecks of production requires the collection of accurate data about all production components, working people and materials from real production conditions. This allows the finding of extreme risk situations and the maximum production capability of the entire work environment, and therefore projecting a coordinated set of production elements in production.

For a successful simulation of production processes it is necessary to establish correct and realistic elements which make up the entire production flow. Through the simulation method, new ways to maximum production capabilities, improvement, upgrading and planning processes, and thus highly risky situation are placed in a controlled production framework. One information-simulation system tested at variable changes production amounts of 1000, 5000, 25000, 100000, 50000, 1000000 and 200000 items. By simulation of the production flow, the financial change of the total costs of a particular financial amount on value of the materials used wanted to be established.

quantity	total cost [finance value]	material cost [finance value]	ratio of total production cost and cost of material
1000	9149	3489	0.3814
5000	22235	9921	0.4462
25000	83615	42078	0.5032
100000	317541	162677	0.5123
500000	1565364	805857	0.5148
1000000	3125113	1609831	0.5151
2000000	6244662	3217779	0.5153

Table 1. Result of simulation testing

The results obtained through simulation testing can establish the relationship of the total work of the production resources with the appropriate work activities and on the other hand with the necessary raw materials for obtaining a finished product. It is expected that the results obtained will yield new production processes which can be influenced in a sense of improving and optimizing the production flow. Furthermore, simulation and assessment of products in a product cycle elements which demand change of existing value standards can be located. Such standards can cover appropriate completion time of particular operations, financial values allocated to a particular resource or through necessary number of work activities on a particular resource. The aim was to investigate to what extent, how and in which time come up significant difference in the change ratio of the value of the material in the production process with a total production value of the product.

Table 1 shows the results of simulation experiments with different quantities of products in production, and the total value of the product, the share prices of materials and ratio of price change for individual quantity.

Experimentally, a different number of completed products in a series were tested (series of 1000, 5000, 25000, 100000, 50000, 1000000 and 200000 products), in order to find the proportion of change of financial value of the total costs and material costs of each series. Total costs include all production activities which describe the production of a product:

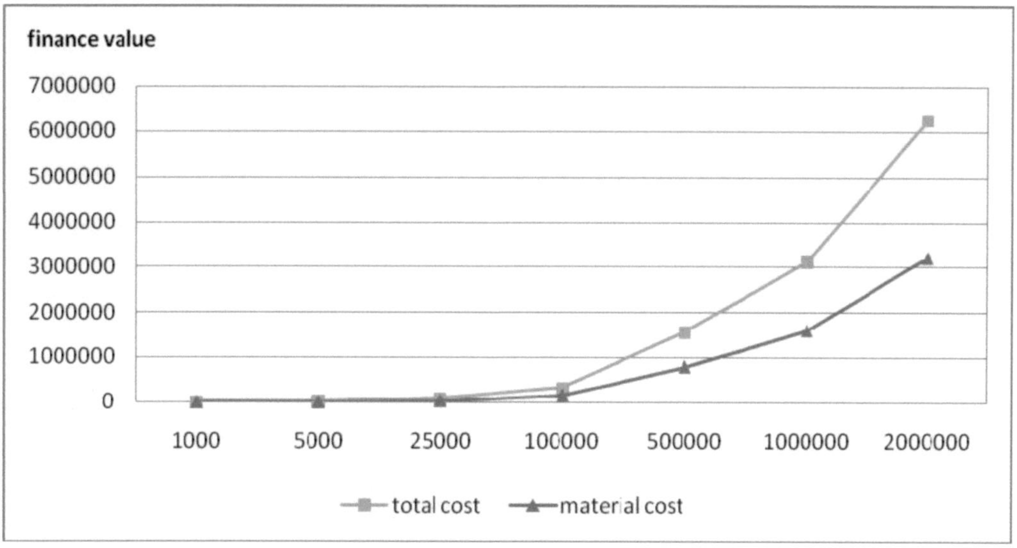

Fig. 7. Changes of finance value on different qualtity

price of working resource and appropriate activities, price of production operations, necessary materials in the production process. In simulating changes of prices for the appropriate series, the proportion of change by which the accuracy and control of cost of the production process of a product can be anticipated.

Figure 7 indicates changes in financial value of a particular series for the entire production costs and materials costs in the production process. From the data obtained, it can be concluded that with the increase in the number of articles in a series there is a higher proportion of total costs and material costs, taking into consideration that the proportion was stabilized in the last series where there was the largest number of products. On the production series of 1000 unit total value of production without the cost of materials amounted to 61.86% of the total cost, on a series of 5000 pieces was 55.38%, for 25000 units was 49.68%, of 100000 pieces is 48.77% for 500000 was 48.52%, for 1 million amounted to 48.49%, and for 2 million has measured 48.47%. It may be noted that the biggest difference between the total cost of production and the share price of materials was up to the quantity of 25000 units, and then there was a stabilization and slight decrease in the ratio.

Figure 8 presents a curve indicating changes in the proportion of total production costs and costs of materials for all experimental series. According to the model and the results it can be concluded and predict that it will further increase production quantities to maintain the current ratio, with a slight change in the share prices of materials in total cost of production. Only in production to 25000 units was recorded considerable changes in the ratio of total production and share materials, and it is area for new further research to develop a new product. It is possible to use the suggested model as a control mechanism in production processes which encompass relating the group of products. At the level of production organization it would be necessary to design models for each group of specific productions in appropriate series for obtaining proportions as control value mechanisms.

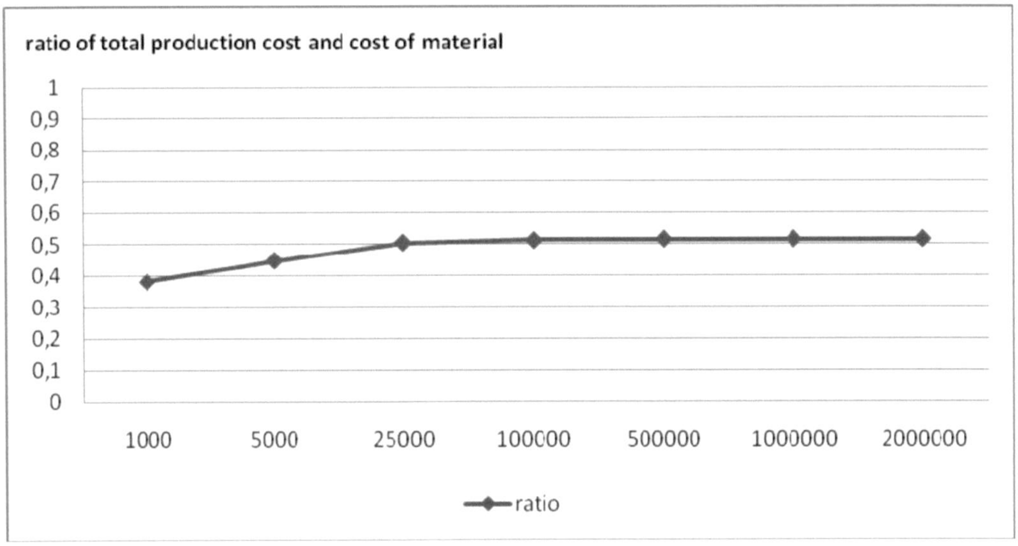

Fig. 8. Change of ratio of total production and cost of material

Analyzing the obtained results, it can be concluded that the total cost of materials on small quantities of one thousand pieces has a smaller share in total price of the product (38.14%), and increasing the amount of two million pieces of material share price increases (51.53%). It's determined that the share prices of materials in the total costs of production has stabilized on quantity of 100000 pieces at 51.23%, for 500000 pieces on 51.48%, and for one million on 51.51%. It also imposes the conclusion that in production of large quantities at one moment comes to stabilizing the ratio of materials cost and total production costs. The moment in which will be stabilized this ratio also depends on the necessary replacement components required in production, or about possible terms of delivery; which condition the additional production capacity. That change of terms of delivery determines the activation of additional production resources, either from its own structure, or from external sources. Compliance the defined terms of planning on the individual resources and departments inside the production structure is one of the main elements of stability in production process.

Further research should be based on the use of new materials and currently available information - production technology. It is also possible that some new materials with good quality characteristics do not satisfied requirements of the market in high production quantities, but in a small zone of production be acceptable. It is also one of the main directions of development of digital - information productions, making a complex and unique products in the minimum quantity (even 1 product) whose realization is fully automated. This includes an acceptable competitive price of finished product.

7. Conclusion

The suggestion for further development of Figure 4 opens up an area for introducing complex mechanisms for reporting on production flows, where the dependency of external inquiries on actually confirmed production offers has to be research, in search for reasons unacceptable on the side of the client. It is also suggested that internal tools be introduced which will construct the inquiry and based on them certain conclusions can be made for new strategic decisions. This opens up a new area for improving production, introducing the system of real simulation of workers according to the effort and productivity in the organization. The system of analysis, comparison and monitoring has to be based on set and realistic values in both information systems, and the results obtained are expected to open new areas for investments.

Such a mechanism demands immediate interaction between users through a web interface with desired time periods and loads in needed resources and workers, comparative prices of production calculations with the post-calculation part, total inquiry calculation, accepted offers, visual representation and numerical values. The results influence daily business decision-making as well as strategic directions in improving the business system. The implementation of such a tool on the existing information structure is possible at the level of the basic model shown in Figure 1, but since such a system does not have qualitative quantitative information from the production of a product itself, adequate conclusions on the production flow is not possible. A concrete application of the suggested mechanism in its full use would be through the model described in Figure 2 where independent inquiries can be placed either to the financial or production system, and can be most outright with targeted inquiries through the integration of both system of the production structure.

8. Acknowledgment

The process of developing complex information structure through the suggested scheme is based on organization structures and resources with high ICT standards. As the existing structure developed, the relationships became more complex and the level of applied knowledge for its maintenance became higher. The last of the suggested models on Figure 4 presents a self-learning structure. Its maintenance requires current knowledge which is constantly subject to further upgrade and change. In that respect the likelihood of survival of structures based on informatics descriptions of production processes is the greatest as is the modification of existing capacities for developing new products based on market demands.

9. References

Nježić, Z. (2011). Prijedlog razrade informacijske strukture grafičkog proizvoda sa normiranjem osnovnih grafičkih procesa, *Zbornik radova Drugoga međunarodnog naučno-stručnog simpozija grafičke tehnologije i dizajna*, ISSN 2232-8831, Kiseljak, Bosna i Hercegovina, 2011

Nježić, Z.; Šimović, V. & Kosić, T. (2009). Projecting of Information System to improve Production Processes, *PRE-CONFERENCE PROCEEDINGS of the Special Focus Symposium on 8th ICESKS: Information, Communication and Economic Sciences in the Knowledge Society*, ISBN 978-953-7210-22-9, Zadar, Croatia, 2009

Nježić, Z.; Šimović, V. & Maletić, F. (2009). Managing IT Systems in a Production Environment, *Proceedings of the 8th WSEAS International Conference on Education and Educational Technology (EDU '09)*, ISSN 1790-5109, Genova, Italy, 2009

Nježić, Z.; Žiljak, V. & Babić, D. (2005). Implementation of Simulative Methods Into Printing Process, *Annals of DAAAM for 2005. & Proceedings of the 16th International DAAAM Symposium Intelligent Manufacturing & Automation*, ISSN 1726-9679, Opatija, Croatia, 2005

Nježić, Z.; Žiljak, V. & Šimović, V. (2006). Virtual Model of Basic Graphic Process, *The 18th International Conference on Systems Research, Informatics and Cybernetics*, ISBN 953-99326-4-5, Baden-Baden, Germany, 2006

Nježić, Z.; Žiljak, V. ; Pap, K. & Sviličić, B. (2003). The stohastic model of simulation of a virtual printing-house, *Advances in printing Science and Technology*, ISBN 953-9676-8-0, Zagreb, Croatia, 2003

Žiljak, V.; Šimović, V. & Pap, K. (2004). Entrepreneurship model: Printing processes simulation with times and prices in the base for normative provisions, *16th International Conference on Systems Research, Informatics and Cybernetics*, ISBN 953-99326-1-0, Baden-Baden, Germany, 2004

Section 3

Emerging Informatics in Railways

10

Digital Railway System

Shi Tianyun et al.*
*Institute of Computing Technologies,
China Academy of Railway Sciences, Beijing,
China*

1. Introduction

1.1 General framework of digital railway system

1.1.1 Construction background of digital railway system

Digital Earth [1] refers to the concept proposed by former US vice president Al Gore in 1998, which is described as a virtual representation of the Earth that is spatially referenced and interconnected with the world's digital knowledge archives. Digital Earth promises to make the unified representative and recognition about the real earth and related phenomenon. Specifically it based on computing technology, multimedia technology and large-scale storage technology, interconnected with broadband network, the use of vast amount geo-referenced information to present earth in three-dimensional description of multi-resolution, multi-scale, multi-dimensional and multi-species, the use of information technology to process the entire planet's natural and social activities of various aspects, maximize the use of geo-information resources, and take it as a tool to transform nature and society, to promote the development of human civilization. Digital Earth is considered to be the best way of integrated use of shared data and information resources available, and the main and core body in the process of sustainable development with information resource. Digital Earth will play important role in social development, economic construction, and national security.

Digital Earth has raised the attention of governments, around support for "Digital Earth" concept and the development of key technologies, and set off a new round of information technology infrastructure and applications development boom on a global scale. Increasingly it has formed a lot of strategic directions, such as Digital China, Digital Government, Digital City, Digital Transportation, Digital Agriculture, Digital Meteorology, etc. National information infrastructure, national spatial data infrastructure and a large number of high-tech project started, and Digital Earth related computing science, large-scale storage, high-resolution satellite images, broadband network, spatial information technology, interoperability and metadata, visualization, and virtual reality, etc. technologies achieved breakthrough progress, and shown great potential for innovation.

With the concept of Digital Earth and Digital China in-depth development and popularization, continue to promote the theory and technology, accelerating the pace of project construction, the concept of Digital Railway gradually formed in the railway

* Wang Yingjie, Li Ping, Guo Ge, Ma Xiaoning, Lu Wenlong, Wu Yanhua and Shi Yi
Institute of Computing Technologies, China Academy of Railway Sciences, Beijing, China

industry. Digital Railway should be the strategic objective of China railway modernization in the 21st century.

1.1.2 Connotation and essential characteristics of digital railway system

1.1.2.1 Definition

Digital railway is new railway information system, which researches digitization of the railway infrastructure(lines, bridges and tunnels, stations, signal system, etc.), mobile equipment (locomotives, cars, EMUs (Electrical Motor Units), etc.) and railway environment (dynamic and static information, multi-resolution and 3D information) based on geographical information system (GIS), Global position system (GPS), Remote system (RS), information system, Internet of Things, virtualization, information integration, etc. to realize overall management and vivid indications of the railway transportation capacity resources and service resources. It internally supports Railway Transport Organization, Passenger & Freight Transport Marketing Services, Enterprise Business Operation Management needs, externally supports visual display of the whole process of passenger travels, freight transportation and query, and synthesizes internal and external information to provide visualization integrated decision support for managers at all levels. It is based on the improvement and transformation of existing railway information system, and has an important role in enhancing the railway management, the level of service and images, and ensuring transport safety [2].

1.1.2.2 Connotation

The concept of Digital Railway has two levels of connotations: the meaning of the first level corresponded with the Digital Earth, is a multi-resolution, three-dimensional representation of China Railway locomotive, car, permanent way, communication & signal, traffic management, etc. related information, and integrated with geographic coordinates, then embedded with large-scale railway associate geographic data and management information; and at the second level, through proper storage management and process with all kinds of data, to make digitalized management for railway transportation industry. Digital dynamic information referenced with static, with a high degree of immersion and presence, in order to facilitate interaction and understanding of the expression to show to the user, makes huge railway system across the country to reproduce the true decision-makers at all levels, to provide a basis for supporting decision-making and production command. Digital Railway will be powerful information infrastructure and resource to support railway modernization construction and operation, and give the decision making organization of railway system the capabilities of meaningful operation, planning and strategy capabilities, and finally realize the idea of "railway in hand". The ultimate goal of the construction of Digital Railway is for servicing with digitalized management to different departments of railway.

In summary, Digital Railway included three aspects of connotation: (1)Digital Railway is a strategic thinking about 21 century China railway modernization development, that will propose integration needs for railway planning, specification, technology, especially information. (2) Digital Railway is a dynamic information mega-system, which provide open, distributed computing capability and full range of services; (3) Digital Railway is virtualized railway, as a digital understanding and reproduction of real railway and its operation [3].

1.1.2.3 The necessity of construction

With the trend of intelligent, green and sustainable development in today, construction and development of Digital Railway still has significance. Digital Railway is the foundation to realize Intelligent Railway development [13], as well as the content of basic building during railway informatization, and the needs of railway modernization for now and the objective of the future.

Government attaches great importance to the development of national railway, invested heavily in rail infrastructure, especially large-scale passenger line construction. In 2010, China railway mileage will reach 110,000 kilometers, among others, above 200 kilometers per hour and intercity passenger rail line will reach 13,000 km, achieve separating from passengers and freights on busy main line, and a large number of modern integrated transport hub in operation. At the period of great construction and development, various kinds of new business applications are emerging, and made strong demand for railway information. At the same time, for the upcoming large-scale railroad network system, existing decentralized information processing methods of information management systems cannot meet the needs of rapid development of railway operations. That makes urgent needs for modern information technology to carry out in depth research and comprehensive application of railway information resources, integrated utilizing geographical information technology, global positioning technology, remote sensing technology, multimedia messaging technology, intelligent image processing technology, virtualization reality technology and network communication technology, etc., and based on information technology promote Digital Railway construction, use of railway information resource, serving railway business operation, to enhance the level of railway operation and management to provide technical support.

1.1.2.4 Essential characteristics

Digital Railway is a comprehensive, large and integrated, complex and arduous mega-systems engineering, and it is a development strategy. Instead, the rail transport system will depend on the digitalized and network-enabled information infrastructure. In the railway transport system, production and management of internal operations and external marketing and passenger services are all part of the effective interaction based on the "digital flow". It develops the railway information system in an innovative way, that achieve digitalize railway management, to make a virtual reproduction of the “real world” railway through the computer and information network. By Digital Railway research and development, archive digitalized railway survey and design, digitalized railway engineering construction, digitalized railway equipment manufacturing, digitalized railway traffic command and control, digitalized railway safety inspection and monitor, and digitalized maintenance and repair, etc., then archive Digital Railway business process reengineering, digital management decision-making, and promote organizational process reengineering. The research and development of Digital Railway will promote management innovation through technology innovation, reduce operating costs, improve efficiency and level of management, facility the connection between the railway and highways, waterways, civil aviation and other modes of transport, provide digitalized passenger and freight transportation service, promote intelligent and integrated transportation systems development.

1.1.3 Construction objectives and research contents of digital railway systems

The objectives of Digital Railway construction include [2]: on the one hand is the realization of Digitalization and Cyberization of the railway business systems, regulating railway foundation information and the methods of information sharing and exchange for dynamic business operation; on the other hand is to establish a railway geographic information platform as the core of information services and sharing for railway systems, ultimately to archive the full sharing of information among railway systems, improve resource utilization efficiency and demonstrate the level of service in the railway.

The research contents of Digital Railway include:

1. Research of Digital Railway architecture, study on hierarchy, logical structure, physical structure of Digital Railway system, and proposed the overall framework.
2. Research of Digital Railway standards. The development of digital spatial data content and standards of the railway, data quality control standards, spatial data exchange standards, spatial information sharing service standards.
3. Research of Digital Railway business application for information exchange. According to the unified planning and need of railway information sharing platform, specifications of the railway business information system output and input of information content and interface specifications.
4. Research of railway spatial data model and structure. Propose Digital Railway data structures of spatial models, and demonstrate the content of spatial database system and logical relationship among them.
5. Research of railway spatial information sharing technologies. Research of railway spatial information sharing technologies, including railway foundational spatial information synchronization and spatial information sharing mechanisms, provide a wealth of spatial data sharing and spatial information services, for all railway information systems.
6. Research of technology solution of core applications. Study on application solution with 3S technologies, virtualization technology, Internet of Things, spatial data querying, information integration and comprehensive application, etc. in railway business operation field.
7. Research of Digital Railway application overall program with internal and external user requirement. In-depth analysis of the various digital application contents and presentation requirements of railway business units and outside users, and propose Digital Railway application overall solution.
8. Research of mechanisms on operation, maintenance, safety & security of Digital Railway information system. Propose Digital Railway information operations, maintenance and updates, and safety & security mechanisms, to ensure that Digital Railway information is updated in real time and efficient maintenance.

1.1.4 General framework of digital railway system

From an engineering perspective, Digital Railway is a network centric geographic information systems engineering, related to information resources, technology, organization, standards and rules, etc., and the key task is to achieve the railway business integration applications and services through the sharing of spatial data based on geographic information platform. Therefore, the Digital Railway construction composed with digital foundational information platform, Digital Railway geographic information platform, Digital Railway information systems, technology systems and information standard systems, and several other components, its general framework shown in Figure 1.

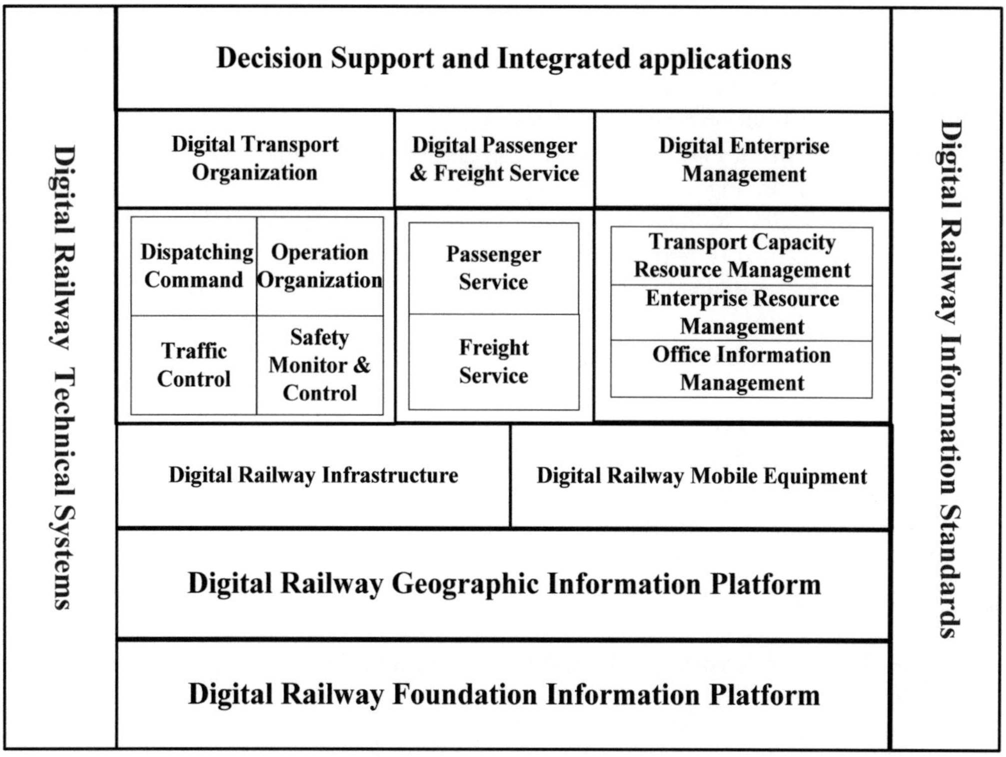

Fig. 1. General Framework of Digital Railway System

Digital Railway foundation information platform

The foundation of Digital Railway is the data in all kinds of railway business operation information systems, and now a large number of railway information system has been put into operation, some systems are under construction. Digitalization for these systems means, according to digital integrated display, publishing, management and decision-making needs, that we should demonstrate information and methods for exchange among these systems(both inside and outside), and we also need construct the railway common information platform and realize dynamic information exchange and sharing of business information. To archive the goal that, on the one hand, to meet the business services and management needs, on the other hand, to satisfy management and decision-making needs at all levels of railway operation.

Digital Railway foundation information platform is an important support for Digital Railway, which includes: network communications platform, information sharing platform, common information platform, information security platform and Digital Railway portal, etc. [4-6]

1. **Network Communication Platform:** Railway network communications platform provide Internet backbone communications infrastructure and intelligent communications management platform for ubiquitous digital network communications environment, including the bearer network (wireless and wired transmission network, switching network, access network), network support

(network management, network synchronization , signaling network) and business-application-centric integrated data network (business network) and other components. Network communication platform provides information network access and digital information transmission services.

2. **Information Sharing Platform:** Information Sharing Platform is the assurance to achieve interoperability among Digital Railway systems. One of the dominated construction principle of Digital Railway Information System is service-oriented. Service-oriented system build method provides support for whole process visualization of Digital Railway operations. Digital Railway information sharing platform uses ESB (Enterprise Service Bus) -based mode to achieve service-based information system interoperability.
3. **Common Information Platform:** Common information platform provides total quality controlled data services for coding data, metadata, and transport common data, geospatial data, and other public base data, including data directory services, security management, quality management, data integration tools for data through the gathering, cleaning and change, and the way the service bus, serving for the Digital Railway information systems information gathering.
4. **Information Security Platform:** Information security platform provides complete roles and authentication system, secure information resources access totally under user access control, security features through network security domain segmentation for Digital Railway, to ensure reliability, availability, confidentiality, integrity, authenticity and controllability.
5. **Digital Railway Portal:** Digital Railway portal is integrated a variety of applications, the unified way that interact with the outside for railway for the access of internet services. It is for passengers, shippers, partners, government and industry authorities to provide interactive information services, e-Commerce, e-Government, e-Collaboration applications such as shared information platform, and to optimize business model, expand market channels, improve customer service and enhance the image of the railway.

Digital railway geographic information platform

The core of Digital Railway is railway geographic information platform. Digital geographic information platform provide a unified national railway map, a unified digital geographic information service for railway information systems, support to achieve the train locating, materials positioning, network planning and other services, and all kinds of information related to railway operations, in a unified interface in the virtual space and time display, achieving convergence and sharing of information

Digital railway information systems

Digital Railway information systems support Digital Railway planning and design, engineering construction, construction and operation management of the entire process, from the composition of a number of information systems. As Digital Railway connotation and core features, and Digital Railway core business value chain, Digital Railway core information systems comprise of planning and design, engineering construction, transport operation organization, passenger and freight services, and business management information systems, etc. Additionally, these information systems highly depend on ubiquitous information provided by Digital Railway infrastructure and Digital Railway mobile equipment.

Digital Rail infrastructure and mobile equipment is an important components of Digital Railway, they use of RFID, Internet of Things technology, the uniform code with the railway line bridge and tunnel infrastructure, locomotives, vehicles, EMU, and railway equipments of communication , signals, traction, power, information, and large parts of the RFID-based unified identity management and all of its static and dynamic information management, to develop standards for RFID applications and fitting processes, to make all parts of railway facilities achieved real-time tracking and timely maintenance, to meet the management needs of Digital Railway to ensure the safety of railway transport.

Decision support and integrated application is the highest level of Digital Railway applications, through data analysis, virtual simulation and presentation, and cross-business collaboration and other technical means to improve the efficiency of railway operations, operational efficiency, and transport security as the purpose, supporting route selection, service program, passenger and freight marketing decisions, security risk identification and early warning, emergency response and other business applications.

Technologies and information standards

A large number of key technologies and information standards support the realization of the concept of Digital Railway development. Key technologies of Digital Railway include, such as 3S (GIS, GPS, RS), virtualization, railway spatial data modeling, mass data storing, spatial information sharing, Internet of Things related, cloud computing, etc. technologies Digital Railway information standards include common railway information coding rules based standards, spatial data content and standards, geospatial data exchange standards, GIS shared services standards, geographic information service based on OGC (Open Geospatial Consortium) standards, SOA (Service oriented Architecture) related standards, etc.

1.2 Geographic information platform of digital railway system

1.2.1 The definition of digital railway geographic information platform

Geographic Information Platform of Digital Railway System is a foundation platform which takes railway spatial information database as the carrier, GIS technologies as the core, achieving railway spatial information and services sharing as the goal. It is responsible for collecting, storing, maintaining and managing of spatial information, which including railway public fundamental spatial information, sharable valuable professional spatial information and related spatial attributed data which gathering from business information systems. Geographic Information Platform also provides spatial information and related services which can be shared to business information systems.

China's railway information systems applied the concept of GIS in varying degrees, and some had already established the GIS subsystem [7], such as information system of permanent way works department (PWMIS), railway land management systems. Ministry of Railways also organize related units to study the overall framework and the programs of railway geographic information systems [8,9]. However, part of the railway business information system uses the different platforms for geographical information, and spatial information sources are not uniform, resulting in spatial information is inconsistent, maintenance workload continued substantial growth, and these are difficult to play overall effectiveness. To this end, an urgent need to tidy plan the construction of Digital Railway from an unified, standardized aspect, and study an advanced application of scientific and rational, safe and reliable railway geographic information platform for railway infrastructure management and maintenance of spatial information, to provide specifications of the railway geospatial data and spatial information services for business information systems of the railway.

1.2.2 The functions of digital railway geographic information platform

Digital Railway geographic information platform railway main functions are as follows:

1. **Railway Spatial Data Management.** Collection, storage, maintenance and management of the national rail spatial information, including common rail base national railway spatial information, and extracted from the business system, there are valuable for sharing of the professional spatial information, metadata and related attribute data. To achieve spatial data of GIS database synchronization and integration between different departments.
2. **Railway Spatial Information Services Management**. Publish spatial information and analysis model, which managed by geographic information, in a standard GIS service delivery style, including spatial data visualization services, GIS data services, GIS function service, GIS directory services. In addition, GIS services can be based on the basic types, custom professional business space in different applications such as passenger and freight space-time statistical analysis of marketing services, and emergency evacuation paths used in service to meet business services for GIS analysis needs.
3. **Railway Geographic Information Service Release.** Provide query, search and locate services on railway spatial information. When the other systems user develop a rail service system, or need to use a GIS data, services, they could through service inquiries, to obtain a specific service path, and call the service and complete implementation of the entire business flow.

1.2.3 The architecture of digital railway geographic information platform

Railway geographic information platform based on the latest Geographic Information shared services model [11]. Geographic information platform is composed by railway spatial data layer, spatial information services layer, rail service interface layer of geographic information, while the necessary network information infrastructure, standards and normative system, security system, so as to ensure the railway geographic information platform running smoothly. Railway systems and other space-related business applications can be built on the basis of geographic information platform, and through the service interface, invoke the railroad railway geographic information platform provided spatial information services. The overall structure is as follows:

1.2.3.1 Data layer

GIS data layer of the railway geographic information platform, responsible for the collection, storage, maintenance and management of the railway spatial information, including railway unified common railway spatial information, and extracted from the business system, there are shared values of the professional spatial information, metadata and related attribute data.

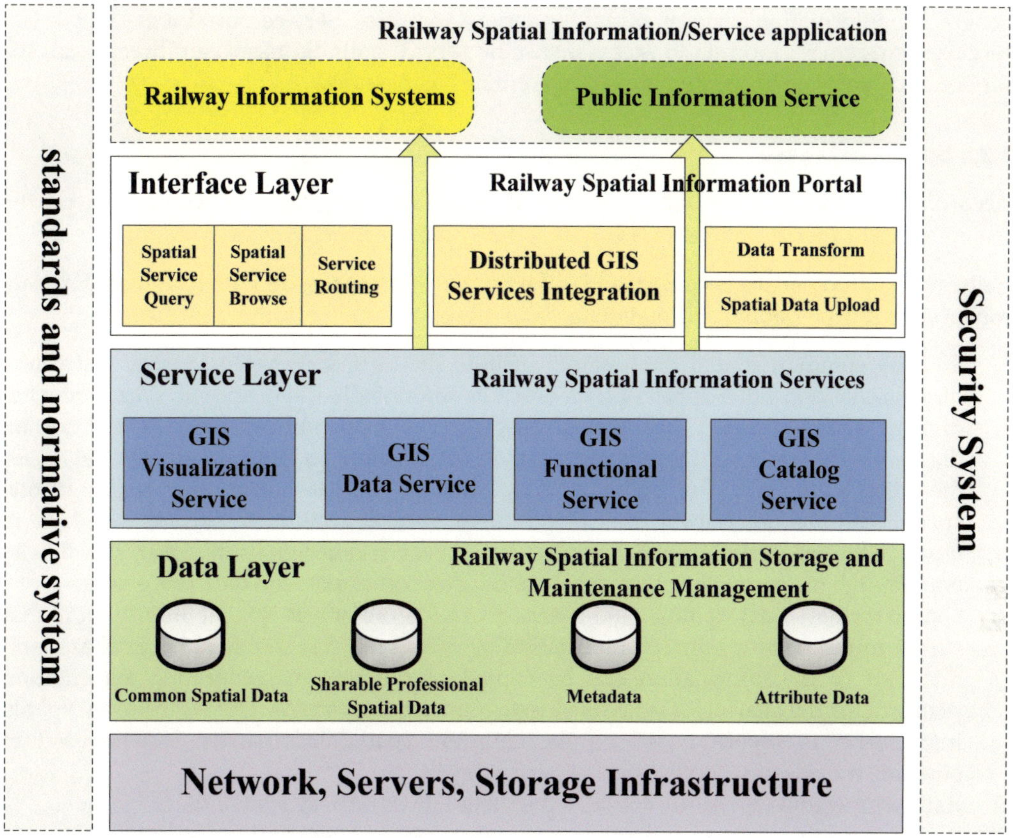

Fig. 2. The Architecture of Digital Railway Geographic Information Platform

1.2.3.2 Service layer

The services layer of railway geographic information platform is the critical part to achieve GIS services. The spatial information services layer serves the system and public, who have the needs for the entire railway geographic information and services, and build a unified, distributed, loosely coupled, space GIS services platform for the railway business functions and information services. Geographic information services layer is responsible for publishing the standard GIS services and GIS spatial analysis models managed by geographic information sharing platform, including spatial data visualization services, GIS data services, GIS functional service, GIS catalog services. In addition, GIS services can be based on the basic types, custom professional business space in different applications such as passenger and freight space-time statistical analysis of marketing services, and emergency evacuation paths used in service to meet business services for GIS analysis needs. needs. It will provide different services for outside and inside users.

1.2.3.3 Interface layer

Railway geographic information platform interface layer is also the railway geographic information services portal, which provides geographic information services portal railway spatial information services available to search and locate. When the other system users develop a rail service system, or need to use a GIS data, services, he can log in railway geographic information services portal for service inquiries. Service portal will call the GIS service management module to access a specific service path. So users can directly call the service and complete implementation of the entire business flow.

1.2.4 Spatial database

According to the railway GIS platform design, the data layer is composed of the maintenance of spatial databases and spatial data management subsystem [10].

Railway spatial database is composed by the railway common spatial data, and spatial data can be shared professional and metadata.

1. Railway common spatial data mainly include different scale vector, raster, and three-dimensional and other types of data (such as multimedia data), specific data content is divided into two areas: the national base railway map, railway lines vertical section diagram. The railway map based spatial information to provide a national basis, the distribution of the railway line, railway bureaus and the main station spatial information; railway line longitudinal vertical section of the line graph is to describe the base railway spatial information, survey and design drawings by the railway line through the vector data formats obtained after conversion and data processing.
2. Shared professional spatial data refers to the professional spatial information that stored in the certain railway information systems, and has the demand to share, and this part of the information can be copied to the railway geographic information platform for the sharing of other business information systems. The professional spatial information is superimposed on the common spatial information can be used to generate the relevant professional expertise layer.
3. Railway metadata is mainly contains the metadata of railway spatial data.

Digital Railway spatial database can be divided into three parts by their contents, which are the national common geographic information data, the railway geographic information data and the sharable railway professional GIS data.

The spatial data maintenance and management sub-system is responsible for the management of the spatial data and metadata, which are stored in geographic information platform, including geographic information platform model and spatial data management, spatial data (vector and raster data) to import, export, convert, copy, append; spatial data quality control, network topology and relationship maintenance; incremental replication and exchange of spatial data; spatial data metadata management, including meta-data collection, management, publishing and navigation.

1.2.5 The application patterns of digital railway geographic information platform

The Application Patterns of Digital Railway geographic information platform includes internal and external service, and they are respectively reflected by Digital Railway Information Sharing Platform service layer and Digital Railway spatial information services portal.

1.2.5.1 The service layer of digital railway information sharing platform

The service layer is a key part of railway geographic platform to realize GIS services, and its core function is to provide GIS services. GIS services in Railway geographic information platform include GIS visualization services, GIS data services, GIS services and directory services functions. The GIS services can be divided into two levels: the first layer for GIS visualization services (map services and OGC services) and GIS data services (data transform service and spatial data upload service), and the second layer for the GIS functional service (map query service, map locate service, map edit service, spatial information service). Which GIS data visualization and GIS services are the basic types of services, GIS capabilities that can achieve some of the major service-specific features and analysis of GIS services, to achieve GIS functional services need to rely on GIS visualization or data services, and when GIS functions called services, they often need to call the GIS visualization or data services.

In addition to providing features of a variety of GIS services at the spatial information services layer, but also must have created publishing services, service interfaces, service management and security management functions, and provide a variety of standard access interfaces such as SOAP (Simple Object Access Protocol), REST (Representational State Transfer), OGC standard services with web services, for the spatial application of business systems.

The railway geographic information platform services layer design shown in figure 3:

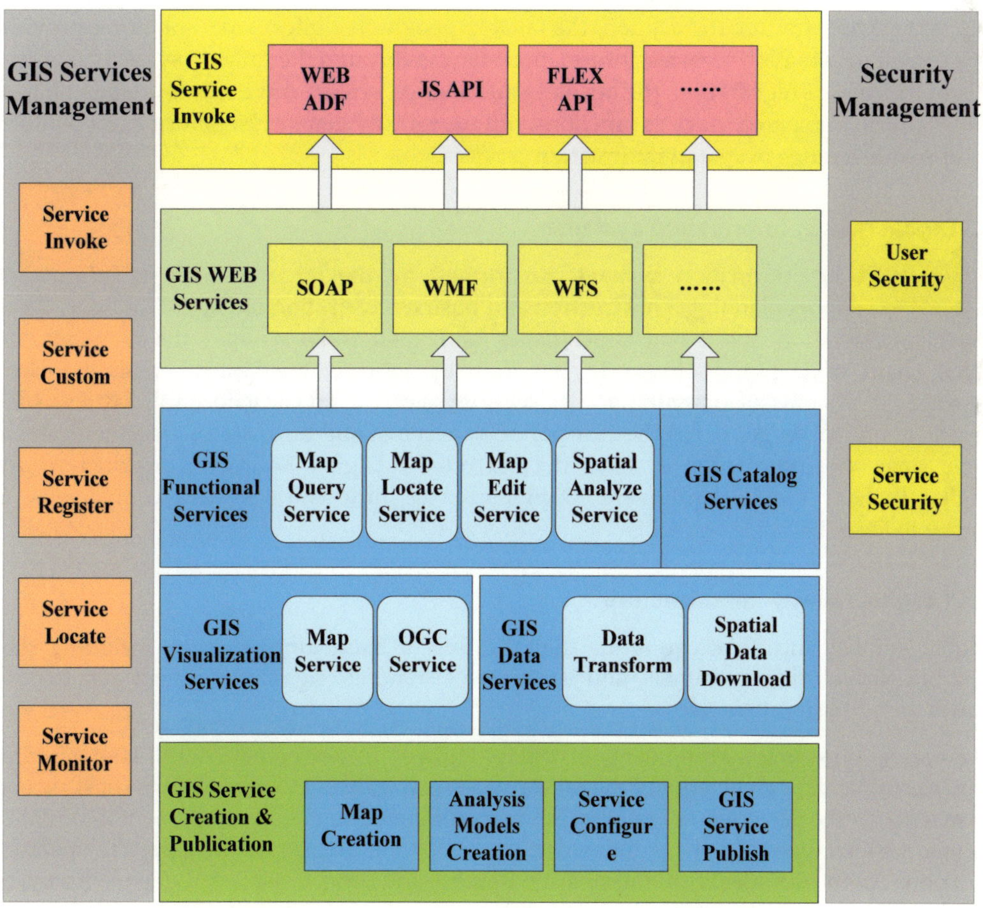

Fig. 3. The Service Layer of Railway Geographic Information Platform

1.2.5.2 Digital railway spatial information service portal

Digital Railway spatial information service portal mainly realize searching and location of railway spatial information services. Through logging spatial information service portal to query, services portal will call the GIS portal service management module to access a specific service path. Service management system called Enterprise Service Bus or GIS services management module, to obtain a specific service path. So users can directly call the service flow path and complete the implementation of the entire business.

Railway spatial information services portal designed the main functions are as follows:

- Distributed GIS Services Integration: integration of data services provide a unified, integrated spatial information services, data services platform is released service.
- Spatial Services Query: allows users to search the spatial information, which published by spatial information service platform through a certain keyword.
- GIS Data Services Browse: enables users to browse the map spatial information service platform for publishing a variety of data services
- Service Routing: after user retrieved service, the service call through the feedback information directly to the user's service call request is forwarded to the service providers.
- Service registration: In addition, the railway geographic information platform provides spatial information services, information sharing through the railway system (platform) in the service registration, the business information system can use Information Sharing Platform for shared services functions, call the railway geographic information platform provide a range of spatial information services.

1.3 Digital railway information systems

Digital Railway information systems are formed by the large number of information systems to support planning, construction and business operation of Digital Railway. Based on the connotation and key characteristics of Digital Railway, and the core business value chain of Digital Railway, Digital Railway information Systems mainly include information systems of planning and design, engineering construction, railway transport organization, passenger & freight transportation services and business management. At the same time, the information systems depend on the Digital Railway infrastructure and Digital Railway mobile equipment. Digital railway information system components, as shown in Figure 4.

1.3.1 Digital railway infrastructure

Digital Railway infrastructure is the digitalization of fixed infrastructure, including road network (lines, bridges, tunnels, and a variety of stations), signal equipment and traction power supply equipment, etc.

The variety of technical equipments of Digital Railway infrastructure should be configured with electronic tags, and layout of the railway lines and stations operate all types of sensors to form a pan in the perception of railway infrastructure environment. Perception of information include various types of railway infrastructure, safety and quality service state, the operation of mobile equipment identification capacity, location and service status, driving environment, wind, rain, snow, earthquake, etc. affect the normal driving state of the weather and the natural environment, goods and passenger service station related information.

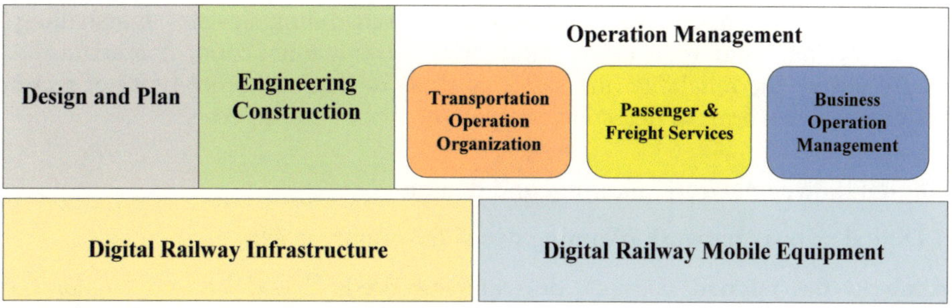

Fig. 4. Digital Railway Information Systems

Various types of sensors of Digital Railway Infrastructure communicate with each other by wireless, cable transmission networks, and rolling stock by means of radio frequency transmission protocol to exchange information. Digital Railway infrastructure contains the station interlocking, line occlusion control, signal control, traction control and power transmission, etc. automatic equipment. Digital Railway infrastructure are more accurate and reliable supporting of ATIS (Automatic Train Number Identification System), disaster prevention and safety monitoring, traffic surveillance, emergency command rescue, transport resource management system implementation.

1.3.2 Digital railway mobile equipment

Digital Railway mobile equipment generally refers to railway mobile transport capacity equipments (including locomotives, vehicles, EMU, etc.) and the digitalization of trains.

Digital Railway mobile equipment percept all kinds of state information of train operation, including their location, speed, power, air resistance, energy consumption, emissions, load and test monitoring equipment state information; position information about itself and the adjacent train; the infrastructure state inspection information around train running alongside; information of natural and meteorological along the train running; automatic access to scheduling and driving instruction program information; locomotives, vehicles and all kinds of EMU state information; state information of cargo and passengers in carriages,and so on.

Digital Railway mobile equipment, through the assembled digital data transmission and communications equipment, realize real-time information communication between the vehicle-based sensors and reliable mass information transmission between train and infrastructure, or between trains. Through real-time dynamic digital platforms, and combine with the digital platforms of operating environment, the model of train status information sensing and monitoring is built, it can realize modern detection for high-speed train, train operation control, digitalization of traction power supply, line public affairs, and digitalization of geographical environment. By data processing integration and intelligent decision-making platform, it can realize the data integration between train and infrastructure, and calculation of self-adaptive, self-test, self-repairing and mandatory safety protection based on knowledge database and intelligent decision. It can provide quality travel services to passengers at journey by building a digital train customer service platform.

Digital Railway mobile equipment has carried a large number of digital train control equipment, including train control, power control, over speed protection control, brake control, automatic control of vehicle equipment, control of the train services, and train monitoring which is interactive with centralized scheduling system, marshalling yard automation systems and road safety monitoring system interaction, it execute the train control. To ensure the reliability and safety of these devices, different types of monitoring systems and various forms of detection equipment must be equipped.

1.3.3 Digital railway network planning and design

1.3.3.1 Digital railway network planning decision support system

According to the railroad network development needs, based on the Digital Railway geographic information platform to provide spatial information services, based on digital model of topography, surface features, geological conditions, and other constraints of line environment, in a different alignment objectives, generate a set of optimal line selection program. For station planning, it will adjacent with the full consideration to stations around the city planning and municipal facilities, combined passenger and cargo location monitoring data, supporting integrated transport and modern logistics system analysis, optimization and smooth convergence of internal and external traffic, the smooth convergence of urban space and the station, and the organization of station function space, etc.

1.3.3.2 Digital aided line design and survey & reconnaissance analysis system

Using of remote sensing, geophysics, in-situ testing, geological exploration, integrated exploration, based on the structure, coupling and system dynamics model survey and calculation methods, auxiliary rolling stock, track, roadbed, bridge and tunnel, the natural environment and other aspects of digital survey data collection, analysis and design, combined with a comprehensive survey and test data management tools to improve the accuracy of the railway survey and design, optimize design, reduce construction costs.

1.3.3.3 Digital railway integrated simulation design system for the design of digital hub station

Modeling and simulation with the design artifact of the marshalling yard, and large or medium-sized terminal station and hub of the total figure, container and rail logistics center, etc., and integrated transport system operating conditions, optimize the real transport operation scenario of the railway station hub of traffic, people, goods, and station equipment, to enable the effectiveness of the design results and reasonable verification. On this basis, to simulate the existing lines in operation, and evaluation of the current operating results, the formulation of emergency response plans to provide effective support for the theory and simulation.

1.3.4 Digital railway construction

1.3.4.1 Digital railway construction project management system

Supporting Digital Railway construction management, including project risk management, project schedule management, project contract management, procurement management, construction management, engineering estimates of integrated management and other digital services, and with the data of operating assets management consistency.

1.3.4.2 Digital railway construction precision apperception and measurement system

Using the track inspection train, digital integrated experimental train, as well as the digital sensors and measurement equipment of the bridge, the tunnels and stations, cable infrastructure and meteorological, geological, hydrological etc.. combined with data processing and testing simulation system to support Digital Railway construction, comprehensive experiment, project acceptance, engineering maintenance.

1.3.5 Digital railway transport operation organization

1.3.5.1 Digital transport command and dispatch system

Includes the Centralized Traffic Control system (CTC), the operation planning management systems, the traffic projections and adjust system, the marshalling yard automation system, etc., and combining with Digital Railway geographic information platform, to digitalize the whole process of the transportation command and dispatch.

1.3.5.2 Digital transport operation organization system

Includes the opening line of program planning system, O-D assisted analysis systems, freight management, passenger transport management, professional transportation management, and automatic train identification system (ATIS) system, etc.

1.3.5.3 Digital transport safety safeguard system

Includes train operation safety monitoring system, emergency rescue command system, hazardous materials safety inspection system, station passenger flow of real-time analysis and early warning systems, security information management system, with simulation of a natural disaster situations, production of railway operations and emergency response and recovery simulation and training capabilities.

1.3.5.4 Digital transportation operations simulation system

Achieve train operation, station operations, transportation security and other aspects of transportation operations virtualization symbiotic simulation, decision support for transport operation organization.

1.3.6 Digital railway passenger & freight transport service

1.3.6.1 Digital passenger service system

Includes ticket sale and reservation system, passenger service system, passenger marketing decision support systems, automatic ticket amount optimize the allocation and pricing adjustments, and provide travel the whole process easy digital navigation services and electronic commerce services.

1.3.6.2 Digital freight services system

Includes freight marketing and capacity allocation system, freight service system, freight marketing decision support systems, to provide cargo tracking, integrated transport and other logistics services.

1.3.7 Digital railway transport capacity and business management

1.3.7.1 Digital transport capacity resource management and maintenance system

For the maintenance, tracking, procurement and operations of the lines, bridge and tunnel, crossing, embankment, repair equipment, communications signals, locomotives, vehicles and other types of capacity resources, provide full life-cycle asset management and effectiveness of accounting services, complement the railway norms, optimizing asset management system, enhance asset management efficiency. Based on the failure mechanism and mode of the capacity resources, and reliability requirements, combined with the economic cost of such repair and maintenance data, forming the maintenance and repair schedule predictive models library and knowledge base, to achieve a reliable forecast maintenance and repair system, the maximum degree of safety, and reduce operating costs and risks.

1.3.7.2 Digital business decision support system

To provide digital-based integrated business information display, statistical analysis and other functions, auxiliary open line programs, asset utilization, operational efficiency and optimize energy efficiency and emissions of other aspects of decision making.

1.4 Digital railway key technologies and information standards

1.4.1 Digital railway key technologies

1.4.1.1 3S Technology and application

3S technology is composition of RS, GIS, and GPS, and it is a modern information technology which is a combination of spatial technology, sensor technology, satellite positioning and navigation technology and computer technology, and highly integrated multi-disciplinary to collect, process, manage, analyze, express, disseminate and apply spatial information. 3S technology is the basis of the construction of Digital Railway. We can use RS technology to get the required railway exploration data, and use GPS technology to solve positioning problem of railway mobile equipment, and GIS technology is the basic displaying platform for development and application of Digital Railway.

1.4.1.2 Railway spatial data modeling Technologies

Data model is an abstraction of real world phenomenon, which describes the basic structure, relationship and the various operations of data. Data model is the formal representation of content and logical organization of relationship of data in database system and it describes and reflects the business activities and information flow in a department or system using abstract form. Railway Geographic Information System requires an efficient data organization mode, which not only can include comprehensive information (including information potentially useful for the future) as possible, but also can be easily and quickly selected.

1.4.1.3 Mass Spatial Data Storage and Access Technologies

Because of the ever mass span geographical spaces of China Railway, the enormous of electronic map, equipment spatial vector image, aerial and satellite photograph, videos along with the rail line, required to study the mass spatial data storage and process technologies, to make railway spatial data management efficient and effective.

1.4.1.4 Railway spatial information sharing technology

The essence of Digital Railway is to establish service and sharing system of railway information whish core is railway spatial information. The core of railway geographic information platform is to provide basic spatial information and sharing professional spatial information. Railway spatial information sharing technology, including synchronization mechanism of railway basic spatial information and service mechanism of railway spatial information, can provides sharing spatial data and rich spatial information services to improve resource comprehensive utilization efficiency. Constantly perfected standards of Digital Railway spatial information is an important means to railway spatial information technology management, and we must make the standards of railway basic spatial information, quality control of railway geographic data, railway geospatial data exchange and sharing services of railway GIS according to the principle that "authoritative data from authoritative department , resources Co-establishing and sharing", to achieve the target that "one base map in railway"

1.4.1.5 Railway spatial information security technology

Sector of Surveying and Mapping have strict regulations in spatial information management, because spatial information interrelates to the national security. Furthermore, digital geographic information is easier to replicate and spread, we must study railway spatial information security technology, and on national spatial data security level, to realize the unified convergence case management of railway spatial information, and take different effective measures to secret-related and public railway spatial information, on the premise of ensuring data or information safety, furthest to realize sharing of railway spatial data.

1.4.1.6 Virtualization technology

Virtualization is a process that to express computer resources using a way which user and applications can easily benefit from. It provides a logical view for data, computing power, storage and other resources, and it is a logical representation of resources which is not subject to physical limitations. Virtualization technology, include network virtualization, system virtualization, computer hardware virtualization, language virtual machine and distributed system simulation technology etc.

Through application of virtualization technology, all the resources of Digital Railway will run transparently on a variety of physical platforms, and it changes logical resource into logical resource, to realize automated allocation of resources. Therefore, we can build Digital Railway under existing applications and platforms using virtualization technology instead of rebuilding a new system.

1.4.1.7 Internet of things related technologies

Under the foundation of computer internet, Internet of Things based on the use of RFID, wireless data communications technology, to construct "Internet of Things" that covered everything in the world. Automatic Train Identification System (ATIS) Implemented by Ministry of Railway is realized using RFID technology. Using technology of Internet of Things, by embedding and equipping sensors into railway lines, bridges, tunnels, culverts, traffic signals and other rail infrastructure, locomotives, vehicles, train-sets and other mobile devices, informatization facility and large fittings, and integrating with the existing information network, can realize overall real-time management of manpower equipment and infrastructure of railway, that is to realize digitalization of railway equipment management, to improve resource utilization and productivity level of railway, and to promote construction of Digital Railway.

1.4.1.8 Cloud computing technology

Digital Railway was supported by a mass of information applications and information processing services, and it needs IT infrastructure and services basis that support the development of the railway business. The traditional construction mode that deploy IT infrastructure according to business information system leads to that information and information technology resources merged into some existing rules and regulations by specialty division. Cloud computing technology provides technical capability and management scheme for construction, maintenance and management of information services and upgrade of information technology infrastructure of Digital Railway and this will improve the ability of information technology of Digital Railway. Cloud computing comes from that business change to virtualization and diversification, and those need information technology to provide business agility, resulting in needs of IT infrastructure integration, data processing tasks and services quality assurance. Cloud computing is a concept and technology system to build a dynamic IT infrastructure, information technology services and information systems architecture. Cloud computing technology offers a way of IT resources development, making information systems to support business to the changing and have dynamic capabilities. Service-oriented hierarchical information services technology, virtualization technology, massive data processing and building mode of centralized data centers in Cloud computing areas provide opportunity to realize alignment of business and IT of Digital Railway.

1.4.1.8 Hybrid system modeling and validation technology

Each system in Digital Railway collects all the physical resources and the environment status information and takes all control decisions according to state changes. State change in physical world is based on continuous model, but control decision is based on discrete model of information space. Predictive maintenance of all kinds of digital equipment in Digital Railway needs continuous and discrete mixed modeling and validation analysis technology - hybrid system modeling and verification techniques. Hybrid systems are a class of widely used computer-based systems, such as embedded systems, information physical integration systems can be considered a typical example of hybrid systems. Currently hybrid automata are the main design modeling language, and reachability test of it is an important way to improve the quality of the system.

At present, the study of hybrid system in the railway has just started, and hybrid systems analysis, hybrid control system design will provide more reliable, more accurate techniques for the analysis, design and verification of massive information physical integration system.

1.4.2 Digital railway core information standards

Precondition of Digital Railway construction is to establish perfect Digital Railway information standards system. Core information standards in Digital Railway standards system include data content (including metadata) standards, data quality control standards, data exchange standards, spatial information sharing service standards, OGC (Open GIS Consortium) standard and SOA (Service Oriented Architecture) standard.

1.4.2.1 Railway common spatial data content and standards

Railway basic spatial data content and standards is a major part of spatial data management standard, including standards of railway basic spatial information, sharing professional spatial information and metadata content.

Digital Railway should establish on the base of international standards, at the same time can achieve expansion and compatibility of state metadata standards. Main reference of international metadata standards in metadata standard construction of Digital Railway list as follows: ISO 19115 metadata standard, ISO 19139 metadata XML Schema implementation standard, ISO 15836 Dublin Core standard.

1.4.2.2 Railway spatial data quality control standards

At present spatial data in each business system of Ministry of Railway independently purchase and make. Because different systems have different requirements of spatial data, in addition to the implementation time of each business systems are not same, leading to spatial data quality irregularity of each department. In construction of Digital Railway, must accord with corresponding national standards and industry standards of spatial data, while take strictly control for spatial data quality to ensure the validity and public of spatial data in storage.

1.4.2.3 Railway spatial data exchange standards

The core figure of Digital Railway is share, so data exchange format standardization of GIS spatial data is also a very important part.

Digital Railway should achieve data exchange between data providers and data users in different GIS platform through data exchange format. Therefore, it should be able to: support the commonly used data formats such as DXF, DWG, TIF, IMG, etc.; support the de facto standard exchange formats such as SHP, E00, etc.; support the national standard exchange formats, such as VCT and so on.

1.4.2.4 Railway GIS shared services standards

The shared services provided by Digital Railway Geographic Information platform should be able to support heterogeneous GIS system even non-GIS system to read and call, to reach the purposes of data integration and function sharing of system. To achieve this purpose, Digital Railway geographic information platform use service-oriented architecture, involves a lot of interoperability standards.

1.4.2.5 OGC standards

For GIS application services of Digital Railway, it is essential to provide standard OGC services. The OGC standard services include WMS (Web Map Service), WFS (Web Feature Service), WCS (Web Coverage Service).

1.4.2.6 SOA architecture standards

In Railway Geographic Information platform, in addition to providing spatial data share using OGC service, should also provide a variety of more advanced GIS map services and geographic analysis services for external which are OGC standards cannot be achieved. We should provide standard Web Services through SOA architecture to provide a variety of GIS mapping services and geographical analysis services. Therefore, Digital Railway construction will also need to follow some of the SOA architecture standards, including WSDL (Web Services Description Language), UDDI (Universal Description, Discovery and Integration), and SOAP protocol (Simple Object Access Protocol).

1.5 Conclusion

Digital Railway is the direction of railway system development and construction, which based on the transformation and improvement of existing railway information system, and it plays an important role to enhance the level of railway management, service and images, and to ensure transport safety. This chapter first discussed the background, content and characteristics of Digital Railway construction, and established a general framework for Digital Railway and analyzed its main study content and basic information platform. Carry out depth research on Digital Railway geographic information platform important part of Digital Railway, analyze its location, function and present the overall structure and application mode. It combined with material carrier and core business of Digital Railway, put forward system composition of Digital Railway information system, including Digital Railway infrastructure and mobile, planning and design, engineering construction, transport organization, passenger and freight services and management applications. Finally, analyze and give key technologies and core information standards of Digital Railway. By the construction of Digital Railway, it will realize the digital upgrade and transform of existing railway system to achieve digital railway operation. The development and construction is a continuing process, and it will lay a foundation for intelligent, green, and sustainable development of the modern railway.

2. References

[1] A. Gore, "The digital earth: Understanding our planet in the 21st century," The *Australian Surveyor*, vol. 43, pp. 89-91, 1998.

[2] Shi Tianyun, Wang Yingjie and Li Ping, "Research on Digital Railway Architecture," *Transportation Systems Engineering and Information Technology*, vol. 10, pp. 29-33, 2010.

[3] Yuan Jingrong, Li Xuewei and Wei Jigang, "Exploratory Study of the Constructure of Digital Railway," *China Railway*, vol. 10, pp. 19-22, 2000.

[4] China Ministry of Railways, "The Strategic Planning of Railway Informatization," ed: China Ministry of Railways, 2005.

[5] Shi Tianyun, Li Ping and Pei Kunshou, "Research on the System Architecture of Railway Common Information Platform," *China Railway*, vol. 8, pp. 12-15, 2007.

[6] Li Ping, Shi Tianyun, Pei Kunshou, "Research on the System Structure of Railway Information Sharing Platform," *China Railway*, vol. 5, pp. 23-26, 2008.

[7] Wang Yingjie, *et al.*, "Review on Applications of GIS in Railways," *China Railway Science*, vol. 23, 2002.

[8] China Academy of Railway Sciences, "Research Report of Railway Geographic Information System," 2003.

[9] Jia Limin and Wang Yingjie, "Architecture of Railway Geographic Information System(RGIS)," *China Railway Science*, vol. 24, pp. 1-6, 2003.

[10] Wang Yingjie and Shi Tianyun, "Research and Design of Railway Geographic Information Sharing Platform," *In Proceedings of the 5th China Intelligent Transportation Anniversary and the Sixth International New Energy Car Innovation Development Forum*, 2009.

[11] Shun GuanFu. *Geographic Information into Third Generation Sharing*. Available: http://media.ccidnet.com/art/2653/20081223/1643471_1.html, 2008.

[12] Sun Yuzhong, "*The* Revival of Virtualization," *Communication of the CCF*, vol. 4, pp. 1-3, 2008.

[13] Liu Weiguo, "The meaning of Modernization, Informatization, Digitalization, Intelligentization and their relations," *China Railway*, vol. 1, pp. 83-86, 2011.

Section 4

Emerging Web Informatics and Applications

11

A Guided Web Service Security Testing Method

Sébastien Salva
LIMOS UMR CNRS 6158, University of Auvergne
France

1. Introduction

For the last five years, the Internet is being revolutionized by becoming a Service-oriented platform. This tremendous inflection point in Computer Science leads to many new features in design and development such as the deployment of interoperable services accessible from Web sites or standard applications, the modelling of high level Business processes orchestrating Web Service sets, or recently the virtualization of service-based applications by means of the Cloud paradigm.

To achieve reliable Web services, which can be integrated into compositions or consumed without any risk in an open network like the Internet, more and more software development companies rely on software engineering, on quality processes, and quite obviously on testing activities. In particular, security testing approaches help to detect vulnerabilities in Web services in order to make them trustworthy. Nevertheless, it is quite surprising to notice that few security testing methods have been proposed for Web Services. This chapter addresses this issue by presenting a formal security testing method for stateful Web Services. Such services are persistent through a session and have an internal state which evolves over operation call sequences. For instance, all the Web Services using shopping carts or beginning with a login step are stateful. The proposed method aims to experiment *black box* Web Services, from which only SOAP messages (requests and responses) are observable. We do not have access to the code, Web services can be experimented only through their interfaces. Our approach is an active Model Based one: it relies on a specification formalized with a model to test Web services by means of test cases generated from the model. Model based testing approaches offer many advantages such as the description of a service without ambiguity. Accompanied with a formal method, some steps of the test can be also automated, e.g., the test case generation Rusu et al. (2005); Tretmans (2008). The use of a model also helps to define a relation between the specification and its black-box implementation to express clearly the confidence level between them. In this paper, we model Web services with Symbolic Transition Systems (STS Frantzen et al. (2005)) describing the different states, the called operations and the associated data.

In literature, for the same reasons, security policies are often described by means of formal rules, which regulate the nature and the context of actions that can be performed. Several security rule languages have been introduced in Cuppens et al. (2005); Senn et al. (2005). We have chosen Nomad (Non atomic actions and deadlines Cuppens et al. (2005)) to model abstract test patterns which can be directly derived from an existing security rule set. Nomad is well suited for expressing properties such as permissions, prohibitions or obligations and is able to take into account response delays. Our approach takes a Web Service specification and applies abstract test patterns on the operation set to generate test requirements called test purposes. These ones, which guide the tests, are then synchronized with the specification to produce the test case suite. The latter checks the satisfiability of the test relation *secure*, which formally defines the security level between the implementation and its specification combined with test purposes. The Amazon E-commerce Web Service (AWSECommerceService) Amazon (2009) is illustrated as an example on which we apply our method.

Another part of the book chapter is dedicated to the experimentation of the method on existing Web Services with an academic tool. The obtained results demonstrate a dramatic lack of security in many Web Services since 11 percent dot not satisfy the restrictions given by our security test patterns.

This book chapter is structured as follows: Section 2 provides an overview of the Web Service paradigm and on some related works about Web Service security testing. Sections 3 and 4 describe the Web service and test pattern modelling respectively. The testing method is detailed in Section 5. In Section 6, we discuss some experimentation results, the test coverage and the complexity of the method. Finally, Section 7 gives some perspectives and conclusions.

2. Web services security overview

Web Services are *"self contained, self-describing modular applications that can be published, located, and invoked across the Web"* Tidwell (2000). To ensure the Web Service interoperability, the WS-I organization has suggested profiles, and especially the WS-I basic profile WS-I organization (2006), composed of four major axes: the Web Service interface description with the WSDL language (Web Services Description Language World Wide Web Consortium (2001)), the definition and the construction of XML messages, based upon the Simple Object Access Protocol (SOAP World Wide Web consortium (2003)), the service discovery in UDDI registers (Universal Description, Discovery Integration Specification (2002)), and the Web service security, which is obtained by using the HTTPS protocol.

It is surprising to notice that security was the poor relation during the rush to Web Services and it is manifest that the HTTPS protocol was not sufficient to fulfill the security requirements of service-based applications. We can now find a tremendous set of documents and specifications related to Service security. The WS-security standard (Web Service Security OASIS consortium (2004)) gathers most of them. This document describes a SOAP rich extension to apply security to Web services by bringing message encryptions, message signing, security token attachment, etc. Both the policy requirements of the server side and the policy capability of the client side can be expressed by means of the WS-Policy specification. Nevertheless, this one is "only" SOAP-based, and defines requirements on encryption, signing or token mechanisms. Higher level rules cannot be expressed with WS-Policy.

Besides these specifications, several academic papers Gruschka & Luttenberger (2006); ISO/IEC (2009); Singh & Pattterh (2010) and the OWASP organization OWASP (2003) focused on Service security in regard to access control by decomposing it into several criteria: availability, integrity, confidentiality, authorization, authentication and freshness and by proposing recommendations for each one. Each criterion can be also modelled formally by means of security rules written with languages such as XACML (eXtensible Access Control Markup Language OASIS standards organization (2009)), Nomad (Security Model with Non

Atomic Actions and Deadlines Cuppens et al. (2005)), or OrBAC (Organisation-based access control Kalam et al. (2003)).

Some other papers, focusing on security rule modelling and formal testing, have been proposed in literature. Modelling specifications for testing and defining formal methods is more and more considered in literature and in industry because this offers many advantages such as the definition of the confidence level of the implementation in comparison with its specification, the coverage of the tests, or the automation of some steps. An overview of model based testing is given in Tretmans (2008).

These works can be grouped into the following categories:

- *Test Generation for Model-based Policies.* Test generation methods for model-based policies construct abstract test cases directly from models describing policies. For instance, Le Traon et al. Le Traon et al. (2007) proposed test generation techniques to cover security rules modelled with OrBAC. They identified rules from the policy specification and generated abstract test cases to validate some of them. Senn et al. showed, in Senn et al. (2005), how to formally specify high-level network security policies, and how to automatically generate test cases, by using the specification. In Darmaillacq et al. (2006), network security rules are tested by modelling the network behaviour with labelled transition systems. Then, test patterns are injected into existing test cases to validate the rules.
- *Random Test Generation:* or fuzzy testing is a technique which automatically or semi-automatically constructs test cases with random values. For instance, in Martin (2006), the authors developed an approach for random test generation from XACML policies. The policy is analyzed to generate test cases by randomly selecting requests from the set of all possible requests,
- *Mutation testing:* usually involve mutation of policies or programs. In Mouelhi et al. (2008), the authors proposed a model-driven approach for specifying testing security policies in Java applications. The policy is modelled with a control language such as OrBAC and translated into XACML. Then, the policy is integrated into the application. Faults are injected into the policy to validate the policy in the application by mutating the original security rules.

Concerning, the Web service security testing, which is the topic of the chapter, few dedicated works have been proposed. In Gruschka & Luttenberger (2006), the passive method, based on a monitoring technique, aims to filter out the SOAP messages by detecting the malicious ones to improve the Web Service's availability. Mallouli et al. also proposed, in Mallouli et al. (2008), a passive testing method which analyzes SOAP messages with XML sniffers to check whether a system respects a policy. In Mallouli et al. (2009), a security testing method is described to test systems with timed security rules modelled with Nomad. The specification is augmented by means of specific algorithms for basic prohibition and obligation rules only. Then, test cases are generated with the "TestGenIF" tool. A Web Service is illustrated as an example.

Our first motivation comes from the paper Mallouli et al. (2009) which describes a testing method from Nomad rules. This one can handle basic rules composed of abstract actions only and can be applied on generic systems. In this book chapter, we intend to propose a specific security testing method which takes into account black box Web Services deployed in a SOAP environment that is used to invoke operations. We claim that SOAP must be considered while testing since it modifies the Web Service behaviour and thus may falsify the testing verdict. So, in Section 3.2 we study the Web service consuming with SOAP and propose a specification completion to take it into account in the test case generation.

We consider the access control-based vulnerabilities expressed in OWASP (2003) to describe some security test patterns composed of actions such as operation requests. Actually, we specialize our test patterns for Web services to experiment our method. So, test patterns are composed of malicious requests (XML and SQL injections) for testing the Web Service availability, authentication and authorization. They also contain different variable domain sets such as *RV* composed of values well-known for detecting bugs and random values, or Inj composed of values for both SQL and XML injections. So, our method covers several categories cited previously (model-based and random testing). Then, we present a dedicated testing methodology, based upon a formal security test relation, denoted *secure* which expresses, without ambiguity, the security level of an implementation with regard to its specification and to a set of test patterns. To check the satisfiability of *secure*, test patterns are translated into test purposes. Then, concrete test cases are generated by means of a synchronous product between the specification and test purposes. Intuitively, we obtain action sequences, extracted from the specification and also composed of the initial test pattern properties. Our test purpose-based method helps to reduce the specification exploration during the test case generation and thus reduces the test costs Castanet et al. (1998).

Prior to present the testing methodology, we define the Web service modelling below.

3. Web Service modelling in SOAP environments

Several models e.g., UML, Petri nets, process algebra, abstract state machines (ASM), have been proposed to formalize Web services. STSs (Symbolic Transition Systems Frantzen et al. (2005)) have been also used with different testing methods Frantzen et al. (2006); ir. H.M. Bijl van der et al. (2003); Salva & Rabhi (2010). The STS formalism offers also a large formal background (process algebra notations, definitions of implementation relations, test case generation algorithms, etc.). So, it sounds natural to use it for modelling specifications and test cases. Below, we recall the background of the STS formalism and the specification completion to take into account the SOAP environment.

3.1 Stateful Web Service modelling

An STS is a kind of input/output automaton extended with a set of variables, with guards and assignments on variables labelled on the transitions. The action set is separated with inputs beginning by ? to express the actions expected by the system, and with outputs beginning by ! to express actions produced (observed) by the system. Inputs of a system can only interact with outputs provided by the system environment and vice-versa.

Definition 1. *A Symbolic Transition System STS is a tuple* $< L, l_0, V, V_0, I, \Lambda, \rightarrow >$, *where:*

- *L is the finite set of locations, with* l_0 *the initial one,*
- *V is the finite set of internal variables, while I is the finite set of external or interaction ones. We denote* D_v *the domain in which a variable v takes values. The internal variables are initialized with the assignment* V_0, *which is assumed to take an unique value in* D_V,

- *Λ is the finite set of symbols, partitioned by $\Lambda = \Lambda^I \cup \Lambda^O$: inputs, beginning with ?, are provided to the system, while outputs (beginning with !) are observed from it. $a(p) \in \Lambda \times I^n_{n\geq 0}$ is an action where p is a finite set of parameters $p = (p_1, ..., p_k)$. We denote $type(p) = (t_1, ..., t_k)$ the type of the variable set p, and D_p the variable domain in which p takes values,*
- *$\rightarrow$ is the finite transition set. A transition $(l_i, l_j, a(p), \varphi, \varrho)$, from the location $l_i \in L$ to $l_j \in L$, also denoted $l_i \xrightarrow{a(p),\varphi,\varrho} l_j$ is labelled by $a(p) \in \Lambda \times I^n_{n\geq 0}$, $\varphi \subseteq D_V \times D_p$ is a guard which restricts the firing of the transition. Internal variables are updated with the assignment $\varrho : D_V \times D_p \rightarrow D_V$ once the transition is fired.*

The STS model is not specifically dedicated (restricted) to Web services. This is why we assume that an action $a(p)$ represents either the invocation of an operation op which is denoted $opReq$ or the return of an operation with $opResp$. Furthermore, Web service are object-oriented components which may throw exceptions. So, we also model exception messages with a particular symbol denoted $!exp \in \Lambda^O$.

For simplicity and to respect the WS-basic profile, we assume that operations either always return a response or never (operations cannot be overloaded). We also assume that STSs are deterministic. As a consequence, we suppose that operations are synchronous, i.e. these ones return a response immediately or do nothing. Asynchronous methods may return a response anytime, from several states and often imply indeterminism.

An immediate STS extension is called the STS *suspension* which also expresses quiescence i.e., the absence of observation from a location. Quiescence is expressed with a new symbol $!\delta$ and an augmented STS denoted $\Delta(STS)$. For an STS $\mathcal{S}$, $\Delta(\mathcal{S})$ is obtained by adding a self-loop labelled by $!\delta$ for each location where quiescence may be observed. The guard of this new transition must return true for each value of $D_{V\cup I}$ which does not allow firing a transition labelled by an output.

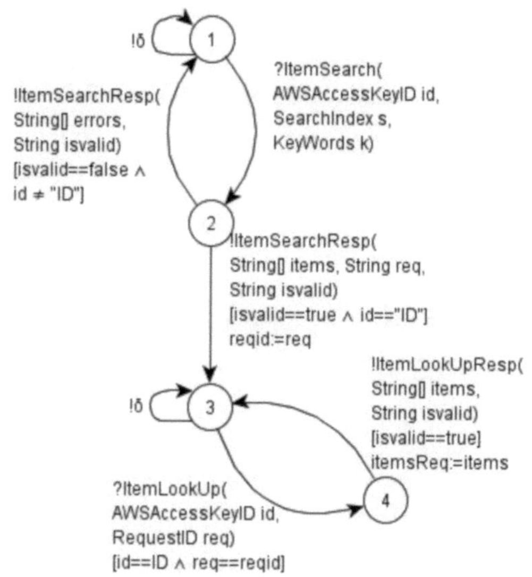

Fig. 1. An STS specification

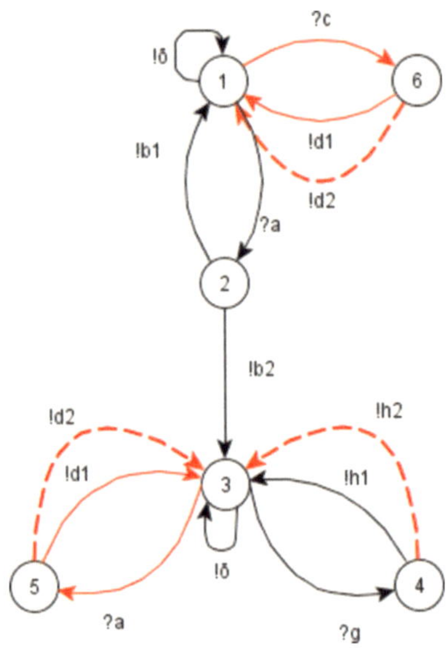

Fig. 2. The completed specification

A specification example, is illustrated in Figure 1. This one describes, without ambiguity, a part of the Amazon Web Service devoted for e-commerce (AWSECommerceService Amazon (2009)). For simplicity, we consider only two operations: *ItemSearch* aims to search for items, and *ItemLookUp* provides more details about an item. The AWSAccessKeyID parameter uniquely identifies the user of the Web service and is provided by Amazon. The SearchIndex parameter is used to identify the item in demand. "book" is a classical value. Notice that we do not include all the parameters for readability reasons.

An STS is also associated to an LTS (Labelled Transition System) to define its semantics. Intuitively, the LTS semantics represents all the functional behaviours of a system and corresponds to a valued automaton without symbolic variables: the states are labelled by internal variable values while transitions are labelled with actions and parameter values.

Definition 2. *The semantics of an STS* $\mathcal{S} =< L, l_0, V, V_0, I, \Lambda, \rightarrow>$ *is an LTS* $||\mathcal{S}|| =< Q, q_0, \sum, \rightarrow>$ *where:*

- $Q = S \times D_V$ *is the finite set of states,*
- $q_0 = (l_0, V_0)$ *is the initial state,*
- $\sum = \{(a(p), \theta) \mid a(p) \in \Lambda, \theta \in D_p\}$ *is the set of valued symbols,*
- $\rightarrow$ *is the transition relation* $S \times \Sigma \times S$ *deduced by the following rule:*

$$\frac{l_i \xrightarrow{a(p),\varphi,\varrho} l_j, \theta \in D_p, v \in D_V, v' \in D_V, \varphi(v,\theta)\ true, v' = \rho(v,\theta)}{(l_i,v) \xrightarrow{a(p),\theta} (l_j,v')}$$

This rule can be intuitively read as follows: for an STS transition $l_i \xrightarrow{a(p),\varphi,\varrho} l_j$, we obtain a LTS transition $(l_i, v) \xrightarrow{a(p),\theta} (l_j, v')$ with v an internal variable value set, if it exists a parameter value θ such that the guard $\varphi(v, \theta)$ is satisfied. Once the transition is executed, the internal variables take the value v' derived from the assignment $\varrho(v, \theta)$. An STS suspension $\Delta(\mathcal{S})$ is associated to its LTS semantics suspension by $||\Delta(\mathcal{S})|| = \Delta(||\mathcal{S}||)$.

Some behavioural properties can now be defined on STS in terms of their underlying semantics, in particular runs and traces.

Definition 3 (Runs and traces). *For an STS $\mathcal{S}$, interpreted by its LTS semantics $||\mathcal{S}|| =< Q, q_0, \sum, \rightarrow>$, a run $q_0\alpha_0...\alpha_{n-1}q_n$ is an alternate sequence of states and valued actions. $RUN(\mathcal{S}) = RUN(||\mathcal{S}||)$ is the set of runs found in $||\mathcal{S}||$. $RUN_F(\mathcal{S})$ is the set of runs of $\mathcal{S}$ finished by a state in $F \subseteq Q$.*
It follows that a trace of a run r is defined as the projection $proj_{\sum}(r)$ on actions. So, $Traces_F(\mathcal{S}) = Traces_F(||\mathcal{S}||)$ is the set of traces of runs finished by states in $F \subseteq Q$.

The traces of a STS suspension $Traces_F(\Delta(\mathcal{S}))$ also called the suspension traces are denoted $STraces_F(\mathcal{S})$.

3.2 The SOAP environment

Web services are deployed in specific environments, e.g., SOAP or REST, to structure messages in an interoperable manner and/or to manage operation invocations. Such environments may modify the observable reactions of a Web service implementation, for instance by adding and modifying the requests and responses. These modifications must be taken into account in testing methods to ensure that the test verdict is not falsified by the environment.

In this book chapter, we consider the SOAP environment only: it consists in a SOAP layer which serializes messages with XML and of SOAP receivers (SOAP processor + Web services) which is a software, in Web servers, that consumes messages (WS-I organization (2006)). The SOAP processor is a Web service framework part which represents an intermediary between client applications and Web services and which serializes/deserializes data and calls the corresponding operations. We summarize below the significant modifications involved by SOAP processors:

- **Calling an operation which does not exist:** this action produces the receipt of a response, constructed by Soap processors, which corresponds to a Soap fault composed of the cause "the endpoint reference is not found". Soap faults are specific XML messages which give details e.g., a cause (reason) about a triggered exception or a crash,
- **Calling an existing operation with incorrect parameter types:** this action produces also the receipt of a Soap fault, constructed by the Soap processor, composed of the cause "Client". This one means that the Client request does not match the Web Service WSDL description,
- **Exception management:** by referring to the WS-I basic profile WS-I organization (2006), when an exception is triggered by a Web Service operation, then the exception ought to be translated into a Soap fault and sent to the Client application. However, this feature needs to be implemented by hands in the operation code. So, when the exception management is implemented, the Soap fault cause is usually equal to "SoapFaultException" (in Java or C# implementations). Otherwise, the operation crashes and the Soap processor may construct itself a Soap fault (or do nothing, depending on the chosen Web Service framework). In this case, the Soap fault cause is different from "SoapFaultException".

In summary, SOAP processors add new messages, called SOAP faults, which give details about faults raised in the server side. They return SOAP faults composed of the causes "Client" or "the endpoint reference not found" if services or operations or parameter types do not exit. SOAP processors also generate SOAP faults when a service instance has crashed while triggering exceptions. In this case, the fault cause is equal to the exception name. However, exceptions correctly managed in the specification and in the service code (with try...catch blocks) are distinguished from the previous ones since a correct exception handling produces SOAP faults composed of the cause "SOAPFaultException". Consequently, it is manifest that SOAP modifies the behaviour of the specification by adding new reactions which must be taken into account while testing.

So, we propose to augment an initial specification with the SOAP faults generated by SOAP processors. We denote $!soapfault(cause)$ a SOAP fault where the external variable *cause* is the reason of the SOAP fault receipt.

Let $\mathcal{S} =< L_{\mathcal{S}}, l0_{\mathcal{S}}, V_{\mathcal{S}}, V0_{\mathcal{S}}, I_{\mathcal{S}}, \Lambda_{\mathcal{S}}, \rightarrow_{\mathcal{S}}>$ be an STS and $\Delta(\mathcal{S})$ be its suspension. $\Delta(\mathcal{S})$ is completed by means of the STS operation *addsoap* in $\Delta(\mathcal{S})$ which augments the specification with SOAP faults as described previously. The result is an STS $\mathcal{S}^{\uparrow}$. The operation *addsoap* is defined as follow: *addsoap* in $\Delta(\mathcal{S}) =_{def} S^{\uparrow} =< L_{\mathcal{S}^{\uparrow}}, l0_{\mathcal{S}}, V_{\mathcal{S}}, V0_{\mathcal{S}}, I_{\mathcal{S}^{\uparrow}}, \Lambda_{\mathcal{S}^{\uparrow}}, \rightarrow_{\mathcal{S}^{\uparrow}}>$ where $L_{\mathcal{S}^{\uparrow}}$, $I_{\mathcal{S}^{\uparrow}}$, $\Lambda_{\mathcal{S}^{\uparrow}}$ and $\rightarrow_{\mathcal{S}^{\uparrow}}$ are defined by the following rules:

Exception to Soapfault:
$$\frac{l_1 \xrightarrow{!exp,\varphi,\varrho}_{\Delta(\mathcal{S})} l_2}{l_1 \xrightarrow{!soapfault(c),\varphi,\varrho}_{\mathcal{S}^{\uparrow}} l_2}$$

Input completion:
$$\frac{l_1 \xrightarrow{?opReq(p),\varphi,\varrho}_{\Delta(\mathcal{S})} l_2, l_1 \xrightarrow{?op_iReq(p),\varphi',\varrho'} l \notin \rightarrow_{\Delta(\mathcal{S})}, ?opReq_i \in \Lambda^I_{\Delta(\mathcal{S})}, l' \notin L_{\Delta(\mathcal{S})}}{l_1 \xrightarrow{?op_iReq(p),\emptyset,\emptyset}_{\mathcal{S}^{\uparrow}} l', l' \xrightarrow{!soapfault(c)),\varphi=[c\neq"CLIENT"\wedge c\neq"the\ endpoint..."],\emptyset}_{\mathcal{S}^{\uparrow}} l_1}$$

SOAPfault completion:
$$\frac{l \xrightarrow{?opReq(p),\varphi,\varrho}_{\Delta(\mathcal{S})} l', \varphi' = \bigwedge_{l' \xrightarrow{!op_iResp(p),\varphi,\varrho}_{\Delta(\mathcal{S})} l''} \neg\varphi}{l' \xrightarrow{!soapfault(c),\varphi',\emptyset}_{\mathcal{S}^{\uparrow}} l}$$

The first rule translates an exception message into a SOAPfault. The second one completes the specification to be input enabled. Indeed, it is stated, in the WS-I basic profile WS-I organization (2006), that any Web service operation can be invoked anytime. So, we assume that each unspecified operation request should return a SOAP fault message. The last rule completes the output set by adding, after each transition modelling an operation request, a transition labelled by a SOAP fault. Its guard corresponds to the negation of the guards of transitions modelling responses. This transition refers to the exception management. When any exception is triggered in the server side, a SOAP fault is sent.

A completed specification example is illustrated in Figure 2 where the solid red transitions represent the operation call completion and the dashed ones the SOAP fault completion. The symbol table is given in Figure 3. For instance, the transition from location 4 labelled by !h2 is added to express that after calling the operation *ItemLookUp* a SOAP fault may be received.

Symb	Message	Guard	Update
?a	?ItemSearchReq(AWSAccessKeyID id,SearchIndex s, KeyWords k)		
?atp	?ItemSearchReq(AWSAccessKeyID id,SearchIndex s, KeyWords k)		TestDom:={Spec(ItemSearch);RV;Inj}
!b1	!ItemSearchResp(String[] errors, String isvalid)	[isvalid==false $\vee$ id<>"ID"]	
!b2	!ItemSearchResp(String[] items, String req, String isvalid)	[isvalid==true $\wedge$ id=="ID"]	reqid:=req
?c	?ItemLookUpReq(AWSAccessKey ID id, RequestID req)		
!d1	!soapfault(c)	[c$\neq$"Client" $\wedge$ c$\neq$"the endpoint..."]	
!d2	!soapfault(c)	[c=="Client" $\vee$ c=="the endpoint..."]	
!ftp	!soapfault(c)	[c=="SOAPFaultException"]	
?g	?ItemLookUpReq(AWSAccessKey ID id, RequestID req)	[id==ID $\wedge$ req==reqid]	
!h1	!ItemLookUpResp(String[] items, String isvalid)	[isvalid==true]	itemsReq:= items
!h2	!soapfault(c)	[isvalid$\neq$true]	

Fig. 3. Symbol table

4. Nomad test patterns

Security policies are more and more expressed by means of formal languages to express without ambiguity concepts such as obligation, permission or prohibition for an organization. A natural way to test policies consists in deriving, manually or semi-automatically, test cases directly from the latter. Usually, we obtain abstract tests, that we call *test patterns*. Some works Mouelhi et al. (2008) have proposed solutions to derive test patterns from basic security rules.

In this Section, to illustrate our methodology and to experiment existing Web services, we propose to formalize some test patterns from the recommendations provided by the OWASP organization OWASP (2003). Thereby, these test patters are specialized for Web services and will help to detect attacks/vulnerabilities such as empty passwords, brute force attack, etc. They are related to the following criteria: availability, authentication and authorization. We do not provide an exhaustive test pattern list, because this one depends firstly of the security policy established by an organization and because an exhaustive list would deserve a separate book of its own. Nevertheless, the following test patterns cover most of the OWASP recommendations. These test patterns are constructed over a set of attacks (brute force, SQL injection, etc.) and model how a Web service should behave when it receives one of them.

As stated previously, we have chosen to formalize test patterns with the Nomad language. Nomad is based upon a temporal logic, extended with alethic and deontic modalities. It can easily express the obligation, the prohibition and the permission for atomic or non-atomic actions with eventually timed constraints. Bellow, we recall a part of the Nomad grammar. The complete definition of the Nomad language can be found in Cuppens et al. (2005).

Nomad notations:
- If A and B are actions, then $(A; B)$ (A followed by B) and $(A \& B)$ (A in parallel with B) are actions
- If A is an action then $start(A)$, $doing(A)$, and $done(A)$ are formulae
- If α and β are formulae, then $\neg\alpha$, $(\alpha \wedge \beta)$, $(\alpha \vee \beta)$, and $(\alpha \Leftrightarrow \beta)$ are formulae
- If α is a formulae, then $\mathcal{O}\alpha$ (α is obligatory), $\mathcal{F}\alpha$ (α is forbidden"), $\mathcal{P}\alpha$ (α is permitted) are formulae
- $\mathcal{O}^{\leq d}A$ represents an obligation with deadline, and is to be read: "it is obligatory that A within a delay of d units of time"
- The last definition concerns the conditional privilege: if α and β are formulae, $(\alpha|\beta)$ is a formula whose semantic is "in the context β, α is true"

As a first step, we augment the Nomad language with this straightforward expression to model the repeating of an action:

If A is an action, then $A^n = A; ...; A$ (n times) is an action.

Now, we are ready for the test pattern description.

4.1 Availability test patterns

The Web Service availability represents its capability to respond correctly whatever the request sent. Especially, a Web service is available if it runs as expected in the presence of faults or stressful environments. This corresponds to the robustness definition *IEEE Standard glossary of software engineering terminology* (1999). So, it is manifest that availability implies robustness. As a consequence, the Web Service robustness must be taken into consideration in availability tests. We studied the Web Service operation robustness in Salva & Rabhi (2010): we concluded that the only robustness tests, which can be applied in SOAP environments without being blocked by SOAP processors, are requests composed of "unusual values" having a type satisfying the Web Service WSDL description. The terms "unusual values" stand for a fault in software testing Kropp et al. (1998), which gathers specific values well-known for relieving bugs. We also defined the operation robustness by focusing on the SOAP responses constructed by Web Services only. The SOAP faults, added by SOAP processors and expressing an unexpected crash, are ignored. This implies that a robust Web Service operation must yield either a response as defined in the initial specification or a SOAP fault composed of the "SOAPFaultException" cause only.

Definition 4. *Let* $\mathcal{S} =< L_{\mathcal{S}}, l0_{\mathcal{S}}, V_{\mathcal{S}}, V0_{\mathcal{S}}, I_{\mathcal{S}}, \Lambda_{\mathcal{S}}, \rightarrow_{\mathcal{S}}>$ *be a STS specification and* $\mathcal{S}^{\uparrow}$ *be its augmented STS. An operation* $op \in \Lambda_{\mathcal{S}^{\uparrow}}$ *is robust iff for any operation request* $?opReq(p) \in \Lambda_{\mathcal{S}^{\uparrow}} \times I^n$*, a SOAP message different from* $!soapfault(c) \in \Lambda_{\mathcal{S}^{\uparrow}} \times I$ *with* $c \neq$ *"SOAPFaultException" is received.*

The first test pattern $T1$ is derived from this definition and expresses that an operation is available if this one does not crash and responds with a SOAP message after any operation request. $T1$ means that if an operation request is "done" then it is obligatory ($\mathcal{O}$) to obtain a response $OutputResponseWS$.

$T1 \longleftrightarrow \forall opReq \in \Lambda^{I}_{\mathcal{S}^{\uparrow}}, \mathcal{O}(start(output\ OutputResponseWS)|\ done(input\ (opReq(p), TestDom := \{Spec(opReq); RV; Inj\})))$ where:

- $OutputResponseWS \longleftrightarrow OutputResponse(p) \vee OutputResponserobust(p)$ corresponds to a response set.
  $OutputResponse(p) = \{!opResp(p) \in \Lambda^O_{\mathcal{S}\uparrow} \times I^n\}$.
  $OutputResponserobust(p) \longleftrightarrow !soapfault(''SOAPfaultException'')$ is the only SOAP fault which should be received according to Definition 4,
- $(opReq(p), TestDom := \{Spec(op); RV; Inj\})$ is a particular input modelling an operation request with parameter values in $Spec(opReq) \cup RV \cup Inj$.
  $Spec(opReq) = \{\theta \in D_{I_{\mathcal{S}\uparrow}}, l \xrightarrow{?opReq(p)\varphi,\varrho}_{\mathcal{S}\uparrow} l' \in \rightarrow_{\mathcal{S}\uparrow}$ and $(l,v) \xrightarrow{?opReq(p),\theta} (l',v') \in \rightarrow_{||\mathcal{S}\uparrow||}\}$ gathers all the values satisfying the execution of the action $?opReq(p)$. These values are given in the LTS semantics (valued automaton) of $\mathcal{S}^{\uparrow}$.
  RV is composed of random values and specific ones well-known for relieving bugs for each classical type. For instance, Figure 4 depicts the $RV(String)$ set, which gathers different values for the "String" type. RANDOM(8096) represents a random value of 8096 characters.
  $Inj \longleftrightarrow XMLInj \cup SQLInj$ corresponds to a value set allowing to perform both XML and SQL injections. $XMLInj$ and $SQLInj$ are specific value sets for the "String" type only. For instance, XML injections are introduced by using specific XSD keywords such as *maxOccurs*, which may represent a DoS (Denial of Service) attack attempt. More details about XML and SQL injections can be found in OWASP (2003).

```
<type id="String">
        <val value=null />
        <val value="" />
        <val value=" " />
        <val value="\$" />
        <val value="*" />
        <val value="&" />
        <val value="hello" />
        <val value=RANDOM(8096)" /></type>
```

Fig. 4. RV(String)

Availability is also ensured in condition that the response delay ought to be limited. This can be written with the test pattern $T2$.

$$T2 \longleftrightarrow \forall opReq \in \Lambda^I_{\mathcal{S}\uparrow}, \mathcal{O}^{\leq 60}(start(output\ OutputResponseWs)|done(input\ (opReq(p), TestDom := \{Spec(opReq); RV\})))$$

This one describes that for each operation request, it is obligatory to receive a response within a delay of 60s.

This test pattern can be implicitly tested if we take into account the notion of quiescence (no response observed after a timeout) during the testing process. Indeed, if quiescence is observed after a delay set to 60s, while an operation invocation, we can consider that $T2$ is not satisfied. So, this test pattern will be implicitly taken into account in Section 5.

4.2 Authentication test patterns

Authentication aims to establish or to guarantee the Client identity and to check that a Client with no credits has no permission. The logon process is often the first step in user authentication. We propose here two classical test patterns relating to this one. We suppose that the logon process is implemented classically by means of specific operation requests gathered in a set denoted $inputAuth \subseteq \Lambda^I$ which are called with authentication parameters (passwords, keys, etc.) and which return SOAP responses. $T3$ refers to the mandatory of returning a fail authentication result each time an authentication request is sent to a Web Service with unusual parameter values such as empty parameters. So, this test pattern covers the well-known empty password vulnerability:

$T3 \longleftrightarrow \forall opReq \in inputAuth,\ \mathcal{O}(start(output\ OutputResponseWS(rlfail))|done(input\ \ (opReq(p), TestDom := \{RV\})))$ where:

$OutputResponseWS(rlfail) \longleftrightarrow OutputResponse(rlfail) \vee OutputResponseFault(p)$. $OutputResponse(rlfail)$ represents an operation response where the message $rlfail$ in $D_{I_{S\uparrow}}$ suggests a failed login attempt. $rlfail$ must be extracted from the specification. $outputResponseFault(p) \Leftrightarrow soapfault(c)$ with $c \neq$ "Client" $\wedge\ c \neq$ "the endpoint reference not found" is a SOAP fault whose cause is different from "Client" and "the endpoint reference not found". The first one means the operation is called with bad parameter types while the second cause means that the operation name does not exist (Section 3.2).

The test pattern $T4$ is dedicated to the "brute force" threat. The latter aims to decrypt or to find authentication parameters by traversing the search space of possible values. A well-known countermeasure is to forbid a new connection attempt after n failed ones for the same user. With $n = 10$, the corresponding test pattern can be written with:

$T4 \longleftrightarrow \forall opReq \in inputAuth,\ \mathcal{O}(start(output\ OutputResponseWS(rlforbid))|(done((input\ \ (opReq(p), TestDom := \{RV\}); output\ outputResponseWS(rlfail))^{10}); done(input\ \ (opReq(p), TestDom := \{RV\}))))$ where:

$OutputResponseWS(rlfail) \longleftrightarrow OutputResponse(rlfail) \vee OutputResponseFault(p)$ is an operation response as previously. The $rlfail$ message expresses a failed login attempt. The message $rlforbid$ indicates that any new connection attempt is forbidden. These messages must be extracted from the specification as well.

4.3 Authorization test patterns

Authorization represents the access policy and specifies the access rights to resources, usually for authenticated users. We define here, two test patterns which aim to check that a user, requesting for confidential data, is really authenticated.

The following test pattern checks that the request of confidential data with the operation set $inputRequestConf$, returns a "permission denied" message if the user is not authenticated (a fail login attempt has been made with the operation request $opReq_2 \in inputAuth$):

$T5 \longleftrightarrow \forall opReq \in inputRequestConf\ \exists op_2Req \in inputAuth, \mathcal{O}(start(output\ OutputResponseWS(rfail))|(done(input\ op_2Req(p)); done(output\ op_2Resp(rlfail)); done(input\ (opReq(p), TestDom := \{Spec(opReq); RV\}))))$ where:

- $opResp_2(rlfail) \in \Lambda^O_{g\uparrow} \times D_I$ is an authorization operation response composed of the $rlfail$ message, which describes a fail login attempt,
- $OutputResponseWS(rfail) \longleftrightarrow OutputResponse(rfail) \vee OutputResponseFault(p)$ describes, as previously, an operation response where the message $rfail$ corresponds to an error message. $rfail$ must be extracted from the specification.

The last test pattern *T6* is dedicated to the receipt of confidential data by means of XML or SQL injections. This one checks that an error message is received when a request containing an XML or SQL injection is sent:

$T6 \longleftrightarrow \forall opReq \in \Lambda^I_{g\uparrow}, \mathcal{O}(start(output\ OutputResponseWS(rfail))|done(input\ (opReq(p), TestDom := \{Inj\})))$

4.4 Attack and vulnerability coverage

Figure 5 describes a non-exhaustive list of attacks and of vulnerabilities which are covered by the previous test patterns. This list is still extracted from the larger one given in OWASP (2003). This table also expresses the portion of Web Service vulnerabilities which shall be detected with the testing method.

Test pattern	Attacks	Vulnerabilities
T1,T2	Denial of service, special character injection, format string attack	Catch null pointer exception, deserialization of unstructured data, uncaught exception, format string, buffer overflow, improper data validation
T3	Format string attack, special character injection	Empty password, improper data validation
T4	Brute force attack	Brute force attack vulnerability, insufficient ID length
T5	Bypassing attacks	Privacy violation, failure to provide confidentiality for stored data
T6	XML, SQL injection	Missing SQL, XML validation, improper data validation

Fig. 5. Attack and vulnerability coverage

4.5 Test purpose translation

Test patterns represent abstract tests that can be used to test several Web services. Such test patterns cannot be used directly for testing since they are composed of abstract operation names. In order to derive and to execute concrete test cases, we shall translate these patterns into test requirements, called test purposes.

Test purposes describe the test intention which target some specification properties to test in the implementation. We assume that these ones are composed exclusively of specification properties which should be met in the implementation under test. Thereafter, we intend to synchronize the STS specification with test purposes, so that final test cases will be composed of both specification behaviours and test pattern properties. So, test purposes must be formalized with STSs as well.

For a specification $\mathcal{S} =< L_{\mathcal{S}}, l0_{\mathcal{S}}, V_{\mathcal{S}}, V0_{\mathcal{S}}, I_{\mathcal{S}}, \Lambda_{\mathcal{S}}, \rightarrow_{\mathcal{S}}>$ we also formalize a test purpose with a deterministic and acyclic STS $tp =< L_{tp}, l0_{tp}, V_{tp}, V0_{tp}, I_{tp}, \Lambda_{tp}, \rightarrow_{tp}>$ such that:

- $V_{tp} \cap V_{\mathcal{S}} = \emptyset$ and V_{tp} also contains a string variable *TestDom* which is equal to the parameter domain provided in test patterns,
- $I_{tp} \subseteq I_{\mathcal{S}}$,
- $\Lambda_{tp} \subseteq \Lambda_{\mathcal{S}}$,
- $\rightarrow_{tp}$ is composed of transitions modelling specification properties. So, for any transition $l_j \xrightarrow{a(p),\varphi_j,\varrho_j}_{tp} l'_j$, it exists a transition $l_i \xrightarrow{a(p),\varphi_i,\varrho_i}_{\mathcal{S}} l'_i$ and a value set $(x_1, ..., x_n) \in D_{V \cup I}$ such that $\varphi_j \wedge \varphi_i(x_1, ..., x_n) \models$ true.

We denote TP the test purpose set derived from test patterns. In particular, a test pattern T is translated into the test purpose set $TP_T \subseteq TP$ with the following steps:

1. T is initially transformed into an abstract test purpose Atp_T, modelled with an STS, composed of generic operation requests. For a test pattern T, we denote OP_T the operation set targeted by the tests in T. For instance $OP_{T1} = \Lambda^I_{\mathcal{S}\uparrow}$,
2. the test purpose set $TP_T = \{tp_T(op) \mid op \in OP_T\}$ is then constructed by replacing generic operation invocations in Atp_T by a real operation name $op \in OP_T$.

For instance, test purpose patterns extracted from the test patterns $T1$ and $T4$ are given in Figures 6 and 7. These STSs formulate the test intention described in $T1$ and in $T4$. $T4$ describes a countermeasure for the brute force threat which is well described in the second test pattern since after ten connection attempts done by the same user, the latter cannot login anymore. *getsender* and *count* are internal procedures which return the IP address of the client and the number of times the client has attempted to connect. From the specification depicted in Figure 2, we also have $TP_{T1} = \{tp_{T1}(ItemSearchReq), tp_{T1}(ItemLookUpReq)\}$. $tp_{T1}(ItemSearchReq)$ is illustrated in Figure 8. It represents a test purpose constructed from $T1$ with the operation "ItemSearch". It illustrates the semantics of $T1$ with a concrete operation name.

Unfortunately, there is no available tool for transforming a Nomad expression into an automaton yet. At the moment, abstract test purposes must be constructed manually.

5. Testing methodology

Now, that Web services, SOAP, and security test patterns expressing security rules, are formalized, we are ready to express clearly the security level of an implementation (relative to its specification and a given set of test patterns). We initially assume that the implementation should behave like its model and can be experimented by means of the same actions. It is represented by an LTS *Impl* and $\Delta(Impl)$ its LTS suspension. The experimentation of the implementation is performed by means of test cases defined with STSs as the specification. Test cases are defined as:

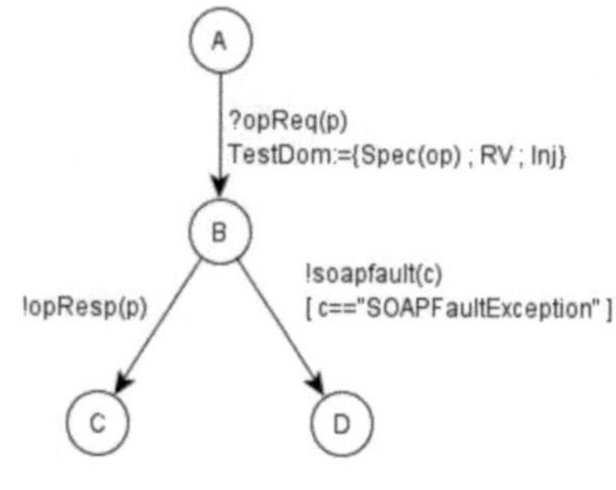

Fig. 6. Test purpose pattern derived from $T1$

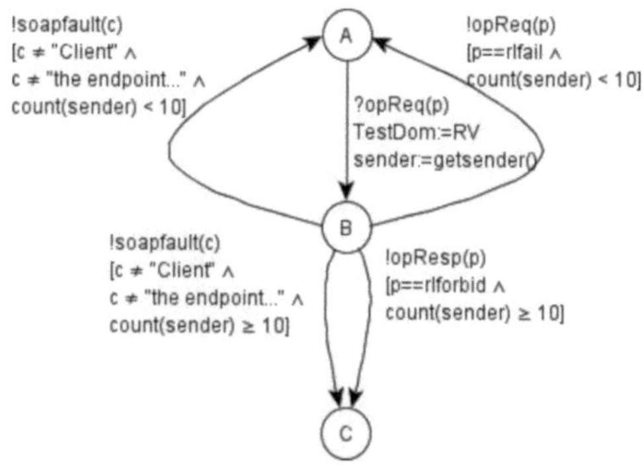

Fig. 7. Test purpose pattern derived from $T4$

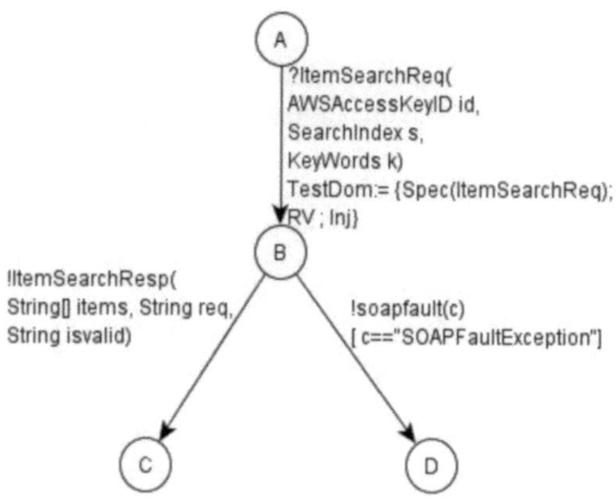

Fig. 8. A test purpose derived from $T1$

Definition 5. *A test case is a deterministic and acyclic STS* $\mathcal{TC} =< L_{\mathcal{TC}}, l0_{\mathcal{TC}}, V_{\mathcal{TC}}, V0_{\mathcal{TC}}, I_{\mathcal{TC}}, \Lambda_{\mathcal{TC}}, \rightarrow_{\mathcal{TC}} >$ *where the final locations are labelled in* $\{pass, fail\}$.

Intuitively, when the test case is executed, *pass* means that it has been completely executed, while *fail* means that the implementation has rejected it.

The proposed testing method constructs test cases to check whether the implementation behaviours satisfy a given set of security test patterns. This can be defined by means

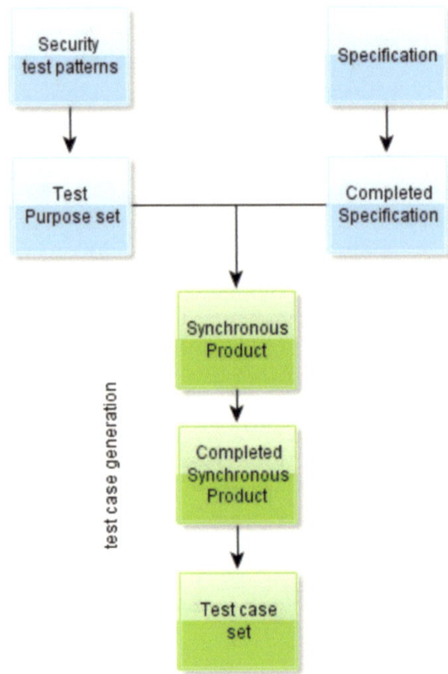

Fig. 9. Test case generation

of a relation based on traces, i.e., the observed valued actions suites expressing concrete behaviours.

More precisely, Since the implementation is seen as a black box, the method checks that the suspensions traces (actions suites) of the implementation can be found in the suspension traces of the combination of the specification with test purposes modelling concrete test patterns. We consider suspension traces, and not only traces, to take into account quiescence, i.e., lack of observation and so response delays. This can be written more formally by means of the following test relation:

$$Impl\ secure_{TP}\ \mathcal{S} \Leftrightarrow \forall tp \in TP, STraces(Impl) \cap NC\_Traces(\mathcal{S}^{\uparrow} \times tp) = \emptyset$$

with TP the test purpose set extracted from the security test patterns, $\mathcal{S}$ the specification, $\mathcal{S}^{\uparrow}$ its suspension and $NC\_Traces(\mathcal{S}^{\uparrow} \times tp) = STraces(\mathcal{S}^{\uparrow} \times tp).\Lambda^0 \cup \{!\delta\} \setminus STraces(\mathcal{S}^{\uparrow} \times tp)$ the non-conformant traces of the synchronous product $\mathcal{S}^{\uparrow} \times tp$.

To check this relation, the test case generation is performed by several steps, summarized in Figure 9 and given below. The main advantage of our model based approach, is that these steps can be automated in a tool.

1. Security test patterns are firstly translated into test purposes modelled by STSs as described in Section 4.5. For a test pattern T, we obtain a test purpose set $TP_T = \{tp_T(op) \mid op \in OP_T\}$ composed of test purposes $tp_T(op)$ with op the tested operation,
2. The specification $\mathcal{S}$ is augmented to take into consideration the SOAP environment, as described in Section 3.2,

3. The augmented specification $\mathcal{S}^{\uparrow}$ and the test purpose set TP_T are combined together: each test purpose $tp_T(op)$ is synchronized with the specification to produce the product $\mathcal{P}_T(op)$ whose paths are complete specification ones combined with the test purpose properties. We denote $Prod_T = \{\mathcal{P}_T(op) = \mathcal{S}^{\uparrow} \times tp_T(op) \mid tp_T(op) \in TP_T\}$ the resulting synchronous product set,
4. The synchronous product locations are labelled by "pass" which means that to reach this location, a correct behaviour has to be executed,
5. Synchronous products are completed on the output action set to express both correct and incorrect behaviours. A completed synchronous product is composed of *Pass* locations to express behaviours satisfying test purposes and *Fail* locations to express that test purposes and thus security test patterns are not satisfied. It results that $Prod_T^{compl} = \{\mathcal{P}_T^{compl}(op) \mid \mathcal{P}_T(op) \in Prod_T\}$ is the completed synchronous product set,
6. Finally, test cases are selected from the completed synchronous products in $Prod_T^{compl}$ by means of a reachability analysis. For a completed synchronous product $\mathcal{P}_T^{compl}(op)$, test cases in $TC_T(op)$ are STS trees which begin from the initial location of $\mathcal{P}_T^{compl}(op)$ and which aim to call the operation op. The reachability analysis ensures that these STSs can be executed on the implementation. For the test pattern T, the test case set $TC_T = \bigcup_{\mathcal{P}_T^{compl}(op) \in Prod_T^{compl}} TC_T(op)$. The final test case set TC is the union of the test case sets TC_T obtained from each test pattern T.

Each of these steps is detailed below. We assume having an augmented specification $\mathcal{S}^{\uparrow}$ and a test purpose $tp_T(op) \in TP_T$ derived from a test pattern T given in Section 4.

5.1 Synchronous product definition

A test purpose represents a test requirement which should be met in the implementation. To test this statement, both the specification and the test purpose are synchronized to produce paths which model test purpose runs with respect to the specification.

Let $tp_T(op) =< L_{tp}, l0_{tp}, V_{tp}, V0_{tp}, I_{tp}, \Lambda_{tp}, \rightarrow_{tp}>$ and $\mathcal{S}^{\uparrow} =< L_{\mathcal{S}^{\uparrow}}, l0_{\mathcal{S}^{\uparrow}}, V_{\mathcal{S}^{\uparrow}}, V0_{\mathcal{S}^{\uparrow}}, I_{\mathcal{S}^{\uparrow}}, \Lambda_{\mathcal{S}^{\uparrow}}, \rightarrow_{\mathcal{S}^{\uparrow}}>$ be two STSs. The synchronous product of $\mathcal{S}^{\uparrow}$ with $tp_T(op)$ is defined by an STS $\mathcal{P}_T(op) = \mathcal{S}^{\uparrow} \times tp_T(op) =_{def}< L_{\mathcal{P}}, l0_{\mathcal{P}}, V_{\mathcal{P}}, V0_{\mathcal{P}}, I_{\mathcal{P}}, \Lambda_{\mathcal{P}}, \rightarrow_{\mathcal{P}}>$, where:

- $L_{\mathcal{P}} = L_{\mathcal{S}} \times L_{tp}, l0_{\mathcal{P}} = l0_{\mathcal{S}} \times l0_{tp}$,
- $V_{\mathcal{P}} = V_{\mathcal{S}} \cup V_{tp}$, $V0_{\mathcal{P}} = V0_{\mathcal{S}} \wedge V0_{tp}$,
- $I_{\mathcal{P}} = I_{\mathcal{S}}$,
- $\Lambda_{\mathcal{P}} = \Lambda_{\mathcal{S}}$,
- $\rightarrow_{\mathcal{P}}$ is defined with the two following rules, applied successively:

$$sync: \frac{l_1 \xrightarrow{a(p),\varphi,\varrho}_{\mathcal{S}^{\uparrow}} l_2, l_1' \xrightarrow{a(p),\varphi',\varrho'}_{tp} l_2'}{(l_1 l_1') \xrightarrow{a(p),\varphi \wedge \varphi',\varrho''=[\varrho;\varrho']}_{\mathcal{P}} (l_2 l_2')}$$

$$assemble: \frac{(l_i l_j) \xrightarrow{a(p),\varphi,\varrho}_{\mathcal{P}} (l_{i+1} l_{j+1}), l_i \neq l0_{\mathcal{S}^{\uparrow}}, (l0_{\mathcal{S}^{\uparrow}} l0_{tp}) \nrightarrow (l_i l_j), l0_{\mathcal{S}^{\uparrow}} \xrightarrow{a_0(p),\varphi_0,\varrho_0} l_1 ... l_{i-1} \xrightarrow{a_{i-1}(p),\varphi_{i-1},\varrho_{i-1}} l_i \in \rightarrow_{\mathcal{S}^{\uparrow}}}{(l0_{\mathcal{S}^{\uparrow}} l0_{tp}) \xrightarrow{a_0(p),\varphi_0,\varrho_0}_{\mathcal{P}} (l_1 l_j) ... (l_{i-1} l_j) \xrightarrow{a_{i-1}(p),\varphi_{i-1},\varrho_{i-1}}_{\mathcal{P}} (l_i l_j)}$$

The first rule combines one specification transition with one test purpose one by synchronizing actions, variables updates and guards. This yields a initial transition set which is completed with the second rule to ensure that there is a specification path such that any synchronized transitions is reachable from the initial location. For sake of readability, we have denoted in the second rule $(l0_{\mathcal{S}\uparrow}l0_{tp}) \nrightarrow (l_il_j)$ to express that there is no path from the initial location to (l_il_j) in $\mathcal{P}_T(op)$.

The synchronous product of the test purpose $tp_{T1}(ItemSearchReq)$ given in Figure 8 with the completed specification is depicted in Figure 10. The synchronized transitions obtained from the first rule are depicted in red. Initially, the test purpose aims to test the ItemSearch operation. So, the synchronous product is composed by the two ItemSearch invocations of the specification combined with test purpose properties.

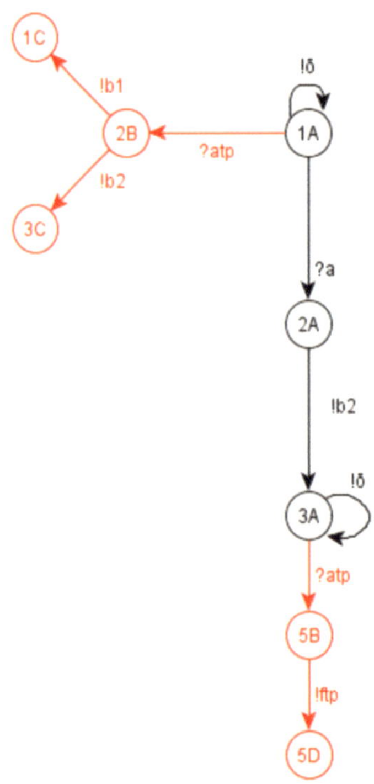

Fig. 10. A synchronous example

5.2 Incorrect behaviour completion

This straightforward part aims to complete synchronous products to express incorrect behaviours. Thanks to this steps, the generated test cases will be composed of final locations labelled either by local verdicts "pass" or "fail". The final test verdict shall be obtained without ambiguity from these local ones.

This completion is made by means of the STS operation *compl* which is defined as follows. For an STS $\mathcal{S}$, $compl\ \mathcal{S} =_{def} \mathcal{S}^{compl} =< L_{\mathcal{S}} \cup \{Fail\}, l0_{\mathcal{S}}, V_{\mathcal{S}}, V0_{\mathcal{S}}, I_{\mathcal{S}}, \Lambda_{\mathcal{S}}, \rightarrow_{\mathcal{S}^{compl}} >$ where $\rightarrow_{\mathcal{S}^{compl}}$ is obtained with the following rule:

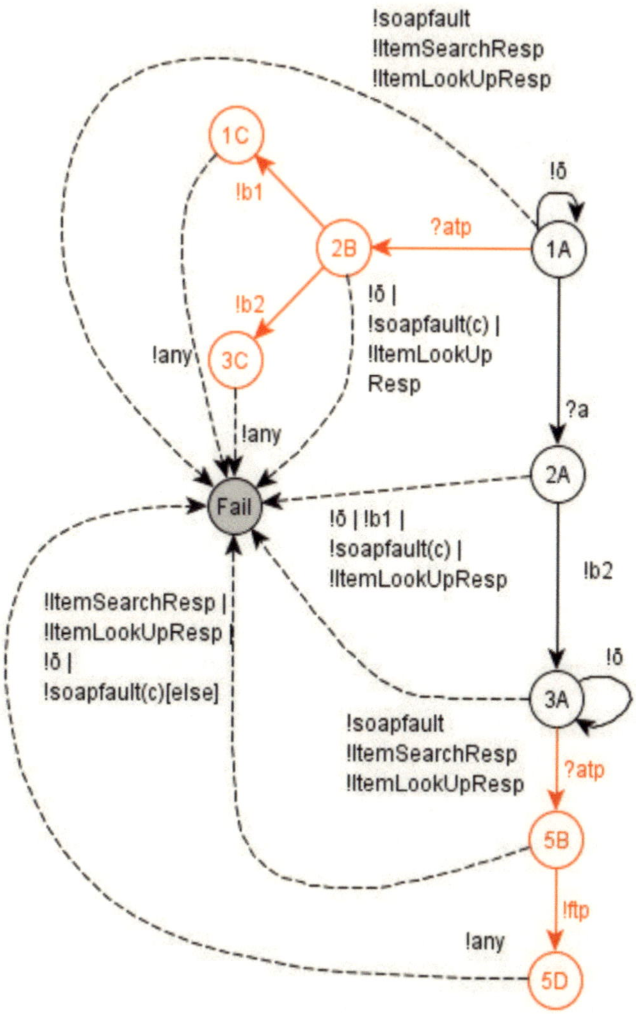

Fig. 11. A completed synchronous example

$$\frac{a \in \Lambda^O_{\mathcal{S}} \cup \{!\delta\},\ \varphi_a = \bigwedge_{l_1 \xrightarrow{a(p),\varphi_n,\varrho_n}_{\mathcal{S}} l_n} \neg \varphi_n}{l_1 \xrightarrow{!a(p),\varphi_a,\emptyset}_{\mathcal{S}compl} Fail}$$

A location l_1 is completed with new transitions to Fail, labelled by unexpected outputs with negations of the guards of transitions in $\mathcal{S}$.

By applying this step on the synchronous product example $\mathcal{P}_{T1}(ItemSearch)$ of Figure 10, we obtain the completed STS depicted in Figure 11. Dashed transitions depict the completion. For sake of readability, we use the label !any to model any output action. Intuitively, the dashed transitions represent unexpected output actions which lead to the Fail location. For instance, the transition $2B \xrightarrow{!\delta} Fail$ expresses that quiescence must not be observed. This transition can be used to test the satisfaction of the test pattern $T2$ (Section 4) directly: if no response is observed after a timeout, we consider that the Web Service under test is not available and therefore faulty.

5.3 Synchronous product path extraction with reachability analysis

Test cases are extracted from the completed synchronous products with Algorithm 1. For a synchronous product $\mathcal{P}_T^{compl}(op)$, the resulting STSs in $TC_T(op)$ are trees which aim to call the operation op, referred in $tp_T(op)$ by extracting acyclic paths of $\mathcal{P}_T^{compl}(op)$ beginning from its initial location and composed of the input action $?opReq(p)$. A reachability analysis is performed on the fly to ensure that these paths can be completely executed.

The algorithm constructs a preamble by using a Depth First Path Search (DFS) algorithm between the initial location l_0 and l_k. A reachability analysis is also performed to check whether the transition t labelled by $?opReq(p)$ is reachable (lines 2-8). In line 9, the value set $Spec(opReq)$, composed of values satisfying the firing of the transition t is generated with the Solving procedure. The Value set $Value(opReq)$, composed of values used for testing op is also constructed according to the $TestDom$ variable provided in test patterns. This set may be composed of values in $Spec(opReq)$, of unusual values in RV or of SQL/XML injection values in Inj (see Section 4). SQL/XML injections are only used if the variable type is equal to "String". If the variable types are complex (tabular, object, etc.), we compose them with other types to obtain the final values. We also use an heuristic to estimate and eventually to reduce test number according to the tuple number in $Value(opReq)$. Intuitively, for a constant denoted Max, if $card(Value(opReq)) > Max$, we reduce the cardinality of $Value(opReq)$ by removing one value of $RV(type(p_1))$, and one of value of $RV(type(p_2))$, and so on up to $card(Value(opReq)) \leq Max$. This part is discussed in the next Section.

The STS tc, modelling a test case, is reset, its variables are initialized with ϱ_0. The previous preamble path and the transition labelled by the operation request $?opReq$ with one value of $Value(opReq)$ are added to the transition set of tc (lines 12-15). Then, the algorithm also adds each next transition $(l_{k+1}, l_f, !a(p), \varphi_{k+1}, \varrho_{k+1})$ with the location l_f labelled by a verdict in $\{pass, fail\}$ and transitions to $Fail$ (lines 16-19). We obtain an STS tree, which describes a complete operation invocation. tc is finally added to $TC_T(op)$.

The "Solving" method takes a path $path$ and returns a variable update ϱ_0 which satisfies the complete execution of $path$. If the constraint solvers Een & Sörensson (2003); Kiezun et al. (2009) cannot compute a value set allowing to execute $path$, then "solving" returns an empty set (lines 21-28). We use the solvers in Een & Sörensson (2003) and Kiezun et al. (2009) which work as external servers that can be called by the test case generation algorithm. The solver Kiezun et al. (2009) manages "String" types, and the solver Een & Sörensson (2003) manages most of the other simple types.

Go back to our example of Figure 11 which depicts the completed synchronous product $\mathcal{P}_{T1}^{compl}(ItemSearch)$. If we suppose having $Spec(ItemSearch) = \{("ID","book","potter")\}$ and $Inj = \{"'or'1' =' 1"\}$, we obtain four test cases, two per value since the operation ItemSearch can be called two times in $\mathcal{P}_{T1}^{compl}(ItemSearch)$. Figure 12 illustrates the two test cases for the SQL injection "' or '1'='1". With the second test case, the operation ItemSearch is firstly called with ("ID","book","potter") to reach the second invocation, which is tested with the value "' or '1'='1".

Algorithm 1: STS extraction from synchronous products

Testcase(STS): TC;
input : An STS $\mathcal{P}_T^{compl}(op)$
output: A test case set $TC_T(op)$
foreach *transition* $t = (l_k \xrightarrow{?opReq(p_1,...,p_n),\varphi_k,\varrho_k}_{\mathcal{P}_T^{compl}(op)} l_{k+1}$ *with* ϱ_k *composed of the assignment* $TestDom := Domain$ *(Section 4.5)* **do**
  repeat
    $path = DFS(l_0, l_k);$
    $\varrho_0 := Solving(path);$
  until $\varrho_0 \neq \emptyset$;
  if $\varrho_0 == \emptyset$ **then**
    go to next transition;
  $Spec(opReq) = \{(x_1,...,x_n) \in D_{(p_1,...,p_n)} \mid (x_1,...,x_n) := Solving(path.t)\};$
  $Value(opReq) := \{(x_1,...,x_n) \in Spec(opReq)$ if $Spec(opReq) \in Domain\} \cup$ $\{(x_1,...,x_n) \in D_{(p_1,...,p_n)} \mid x_i \in RV(type(p_i))$ if $RV \in Domain\} \cup$ $\{(x_1,...,x_n) \in D_{(p_1,...,p_n)} \mid ((x'_1,...,x'_n) \in Spec(opReq), x_i = x'_i$ if $type(p_i) \neq "String", x_i \in Inj$ if $type(p_i) == "String")$, if $Inj \in Domain\};$
  foreach $(x_1,...,x_n) \in Value(opReq)$ **do**
    $STStc := \emptyset;$
    ϱ_0 is the variable initialization of tc;
    $\varphi_{tc} := [p_1 := x_1, ..., p_n := x_n];$
    $\rightarrow_{tc} := \rightarrow_{tc} \cup path.(l_k \xrightarrow{?opReq(p_1,...,p_n),\varphi_k \cup \varphi_{tc},\varrho_k} l_{k+1});$
    foreach *transition* $t' = l_{k+1} \xrightarrow{!a(p),\varphi,\varrho} l_{k+2}$ **do**
      $\rightarrow_{tc} := \rightarrow_{tc} \cup t';$
    foreach *transition* $t' = l \xrightarrow{!a(p),\varphi,\varrho} Fail$ *such that* l *is a location of path* **do**
      $\rightarrow_{tc} := \rightarrow_{tc} \cup t';$
    $TC_T(op) := TC_T(op) \cup tc;$

$Solving(path\ p) : \varrho;$
$p = (l_0, l_1, a_0, \varphi_0, \varrho_0)...(l_k, l_{k+1}, a_k, \varphi_k, \varrho_k);$
$c = \varphi_0 \wedge \varphi_1(\varrho_0) \wedge ... \wedge \varphi_k(\varrho_{k-1});$
$(x_1,...,x_n) = solver(c)$ //solving of the guard c composed of the variables $(X_1,...,X_n)$ such that $c(x_1,...,x_n)$ true;
2 **if** $(x_1,...,x_n) == \emptyset$ **then**
  $\varrho := \emptyset$
else
  $\varrho := \{X_1 := x_1, ..., X_n := x_n\}$

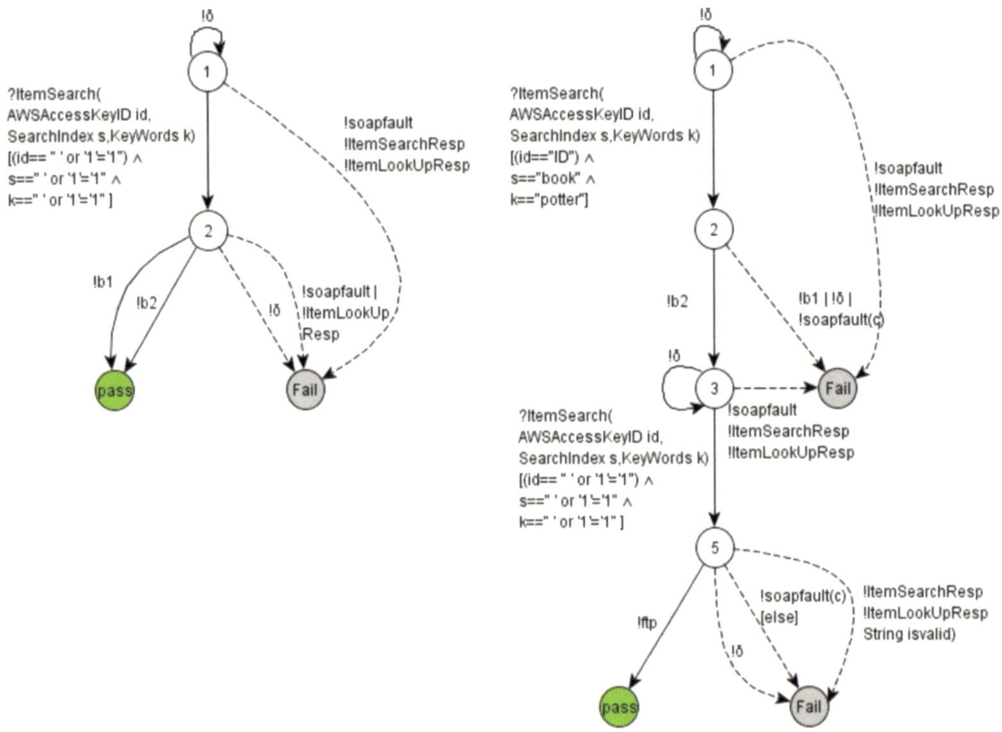

Fig. 12. Test case examples

5.4 Test verdict

In the test case generation steps, for a test purpose $tp \in TP$, we have defined the completion of the product $\mathcal{S}^{\uparrow} \times tp$ to recognizes non-conformant behaviours leading to its Fail states. So, the non-conformant trace set $NC\_STraces(\mathcal{S}^{\uparrow} \times tp)$ can be also written with the expression $STraces_{Fail}((\mathcal{S}^{\uparrow} \times tp)^{compl})$, which represents the suspension trace set leading to Fail. As a consequence, the $secure_{TP}$ relation can be also defined by:

$$
\begin{aligned}
Impl\ secure_{TP}\ \mathcal{S} &\Leftrightarrow \forall tp \in TP, STraces(Impl) \cap NC\_STraces(\mathcal{S}^{\uparrow} \times tp) = \emptyset \\
&\Leftrightarrow \forall tp \in TP, STraces(Impl) \cap STraces_{Fail}((\mathcal{S}^{\uparrow} \times tp)^{compl}) = \emptyset
\end{aligned}
$$

Now, it is manifest that the test case set, derived by our method, allows to check the satisfaction of the relation $secure_{TP}$ since a test case $\mathcal{TC} \in TC$ is selected in the product $(\mathcal{S}^{\uparrow} \times tp)^{compl}$. So, when a test case yields a suspension trace leading to a Fail state, then the implementation does not respect test purposes and security test patterns.

For a test case $\mathcal{TC}$, the suspension traces of $\mathcal{TC}$ are obtained by experimenting the implementation $Impl$. This execution of one test case $\mathcal{TC}$ on $Impl$ corresponds to the parallel composition of the LTS semantics $tc = ||\mathcal{TC}||$ with $\Delta(Impl)$, which is modelled by the LTS $\Delta(Impl)||tc =< Q_{Impl} \times Q_{tc}, q0_{Impl} \times q0_{tc}, \sum_{Impl}, \rightarrow_{\Delta(Impl)||tc}>$ where $\rightarrow_{\Delta(Impl)||tc}$ is given by the following rule:

$$\frac{q_1 \xrightarrow{a}_{\Delta(Impl)} q_2,\ q_1' \xrightarrow{a}_{tc} q_2'}{q_1 q_1' \xrightarrow{a}_{\Delta(Impl)||tc} q_2 q_2'}$$

Pragmatically, the tester executes a test case by covering branches of the test case tree until a *Pass* or a *Fail* location is reached. If a test case transition corresponds to an operation invocation, the latter is called with values given in the guard. Otherwise, the tester observes an event such as a response or quiescence. It searches for the next transition, which matches the observed event, and covers it.

Now, we can say that the implementation $Impl$ is $secure_{TP}$ or in other terms, satisfying a test purpose set TP, if for all test case $\mathcal{TC}$ in TC, the execution of $\mathcal{TC}$ on $Impl$ does not lead to a Fail state.

6. Experimentation and discussion

This section illustrates the benefits of using our method for security testing by giving some experiment results. We also discuss about the test coverage and the methodology complexity.

6.1 Experimentation results

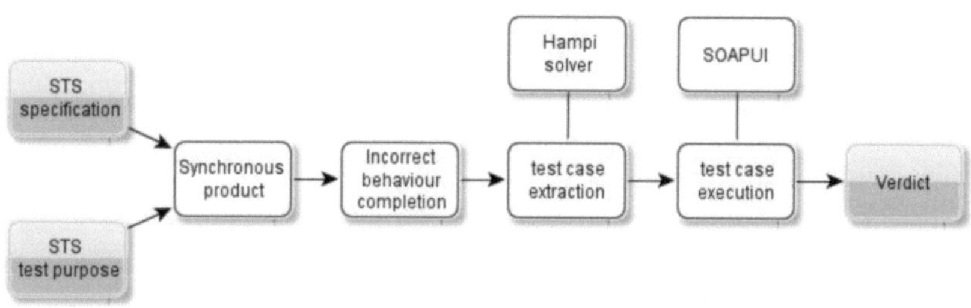

Fig. 13. Test tool architecture

We have implemented a part of this methodology in a prototype tool to experiment existing Web services. The tool architecture is illustrated in Figure 13. It performs the steps described in Section 5 i.e., synchronous products between test purposes and STS specifications, the completion of the synchronous products to add incorrect behaviours, and the test case extraction. Finally, test cases are translated into XML semi-automatically to be executed with the SOAPUI tool Eviware (2011), which is a unit testing tool for Web services. For simplicity, we have only considered String type parameters and the Hampi solver to generate values for the test case generation. To obtain a reasonable computation time, the String domain has been limited by bounding the String variable size with ten characters and by using a set of constant String values such as identification keys. We have also limited the test case number to 100. The experimentation is based upon six initial abstract test purposes, one for each test pattern given in Section 4.

Firstly, we experimented our methodology on the whole Amazon AWSECommerceService (2009/10 version) Amazon (2009). The current test purpose set had not risen security issues. Actually, this Web Service is taken as example in several research papers and many new versions of this service have been released to improve its reliability and its security. Therefore, these results are not surprising.

Web Service (WSDL)	test number	Availability	Authentication	Authorization
http://research.caspis.net/webservices/flightdetail.asmx?wsdl	56	0	0	1
http://student.labs.ii.edu.mk/ii9263/slaveProject/Service1.asmx?WSDL	60	0	1	1
http://biomoby.org/services/wsdl/www.iris.irri.org/getGermplasmByPhenotype	26	0	6	0
http://www.infored.com.sv/SRCNET/SRCWebServiceExterno/WebServSRC/servSRCWebService.asmx?WSDL	20	10	0	0
http://81.91.129.80/DialupWS/dialupVoiceService.asmx?WSDL	22	0	0	2
http://81.91.129.80/DialupWS/SecurityService.asmx?WSDL	18	0	0	3
https://intrumservice.intrum.is/vidskiptavefurservice.asmx?WSDL	66	6	1	0
http://www.handicap.fr/server_hanproducts.php?wsdl	78	2	0	4
https://gforge.inria.fr/soap/index.php?wsdl	100	1	0	0
http://193.49.35.64/ModbusXmlDa?WSDL	30	2	0	0
http://nesapp01.nesfrance.com/ws/cdiscount?wsdl	30	2	0	2
http://developer.ebay.com/webservices/latest/ShoppingService.wsdl	30	10	0	0

Fig. 14. Experimentation results

We also tested about 100 other various Web Services available on the Internet. Security vulnerabilities have been revealed for roughly 11 percent although we have a limited test purpose set. 6 percent have authorization issues and return confidential data like login, password and user-private information. Figure 14 summarizes our results.

Different kinds of issues have been collected. For instance, the Web Service *getGermplasmByPhenotype* is no more available when this one is called with special characters. Here, we suspect the existence of the "improper data validation" vulnerability. Authorization issues have been detected with *server_hanproducts.php* since its returns SOAP responses containing confidential data, such as table names and database values. Similar issues are raised with the Web Service *cdiscount*. So, these ones fail to provide confidentiality for stored data. With *slaveProject/Service1.asmx*, the "brute force" attack can be applied to extract logins and passwords.

The experimentation part has also revealed that other factors may lead to a fail verdict. For instance, the test of the *Ebay shopping* Web Service showed that quiescence was observed for a third of the operation requests. In fact, instead of receiving SOAP messages, we obtained the error "HTTP 503", meaning that the Service is not available. We may suppose here that the server was experiencing high-traffic load.

Step	Complexity	Location nb	Transition nb
Synchronous product	nn′+(n+k)n′	k	n
Completion	k	k+1	n+kn
Test case extraction	(k+1+n+kn)n×Value(opReq)	/	/

Fig. 15. Time complexity of the methodology

6.2 Discussion

Both the complexity and test coverage was left aside in the methodology description. These ones can now be discussed:

- *Methodology complexity:* the whole methodology complexity is polynomial in time in the worst case (with large test purposes testing exhaustively the implementation). This complexity is summarized in Figure 15, for one test purpose and with n (n') the specification (test purpose) transition number, k (k') the specification (test purpose) location number respectively. The *location nb* (*Transition nb*) column gives the location number (transition number) of the resulting STS once the step is achieved. In the experimentation part, we have observed that this complexity is strongly reduced since the synchronous product step produces STSs with a few more locations and transitions than the specification ones. Nevertheless, this complexity also depends on the number of testing values in $Value(opReq)$. So, if $Value(opReq)$ is large, both the complexity and the test case number may manifestly explode. This is why we implemented a heuristic which limits the test case set, by limiting the Max value in the test case extraction algorithm (Algorithm 1). When the test case number is limited to 100, testing one Web Service with our tool takes at most some minutes. The execution of 1500 tests require less than one hour. The whole test cost naturally depends on the test case number, but also on the delay required to observe quiescence. We have set arbitrarily this delay to 60s but it may be necessary to augment or to reduce it,
- *test coverage:* the test coverage of the testing method depends on the test pattern number and on the Max parameter, which represents the test number per operation. Firstly, the larger the test pattern set, the more issues that will be detected, while testing. However, our experiment results show that a non exhaustive test purpose set is already able to detect issues on a large number of Web services. The method is also scalable since the predefined set of values RV and Inj can be upgraded easily.

  The test coverage depends, besides the test pattern number, on the number of parameters per operation: the higher the number of parameters, the more difficult it will be to cover the variable space domain. This corresponds to a well-known issue in software testing. So, we have chosen a straightforward solution by bounding the test case number per operation. The Max value must be chosen according to the available time for test execution but also according to the number of parameters used with the Web service operations so that each parameter ought to be covered by a sufficient value set. For instance, for one operation composed of 4 parameters, each covered with at least 6 values, the Max parameter must be set to 1300 tests. Nevertheless, as it is illustrated in our results, a lower test case number (100 tests) is sufficient to discover security issues. There exist other interesting solutions, for the parameter coverage, which need to be investigated, such as *pairwize* testing Cohen et al. (2003) which requires that, for each pair of input parameters, every combination of values of these two parameters are covered by a test case.

7. Conclusion

We have introduced a security testing methodology dedicated for stateful Web Services. This one takes STS specifications and a Nomad test pattern set, which are translated into test purposes to check the test relation $secure_{TP}$. The specification is completed to take into account the SOAP environment while testing. Test cases are generated by means of a synchronous product between test purposes and the completed specification.

The first concluding remark, raised by our experimentation, is that SOAP Web Services are not a "security nightmare". Several companies have taken into consideration the Web Service security standards. For instance, the Amazon Service is based upon some features proposed by the WS-Security specification (timestamps, etc.). Nevertheless, our experiment results have revealed that 11 percent of the tested Web Services are vulnerable. And, we believe that this number should increase with a larger test pattern set. This leads to the first perspective. Our work is based upon the recommendations for Web Services, provided by the OWASP organization. These ones do not propose formal security rules. However, it sounds interesting to dispose, in an open-source community, of a large formal rule set, independently of the language used for modelling them. Such a rule set would be interesting to derive easily test patterns and to define the vulnerability coverage of our testing method.

Our testing tool is a prototype which requires further improvements. To the best of our knowledge, there is no Nomad parser or analyzer to translate Nomad expressions into an automata-oriented model. So, abstract test purposes are currently constructed by hands. An automatic generation would be more pleasant. The value sets, used for the test case generation can be manually modified but stay static during the test case generation. Furthermore, to avoid a test case explosion, the cardinality of these sets is reduced independently of the Web Service under test. It could be more interesting to propose a dynamic analysis of the parameter types to build a list of the most adapted values. It could be also interesting to analyze the values leading to more errors while testing and to set a weighting at each of them.

The experimentation part has also revealed that other external factors, e.g., high traffic load, may lead to a fail verdict. Such external factors show the limitations of our testing method, which cannot take them into account. A possible solution would be to complete it with a monitoring method which could detect security issues over a long period of time.

8. References

Amazon (2009). Amazon e-commerce service (ecs).

Castanet, R., Kone, O. & Laurencot, P. (1998). On the fly test generation for real time protocols, *International Conference on Computer Communications and Networks,* p. 378.

Cohen, M. B., Gibbons, P. B. & Mugridge, W. B. (2003). Constructing test suites for interaction testing, *Proc. Intl. Conf. on Software Engineering (ICSE)*, pp. 38–48.

Cuppens, F., Cuppens-Boulahia, N. & Sans, T. (2005). Nomad : A security model with non atomic actions and deadlines, *Computer Security Foundations. CSFW-18 2005. 18th IEEE Workshop*, pp. 186–196.

Darmaillacq, V., Fernandez, J., Groz, R., Mounier, L. & Richier, J.-L. (2006). Test generation for network security rules, *Testing of Communicating Systems (TestCom)*, Vol. 3964, LNCS, Springer, pp. 341–356.

Een, N. & Sörensson, N. (2003). An extensible SAT-solver, *Proc. 6th International Conference on Theory and Applications of Satisfiability Testing*, Vol. 2919, LNCS, Springer, pp. 502–518.

Eviware (2011). Soapui. http://www.soapui.org/.

Frantzen, L., Tretmans, J. & de Vries, R. (2006). Towards model-based testing of web services, *in* A. Bertolino & A. Polini (eds), *in Proceedings of International Workshop on Web Services Modeling and Testing (WS-MaTe2006)*, Palermo, Sicily, ITALY, pp. 67–82.

Frantzen, L., Tretmans, J. & Willemse, T. (2005). Test Generation Based on Symbolic Specifications, *in* J. Grabowski & B. Nielsen (eds), *Formal Approaches to Software Testing – FATES 2004*, number 3395 in *Lecture Notes in Computer Science*, Springer, pp. 1–15.

Gruschka, N. & Luttenberger, N. (2006). Protecting web services from dos attacks by soap message validation, *in Proceedings of the IFIP TC11 21 International Information Security Conference (SEC)*.

IEEE Standard glossary of software engineering terminology (1999). *IEEE Standards Software Engineering 610.12-1990. Customer and terminology standards*, IEEE press.

ir. H.M. Bijl van der, Rensink, D. A. & Tretmans, D. G. (2003). Component based testing with ioco.
URL: *http://doc.utwente.nl/41390/*

ISO/IEC (2009). Common Criteria for Information Technology Security (CC), *ISO/IEC 15408, version 3.1, ISO/IEC 15408*.

Kalam, A. A. E., Benferhat, S., Miège, A., Baida, R. E., Cuppens, F., Saurel, C., Balbiani, P., Deswarte, Y. & Trouessin, G. (2003). Organization based access control, *Proceedings of the 4th IEEE International Workshop on Policies for Distributed Systems and Networks*, POLICY '03, IEEE Computer Society, Washington, DC, USA, pp. 120–132.
URL: *http://dl.acm.org/citation.cfm?id=826036.826869*

Kiezun, A., Ganesh, V., Guo, P. J., Hooimeijer, P. & Ernst, M. D. (2009). Hampi: a solver for string constraints, *ISSTA '09: Proc of the eighteenth international symposium on Software testing and analysis*, ACM, New York, NY, USA.

Kropp, N. P., Koopman, P. J. & Siewiorek, D. P. (1998). Automated robustness testing of off-the-shelf software components, *FTCS '98: Proceedings of the The Twenty-Eighth Annual International Symposium on Fault-Tolerant Computing*, IEEE Computer Society, Washington, DC, USA, p. 230.

Le Traon, Y., Mouelhi, T. & Baudry, B. (2007). Testing security policies: going beyond functional testing, *ISSRE'07 (Int. Symposium on Software Reliability Engineering)*.
URL: *http://www.irisa.fr/triskell/publis/2007/letraon07.pdf*

Mallouli, W., Bessayah, F., Cavalli, A. & Benameur, A. (2008). Security Rules Specification and Analysis Based on Passive Testing, *in* IEEE (ed.), *The IEEE Global Communications Conference (GLOBECOM 2008)*.

Mallouli, W., Mammar, A. & Cavalli, A. R. (2009). A formal framework to integrate timed security rules within a tefsm-based system specification, *16th Asia-Pacific Software Engineering Conference (ASPEC'09), Malaysia*.

Martin, E. (2006). Automated test generation for access control policies, *Companion to the 21st ACM SIGPLAN symposium on Object-oriented programming systems, languages, and applications*, OOPSLA '06, ACM, New York, NY, USA, pp. 752–753.
URL: *http://doi.acm.org/10.1145/1176617.1176708*

Mouelhi, T., Fleurey, F., Baudry, B. & Traon, Y. (2008). A model-based framework for security policy specification, deployment and testing, *Proceedings of the 11th international conference on Model Driven Engineering Languages and Systems*, MoDELS '08, Springer-Verlag, Berlin, Heidelberg, pp. 537–552.

OASIS consortium (2004). Ws-security core specification 1.1. http://www.oasis- open.org/committees/tc_home.php?wg_abbrev=wss.

OASIS standards organization (2009). Xacml (extensible access control markup language). URL: *http://xml.coverpages.org/xacml.html*

OWASP (2003). Owasp testing guide v3.0 project. URL: *http://www.owasp.org/index.php/Category:OWASP_Testing _Project#OWASP_Testing_Guide_v3*

Rusu, V., Marchand, H. & Jéron, T. (2005). Automatic verification and conformance testing for validating safety properties of reactive systems, *in* J. Fitzgerald, A. Tarlecki & I. Hayes (eds), *Formal Methods 2005 (FM05)*, LNCS, Springer.

Salva, S. & Rabhi, I. (2010). Stateful web service robustness, *ICIW '10: Proceedings of the 2010 Fifth International Conference on Internet and Web Applications and Services*, IEEE Computer Society, Washington, DC, USA, pp. 167–173.

Senn, D., Basin, D. A. & Caronni, G. (2005). Firewall conformance testing, *Testing of Communicating Systems (TestCom)*, Vol. 3502, LNCS, Springer, pp. 226–241.

Singh, M. & Pattterh, S. (2010). Formal specification of common criteria based access control policy, *International Journal of Network Security*, pp. 139–148.

Specification, O. U. (2002). Universal description, discovery and integration. http://www.oasisopen.org /cover/uddi.html.

Tidwell, D. (2000). Web services, the web's next revolution, *IBM developer Works*, IBM books.

Tretmans, J. (2008). Model Based Testing with Labelled Transition Systems, *in* R. Hierons, J. Bowen & M. Harman (eds), *Formal Methods and Testing*, Vol. 4949 of *Lecture Notes in Computer Science*, Springer Berlin / Heidelberg, Berlin, Heidelberg, chapter 1, pp. 1–38. URL: *http://dx.doi.org/10.1007/978-3-540-78917-8_1*

World Wide Web Consortium (2001). Web services description language (wsdl).

World Wide Web consortium (2003). Simple object access protocol v1.2 (soap).

WS-I organization (2006). Basic profile. URL: *http://www.ws-i.org/docs/charters/WSBasic_ Profile _ Charter2-1.pdf, (accessed May 1, 2010)*

12

Autonomous Decentralized Multi-Layer Cache System to Low Latency User Push Web Services

Hironao Takahashi[1,2], Khalid Mahmood Malik[2] and Kinji Mori[1]
[1]*Department of Computer Science, Tokyo Institute of Technology Tokyo,*
[2]*DTS, Inc 3-39-5 Higashi Ueno Taitou-ku Tokyo,*
Japan

1. Introduction

Emerging rich interactive Web services require timeliness and high availability. These applications are usually characterized as high I/O intensive service model such as e-commerce services, medical sciences including healthcare and digital imaging. [1,3]. These applications require continuous operation, non-stop service system and timeliness to achieve high assurance to meet Service Level Agreement (SLA). SLA is the explicit requirement of the Quality of Service (QoS), such as reliability and timeliness. SLA requirement in the emerging applications on the Internet needs Autonomous Decentralized System (ADS) [8] characteristics [2,4].

The usage of Web services on the Internet is increasing exponentially and giving rise to very large online community. Web service community behavior shows power functions (from 2.1 to 4) that is called "small world". Therefore, some web sites are much more popular and hence highly I/O intensive. In these websites, there is considerable response time delay due to increasing demand of user push type I/O request and its data coherence. Faded Information Field (FIF) technology supports pull type of read event access enhancement while Autonomous Decentralized System by different class of nodes by its service level. But Web services require interoperable communication for user push type also. Traditional system does not meet the dynamic demand and it doesn't have Multi layer-cache concept. To enhance the user push type I/O performance, there are two approaches. One is the cache node approach and the other is selecting a high performance device. Each of them has pros & cons. High speed device such as NAND Flash SSD has less capacity and very limited write life cycle time. Proxy cache node effects for read event but it doesn't achieve write event on each node dynamically. Thus the interoperable I/O performance is not enhanced by existing approaches. How to solve these issues by the system architecture is proposed by this paper. First is to achieve timeliness user pushing type I/O performance by using write back cache processing node (P-Node). Second is to maintain online property by trio nodes by dual data field configuration. The third is data availability which is achieved by dividing processing node and content node in two data fields and duplicating data storage partitions. This system architecture has two data fields with trio nodes Autonomous Decentralized

Multi Layer cache system. Processing node (P-Node) has L3 cache and it performs low latency of time response. L3 cache is dedicated block cache memory on P-Node. Because operating system managed memory doesn't hold specific block data of application services inside of the memory [10, 11], there have been a number of efforts to improve I/O performance however these are substantially different from our work. In [12], the author proposes Unified Buffer Cache (UBC). The focus is to unify the file system and virtual memory caches of file data to improve I/O transactions. However it is an unmanaged one level cache that is very much different from the L3 cache. Similarly [13], [14] provide solution for high I/O, based on RAM disk memory [18] and solid-state disk, and is altogether different from L3 block cache [16]. Other side of block cache is L4 cache. It is inside block device in the Content Node (C-Node). Pre-fetching read is performed by C-Node L4 cache. Thus, two different cache nodes manage user pushing type services model with low latency time web service.

Section 1 is introduction and section 2 is Autonomous multi-layer cache system architecture. Section 3 is its evaluation and section 4 concludes our work.

2. Autonomous multi-layer cache system architecture

2.1 System architecture

Autonomous decentralized multi-layer cache system is designed to achieve low latency user push web service. The system architecture is shown as Figure 1.

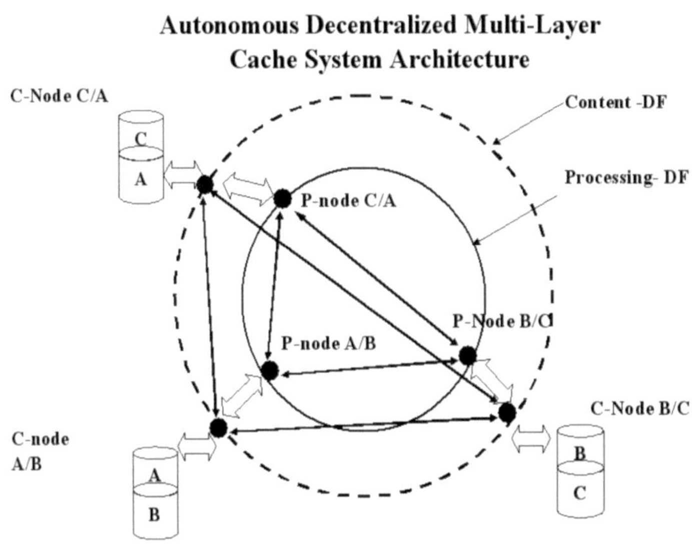

Fig. 1. Autonomous Decentralized Multi-Layer Cache system architecture

The system has following features.

1. Dual Data Fields for Processing and Content.
2. Processing Data Field for Process trio Node group.
3. Content Data Field for Content Trio Node group.
4. P-Node and C-Node are configured Trio Node group on each Data Field.
5. Data availability is achieved by dual storage disk partitions.

6. To achieve the timeliness I/O, the dedicated block cache is implemented on both Nodes.
7. Write event performed by L3 cache on P-Node.
8. Data availability achieved by duplicated storage partitions on each C-Node.

The storage space for all data is at C-node trio group. Each C-Node is connected three of them. To execute C-Node application program, P-Node is always required. Therefore, group creation process is required initially.

2.2 Initialization

Initialization process is shown in Figure-2.

1. C-Node broadcasts its own node status.
2. When other C-Node receives their node status, reply to it with own node status via Content Data Field.
3. Created Trio C-Node group, broadcasts the request of P-Node availability via C-DF.
4. Receive the initialization request from C-Node, P-node reply their node status.
5. C-Node notices P-Node for P-Node trio group creation.
6. P-Node is created by nearest P-Node autonomously.
7. Once P-Node trio group and C-Node trio group is created, P-Node starts to mount C-Node storage partitions.
8. Here, P-Node has two mounting points on C-Node. P-Node mounts one storage partition via L3 cache space and another storage partition is mounted via non L3 cache space.
9. P-Node manages two storage partitions now. The data availability is achieved by the duplicate storage partitions.

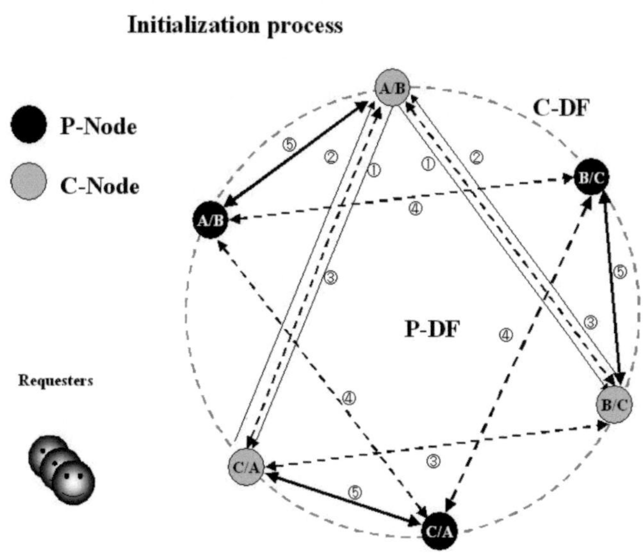

Fig. 2. Initialization process

10. C-Node (A/B), C-Node (B/C) and C-Node(C/A). Therefore, P-Node trio group also has same storage partition as P-Node (A/B), P-node (B/C) and P-Node (C/A).

After mounting of C-Node successfully, application program and service are loaded from C-node. Now P-Node is ready to start web service for C-Node.

2.3 Processing Node (P-Node) autonomous failure sense and replacement process

Processing node (P-Node) is timeliness high I/O response event execution node. To execute timeliness event, P-Node has L3 cache space in its local memory to do one hop write event. Each P-Node in trio group communicates with each other. When, one of P-node fails, other P-node in trio group detects the status. The failure replace process is shown in Figure 3. In this case, P-Node (A/B) is failed and P-Node (B/C) detected this status by the event of co-related storage partition as "B". P-Node (B/C) broadcasted the message for inquiry of available extra P-Node via P-DF (Step-1). There are three P-nodes available and the nearest position P-Node is to be the candidate of new member node. The fastest replier P-Node is selected by this policy (Step-2). P-Node (B/C) and P-Node (C/A) are creating new P-Node connection (Step-3). New P-Node (A/B) starts to mount C-Node (A/B) and load application program from C-Node (A/B). During the creation of new P-Node (A/B), the service for storage partition "A", "B" and "C" are sustaining by P-Node (B/C) and P-Node (C/A). P-Node doesn't have any application program and its data. These data and service program are stored in C-Node. Therefore, P-Node replacement event can be so easy and so quickly for change. The data in L3 cache on failure P-Node (A/B), the possibility of dirty data on storage partition "A". This dirty data "A" is flushed by P-Node (C/A) message. Therefore, write dirty data coherency is protected.

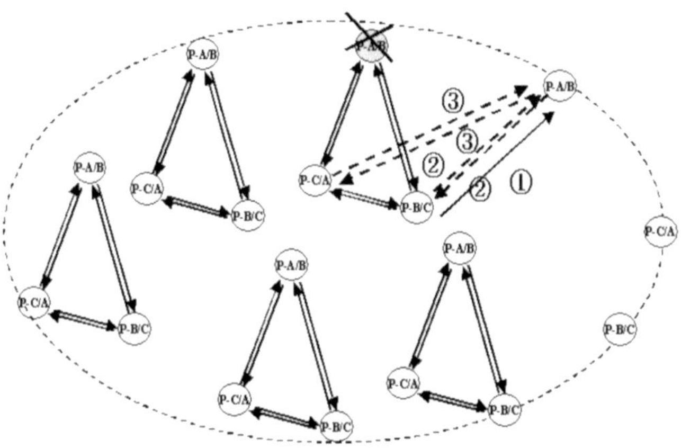

Fig. 3. P-Node (A/B) replacement process

2.4 Processing Node (P-Node)

Processing Node (P-Node) has L3 cache in its local memory space. Unlike OS local memory and UBC, this cache space is storage block address cache and is generated by cache control software with RAM disk driver. Therefore, L3 cache is not visible from OS. The main purpose of L3 cache is timeliness write I/O event execution by write back cache policy. Each P-Node is mounted two partitions on C-Node and one side of partition is mounted through

L3 write back cache. L3 write back cache holds write data until the dirty flush timing comes. At the flush time L3 cache autonomously flush the dirty data. The summarization of P-Node features is following. 1) Three nodes are collaborating as trio node group. 2) Write event request executes by L3 cache write back policy in local memory space. 3) Each P-Node is mounted two storage partitions on C-Node to maintain its data availability. 4) Minimized write I/O latency. 5) Autonomous read cache node expansion. The uniqueness of P-Node is trio node configuration. Each node has two storage partitions and three nodes that have mirroring partitions as mirrored. Therefore, if one P-Node fails, other node can continue the system operation and maintain its availability. But, the main purpose of two partitions are mirrored by three nodes is write back cache with no dirty data flushing policy. Because P-Node achieves timeliness write I/O event without any write speed performance drop. P-Node receives write event request by its L3 write back cache. Creating dirty data flush is done by other P-Node that was mounted on same partition without L3 write-back cache.Figure 4 shows L3 block cache P-Node.

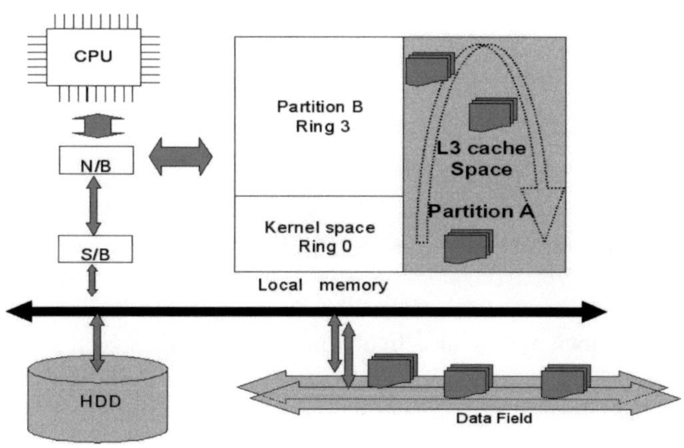

Fig. 4. L3 Block cache P-Node

Other space is OS memory space. Other one of node service runs on this memory space. L3 block cache policy is always write-back cache and other one is no write-back policy. The P-Node performs the high I/O response from the request by L3 block cache and performs write eventually coherency process. Thus, P-Node activates by two nodes minimum and they achieve low latency write event manner.

There are three features of L3 cache. Firstly it converts local memory into I/O block device cache, and mounts this on C-Node target device. Secondly cache policy selection as per the application requirement, and lastly an appropriate technique to search and access the data efficiently in the L3 block cache. The selection of block device is very flexible, for instance if system needs more high I/O speed for I/O and network transactions then the local memory is the ultimate choice. The local memory is transformed to a block I/O device to behave as a cache layer. Consequently it performs high I/O transactions and significantly improves response by utilizing bandwidth equal to the local memory. L3 cache management software detects the block address, which was requested, and keeps this data on the cache device. So, most of the requests are fulfilled from the cache. If the requested block data is not available on the cache, then it is accessed from target storage device. The third function of the L3 block cache technology as shown as Table -1 is search algorithm to look for data on the L3 block cache efficiently. A new cache search algorithm quickly searches required block of data for I/Os to further reduce the latency of time. The L3 block cache consisting of blocks is divided into groups where each group contains equal number of blocks. The jumping algorithm first points to the required group for which that sector corresponds and then search to the required block of data in the group. Jumping algorithm enhances much higher search time than standard sequential search technique for sequential requests. If the requests are randomly distributed, then more advantage is expected than standard search. Investigation for the value of number of column for block I/O data is carried out. In the current paper the value is 32, but If CPU performance is higher, then 64 or 128 may be selected as this tradeoff depends upon the CPU specifications.

Group 1 ⇨	Block 1	Block 2	Block 3	Block 4	Block 5
Group 2	Block 1	Block 2	Block 3	Block 4	Block 5
Group 3	Block 1	Block 2	Block 3	Block 4	Block 5

Table 1. P-Node L3 block cache jumping search table

In order to elaborate this mechanism, following is its example. This simple code describes how to search desired block of data effectively on the L3 block cache:

```
IRP Offset =0;
IRP length = 2048;
NrBlocks = ((offset + NrSectors - 1)>> *(targetDisk->SectorPerBlock2)) +1;
NrBlocks = ( ( 0 + 4  - 1)>> 3  ) +1;
Index = (ULONG) ((blockSector.QuadPart) % (targetDisk->NrBlocks));
Index = 1 % 100 = 1;
RowIndex = (Index / (targetDisk->index Columns));
ColumnIndex = 0%32= 0;
Block = _SearchBlock (targetDisk, blockSector, RowIndex, Column Index);
Block = _SearchBlock (targetDisk, 0, 0, 0);
```

Block of data will be searched in the list attached on this index that whether it exists on L3 block cache or not. Hashing technique is useful for large size data but it is weak for small set of data. Also when the data address has conflict, open address method is used to resolve the issue.

2.5 Content Node (C-Node)

Content node (C-Node) has all of service application program and data related to each storage partition. Each C-Node is configured trio group autonomously. The storage partition is encapsulated L4 block cache. The L4 cache is dedicated device block cache and it has write back policy. The request from P-node is entertained in write back cache manner.

Therefore, write event latency of time to be shorter than non L4 cache C-Node model. C-Node is Content Node that has dynamic data availability function for web application services. There is iSCSI base connection from P-Node to C-Node and it enables to connect P-Node for high I/O response execution. The capacity of storage is virtualized value that was shown and it is showing multi Terabyte storage capacity. C-Node has two partitions regularly and they are mirroring by the trio nodes as shown in Figure 5. The disk partitions inside of C-Node are main pool and sub pool such as "A" and "B", "B" and "C" and "C" and "A". Therefore, if "A" partition disk is failed; other duplicated partition can be used for maintaining the service. C-Node is connecting Data Filed and is waiting the event from upper P-Node. When P-Node receives the storage mount point from C-Node, P-Node mounts to C-Node and starts each service from each partition. Once each service is started, C-Node tries to maintain frequently accessed block address for each service on L4 cache to enhance the cache hit availability.

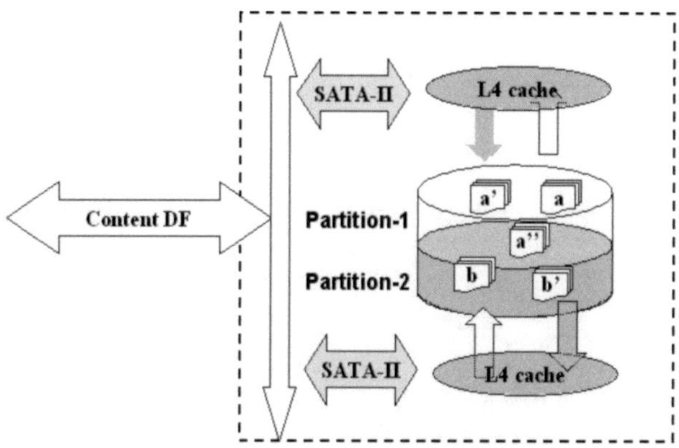

Fig. 5. L4 cache design diagram

Thus, L4 cache on C-Node holds the most used block data on the L4 cache and is utilized for P-Node expansion when service demand is increased. Generally, C-Node can connect other C-Node whenever P-Node in Data Field requests new extra storage capacity. The process of expansion event for C-Node executes by block data analysis monitor in P-Node. The block data analysis tool gets the block address total sum in the sampling time and if the total block address exceeds the threshold value, this P-Node broadcasts the expansion request to extra C-Node autonomously. The threshold value considers the balance L3<L4 to maintain timeliness I/O performance. C-Node has L4 cache that is located inside of each storage drive. The L4 cache implements pre-fetching technology to reduce the first read cache penalty. The accuracy of read cache hit ratio is determined by algorithm. There are many cache pre-fetching techniques available such as Least Recently Used (LRU), First In First Out (FIFO), Hidden Markov and NN+ CBR. In this case, LRU model is selected. C-Node autonomous storage node functions were implemented by following independent modules. 1) L4 cache layer management module. 2) Failure sense and event notice module. 3) Autonomous Local storage duplication module. 4) Pre-fetching read module. L4 cache enhances read / write cache hit ratio by dedicated L4 block cache space. Event the first read cache penalty, C-Node pre-fetches the most possible read data by its pre-fetching technique. Therefore, the almost read penalty is less than direct storage access. The basic features of L4 cache are 1) Loosely connection, transparency 1GB block cache.2) Write-back policy with

pre-read cache implementation and 3) Pre fetching boot up file, 4) Internal UPS that has automatic shutdown function acts whenever un-properly shutdown or upper system power fail re-securing dirty data on the cache table. 5) Can be expandable the total number of L4 cache size by multiple number of L4 cache drive.

This L4 cache space is completely individual autonomous memory space on the device. Today, there are many RAID storage subsystems available. But seeing from the individual device point of view, there are some difference points. RAID controller has buffer cache memory for RAID sets. But, this is the unified block cache space and it for block cache of RAID set and its volume. Also it is not safety idea when RAID subsystem electric power failure occurs. P-Node L4 cache is loosely connection individuality block cache. Only L4 cache device achieves no risk with high I/O speed with assurance benefit. Figure 6 is L4 cache block diagram in C-node. In this general case of design, 1GB DRAM for L4 cache memory with Flash SSD is target mounted device. Internally, 64bit based DRAM assigned and its I/O performance shows more than 270MB/s with 40KIOPS transaction performance under MLC SSD configuration.

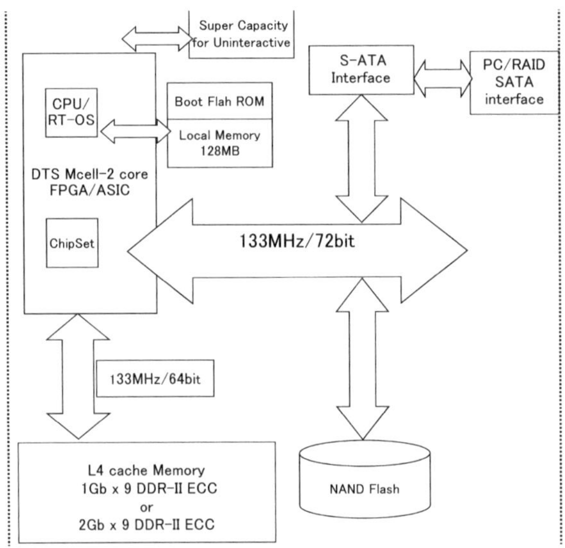

Fig. 6. L4 cache design diagram

2.6 Write data coherency process by P-Node

When write data request received from out side requester, two P-Nodes that are mounted C-Node application program partition execute the write request event by L3 cache P-Node and non-L3 cache P-Node. For instance, If Write event required at storage partition "A", there are two P-Node related this event as P-Node (A/B) and P-Node (C/A). In this case, P-Node (A/B) has L3 cache for "A" and P-Node (C/A) hasn't. The ACK for write event requester replied by P-Node (A/B) using L3 write back cache is by one hop. Then P-Node (A/B) is holding dirty data. Another P-Node (C/A) executes write event to C-Node (C/A). It also does C-Node (A/B) by write event broadcast message via C-DF. Once received write event request from P-Node (C/A). Both of C-Node (A/B) and C-Node (C/A) have done the write event and ACK to P-Node (C/A) that the event is completed. When P-Node (C/A) received it from both of C-

Node, P-node (C/A) signal cast to P-node (A/B) the message of write event was done. Then P-node (A/B) flag off of write dirty and open the memory space for new write event entry. Therefore, always write-data response time is maintaining high I/O response by L3 write-back cache with non-L3 write-through cache without cache memory size limit.

2.7 Read event by L3/L4 cache

L3 cache on P-Node effects read I/O event also. L3 cache is dedicated storage cache on P-Node and it maintains the data inside of L3 cache. The read event process is following. a) When received the read event "A" from requester, there are two P-Nodes that are related partition "A". b) One of P-Node has L3 block Cache space and other is no cache space of dedicated "A" partition. It just mounts "A" partition. c) When executes read event of "A" partition, the one of P-Node which has L3 cache for partition "A" executes the read event if L3 cache space holding the read event data and broadcast its acknowledge via data field as timeliness manner. d) Other one of P-Node executes by traditional read event execution if read data detects inside of memory space. e) The fastest read event executed node broadcasts the result of read request event to other nodes with event message. f) Once received the read event result from any P-Nodes, this node stops the read event execution. g) Eventually, the fastest P-Node result reaches the requester. P-Node read event is very flexible process. If one of node holding data for the event, anyone can be the fastest replier. Other node that has data for read request is stopped by the fastest node action. When the read event access size exceeds more than L3 cache, L4 cache on C-Node has possibility to maintain the next priority data. C-Node manages the size of L4 cache if P-Node L3 cache size exceeds L4 cache, C-Node expands the L4 cache capacity inside C-node disk configuration change and it maintains the ratio "L3<L4".

2.8 Content Node (C-node) failure sense and replace

When the event of C-Node failure occurs, co-related P-Node detects C-Node status by its response behavior. For example, C-Node (A/B) is mounted by P-Node (A/B), therefore, P-Node (A/B) detects C-Node (A/B) failure by no response or reply timeout. P-Node (A/B) single casts the message of call extra C-Node via C-DF. If an unassigned C-node is existing, then this C-node broadcasts the status to related C-Node in trio group. The nearest C-Node becomes the new member of C-Node trio group and starts to communicate with three as new trio group. The application is stored another size of C-Node with latest data, C-Node (B/C) provides "Storage partition "B" and C-Node (C/A) supplies storage partition "A" Thus, data duplication is time consuming work but this event runs on only C-DF. Therefore, seeing from out band requester, it is hidden internal task and less impact for out band service. This is one of the advantages by dual data field design. After duplication event is finished, New C-node (A/B) is released to P-Node (A/B). Even before complete this duplication event; other two of C-Nodes with three P-Nodes can sustain the operation without any service interruption.

3. Evaluation

3.1 Determination of geometrical architecture

Write I/O event requires two L3 cache nodes to manage write-data coherency by Eventually Consistent manner. This process is utilized by two L3 cache nodes with two L4 C-Nodes for assurance purpose. One of C-Node is mounted one of L3 cache node and other one is mounted no L3 cache as standard drive access way. Therefore, two P-Node with two C-Node partitions are required to maintain high latency of I/O. Thus, two partitions are required physically to achieve low latency of time for the write event. But, in two node configuration, there is no assurance policy against one node failure. Seeing from online function sustainability, three nodes is minimum number for a group. Each P-Node is connecting C-Node for its representative. Therefore, the combinations between P-Node and C-Node require the same number of nodes. To consider the online availability, the number of nodes is determined by Scale-out for the system. The latency of time and its overhead and threshold value are evaluated. Then it is determined about the number of nodes which can be easily managed. About online availability, what is the best number of node on each Data Field is evaluated. Proposing architecture has trio node group and when the event of one of node failed, the node availability of system level is 7/8. If node number n is same as node number n, its redundancy is much higher than Trio node n=3. But there are so many data communication on Processing Data Field and Content Data Field. For example, Dual node is 3/4, Trio node is 7/8 and Quad node is 15/16. 3/4 < 7/8 < 15/16 Therefore, quad node is higher than others. But, IO transaction is n*(n-1)/2 by Metcalfe's law. Therefore, its network overhead is

NP *(dual)* = 2*1/2 = 1
NP *(Trio)* = 3*2/2 = 3
NP *(Quad)* = 4*3/2 = 6

Moreover, management cost of cache coherency and cache size on each node is 1/n size from original cache size. Therefore, ½, 1/3 and ¼ cache size is utilized. It significantly reduces cache size. This matter generates very big impact of cache performance and less cache hit ratio. Therefore, Trio node plus two partitions is much better architecture in comparison with other number of nodes architecture.

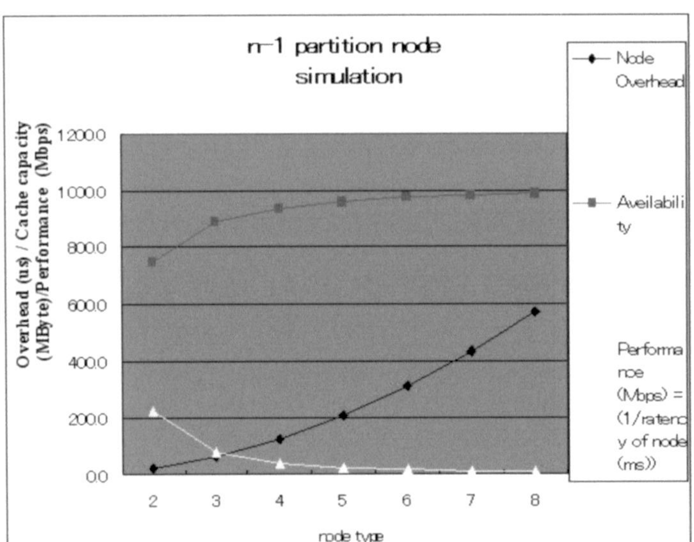

Fig. 7. n-Node simulation

Figure 7 shows n-Node simulation. The availability of Two-Nodes is 0.75 and Trio-Nodes is 0.888 and Quad-node is 0.937. But, node overhead is increasing by number of node. Two-Node is 22msec and Trio-node is 64mSec and Quad-Node is 126mSec. Seeing from balance point of view, two-Node is minimum overhead model but in one node failure, there are no redundancy nodes. It is risky from availability point of view. Therefore Trio-Node is better than other configurations. Also proposing system has dual data fields. It has high adaptability too.

3.2 P-Node + C-Node performance evaluation by XDD bench

In this section we evaluate C-Node L4 cache management policy as L3<L4. The objective of this experiment is to carry out performance evaluation of P-Node + C-Node using L3/L4 cache (combined performance gain due to L3 and L4 caches). This evaluation shows that the high I/O cache node doesn't maintain the I/O performance gain stable. The I/O performance gain calculates by Amdahl's law as shown in equation (1).

$$G_i = \frac{1}{1 - C_i + \frac{C_i}{X_i}} \prod_{j=1}^{m} L_{i,j}. \tag{1}$$

Gi = cache gain,
Ci = cache hit ratio
Xi= cache device speed gain compare target device speed.
Lij = overhead for cache program.

Therefore, if the access doesn't hit the cache, performance drops more than original target drive speed because cache overhead exists. To manage this cache behavior, multi-layer cache system architecture with balanced cache ratio is key factor. This experiment carries out two scenarios under this hardware and XDD benchmark test was utilized as shown in Table 2.

Machine	HP DL-145
CPU	AMD Opteron(tm) Processor 248 2210.364MHz x 2
OS	Linux Redhat 4
System RAM	Total 4 GB
DTS cache L_3	1GB (write Back) / 3GB OS space
DTS cache L_4	L3 < L4 2GB, (by L4 drive x 2) L3 > L4 0.03GB, (by HDD x 2)
Be Benchmark tool	XDD65.013007

Table 2. System specifications for system configuration

The evaluation of I/O performance of L_3 cache on P-Node against OS UBC cache has been carried out on Linux Kernel 2.6.24 rt27 32bit by XDD65.013007 as shown in Figure 8 (a), (b) and (c). In this scenario sequential read and write data types are utilized. Interoperable (two way) I/O types read/write (50% 50%) are evaluated in this scenario. The test files are 4KB, 64KB and 128KB on each access type for L3 cache in comparison with OS based UBC cache.

The total memory size is 4GB in the computer and it is assigned 3GB OS area and 1GB L3 cache. UBC utilizes full size of 4GB memory without any limitation. L3 cache policy was designed write back policy with read through. The reason of read through cache on UBC is because it is read buffer cache when read event is on the buffer space. L3 cache dedicates the write event and holds write event data for the read event. The result shows that L3 cache gives double performance than UBC buffer at sequential read and write test. Other result at read/write 50%/50% shows 13706.78 IOPS with L3 cache in comparison to 2745.08 for UBC. It is five times gain at read/write 50%/50% compare UBC cache node system. L3 cache is dedicated storage partition block cache and it manages write back policy by L3 cache and read from L3 cache. Therefore, interoperable I/O performance is very effectiveness event. This result shows the proof of performance effects by L3 cache compare unified buffer space.

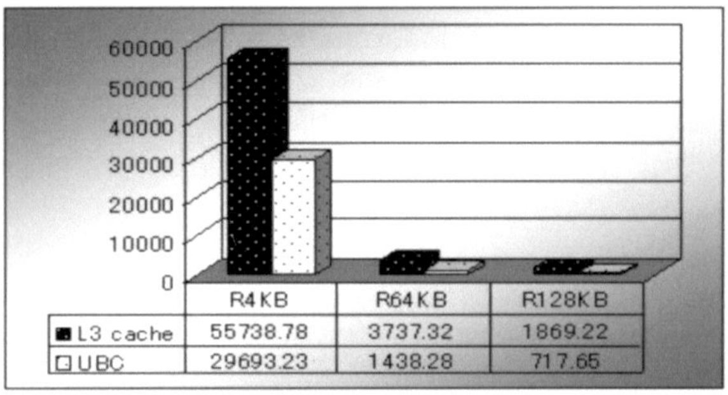

(a) Read sequential

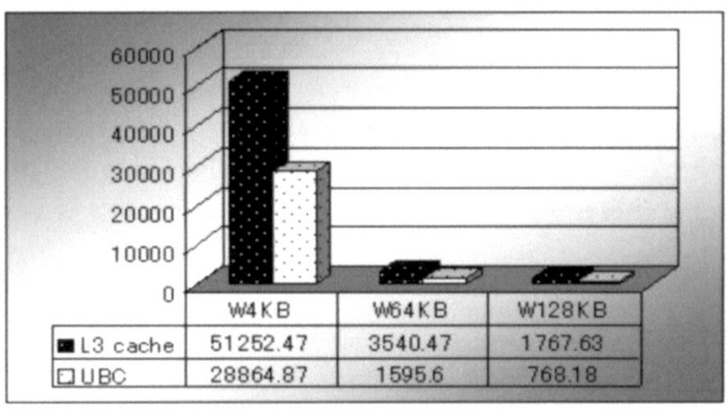

(b) Write sequential

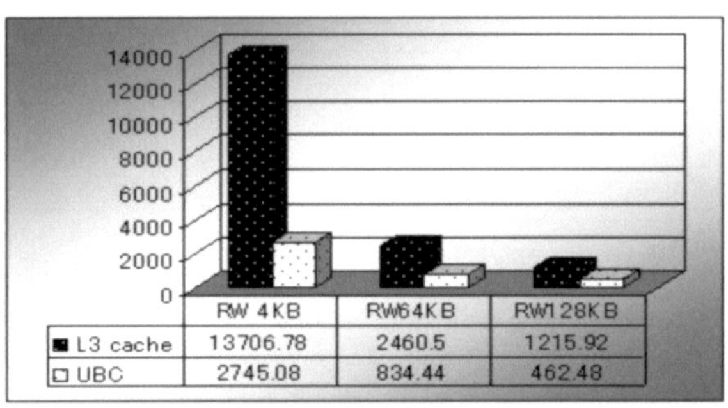

(c) Read/write 50% / 50%

Fig. 8. L3 cache VS OS UBC cache I/O performance.

4. Conclusion

Web service is heterogeneously demand model in today. User push type web service is so popular such as twitter and SNS. The demand from them is web evolving target model behavior. Therefore, web service needs adaptability, online expandability and data availability. Increasing user push type web service demand has dynamic behavior. Therefore the management of the coherency of written data is also a big issue. Proxy server is read cache model and it is data duplication model but it doesn't support duplication write data event dynamically. It also doesn't support coherency of write data too. Maintaining the low latency of time, single Data Field model can't achieve these issues with limited size of write cache memory space. The proposed system architecture ensures 1) Adaptability for user push type web service demands and 2) online node sustainability and 3) low latency of write data without write cache size limit and 4) P-node /C-Node cache autonomous contribution. Utilize L3 cache and L4 cache benefits by P-Node/C-Node L3/L4 cache. The write data coherency issues, P-Node plus C-Node write eventually Consistency process is enabled it. The concept is always executed by L3 cache P-Node and it guarantees the write event latency minimum network hops. Therefore, it achieves the low latency of time write I/O event for real time web application. P-Node also performs read data performance by L3 cache. L3 cache on P-Node evaluation shows double performance in comparison with UBC cache at sequential read and write test. Other results in case of read/write 50%/50% shows 13706.78 IOPS compare 2745.08 for UBC. It is five times faster than UBC cache node system. This is the proof of performance effects by L_3 dedicated cache for low latency web service in comparison with unified buffer on autonomous node.Thus, the layer cache node would be utilized under many massive I/O applications by its autonomous decentralized node. Co-related P-Node and C-Node show high I/O advantage with dynamic data availability. Therefore, Autonomous multi-layer cache system architecture is the solution for interoperable communication with low latency of time web service with dynamic data availability. Our next step is variable service application level evaluation and autonomous node community expansion / reduction technology design.

5. References

[1] I.-L. Yen, R.Paul and K. Mori. Towards integrated methods for high-assurance systems. IEEE Computer, 31(4):32-34, April 1998.

[2] K. Mori. Autonomous decentralized systems: concept, data field architecture and future trends. In Proc. of ISADS, IEEE, pages 28-34, 1993

[3] H.F. Ahmad and Mori. Autonomous Information Service System: Basic Concept for Evaluation, IEICE Transactions on Fundamentals of Electronics and Computer Sciences, Vol. E83-A, No.11 pp.2228-2235, November 2000

[4] Leguizamo, C.P. Kato, S. Kirai, K. Mori, K. Autonomous Decentralized Database System for Assurance in Heterogeneous e-Business. Proceeding of COMPSAC, p589-p595, IEEE, May 2000

[5] S. Przybylski,M. Horowitz, J. Hennessy, Characteristics of performance-optimal multi-level cache hierarchies, Proc of the 16th Annual International Symposium on Computer Architecture pp. 114 - 121 (1989).

[6] Moore's law www.intel.com/technology/mooreslaw/ index.htm

[7] Elizabeth Varki, Arif Merchant, Jianzhang Xu, and Xiaozhou Qiu. Issues and Challenges in the Performance Analysis of Real Disk Arrays. IEEE Transactions on Parallel and Distributed Systems, 15(6):559–574, 2004.

[8] ADS protocol specification R3.0 , MSTC/JOP 1101-19999/09/3

[9] Dai Kobayashi, Akitsugu Watanabe, Toshihiro Uehara, Haruo Yokota, A high-availability software update method for distributed storage systems: Research Articles, Systems and Computers in Japan, Vol 37, Issue 10, Pp 35-46 (2006)

[10] Daniel P. Bovet, Marco Cesati : Understanding the Linux Kernel , O'reilly Press, pp.422-498 (2001).

[11] Maurice J. Bach : The Design of The UNIX Operating system, Bell Labs Press, pp.264-287 (1986)

[12] Chuck Silvers, UBC : An efficient Unified I/O and Memory Caching Node for Netbsd, Proceedings of FREENIX Track: 2000 USENIX Annual Technical Conference, San Diego, California, USA, June 18–23, 2000

[13] White Paper, Using Real-Time I/O Signature Analysis to Identify Performance Improvement Options for Database Applications, http://www.soliddata.com/pdf/WP_IOSignatures_v2.pdf, Solid Data Systems Inc, July 2006.

[14] Wade Tuma, Comparisons of Drive Technologies for High-Transactions Databases, http://www.soliddata.com/pdf/WP_Drive_Comparison_v2.pdf, Solid Data Systems, Inc. (August 2007)

[15] Mohamed Zahran, Kursad Albayraktaroglu and Manoj Franklin, Non-Inclusion Property in Multi-level Caches Revisited, IJCA, Vol. 14, No. 2, pp.1-10, (2007)

[16] Hironao Takahashi, Hafiz Farooq Ahmad, Kinji Mori, Layered Memory Architecture for High IO Intensive Information Services to Achieve Timeliness, 11th IEEE High Assurance Systems Engineering Symposium Nanjing, China, December 3 - 5, 2008

[17] S. Pai, Vivek ; Druschel, Peter ; Zwaenepoel, Willy, "IO-Lite: a unified I/O buffering and caching system", ACM Transactions on Computer Systems (TOCS), Vol. 18, No. 2, 2000, p. 37-66.

[18] RAMDISK browsed at sep 20th 2009 http://www.vanemery.com/Linux/Ramdisk/ramdisk.html

[19] S. Przybylski,M. Horowitz, J. Hennessy, Characteristics of performance-optimal multi-level cache hierarchies, Proc of the 16th Annual International Symposium on Computer Architecture pp. 114 - 121 (1989).

[20] Hironao Takahashi, Hafiz Farooq Ahmad, Kinji Mori, "Balanced Memory Architecture for High I/O Intensive Information Services for Autonomous Decentralized System", The 9th International Symposium on Autonomous Decentralized Systems (ISADS 2009), Athens, Greece, March 23-25, 2009, pp 93-99

13

Authentication of Script Format Documents Using Watermarking Techniques

Mario Gonzalez-Lee, Mariko Nakano-Miyatake and Hector Perez-Meana
National Politechnics Institute,
Mexico

1. Introduction

The electronic document authentication is a subject of active research because, with the release of very efficient program for documents, images and video processing, the manipulation of such digital content becomes easier. Then, the development of efficient methods allowing the protection of sensitive digital material, avoiding unauthorized manipulations, without degradation of the original materials is a very important task that has found application in the solution of many practical problems in the financial, banking, insurances, legal, and Government fields, among others.

Thus digital content authentication and protection algorithms, for using in several practical applications, have been proposed during the last decade some of them use fragile or semi-fragile watermarking algorithm, fingerprints for document leakage investigations and robust watermark for copyright protection.

Most of these schemes consider the document to be protected as an image, without taking in account that in a more natural scenario, a digital document is in fact stored using an electronic format such as PDF, postscript and word files, etc., especially with the increasing use of digital signatures.

This chapter presents an authentication scheme for script format digital documents using watermarking techniques that are capable to achieve an accurate verification that makes possible to detect malicious and unauthorized documents manipulations. The remaining of this chapter is organized as follows, first, a review of similar works for document watermarking, followed by detailed background in sections 2 and 3, then, the document watermarking approach is presented in section 4, the results are presented in section 5 and finally some conclusions where the main achievements of this watermarking approach will be discussed, and in the end, the references used in this chapter are listed.

1.1 Previous works

Several schemes have been developed to authenticate digital documents which embed invisible watermark into digital documents, most of them considering the digital documents as binary images. Yang and Kot proposed a document authentication scheme, in which an authentication code is embedded by changing the spaces size between consecutive words and characters (Yang & Kot, 2004). The main drawback of this scheme is its high computational complexity and vulnerability against noise.

Huang proposed an authentication method for binary images including text documents (Huang et al., 2004), in which firstly the binary image is segmented in blocks and then some pixels in each block are rearranged in order to enforce a given relationship between the total number of black and white pixels in it. During the authentication process, this relationship is verified for each block in order to authenticate the block. If this relationship is satisfied the block is considered as authentic, otherwise the block is considered as tampered. The principal disadvantage of this method is that a degradation introduced in the encoded binary image is noticeable.

Wu and Liu proposed binary image block-wise authentication scheme, in which flippable pixels in each block are manipulated in order to embed a watermark bit in the block (Wu & Liu, 2004). Here the embedded watermark is imperceptible, because fliping flippable pixels do not cause any distortion of the binary image. However, in general, the watermark embedding payload is very low compared with the number of flippable pixels into the image.

To improve the embedding payload, Gou and Wu introduced the concept of "super-pixels" and wet paper coding into the Wu and Liu's scheme (Gou & Wu,, 2007). The "Super-pixels" form a set of individually non-flippable pixels, which can be removed or added together without causing visual distortion. Also Wu and Liu reported that their authentication scheme is robust to printing and scanning operations. However during the scanning process, a rotation, even with angles smaller than one degree may results in an embedded watermark signal lost.

Document authentication schemes for formats such as Portable Document Format (PDF) or PostScript had received few attention among researchers although many official documents are stored using this type of formats. In (Zhu et al., 2007), a document authentication method using render sequence encoding is proposed, in which the encoding process is based on modulate the display sequences using a Document Description Language (DDL), such as PostScript, PDF, Printer Control Language, etc. In the render sequence, predefined characters are permuted by a user's secret key; and then during the authentication process, the document is considered as authentic if the permutation corresponds to the secret key used in embedded stage. This scheme determines correctly if a document is authentic or not, however there are two inconveniences that may limit its practical use. Firstly the size of the encoded document file is considerably increased compared with the original file size, and the second one is the fact that the structure of the encoded render sequence is unnatural, and as a consequence, it can be easily detected by an unauthorized person, doing it possible the used of reverse engineering to tamper the document.

To solve these problems, Gonzalez-Lee proposed a watermarking-based document authentication scheme, in which character metrics are used to embed a watermark sequence (Gonzalez-Lee et al., 2009). The advantage of proposed scheme is that the watermarked file size is not changed compared with original file size and also the watermarked file conserves its original appearance, enhances in this form its security because the watermark presence is not evident.

Finally, we would like to discuss the previous work in document security done by the main promoters of electronic document schemes, the PDF uses a scheme with several variants of permissions that allow user to do different tasks, for example, permissions for printing or even copy portions of the document (done by CTL+C, CTL+V shortcuts), a password protected document will ask for the password when one wants to perform one of the described task. Unfortunately, this scheme is tied to Acrobat Reader and the security can be override as easy as to use another PDF viewer, for example Gnome Document Viewer available in most Linux distributions, that viewer won't ask for any password for printing or to copy portions of the document. Another possibility is that the security relies on hiding the document contents; in this case, the viewer doesn't allow anyone to see the contents of the document unless the right password is given. Again this scheme can be easily broken with the use of free tools, for example PDFcrack (Noren, 2008); by using this tools, anyone can break the password within a couple of days with a consumer computer. Once Broken, the attacker will be able to view the document contents, and save an unprotected copy of the document which can be modified, and even saved with the same password so the legitimate document is replaced by the tampered document and the user is unaware of this. More on the security model of PDF can be read in (Adobe, 2006).

2. Document description languages

Computer languages such as C language are general propose, they can be used for developing a broad spectrum of applications; others like Fortan and Matlab are designed for numerical calculations so their respective instruction sets facilitate greatly calculations in engineering field. One can easily think on many useful instructions or functions that facilitate coding complex programs, for example, the function sin(x) is very useful in engineering computing programs but it is of little use in describing an electronic document.

In order to achieve an efficient description of the basic elements that allow the creation of a practical document, we need a proper computer language that meets the challenge of describing properly an electronic document, this computer language is called a Document Description Language or DDL for short, and thus a DDL is a computer language which instruction set is designed to contain commands for common tasks needed to draw a document.

A DDL is designed to facilitate the description of a document, in other words, their instruction set are very handy for common task such as to indicate where to draw a given set of characters (e.g. a row or a paragraph), which font size, and other properties according to the desired document layout. It is hard to imagine trying to describe a web page using C or Matlab instruction set, so, the scope and propose of DLL's is evident.

We can mention many implementations of practical DDL's, for example, for describing Web pages we can use the Hiper Text Markup Language (HTML), and for electronic documentation, we can choose among PostSript, Portable Document Format (PDF), Open Document Format (ODF) used by the OppenOffice.org and LibreOffice projects.

As discussed above, there are many DDL's, most of them are different radically, this difficult the development of a universal approach that can be used for every DDL. In most cases, a given watermarking approach can be adapted for several DDL's, but in other cases, we must to design a completely different paradigm.

Finally, we wish to point out that a DDL is like any other computer language, it provides an instruction set but those instructions must be properly structured, in next section, a discussion on this subject is carried out.

3. Document Description Scripts

In previous section, we discussed the scope of DDLs, in this section we'll introduce a new concept: the Document Description Script or DDS for short. Let's state this: a DDL is an instruction set, these instructions are unable to perform anything unless they are properly structured and proper parameters are given.

Most of the time, for any computer language, instructions are written in a file known as a sourcecode and then compiled in order to generate a computer program (sometimes, the sourcecode is not compiled but interpreted instead), sometimes these source code is also called a script; a DDS shares this concept, the DDS contain a set of instructions properly structured, they are written in a script what we call a document and this document is interpreted by a document viewer, so this viewer interprets how to draw a document in a computer screen or how to print it.

For example, in Fig. 1; a part of the DDS as used for the ODF, PostScript and PDF is shown. Of course, it lacks many essential elements, but the aim is to show the nature of those approaches.

In Fig. 1(a), we can see that the text "This is a text document showing a DDL with a xml approach" is to be drawn in the page, we can identify the special tags body to indicate that the body of the document is to begin, and then the special tag text indicates that the enclosed stream is the text of the document and furthermore, the special tag `text:p text:style-name="Standard"` indicates that the enclosed paragraph and this text has the style Standard (12 pt Times Roman font, normal weigth), usually a document has several paragraphs and several styles including user defined styles, for example bold letters with font size 14 pt and Arial font, and the way to define which parts of the whole text has to be in this style is by means of these command sequence.

In Fig. 1(b) the command sequence to draw the text "this is a text document showing a DDL with a PostScript approach" is illustrated, it is clear how different DDL's approach the same task in different ways, not necessarily better yet different. In this slice of code, one can identify a command used to position the text in a given point in the page ("`100 50 moveto`" positions the beginning of the text at the point (100,50)), and then, the character stream is given, note the special delimiters "`(`" and "`)`" which enclose the characters to be drawn and finally the instruction "`show`" that draws the given stream in the page. And in Fig. 1(c) it is shown the corresponding script slice to approach the same task, one can see that it is almost the same as done using the postscript approach, not surprisingly since it is know that PDF is an evolution from Postscript.

We would like to emphasize that not all DDL's use the same instruction set for document descriptions, furthermore, in most cases DLL's differ greatly, thus in the remaining of this chapter, we well focus in DDL in which character metrics are available so an automated system can locate an process them, and illustrative examples will be carried out using the postscript DDL because is better documented and easier to understand; since postscript is

```
<office:body>
      <office:text>
         <text:p text:style-name="Standard">
            This is a text document showing a DDL with a xml
            approach
         </text:p>
      </office:text>
  </office:body>
 </office:document-content>
```

(a)

```
100 50 moveto
(this is a text document showing a DDL with a PostScript
approach)
show
```

(b)

```
100 50 Td
(This a text document showing a DDL with a PDF approach) Tj
```

(c)

Fig. 1. Example of a DDS, one can notice how a Language is used to describe the structure of an electronic document. The same text was written with a) the ODF; b) the Postscript Language and c) the PDF.

considered the basis of PDF, it is feasible that if you understand the postscript it will be in fact easier to understand the PDF internals, conversely, it will be more difficult to proceed the other way.

A typical approach is depicted in Fig. 2. In this figure we can see that the most important parts of the script file are the header and the body. The former is called Encapsulated PostScript or EPS, it contains information about the version of the standard used in the document; in addition, it contains other useful data such as the number of pages, the bounding box, etc. The latter, that is to say, the body contains the whole contents of the document organized in pages (each one can be recognized easily by the special command

```
%!PS-Adobe-2.0
%%Pages:  2
%%Creator: Txt2Ps
%%Title: A Simple Document.
%%PageOrder: Ascend
%%BoundingBox: 0 0 615 792
%%CreationDate: Fri Jul  9 17:31:33 2010
%%BeginSetup
%%PaperSize: Letter
%%EndSetup

/Times-Roman      findfont
12          scalefont    setfont

%%Page: 1 1
%%                  %%                  Page                  Contents
%%%%%%%%%%%%%%%%%%%%%%%%%%%%%%%%%%%%%%%%%%%
showpage

.
.
.
%%Page: N N
%%                  %%                  Page                  Contents
%%%%%%%%%%%%%%%%%%%%%%%%%%%%%%%%%%%%%%%%%%%
showpage
```

Fig. 2. Example of a basic DDS of PostScript.

`showpage` which is used to mark the end of a page and tell the document interpreter that the page must be drawn). In this example, the actual contents of the page is not shown, a comment is shown instead. The first lines illustrate a header, then, the marker `%%Page: x x` is used to begin the page x, and the command `showpage` marks the end of the page.

In the examples ahead, all this structure will be omitted and just the contents will be illustrated in order to keep the examples small and to focus in the parts of the script that are processed.

3.1 Character metrics

In last section, the basic concepts of DDS's and their role was described, in this section we will go deeper in the internals of the document description scripts.

Let's first introduce the character metrics concept.

A character metric is the distance between consecutive characters, another way to understand the character metrics is as the distance that "the cursor" must be advanced to place next character. A character has two metrics, called m_x and m_y, that are the distance in the x-axis and the y-axis where the next character must be placed (see Fig. 3). Since some languages have different writing styles, the metrics should agree with this, and thus we can have vertical documents, like Japanese in which $m_x=0$ and $m_y \neq 0$, and horizontal documents like in English in which $m_x \neq 0$ and $m_y=0$, and the seldom used, diagonal documents, which are mostly used in graphic design field, even when seems that this class apply only for line shapes, here consider that any text in which $m_x \neq 0$ and $m_y \neq 0$ holds is a diagonal document. Fig. 4 shows examples of each type of documents.

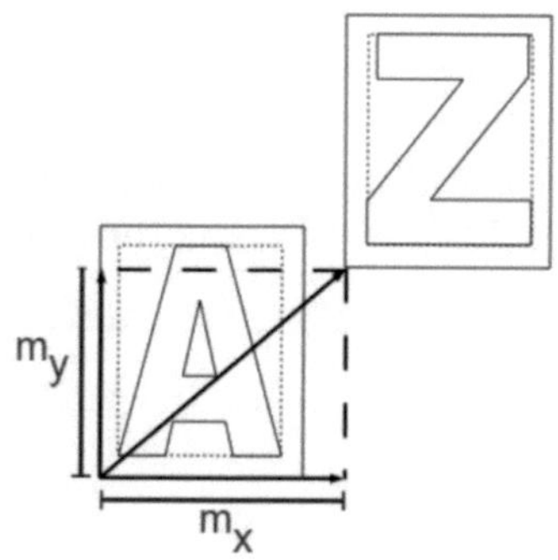

Fig. 3. The character metrics.

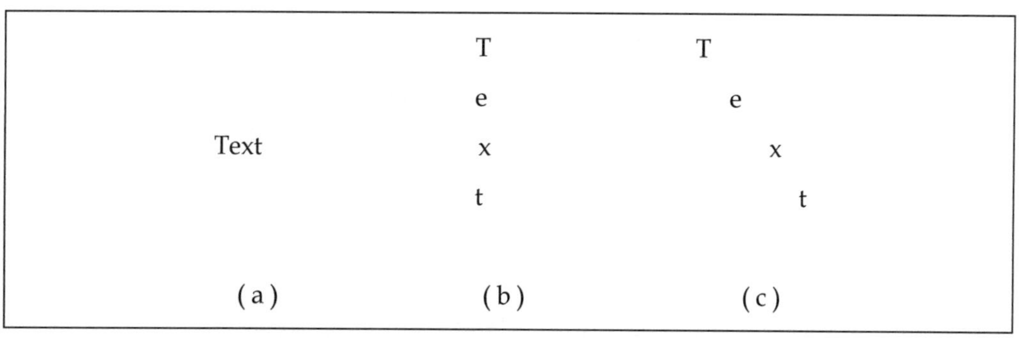

Fig. 4. Types of documents. a) Horizontal document, b) Vertical document and c) diagonal document.

More information on character metrics can be read in (Turner, 2000).

As mentioned above, the actual contents of a page is enclosed in special tags; for text documents, the text is organized in rows. In Fig. 5 it is shown an example of a simple row definition. Firstly, the position for the row within the page is set at (52,742) by the command

```
50      742  moveto   (C Language History)

[ 8.100947  3.930948    7.540798    5.871108    6.430798
  6.430798  6.430798    5.871108    6.430798    5.871108
  3.930948  8.650798    4.210798    5.320798    4.210798
  6.430798  4.761107    6.430798    ] xshow
```

Fig. 5. Example of an actual row definition.

`moveto` and then the text "C Language History" is the contents of the row and the following vector contains the metrics for each character in the row, generally, the characters does not full fill the page width, so a small constant should be added to each metric in order to fit the page width, that is to say, to left and right justify the text, next, the command `xshow` indicates that this row must be drawn with given metrics, however nothing is actually drawn until a `showpage` command is encountered.

As depicted in Fig. 5, we can find a rich source of data that can be modified in order to either hide information to implement a steganographic system or to embed digital watermarks. A natural question is that if such modifications could have side effects such as visual distortion, but consider that each unit of metrics is in fact 1/72 inches, that it to say, a metric of 1.0 = 1/72 inches, so the changes are mostly imperceptible. More about DDS languages can be read on (Adobe, 1999),(Adobe,2006) and (Reid, 1990).

In next section, we will discuss a watermarking system that uses character metrics in order to embed digital watermarks.

4. Document watermarking approach

Watermarking for authentication schemes differ from copyright enforcement schemes, in the latter, the watermark integrity is crucial, since no matter what attack is carried out on the protected material, the watermark should be still detected, of course damaged yet detectable. In authentication applications, the watermark should be fragile, any modifications should damage the watermark seriously so the system would be unable to detect the watermark, and in other words, any modification on the protected media would render the watermark undetectable by the system. These kinds of applications are intended to prevent frauds or moral damages.

4.1 Attack scenario to watermark

As stated in last section, in watermarking for authentication applications, a natural attack scenario is as follows: an attacker trying to modify a protected digital material in order to change the meaning of this material. An example of this is an electronic document that is modified to change the message contained in this document to commit fraud. Such attack is feasible due to the existence of free tools such as PDFedit, (Hocko, 2009).

In order to carry out a successful attack, the attacker must achieve the following goals:

- Change the meaning of the original message in the protected document so it matches some desired meaning, usually malicious, in a way that is not possible to figure the modification out.

- Preserve as much as possible of the watermark, so an automatic verification system still be able to detect it an thus to validate the document as a legitimate one.

From this situation is evident the need of a document authentication system based on fragile watermarking, so even if the modification of the document is small, the watermark shall be no detectable.

4.2 Watermarking using character metrics

In section 3.1, the metrics of characters were described, in this section; we discuss a model for watermarking using characters metrics. This model is depicted in Fig. 6. In this model, some edition software takes the raw text so it can build a well formed DDS from the input data; the edition software uses the instructions in a DDL data base so the resulting DDS follows the file standard. Then, the watermarking algorithm embeds a watermark generated using some secret key in the resulting script, the final product is a watermarked DDS.

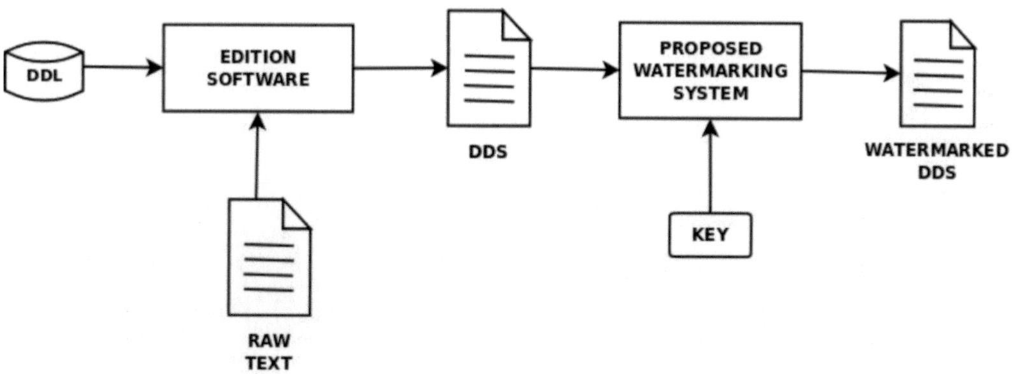

Fig. 6. Watermarking model for electronic documents in a DDS approach.

There are many software capable of producing high quality documents, we will assume that such software is provided by third party, yet the resulting documents follow some standard. So, the watermarking system has to be designed to interpret the input DDS in order to process it under this assumption.

Next, we will introduce a watermarking scheme which relies on the modification of character metrics for watermark embedding; a question might be arisen regarding the distortion caused by the metrics modification, in this subject, we must consider that a unit of metrics equals 1/72 inches, so small modifications should be negligible.

The watermark $W=[w_i], i=1,2,...,N$ is a binary (-1 or 1) pseudo random sequence with zero mean an variance 1. Without losing generality, we will assume that we are dealing with horizontal documents; the extension to vertical and diagonal documents is easily carried out.

The whole document is interpreted and then we can form two vectors named $C=[c_i], i=1,2,...,N$ and $M=[m_i], i=1,2,...,N$, the former is the vector of the characters of the document, and the latter is a vector of their metrics. The character metrics are firstly modified as follows:

$$m'_i = m_i + \frac{ASCII(c_i)}{1000} \tag{1}$$

Where c_i is the i-th character in the document and $ASCII(c_i)$ is the ASCII value of character c_i. For example, if $c_i = A$, $ASCII(c_i) = 097$.

The watermark is embedded using a multiplicative rule as follows:

$$M_i = m'_i(1 + gw_i) \tag{2}$$

where M_i is the watermarked metric corresponding to the i-th character, this is another vector named $M' = [M_i], i = 1,2,...,N$ and w_i is the i-th watermark bit, g is the gain factor; in experimental results, we found that a good value for g is one that just crosses the threshold as depicted in Fig. 7, that keeps a balance between the watermark imperceptibility and tamper detection capability.

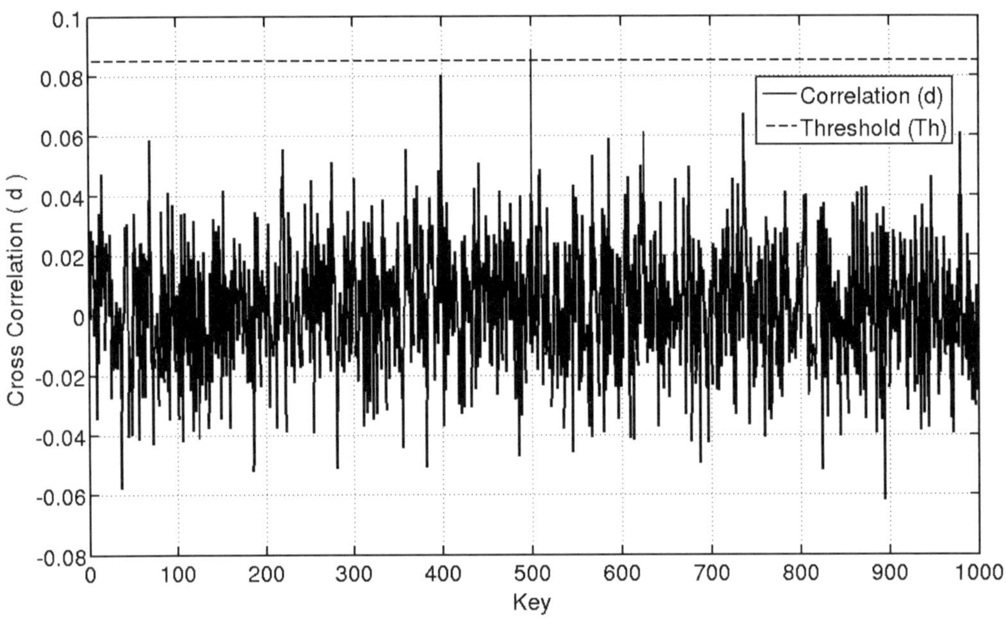

Fig. 7. Watermarking detection, the watermark was generated using key number 500. The use of a gain value that barely crosses the threshold is advised.

Then, the watermarked metrics vector M' replaces the original metrics vector M. Finally, the vectors C and M' are used to re-assemble the document, for better understanding see Fig. 8.

On the other hand, for detecting the watermark, we need to retrieve the watermarked metrics vector from the file, so we have the vector $\tilde{M} = [\tilde{m}_i], i = 1,2,...,N$. Where $\tilde{m}_i$ is the extracted metric. Then the presence of the watermark can be assessed by computing the Cross Correlation (d) between the retrieved watermark $\tilde{M}$ and the watermark W as follows:

$$d = \frac{1}{N}\sum_{i+1}^{N} \tilde{m}_i w_i \tag{3}$$

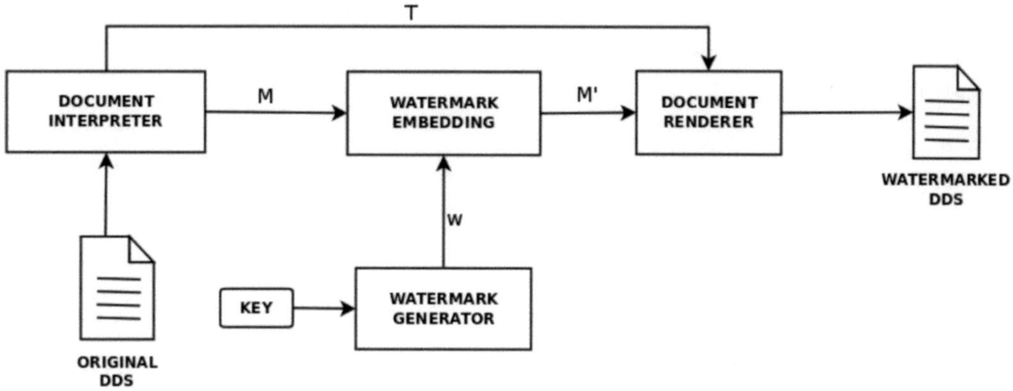

Fig. 8. Detailed block diagram of the Watermarking algorithm.

The value of d must be compared with the threshold Th and if $d \geq Th$ holds, then the watermark is present and thus the document is considered as authentic, otherwise, as tampered. The threshold is computed as:

$$Th = 2.8\sqrt{2\frac{\sigma^2}{N}} \tag{4}$$

Where σ^2 is the variance of the vector of metrics $\tilde{M}$.

Equations (4) is a modification from the one proposed by Piva as the optimal threshold for correlation-based detectors, and since proposed system holds the same asumptions as presented in (Piva, 1998), equation (4) holds, however, in order to achieve accurate results for the intended application, the value of '3.3' from the original equation was changed for '2.8' because in this way a lower value of embedding gain can be set, this helps to make the watermark very fragile, so a lower value of Th is desirable because it helps to reduce false positive error rate (a false positive is when the system decides that a tampered document is authentic; false negative occurs when the system decides that an authentic document is tampered). A block diagram for the watermark detection process is shown in Fig. 9.

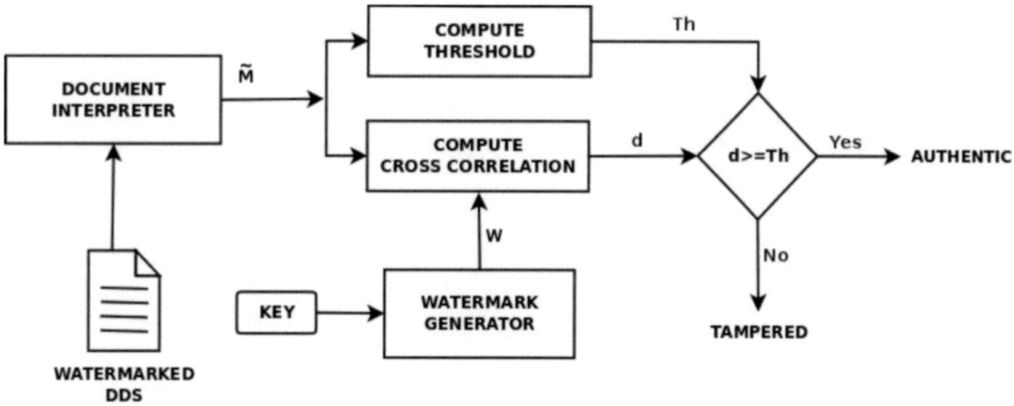

Fig. 9. Watermarking detection.

Experimental results and discussions will be carried out in next section.

5. Results and discussions

Although there is not a standard benchmark for document watermarking systems, we will present results for common concerns in watermarking electronic documents such as watermark imperceptibility, tamper detection capability and practical considerations.

5.1 Watermark imperceptibility

Since electronic documents are not images we cannot assess the distortion caused by the watermarking process using common distortion measures such as the Peak Signal to Noise Ratio (PSNR) or the Mean Absolute Error (MAE), because of this, the distortion assessment was carried out using a Mean Opinion Score (MOS) evaluation.

The MOS evaluation was set this way: twenty pair of different documents (each pair consisted of the original and the watermarked document) were shown to 100 observers whose gender and ages are distributed as described in Tab. 1.

Age (years)	Female	Male
20-30	33	32
30-40	4	10
40-50	2	7
50+	3	9

Table 1. Age and gender distribution of MOS observers.

The observers were asked to assess the difference between the original and watermarked documents, and to assign a score according to Tab. 2. And the average result of the MOS was a 4.6 which confirms the watermark imperceptibility. The observers argued the following reason to score other than 5:

- The ink of the letters is uneven.
- The text is misaligned to the paper sheet.
- The paper whiteness is slight different.

Since the observers were aware that they must find differences, they pointed out what they though could be the difference, and even when these differences in fact existed, they were caused directly either by the printer or by the composition of the paper.

Score	Meaning
5	There is not any perceptible difference
4	There is a slight difference that can be ignored
3	There is a slight difference which cannot be ignored
2	There is a noticeable difference
1	It is evident the difference between the two documents

Table 2. MOS evaluation criteria.

To further support the results of the MOS, we present a measure of the distortion of the metrics compared with the original metrics (see Fig. 10). It can be seen that when a character with high ASCII value appears in the document, the distortion becomes larger although it is too small to cause significant distortion.

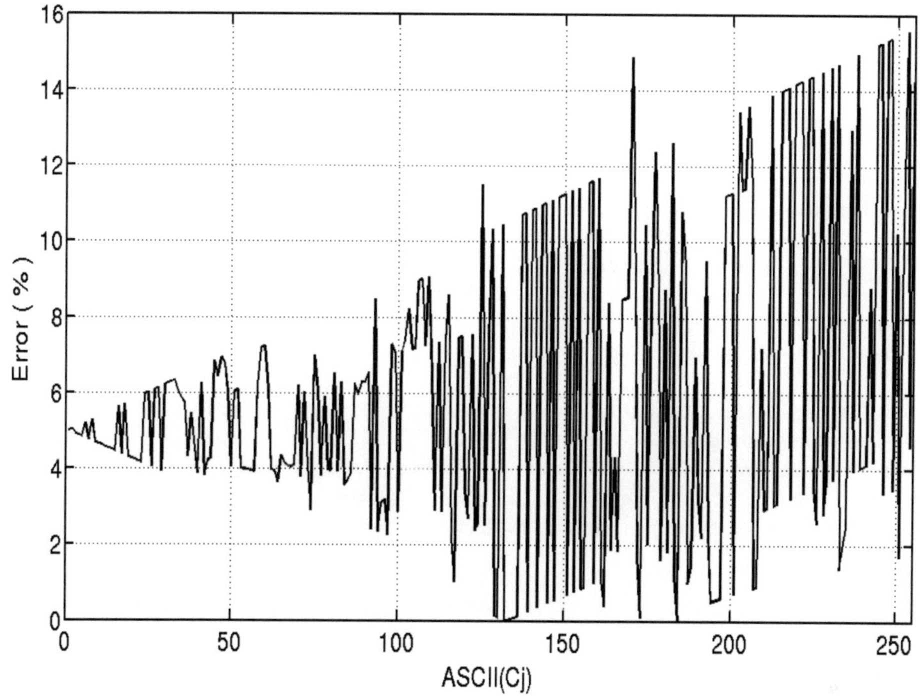

Fig. 10. Error percentage for each character in the ASCII code for some random watermark; the maximum distortion is about 16 %.

In Fig. 11 a pieces of a document and its watermarked version is shown.

5.2 Tamper detection capability

Let's consider two possibilities to tamper a document, in the first one, the attacker changes characters according to convenience without changing the metrics because he expects that this won't damage the watermark, if the attack is carried out this way, we can expect a document as shown in Fig. 12. It is quite evident that some modifications were made, so any human can easily detect the tamper even if the original document is not available for comparison. Now, consider another variant, the attacker have knowledge of the file standard so he has the needed skills to modify the document to preserve its natural look, to achieve this goal, the attacker must to re-compute the metrics related to the tampered characters, as expected, the more tampered characters, the more the damage to the watermark, in Fig. 13 we show a typical behaviour of this phenomena, we can see that once the correlation value d is below the threshold value, it never surpasses it again, furthermore,

C Language History

The initial development of C occurred at AT&T Bell Labs between 1969 and 1973; according to Ritchie, the most creative period occurred in 1972. It was named "C" because many of its features were derived from an earlier language called "B", which according to Ken Thompson was a stripped-down version of the BCPL programming language.

The origin of C is closely tied to the development of the Unix operating system, originally implemented in assembly language on a PDP-7 by Ritchie and Thompson, incorporating several ideas from colleagues. Eventually they decided to port the operating system to a PDP-11. B's lack of functionality to take advantage of some of the PDP-11's features, notably byte addressability, led to the development of an early version of the C programming language.

(a)

C Language History

The initial development of C occurred at AT&T Bell Labs between 1969 and 1973; according to Ritchie, the most creative period occurred in 1972. It was named "C" because many of its features were derived from an earlier language called "B", which according to Ken Thompson was a stripped-down version of the BCPL programming language.

The origin of C is closely tied to the development of the Unix operating system, originally implemented in assembly language on a PDP-7 by Ritchie and Thompson, incorporating several ideas from colleagues. Eventually they decided to port the operating system to a PDP-11. B's lack of functionality to take advantage of some of the PDP-11's features, notably byte addressability, led to the development of an early version of the C programming language.

(b)

Fig. 11. Sample documents. a) Original document. b) Watermarked document.

C Language History

The initial development of C occurred at my l aboratori es bet ween 2008 and 2011 according to Reut ers, the most creative period occurred in 2010. It was named " C" because i t i s easy t o pronou nce derived from an earlier language called "B", which according to many s ou r ces was a stripped-down version of the BCPL programming language.

The origin of C is closely tied to the development of the Li nux operati ng s yst e m originally implemented in assembly language on a HP - 48GX by our researc h g roup, incorporating several ideas from colleagues. Eventually they decided to port the operating system to a PDP-11. B's lack of functionality to take advantage of some of the PDP-11's features, notably byte addressability, led to the development of an early version of the C programming language.

Fig. 12. Example of a malicious modification; only the characters were changed whilst the metrics remain unchanged. The modifications can be easily spotted.

even when the threshold seems to possess a parabolic like shape and in some point it decreases, the correlation value is below the threshold. A close up of Fig. 13 is shown in Fig. 14, in this figure we can see the point in which the correlation goes below the threshold, in this case, when about 0.6% of characters are tampered

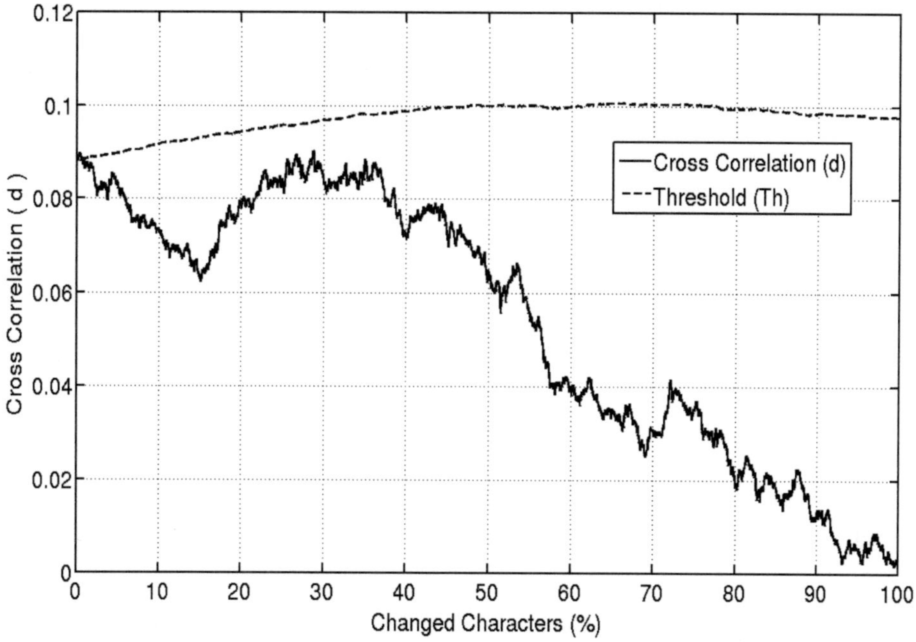

Fig. 13. System response as the percentage of tampered characters varies from 0% to 100%.

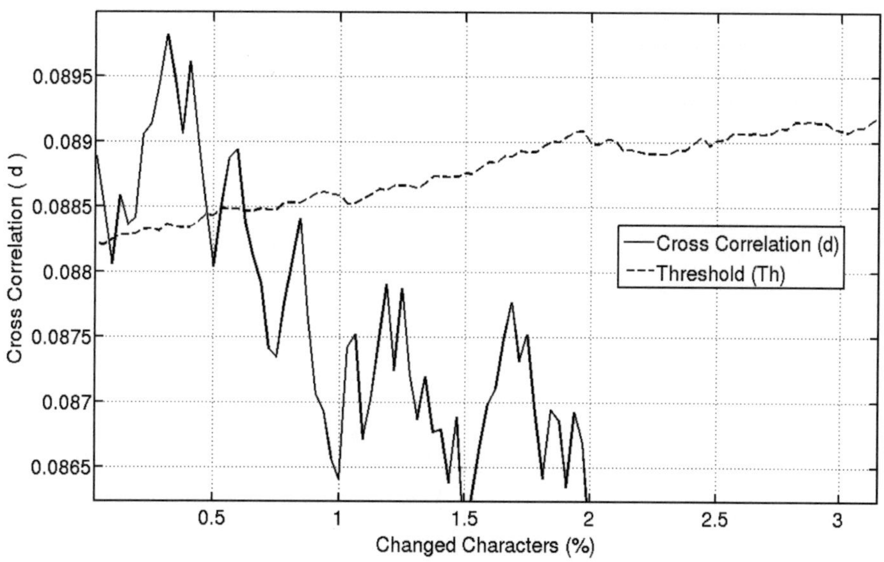

Fig. 14. System response as the percentage of tampered characters varies from 0% to 3.125%.

In Tab. 3 we present results for 10 different documents, showing the percentage of tampered characters that had to be tampered so the system considers them as tampered. High values in the table are explained as follows, as seen in Fig. 13 and Fig. 14, the correlation value does not decrease monotonically because the metrics are highly correlated to the watermark, this causes oscillations specially in low percentages of tampering, so the reported percentages are those in which the correlation don't crosses the threshold anymore.

Document Sample	Gain (g)	Altered Characters (%)
1	0.020	0.625
2	0.0140	1.570
3	0.0140	22.76
4	0.0190	2.510
5	0.0120	20.09
6	0.0135	2.003
7	0.0200	12.46
8	0.0160	6.308
9	0.0170	0.675
10	0.0175	0.453

Table 3. Percentage of minimum altered characters the system can determine that the document is tampered.

5.3 Practical considerations

The system described above has a very low complexity, for embedding a watermark of length N, 5N multiplications are needed, the average execution time in a consumer laptop is depicted in Fig. 15. It can be seen that the system clearly meets a wide spectrum of practical needs; one can ensure that the system can process a document with hundreds of pages in few seconds, which should be good enough for most practical scenarios.

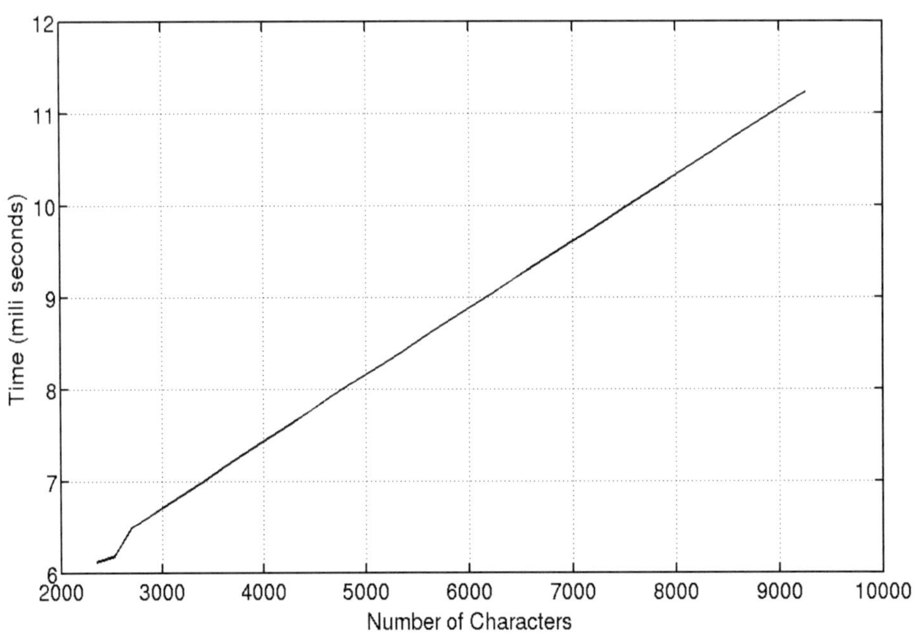

Fig. 15. Execution times for documents as the number of characters varies.

6. Conclusions

Through the development of this work, the following conclusions can be reached: Watermarking DDS format documents is a feasible and low complexity task that accomplishes a reliable electronic document authentication schemes with many desirable characteristics such as imperceptibility and very good tamper detection capabilities. Recall that many works in the field of document authentication are developed considering electronic documents as binary images, thus the development of watermarking systems in script format is a rich research field.

Results show that watermark imperceptibility is highly achieved as described in section 5.1, and considering the results of the MOS test, we can conclude that the proposed watermarking system will meet almost any imperceptibility requirements. Another important achievement is the tamper detection capability, that proved to be reliable even in the worst case of our tests, however, if this is a concern, a future work could perform verifications in smaller blocks, for example, the verification can be done in streams of 100 characters, so the 22.7% of characters that must be tampered, and 23 characters altered out of 100 is more likely to be a harmless modification since would be more difficult to have an attack useful to the proposes of any attacker.

Finally, the scheme discussed in this chapter is not intended to replace any security measures implemented in the different electronic document schemes such as the ones implemented in the ODF or in the PDF, but it would be advised to complement the current ones so a more secure electronic document model could be achieved.

7. Acknowledgments

The authors would like to thank the Council of Science and Technology (CONACYT) in Mexico and to the National Polytechnic Institute (IPN) of Mexico for support this work.

Examples in this chapter were chosen to mention C language in memory of its creator Dennis Ritchie, who passed away last October 12th, 2011. C language was extensively used during the development of this research.

8. References

Adobe, (1999). PostScript Language Reference, Third edition. Addison-Wesley Publishing Company Inc., ISBN 0-201-37922-8, U.S.A.

Adobe, (2006). PDF Reference: Adobe Portable Document Format Version 1.7, Sixth Edition. Adobe Press, ISBN 0-321-30474-8, U.S.A

Gonzalez-Lee, M.; Santiago-Avila, C.; Nakano-Miyatake, M. & Perez- Meana, H.; (2009) Watermarking based Document Authentication in Script Format. *Proc. 52th IEEE Midwest Symp. on Circuits and Systems*, ISBN 978-1-4244-4479-3. Cancun, Mexico. August, 2009.

Gou, H. & Wu, M. (2007) Improving Embedding Payload in Binary Images with Super-Pixels. Proc. *IEEE Int. Conf. Image Processing*, ISBN 1-4244-1437-7. San Antonio, U.S.A , September, 2007.

Hocko, M.; Mišutka, J. & Petříček, M.; (2009). *PDFedit. In PDFedit pdf manipulation library, gui, tools.* Available from:
http://pdfedit.cz/en/index.html.

Huang, P.; Wu, D. & Tsai, W. (2004) A Novel Block-Based Authentication Technique for Binary Images by Block Pixel Rearrangements. *Proc. IEEE Int. Conf. on Multimedia and Expo (ICME) 2004*, ISBN 0-7803-8603-5. Taipei, Taiwan. June, 2004.

Noren H. (2008) pdfcrack, *In PDFcrack – A Password Recovery Tool for PDF- Files. October 2011.* Available from:
http://sourceforge.net/projects/pdfcrack/.

Piva, A.; Barni, M. & Capellini V. (1998). Threshold selection for correlation-based watermark detection. *Procedings of COST254 Workshop on intelligent communication. ISBN* _____. L'Aquila, Italy. April, 1998.

Reid, G.C.; (1990); Thinking in PostScript; Addison-Wesley Publishing Company Inc.; ISBN0-201-52372-8; U.S.A.

Turner D. (2000); Glyph , In: *Freetype Glyph Conventions.* October 2011. Available from:
http://www.freetype.org/freetype2/docs/glyphs/index.html.

Wu, M. & Liu, B. (2004) Data Hiding in Binary Image for authentication and Annotation. *IEEE Trans. on Multimedia* Vol. 6 No. 4. April, 2004. pp. 528-538. ISSN 1520-9210.

Yang, H. & Kot, A.C. (2004). Text Document authentication by Integrating Inter Characters and Spaces Watermarking, *Proc. IEEE Int. Conf. On Multimedia and Expo (ICME) 2004.* ISBN 0-7803-8603-5. Taipei, Taiwan. June, 2004.

Zhu, B.; Wu J. & Kankanhalli, M.S. (2007) Render Sequence Encoding for Document Protection. *IEEE Trans. on Multimedia* Vol. 9, No. 1, January, 2007. pp. 16-24. ISSN 1520-9210.

14

Running: A Mixed Language Software as an e-Learning Solution for the State Budget Management

[1]Guillaume Koum and [2]Innocent Dzoupet
[1]Computer Sciences, Mathematics and Systems Simulation Laboratory-Polytechnic National HighSchool, Yaounde,
[2]iTech Company, Yaounde,
Cameroun

1. Introduction

Governments' attitude relevant to financial information systems consists to computerize systems, following sectors of activities which give name to computer applications such that:

- Taxes
- Customs
- Treasury
- Budget
- Etc...

Otherwise, research has shown that, for technology to be effective tool in the learning process, three conditions must be met. (1) there needs to be high-quality content that is relevant to the learning needs of the students and to the education system of the country; (2) teachers must be trained to integrate the new digital resources into their teaching practices; (3) technical support must be readily available to address any problems that arise [1].

In the State budget management a Government in achieving the objectives outlined in the finance law, undertakes at least two key activities which are to [2]:

- Coordinate the State Budget process by the ministry of Finance
- Work with other State Government ministries to monitor and assess financial and non-financial performance against Budget forecasts.

In open source software development, many issues are solved by integrating the users of the software in the development process, or even letting these users build the system themselves. Education requirements in languages training can be derived from software engineering. If the application is fully bilingual, it must provide the ability to receive the data in the two languages without showing a preference for either language. For us, we admit that these languages are French and English. So the interface to the data provider allows for the selection of available data in both French and English. Whenever both French and English are used on the same page, the language of each passage of text is indicated.

Electronic learning (e-learning) is a concept where teaching programmes conceived elsewhere are presented on the Web, under the supervision of a lecturer. Lessons organised in chapters are proposed on the Web. The lecturer must follow the sequential presentation of the material. The domains of application include the learning of a new language [3]. Consequently the user can learn either French or English with the described system.

We consider that the current system is partially bilingual. We assure that there is not a need of standard for the data interface and that the e-Government agreement is not relevant. The mixed language content is visible on buttons as well as in the texts.

An electronic issue management system, alternatively known as a help desk system, refers to a computer application that can be used to electronically automate the process of managing business issues, including problems, defects, tasks, changes or new requests. The difficulties found in using such a system are often from the lack of expertise to resolve the issues that are stored by the system. Ontology and case-based reasoning are suited to better provide structured information and enable the capturing of tacit knowledge of experts of the domain [4], [5].

An informal ontology may be specified by a catalog of types that are either undefined or defined only by statements in a natural language. A formal ontology which can be compared to a terminological ontology is specified by a collection of names for concept and relation types organized in a partial ordering by the type-subtype relation [6], [7]. A formal ontology is further distinguished by the way the subtypes are distinguished from their super-types: an *axiomatic ontology* distinguishes subtypes by axioms and definitions stated in a formal language, such as logic or some computer-oriented notation that can be translated to logic; a *prototype-based ontology* distinguishes subtypes by a comparison with a typical member or *prototype* for each subtype.

We use both terminological and prototype-based ontology to conceptualize translation issues as far as the State management budget is concerned. We implement all this in a case-based reasoning (CBR) system. Several issues in knowledge representation and ontology are closely related to CBR due to the fact that CBR is richer not only in the complexity of case-base design but also in the background of knowledge representation

The chapter is organized as followings. After the introduction, the first section talks about multilingual and bilingual software. The way bilingual software can maintain interface in two languages is underlined. Mind mapping is considered as a translation technique. The second section presents the mechanisms surrounding the preparation and execution of the State budget. The third section is dedicated to different ontology models required for the system. The fourth section presents case-based reasoning (CBR), a technique in artificial intelligence field conducive to learning. CBR is associated with the prototype-based ontology to solve language translation problems. The fifth section describes RUNNING application through variety of functionalities. The sixth section shows some results of the system about State revenue and expenditure. Finally, the chapter is concluded with perspectives expected.

2. Bilingual software

2.1 Multilingual software

Writing multilingual software has never been easy {8]. Translating user interface is only half of the task. It is mandatory for user satisfaction. The screen must not contain text in more than one language. This is why the language choice is an acquired. One has to remember about many different things, such as time/date format, money symbol and a lot of other things. But even translation interface used to be very difficult task because most programming environments lack usable tools for it. For example, in Visual C++ to create multilingual software one has to manually translate *.rc file and then after every change to resources, one has to manually retranslate *.rc file. Even languages that were designed with creating multilingual software in mind, such as Java and .NET, there are no built-in tools for translation.

In this regard, the Multi-Language Add-In for Visual Basic 6 provides a general solution for creating and maintaining Visual-Basic projects with support for multiple languages [9].

This involves the following basic steps:

1. Identifying the strings to be translated.
2. Specifying the languages to be supported.
3. Translating the strings into each language.

The Multi-Language Add-In supports these steps as follows:

Identifying the strings to be translated

- The Add-In scans the controls on all Forms, UserControls and UserDocuments to find the text properties which require translation.
- The relevant properties are defined in a Controls Database. This database already supports most commonly used controls and can easily be extended to support any other controls used in each project.
- The Add-In scans program code for strings which may require translation. The strings are displayed in a table where are selected the strings which require translation.
- When a line is selected in the table, the corresponding line is displayed in the Visual Basic Editor.

Specifying the languages to be supported

- When Multi-Language support is added to a project, the original language is specified.
- Additional languages are added using a simple dialog.

Translating the strings into each language

- The strings from controls and the strings from source code are displayed in two separate tables.
- In each table, there is a row for each string and a column for each language.
- The strings can be edited in the table.
- The strings are stored in a project database.

2.2 User Interface in bilingual software

Bilingual software must support and facilitate the entry of data from users and collection of data from other systems and sources in both French and English for instance. The data held, managed and processed by a software application is usually derived from inputs external to the application [10].

Where a manual user interface is used to enter data, this interface should allow for the entry of all language-sensitive items in both languages. To achieve this, data entry fields can either be placed in parallel or sequentially on the same area of the interface or they can be arranged in different places, but linked to the same interface state.

Placing the data entry fields for each language on the same page is more straightforward for the user, making the requirement to enter both languages more explicit. Where the data entry fields for each language are placed separately, it is important that they occur within the same user 'state' where the user should be expected to enter data for both languages before progressing to the next step in their interaction with the application. One language is given prominence and should be the preferred language for the user.

In general, bilingual software applications ensure equal treatment of all languages and encourage entry of data for all supported languages. Since data isn't always available in both languages, it is important for a software application to allow users to enter data in a single language. However, there is the potential for users to neglect to enter data in the alternate language, even when it is available and the software application discourages this. Where the layout of the interface doesn't make it completely clear and evident that there is the capability to enter both languages, indicators must be located alongside those fields that require bilingual entry. Ideally, this indicator can also provide a link to where the equivalent data entry field in the alternate language is located.

Ideally, all data are held in both languages, with a full bilingual dimension. However the reality is that some data might be available in one language and not the other. The system is then partially bilingual. The design of the data search capability must be such that the user is provided with the maximum flexibility in how to search, what language to use for the search and what data to search.

2.3 Languages translation and mind mapping

On a very early stage of studying a language, students first check the words in a dictionary, they try then to link them together, often consult grammar books. However, once there is advance in studies, the process of getting the words' meanings and the process of re-constructing the sentence into the target language comes automatically and naturally together and this perhaps constitutes the difference between a language learner and a translator.

Professional translators work with more than words: they translate concepts as well [11]. This may mean that the sentence structure will differ greatly from the original text, and the entire vocabulary may differ from "dictionary" definitions, depending upon the register of the text. Sometimes a single sentence may be translated as two sentences, or two sentences may be combined into one. During the course of revision, sentence structure may be changed, and the translator may even come up with more effective ways of expressing concepts contained in the text

Translation techniques depend of what kind of texts to translate. If it is a legal or engineering text then terminology (words) is more important, then perhaps translating literally on first draft is satisfactory, but not desirable either. If it is an economic or a financial text, then this method will not work as it is first necessary to summarize the meaning of the whole text, not just the words or indeed the sentences.

However in general, professional translators are characterized by a lack of mind.

Memory is more than recalling information for exams or trivial games. It's an important work skill that users can develop and improve, because the ability to remember is a major advantage with tips like:

- remembering key statistics during a negotiation;
- quoting a precedent-setting action when making a decision;
- impressing clients with knowledge of their product lines:
- Etc….

Mind maps (also called concept maps or memory maps) are an effective way to link ideas and concepts in human brain, and then "see" the connections firsthand [12].

Mind mapping tends to focus on remembering facts and details. Consequently, memorizing correct responses is more important than understanding the concept. Mind mapping is a note-taking technique that records information in a way that shows how various pieces of information fit together. There's a lot of truth in the saying "A picture speaks a thousand words", and mind maps create an easily-remembered "picture" of the information on is trying to remember.

This technique is very useful to summarize and combine information from a variety of sources. It also allows thinking about complex problems in an organized manner, and then presents findings in a way that shows the details as well as the big picture.

The mind map itself is a useful end product. Nevertheless, the process of creating the map is just as helpful for the memory. Since languages translators does not have mind, if their support tools are associated with mind mapping a new approach can be defined to implement language translation assistants for some domain of activities. In particular remembering terminology is necessary.

3. State budget process

Preparation of the Government's annual budget is the responsibility of the staff of the General Direction of Budget. The execution and implementation of the budget is an on-going annual cycle comprised of the following highlights [13].

3.1 Financial analysis of actual and projected expenditure

At the end of a fiscal year, the Budget team reviews the financial data for each ministry and program. This analysis provides important insights into how State Government raises revenue and spends money. Generally these insights lead to assist the development of the Government's budget proposal for the coming fiscal year.

3.2 Preparation of the budget

Following ministerial responses to credits requirements, the Budget team prepares the ministry's recommended budget proposal. A document filled at this occasion is sent back by the branch ministries to the ministry of Finance.

3.3 Submission of the budget to the National Assembly

The Government presents the budget proposal to the Legislature during an annual budgetary session. According to the fiscal regime of the State, the Government shall propose this budget document to the National Assembly with a delay before the budgetary session.

3.4 Budget enactment

The National Assembly must consider and adopt the final version of the appropriation bill within a fixed time following the beginning of the session. The consideration of the budget proposal starts in the finance and budget Committee[1]. Here budget discussions are conducted by the Committee President to resolve all major budget issues. At the end of the discussions and after all the budget analyses, the Committee then develops its budget recommendations for consideration by the entire house in the plenary session.

The adoption of the final version of the bills takes place in the plenary session in the presence of the entirety of the House and the whole Government team. Presided over by the Speaker of the House, this adoption goes through two steps including the budget hearings known as the parliamentary debate and the passing or the vote on the bills. At the beginning of the parliamentary debate, the Head of Government presents the information on the trends of the national economy, the public finances guidelines and the development of major investment projects. Then follows the questions and answer session during which Cabinet Ministers are called upon by parliamentarians to defend their budget requests.

The passing of the finance law like that of other legislations is conducted by the Speaker of the House at the floor of the entire House. Unlike other legislations, the finance law must be debated and passed in two separate and sequential steps. First, the first part of the finance law is debated and passed. It is only after the adoption of the first part that the second part of the finance law may be debated and passed.

3.5 Budget promulgation

Once the National Assembly considers the budget proposals and adopts the final version of the appropriation text, it forwards it to the Presidency of the Republic. The President of the Republic signs it into law within a fixed period following the receipt.

3.6 Budget implementation

After law promulgation, the implementation of the State budget begins. Ministries can then spend the appropriated funds. At the same time, the General Direction of Budget prepares the financial statements describing the prior fiscal year. At this point, the budget process begins a new exercise for the next fiscal year. During the fiscal year, the legislature may deem it necessary to adjust the current year's budget. This change is implemented via the Budget Adjustment Act.

---

[1] The finance and budget Committee is made off of a certain number of parliamentarians. Other Committees are set up at the National Assembly.

4. Ontology spot

The subject of *ontology* is the study of the *categories* of things that exist or may exist in some domain [13], [14]. The product of such a study, called *ontology,* is a catalog of the types of things that are assumed to exist in a domain of interest D from the perspective of a person who uses a language L for the purpose of talking about D. The types in the ontology represent the *predicates, word senses,* or *concept and relation types* of the language L when used to discuss topics in the domain.

4.1 Terminological ontology

In a terminological ontology categories need not be fully specified by axioms and definitions. An example of a terminological ontology is WordNet [15], whose categories are partially specified by relations such as subtype-supertype or part-whole, which determine the relative positions of the concepts with respect to one another but do not completely define them.

For this purpose; information in WordNet is organized around logical groupings called synsets. Each synset consists of a list of synonymous words or collocations, and pointers that describe the relations between this synset and other synsets. Two kinds of relations are represented by pointers: lexical and semantic. Lexical relations hold between semantically related word forms; semantic relations hold between word meanings.

Formal concept analysis approach is adopted for the terminological ontology construction. Formal background is constructed based on the concept of commitment order linked to other concepts. In the formal background, the object is one document concerning the information for supplier or beneficiary and the properties are the ontology concepts. The concepts and classification relationships between concepts are structured in the form of concept trees and translated into ontology.

Commitment and order are **direct antonyms**, a pair of words between which there is an associative bond resulting from their frequent co-occurrence. Commitment order can also be considered as a **holonym (Y** is a holonym of **X** if **X** is a part of **Y). A meronym** is the name of a constituent part of, the substance of, or a member of something **(X** is a meronym of **Y** if **X** is a part of **Y).** So, all proprieties in this document are meronyms **(**except commitment order which is a holonym**).**

Regarding the State budget management, the commitment order in the information for the supplier or beneficiary document appears every time a nature of voucher is indicated. They are three boxes with the words "Nature of document".

- The certificate of indebtedness: it is accompanied by a commitment order in two copies the green original and the yellow duplicate.

The supplier shall:

1. Fill the order specified on the commitment order or documents attached thereto.
   Commitment order or any other orders should not be filled unless they are accompanied by a certificate of indebtedness.
   Only the Certificate of indebtedness commits the state and makes settlement possible.

2. After filling the order forward to issuing service indicated on the document
   a. The Certificate of indebtedness the following information
      the amount invoiced
      the method of settlement requested
      references of attached invoices.
   b. An original and a duplicate of the invoice(s) for which settlement is being requested.
   c. The yellow duplicate of the commitment order (the supplier should keep as proof the rein original of the commitment order).
   d. For contracts: a registered copy of the contract.

If the order is to be continued, the supplier should receive a new certificate of indebtedness with which to invoice subsequent order, in which case points (a) and (b) above should be observed.

The certificate of indebtedness should accompany the advice of settlement for the previous orders filled.

- The advice of settlement, as its name indicates, is a simple notice sent at the end of the transaction to the beneficiary of commitment order to inform him that the Treasury has effected settlement.

It is in beneficiary's interest to ensure that the amount and method of settlement shown on the advice of settlement are consistent with the information he supplied on the certificate of indebtedness.

Where the need arises, he should contact the treasury sub-department of expenditure

- The advice of cancellation: it is possible for the issuing service to cancel a commitment order wholly or in part.

In the event of total cancellation, the order should not be filled at all, no settlement can be made.

Where the cancellation is partial, the advice of cancellation should be accompanied by a new certificate of indebtedness showing only the amount corresponding to that part of the initial commitment that has not been cancelled.

In either case, the supplier or beneficiary should be sure to contract the issuing service

If that was not done at the time cancellation procedure were initiated.

A methodology based on Mind Maps captures all and only the knowledge we need for a scope of the commitment order. The borders among proprieties are traced by the tree branches and eliminate synonyms not in the lexical sense but in the semantic sense. The ontology model avoids the management of conflicting knowledge as a terminological issue.

A good Mind Map shows the "shape" of the subject, the relative importance of individual points, and the way in which facts relate to one another. A complete Mind Map may have main topic lines radiating in all directions from the center. Sub-topics and facts will branch off these, like branches and twigs from the trunk of a tree. The title of the subject explored is written in the center of the page (Commitment order in Figure1)

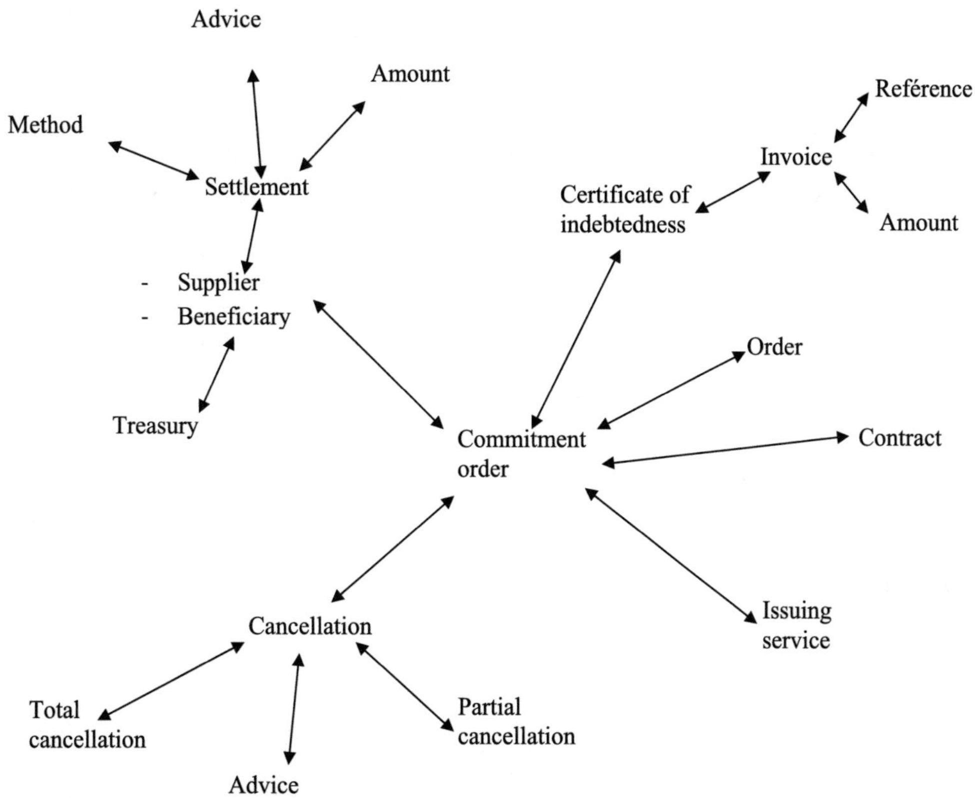

Fig. 1. Terminological ontology

4.2 Prototype-based ontology

A prototype-based ontology is described as a terminological ontology whose categories are distinguished by typical instances or *prototypes* rather than by axioms and definitions in logic [16].

For every category c in a prototype-based ontology, there must be a prototype p and a measure of *semantic distance* $d(x, y, c)$, which computes the dissimilarity between two entities x and y when they are considered instances of c. Then an entity x can be classified by the following recursive procedure:

- Suppose that x has already been classified as an instance of some category c, which has subcategories $s_1,...,s_n$.
- For each subcategory s_i with prototype p_i, measure the semantic distance $d(x, p_i, c)$.
- If $d(x, p_i, c)$ has a unique minimum value for some subcategory s_i, then classify x as an instance of s_i, and call the procedure recursively to determine whether x can be further classified by some subcategory of s_i.
- If c has no subcategories or if $d(x, p_i, c)$ has no unique minimum for any s_i, then the classification procedure stops with x as an instance of c, since no finer classification is possible with the given selection of prototypes.

Since a prototype-based ontology depends on examples, it is often convenient to derive the semantic distance measure by a method that learns from examples, such as statistics, cluster analysis, or neural networks.

We may allow an individual in our ontology to have multiple prototypes. Therefore we represent this relationship between Individuals with some hasPrototype property. So we need a way to define multiple inheritance mechanism on instances (and that is exactly what the hasPrototype property would do).

For the translation to be performed, some text analysis is required. Keyword counts are a simple analytical technique, but they ignore sentence structure. This is why a prototype-based ontology can be necessary in order to give a normal sense to sentences. While considering a sentence which is a text as an object, we can define prototypes on it. Moreover a sentence drains an idea and can be limited to a single term.

Example 1

There may be an object Regional_HospitalA in region A. Then, we proceed to create object Regional_HospitalB by specifying Regional_ HospitalA as its prototype, as well as specifying that Regional_HospitalB is situated in region B.

We precise that Regional_HospitalB has the same properties as Regional_HospitalA, except that its region is B.

We could choose to describe it like this:

```
 Individuals = {Regional_HospitalA, Regional_HospitalB, A, B}


Regional_HospitalA  hasRegion A

Regional_HospitalB  hasRegion B


Regional_HospitalB  hasPrototype Regional_HospitalA
```

While reasoning, we ignore the inherited property value if the object redefines it itself. In this case, the information that Regional_HospitalB is in region B should have priority over the information that Regional_HospitalB may be situated in region A because it is like Regional_HospitalA.

If there is no translated information on region B to be recorded by the user during its work, search through input ontology (investments list in the investment budget) and output ontology (projects list in the appropriate program) helps to solve the problem.

Input ontology

We consider the concept All State revenue. It can represent the foundation of the input ontology illustrated in Figure2.

Output ontology

We consider the concept « All State expenditure ». It can constitute the basis of the output ontology presented in Figure3.

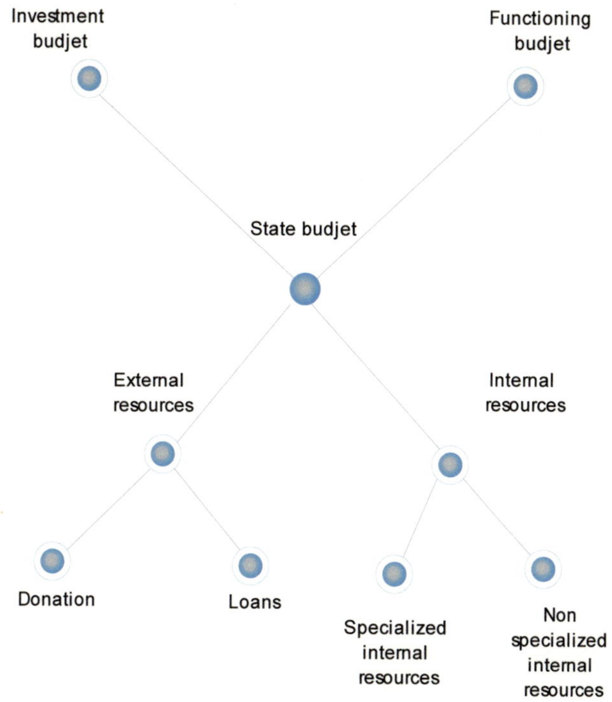

Fig. 2. Input ontology

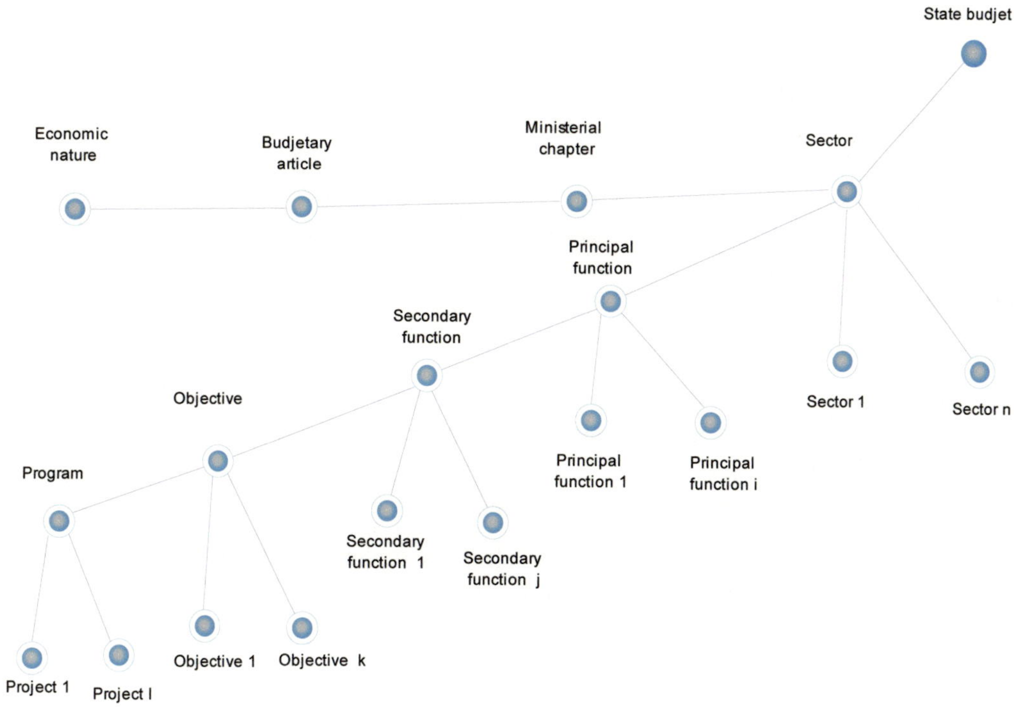

Fig. 3. Output ontology

Budgetary ontology

The finance law is a law of the land and provides for and authorizes all State revenue and expenditure for the upcoming fiscal year. It is founded on a budgetary ontology presented in figure....

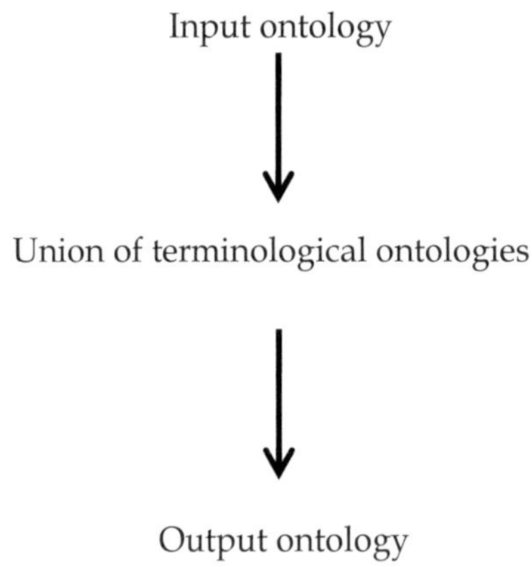

Fig. 4. Budgetary ontology

5. Case-based reasoning

5.1 Principle

Case-based reasoning (CBR) is the process of solving new problems based on the solutions of similar past problems [17], [18]. A new problem is solved by finding a similar past case, and reusing it in the new problem situation. The knowledge and reasoning process used by an expert to solve the problem is not recorded, but is implicit in the solution.

To solve a current problem: the problem is matched against the cases in the case base, and similar cases are retrieved. The retrieved cases are used to suggest a solution which is reused and tested for success. If necessary, the solution is then revised. Finally the current problem and the final solution are retained as part of a new case.

All case-based reasoning methods have in common the following process:

- retrieve the most similar case (or cases) comparing the case to the library of past cases;
- reuse the retrieved case to try to solve the current problem;
- revise and adapt the proposed solution if necessary;
- retain the final solution as part of a new case.

Retrieving a case starts with a (possibly partial) problem description and ends when a best matching case has been found. The subtasks comprise:

- identifying a set of relevant problem descriptors;
- matching the case and returning a set of sufficiently similar cases (given a similarity threshold of some kind); and
- selecting the best case from the set of cases returned.

Some systems retrieve cases based largely on superficial syntactic similarities among problem descriptors, while advanced systems use semantic similarities.

Reusing the retrieved case solution in the context of the new case focuses on: identifying the differences between the retrieved and the current case; and identifying the part of a retrieved case which can be transferred to the new case. Generally the solution of the retrieved case is transferred to the new case directly as its solution case.

Revising the case solution generated by the reuse process is necessary when the solution proves incorrect. This provides an opportunity to learn from failure.

Retaining the case is the process of incorporating whatever is useful from the new case into the case library. This involves deciding what information to retain and in what form to retain it; how to index the case for future retrieval; and integrating the new case into the case library.

5.2 Learning in Case-Based Reasoning

A very important feature of case-based reasoning is its coupling to learning. CBR is an approach to incremental, sustained learning, since a new experience is retained each time a problem has been solved, making it immediately available for future problems. Learning in CBR occurs as a natural by-product of problem solving. When a problem is successfully solved, the experience is retained in order to solve similar problems in the future. When an attempt to solve a problem fails, the reason for the failure is identified and remembered in order to avoid the same mistake in the future.

Case-based reasoning allows learning from experience, since it is usually easier to learn by retaining a concrete problem solving experience than to generalize from it.

5.3 Tradeoff between prototype-based ontology and case-based reasoning

The establishment of prototype-based ontology lays the foundation for case knowledge sharing. The tradeoff associates prototype-based ontology and case based reasoning technology in State budget management. The system structure of translation process is designed on the basis of prototype-based ontology and case-based reasoning theory and its application. The system not only considers the full use of bilingual domain experts' experiences and knowledge, but also can supports sharing and reuse of case knowledge in budgetary case bases. So, it solves the problem of knowledge reuse generated for those learning one or the other language with focus on budgetary domain. Also a simple semantic similarity algorithm can be admitted and used to compute similarity between new case and a case from case bases. So the real meaning of each term or sentence in different case expression is discovered and they are recorded in case bases with their mapping relation.

Example 2

We suppose that there exists an object Regional_RoadA1A2 in region A. Then, we need to create object Regional_RoadB1B2 in region B by specifying Regional_ RoadA1A2 as its prototype.

We indicate that Regional_RoadB1B2 has the same properties as Regional_RoadA1A2, except that its region is B.

As in example1, we could choose to describe it like this:

```
 Individuals = {Regional_RoadA1A2, Regional_RoadB1B2, A,B}

Regional_RoadA1A2 hasRegion A
Regional_RoadB1B2 hasRegion B

Regional_RoadB1B2 hasPrototype Regional_RoadA1A2
```

If there is no translated information on region B at the disposal of the user, we have to refer first to object Regional_HospitalB which already is known (example1).

Regional_HospitalB is linked to Regional_RoadB1B2 through the adjective Regional, in one of the terminological ontologies. The noun issuing from it is RegionB.

Two lessons can be observed from this situation.

- Regional_RoadB1B2 inherits from Regional_RoadA1A2 and from Regional_HospitalB because of hasPrototype propriety.
- The translation of RegionB's characteristics already done constitutes the most similar case retrieved, that must be reused, revised (a region is presented differently whether it is roads or hospitals) and retained, according to CBR schema (Figure5).

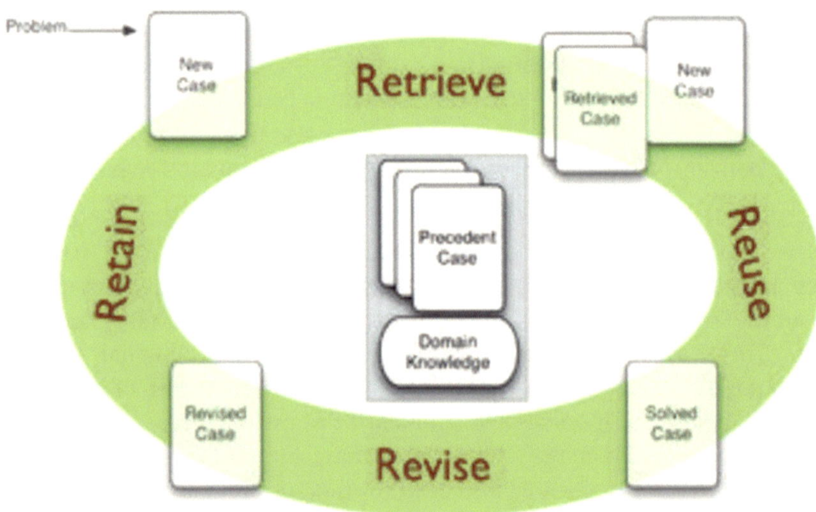

Fig. 5. CBR schema

The leaning cycle is then schematized in Figure6.

6. Running application

6.1 Presentation

RUNNING is a partially bilingual application. It is written in open source engineering through Symfony [19], a web application framework for PHP projects. Symfony aims to

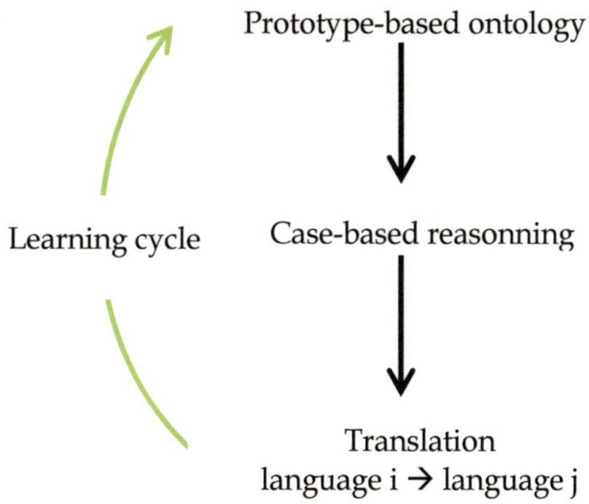

Fig. 6. Translation process

speed up the creation and maintenance of web applications, and to replace the repetitive coding tasks by power, control and pleasure. Symfony is a full-stack framework, a library of cohesive classes written in PHP. It provides an architecture, components and tools for developers to build complex web applications faster.

RUNNING can motivate users (either of French or of English) in the following categories:

- Drill-and-practice (vocabulary training with the state budget concepts)
- Tutorials (basic knowledge and facts required in the state budget operations)
- Etc...

6.2 System

RUNNING comprises the following modules:

- Management of service providers: It allows service providers identification.
- Management of beneficiaries: It identifies and treats beneficiaries.
- Management of executing agents: It identifies and treats credits managers.
- Opening of accounts: It concerns the opening of credits.
- Management of commitments: It allows provisions and cancels credits reservation.
- Management of settlements: It settles the expenditure or the canceling by the credits manager.
- Data restitutions: It prints reports on the state budget following up.
- Resources identification: It proceeds at resources identification, as loans and legs.
- Projects and programs identification: It establishes various projects and programs.
- Treatment of reception unit of the expenditure: The budgetary line is implicated.
- Allocation of credits by nature to the reception unit: The projection by nature is performed.
- Treatment of tenders: Calls of tenders are treated.
- Implementation of amendments: Amendments are implemented.
- Followings up of the state budget: Followings up activities are concentrated in this restitution.

- Secure access by level of confidentiality: It covers security issues.
- Documentation and online tutorials. The teaching component is recorded.

RUNNING offers a subsidiary mechanism of improving bilingual skills of users regarding the State budget management.

Budgetary ontology in language i ⟶ Translation process ⟶ Budgetary ontology in language j

Fig. 7. Budget translation

7. Results

7.1 Results about state revenue

Screens are presented that express State revenue in terms of resources and new financing. RUNNING exploits the input ontology to help users who need to learn how to translate what contributes to budget revenue.

Screen1 displays the resource list constituted of internal and external resources. Internal resources comprise mainly variety of taxes and custom fees. An example of an external resource is the public debt. It can be a bilateral or a multilateral external resource. Resources are listed in French and in English.

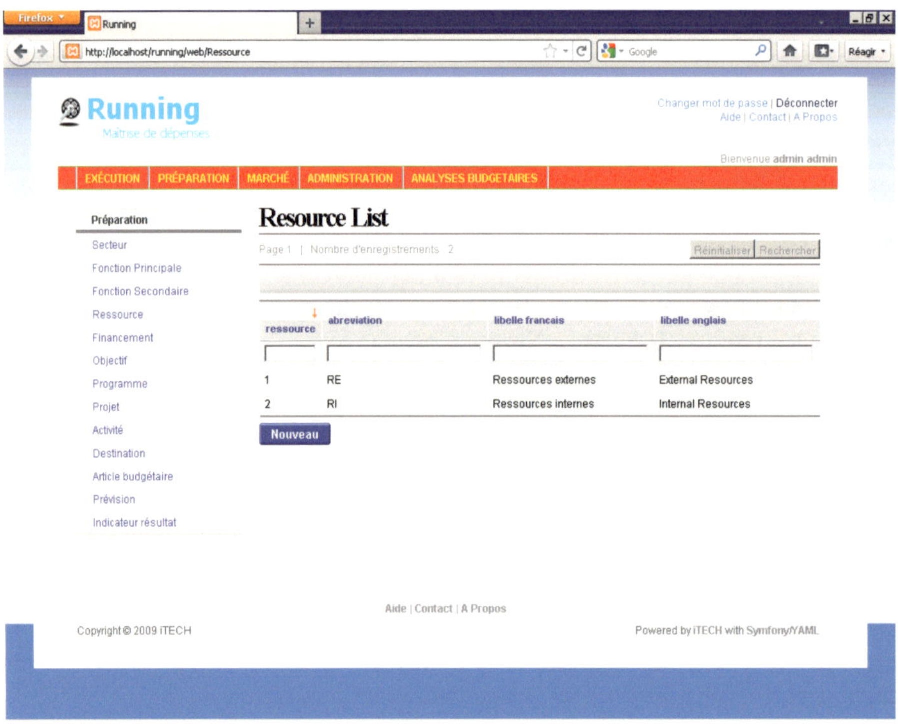

Screen 1. Resource List

Screen2 concerns new financings. They can be provided by financial markets through public titles. In the level of enterprises, securities are strengthened in a financial market for the compartment of the titles of capital and for the compartment of the titles of credit. The wording is introduced in French and in English.

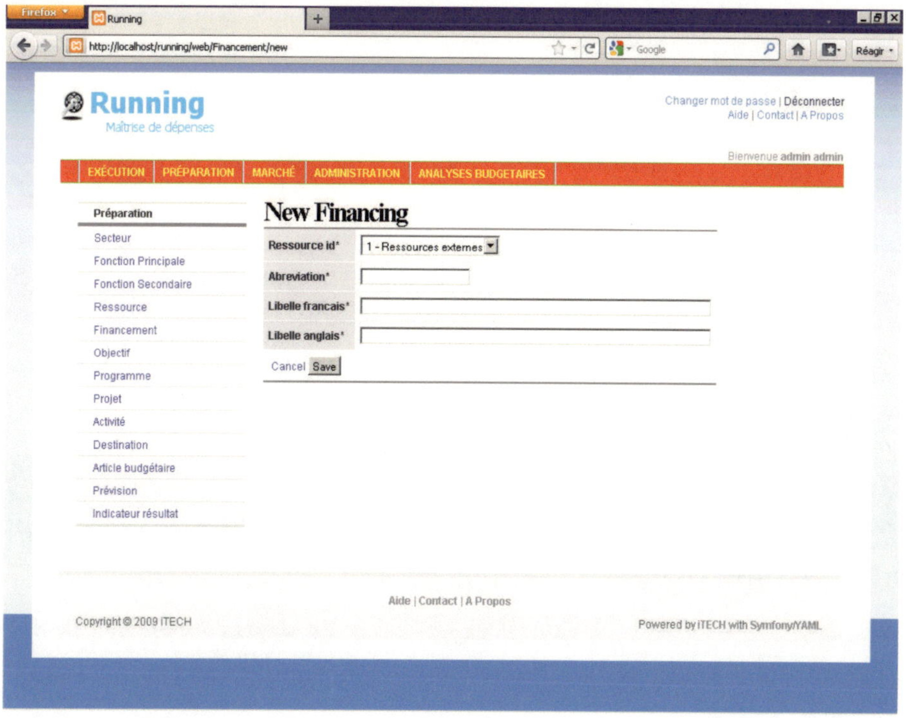

Screen 2. New Financing

7.2 Results about state expenditure

A project is a one-time effort that produces a specific result. A project is a part of a program. Here are some projects whose translation is studied in example1 and example2:

- Roads construction
- Hospitals building;
- Etc…

Screen3 offers a summary field which contain the project scope. The scope is the description of the boundaries of the project. It defines what the project will deliver. It is the view all stakeholders have from the project, a definition of the limits of the project. In the summary field, requirements must be specified. The scope must be written in French and English.

Screen4 allows the description of an activity through the summary field. An activity is a component of a project. It is constituted of sequences and dependencies. At this level durations are determined and the network diagram for the project schedule is developed. The summary field must contain these activity details in French and in English except the network diagram.

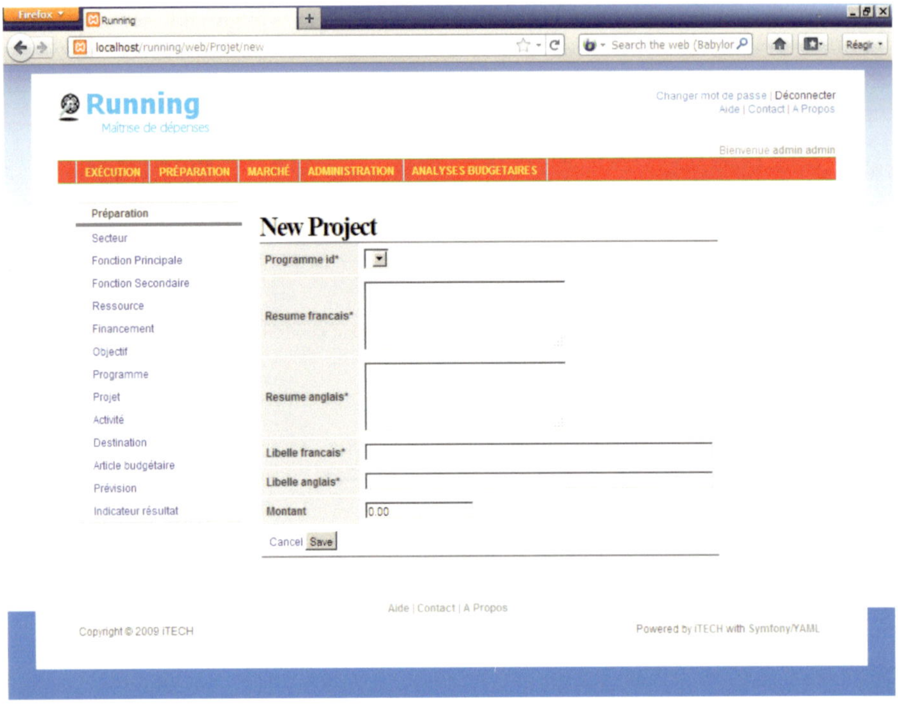

Screen 3. New Project

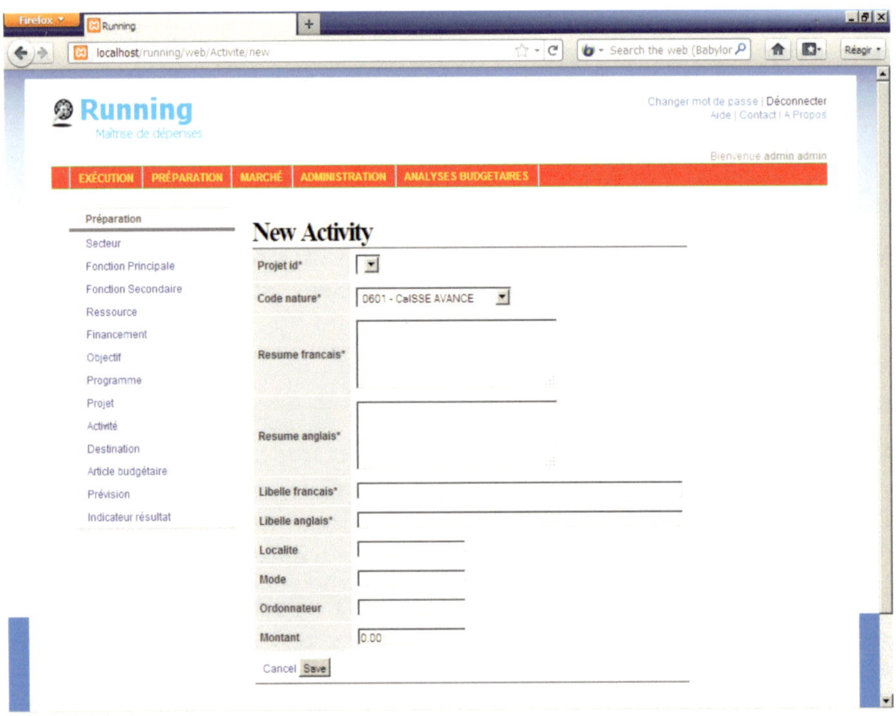

Screen 4. New activity

8. Conclusion

For each year, the financial law provides for and authorizes all State revenue and expenditure and presents all the programs aimed at attaining economic, social and cultural objectives. The financial law is applied in the Budget Domain which requires a strong knowledge management. In presence of two languages (French and English in our case) bilingual interfaces need hard efforts of language translation.

When organizations are facing language translation issues, here are some mistakes to avoid:

- Asking users to specify details about the translation rather than using a conform idea to record that information
- Allowing service staff to select or influence potential users, for instance, by transferring some works but not others to particular persons
- Not sharing translation results with service staff

In this chapter, we specify a system allowing users to communicate with RUNNING application and to improve their bilingual skills by learning the vocabulary related to State budget management. An ontological system is developed to bring adequate terminology and knowledge to non-expert users in bilingualism. The term ontology corresponds to a formal structure expressed in different models and different degrees. The budgetary ontology represented has three stages;

- Input ontology
- Union of terminological ontologies
- Output ontology

This decomposition is aimed to conceptualize the domain in such a way that data semantics is well described and understood. Reasoning mechanisms are also précised for users' experience.

The public sector area is characterized by a wide range of task and work arrangements. Some processes in financial applications are still limited to simple processes of registering, accounting and calculating. RUNNING application is provided with value-added features facilitating users to be accommodated with budgetary concepts in French and in English simultaneously.

Besides, decision-making in public administration occurs at organizational or policy level but it is also characteristic of its operative work. Thereby, public agents must be able to access information and knowledge to help their tasks, so that decision-making can take advantage of this evolution.

RUNNING is an application in which the user finds material of Computer-Aided Learning to be more bilingual by understanding complex terms, as far as the State budget management is concerned. Web and open source development characters give it the ability to be migrated in other technical domains where the language translation can represent a difficult problem to be solved by users. This is an interesting way of learning words and notions tied to a specific field of activities.

9. Acknowledgements

Authors like to thank Dr. Mathias Ariel Ngnitedem, Nelson Mandela School of Public Policy and Urban Affairs, Southern University and A&M College (Baton Rouge, Louisiana, USA) for his helpful contribution and knowledge of budgetary domain.

10. References

[1] Jerome Fonin. (2002). Logical Framework and Risk Analysis for a National Distance Education (NDE) Project. Cameroon case Study. Proc. First National Seminar on Distance Education- Yaounde, pp 40-46.

[2] Malcolm Holmes and al. (1998). Handbook of public expenditure management. World Bank. Washington. ISBN 0-8213-4752-7.

[3] Kolyang. (2002). Research and Education Quality Improvement through Information and Communication Technologies and Distance Learning. Proc. First National Seminar on National Distance Education- Yaounde, pp 26-32.

[4] Schank Roger C., & Christopher K. Riesbeck, eds. (1981) Inside Computer Understanding, Lawrence Erlbaum Associates, Hillsdale, NJ.

[5] Schank Roger C., Alex Kass, & Christopher K. Riesbeck (1994) Inside Case-Based Explanation, Lawrence Erlbaum Associates, Hillsdale, NJ

[6] Sowa, John F. (1999c) "Ontological categories," in L. Albertazzi, ed., Shapes of Forms: From Gestalt Psychology and Phenomenology to Ontology and Mathematics, Kluwer Academic Publishers, Dordrecht, 1999, pp. 307-340.

[7] Sowa John F. (2000b) "*Ontology, metadata, and semiotics,*" in B. Ganter & G. W. Mineau, eds., Conceptual Structures: Logical, Linguistic, and Computational Issues, LNAI 1867, Springer-Verlag, Berlin, 2000, pp. 55-81.

[8] V. Prasanna Venkatesan (2010). Armms - An Architectural Reference Model for Multilingual Software (Chapter 6). VDM Verlag Publisher.

[9] Francesco Balena (1999). Programming Microsoft Visual Basic 6.0 Microsoft Press

[10] Dr International. (2002). Developing International Software. Microsoft Press, ISBN 0-7356-1583-7.

[11] Andrew Chesterman (1997). Memes of Translation: The Spread of Ideas in Translation Theory. Benjamins Translation Library Series, No. 22.

[12] Tony Buzan, Barry Buzan (1996). The Mind Map Book: How to Use Radiant Thinking to Maximize Your Brain's Untapped Potential. Plume Publisher.

[13] Helen Steward. (1997).The Ontology of Mind: Events, Processes, and States. Clarendon Press-Oxford.

[14] John Heil. (2003). From an Ontological Point of View. Clarendon Press-Oxford. Christiane

[15] Fellbaum (1998). WordNet: An Electronic Lexical Database. MIT Press.

[16] Eduardo Mena, Arantza Illarramendi (2001). *Ontology-based* query processing for global information system . Business & Economics

[17] Janet Kolodner (1993).Case-based reasoning. Morgan Kaufmann Publishers

[18] Ian Watson (1997). Applying Case-Based Reasoning Techniques for Enterprise Systems. Morgan Kaufman Publishers

[19] Fabien Potencier, Hugo Hamon (2009). Symfony. Eyrolles Collection.